POSTMODERN
SOCIAL
THEORY

POSTMODERN SOCIAL THEORY

George Ritzer
University of Maryland

THE McGRAW-HILL COMPANIES, INC.
New York   St. Louis   San Francisco   Aukland   Bogotá
Caracas   Lisbon   London   Madrid   Mexico City   Milan
Montreal   New Delhi   San Juan   Singapore   Sydney   Tokyo   Toronto

McGraw-Hill

A Division of The **McGraw·Hill** *Companies*

This book was set in Times Roman by Ruttle, Shaw & Wetherill, Inc.
The editors were Jill S. Gordon and Katherine Blake;
the production supervisor was Leroy A. Young.
The cover was designed by Caryl and Scott Silvers.
Project supervision was done by Hockett Editorial Service.
Quebecor Printing/Fairfield was printer and binder.

POSTMODERN SOCIAL THEORY

Permissions Acknowledgments appear on pages v–viii and on this page by reference.

This book is printed on acid-free paper.

1 2 3 4 5 6 7 8 9 0 FGR FGR 9 0 9 8 7 6

ISBN 0-07-053019-X

Library of Congress Cataloging-in-Publication Data

Ritzer, George.
    Postmodern social theory/George Ritzer.
       p.   cm.
    Includes bibliographical references and index.
    ISBN 0-07-053019-X
    1. Postmodernism—Social aspects.   2. Sociology—Philosophy.
I. Title.
HM73.R534   1997
301'.01—dc20   96-21073

http://www.mhcollege.com

PERMISSIONS ACKNOWLEDGMENTS

Grateful acknowledgment is made for permission to quote from the following previously published sources.

Chapter 1

Baudrillard, Jean. *The Transparency of Evil: Essays on Extreme Phenomena.* London: Verso, 1993.

Bauman, Zygmunt. *Intimations of Postmodernity.* London: Routledge, 1992. Reprinted by permission of Routledge, UK.

Denzin, Norman. "Postmodernism and Deconstructionism." In *Postmodernism and Social Inquiry,* edited by David R. Dickens and Andrea Fontana, 182–202. New York: Guilford Press, 1994. Reprinted by permission of Guilford Press.

Denzin, Norman. "Re-reading the Sociological Imagination." By Norman Denzin. *The American Sociologist* (fall 1989): 238–282. Copyright © 1989 by Transaction Publishers; all rights reserved. Reprinted by permission of Transaction Publishers.

Kellner, Douglas. "Introduction: Jameson, Marxism, and Postmodernism." In *Postmodernism: Jameson: Critique,* edited by Douglas Kellner. Washington, D.C.: Maisonneuve Press, 1989. Reprinted by permission of Masionneuve Press.

Spivak, Gayatri. "Translator's Preface." In Jacques Derrida, *Of Grammatology,* ix-lxxxvii. Baltimore: The Johns Hopkins University Press, 1974. Reprinted by permission of The Johns Hopkins University Press.

Chapter 2

Antonio, Robert J. "Nietzsche's Antisociology: Subjectified Culture and the End of History." *American Journal of Sociology* 101 (1995): 1–43. Copyright © 1995 by The University of Chicago. All rights reserved. Reprinted by permission of The University of Chicago Press.

Rorty, Richard. *Philosophy and the Mirror of Nature.* Copyright © 1979 by Princeton University Press. Reprinted by permission of Princeton University Press.

Spivak, Gayatri. "Translator's Preface." In Jacques Derrida, *Of Grammatology,* ix-lxxxvii. Baltimore: The Johns Hopkins University Press, 1974. Reprinted by permission of The Johns Hopkins University Press. Copyright © 1969 by Editions Gallimard. Reprinted by permission of Georges Borchardt, Inc.

Chapter 3

Foucault, Michel. *The Archaeology of Knowledge and the Discourse of Language.* New York: Harper Colophon, 1971/1976. Copyright © 1969 by Éditions Gallimard. Reprinted by permission of Georges Borchardt, Inc.

Foucault, Michel. *The Birth of the Clinic.* New York: Vintage, 1975. Translation copyright © 1973 by Tavistock Publications, Ltd. Reprinted by permission of Pantheon Books, a division of Random House, Inc.

Foucault, Michel. *Discipline and Punish: The Birth of the Prison.* New York: Vintage, 1979. Copyright © 1975 by Éditions Gallimard. Reprinted by permission of Georges Borchardt, Inc.

Foucault, Michel. *Madness and Civilization.* London: Tavistock, 1967. Reprinted by permission of Tavistock Publications.

Foucault, Michel. *The Order of Things: An Archaeology of the Human Sciences.* New York: Vintage, 1973. Copyright © 1966 by Éditions Gallimard. Reprinted by permission of Georges Borchardt, Inc.

Chapter 4

Foucault, Michel. *The History of Sexuality.* Vol. 1, *An Introduction,* translated by Robert Hurley. New York: Vintage, 1980. Copyright © 1976 by Éditions Gallimard. Reprinted by permission of Georges Borchardt, Inc.

Foucault, Michel. *The History of Sexuality.* Vol. 2, *The Use of Pleasure.* New York: Pantheon Books, 1985. Copyright © 1984 by Éditions Gallimard. Reprinted by permission of Georges Borchardt, Inc.

Foucault, Michel. *The History of Sexuality.* Vol. 3, *The Care of the Self.* New York: Pantheon Books, 1986. Copyright © 1984 by Éditions Gallimard. Reprinted by permission of Georges Borchardt, Inc.

Chapter 5

Baudrillard, Jean. *For a Critique of the Political Economy of the Sign.* United States: Telos Press, 1981. Reprinted by permission of Telos Press.

Baudrillard, Jean. *Fatal Strategies.* New York: Semiotext(e). Foreign Agent Series, 1990. Reprinted by permission of Semiotext(e).

Baudrillard, Jean. *The Mirror of Production.* St. Louis: Telos Press, 1975. Reprinted by permission of Telos Press.

Baudrillard, Jean. *Symbolic Exchange and Death.* London: Sage, 1993. Reprinted by permission of Sage Publications.

Baudrillard, Jean. *The Transparency of Evil: Essays on Extreme Phenomena.* London: Verso, 1993.

Bauman, Zygmunt. *Intimations of Postmodernity.* London: Routledge, 1992. Reprinted by permission of Routledge, UK.

Gane, Mike, ed. *Baudrillard Live: Selected Interviews.* London: Routledge, 1993. Reprinted by permission of Routledge, UK.

Poster, Mark, ed. *Jean Baudrillard: Selected Writings.* Stanford: Stanford University Press, 1988. Reprinted by permission of Stanford University Press, and Blackwell Publishers.

Chapter 6

Baudrillard, Jean. *For a Critique of the Political Economy of the Sign.* United States: Telos Press, 1981. Reprinted by permission of Telos Press.

Baudrillard, Jean. *Fatal Strategies.* New York: Semiotext(e). Foreign Agents Series, 1990. Reprinted by permission of Semiotext(e).

Baudrillard, Jean. *The Illusion of the End.* Palo Alto: Stanford University Press, 1994. Reprinted by permission of Stanford University Press.

Baudrillard, Jean. *The Mirror of Production.* St Louis: Telos Press, 1975. Reprinted by permission of Telos Press.

Baudrillard, Jean. *Simulations.* New York: Semiotext(e). Foreign Agents Series, 1983. Reprinted by permission of Semiotext(e).

Baudrillard, Jean. *Symbolic Exchange and Death.* London: Sage, 1993. Reprinted by permission of Sage Publications.

Baudrillard, Jean. *The Transparency of Evil: Essays on Extreme Phenomena.* London: Verso, 1993.

Gane, Mike, ed. *Baudrillard Live: Selected Interviews.* London: Routledge, 1993. Reprinted by permission of Routledge, UK.

Chapter 7

Bowie, Malcolm. *Lacan.* Cambridge: Harvard University Press, 1991.

Deleuze, Gilles, and Felix Guattari. *Anti-Oedipus: Capitalism and Schizophrenia.* New York: Viking Penguin, 1972.

Derrida, Jacques. *Writing and Difference.* Chicago: University of Chicago Press. Copyright © 1978 by The University of Chicago. Reprinted by permission of The University of Chicago.

Jameson, Fredric. "Postmodernism, Or, The Cultural Logic of Late Capitalism." *New Left Review* 146 (1984): 59–92.

Lyotard, Jean-François. *The Postmodern Condition: A Report on Knowledge.* Translated by Geoff Bennington and Brian Massumi. Minneapolis: University of Minnesota Press, 1984. English translation and Foreward copyright © 1984 by the University of Minnesota. Original, French-language edition copyright © 1979 by Les Éditions de Minuit. Reprinted by permission of the University of Minnesota Press, and Manchester University Press.

Lyotard, Jean-François. *The Postmodern Explained: Correspondence 1982–1985.* Translated by Don Barry, Bernadette Maher, Julian Pefanis, and Morgan Thomas. Minneapolis: University of Minnesota Press, 1993. English translation copyright © 1992 by Power Publications, Sidney, Australia. North American edition copyright © 1993 by the Regents of the University of Minnesota. Original, French-language edition copyright © 1988 by Éditions Galilée, Paris. Reprinted by permission of the University of Minnesota Press.

Spivak, Gayatri. "Translator's Preface." In Jacques Derrida, *Of Grammatology,* ix-lxxxvii. Baltimore: The Johns Hopkins University Press, 1974. Reprinted by permission of The Johns Hopkins University Press.

Chapter 8

Bauman, Zygmunt. *Intimations of Postmodernity.* London: Routledge, 1992. Reprinted by permission of Routledge. UK.

Bauman, Zygmunt. *Postmodern Ethics.* Oxford: Basil Blackwell, 1993. Reprinted by permission of Blackwell Publishers.

Beck, Ulrich. *Risk Society: Towards a New Modernity.* London: Sage, 1992. Reprinted by permission of Sage Publications.

Giddens, Anthony. *The Consequences of Modernity.* Stanford, Stanford University Press, 1990. Reprinted by permission of Blackwell Publishers.

Giddens, Anthony. *Modernity and Self-Identity: Self and Society in the Late Modern Age.* Stanford: Stanford University Press, 1991. Reprinted by permission of Blackwell Publishers.

Chapter 9

Best, Steven, "Jemeson, Totality, and the Poststructuralist Critique." In *Postmodernism: Jameson: Critique,* edited by Douglas Kellner, 333–368. Washington, D.C.: Maisonneuve Press, 1989. Reprinted by permission of Masionneuve Press.

Bordo, Susan. "Feminism, Postmodernism, and Gender-Skepticism." Reprinted from *Feminism/Postmodernism,* edited by Linda Nicholson (1990), 122–156, with permission of the publisher, Routledge: New York.

Butler, Judith. "Contingent Foundations." Reprinted from *Feminist Contentions: A Philosophical Exchange,* edited by Selya Benhabib, Judith Butler, Dricilla Cornell, and Nancy Fraser (1995), 33–57, with permission of the publisher, Routledge: New York.

Cixous, Helene. "The Laugh of the Medusa." *Signs* 1 (4) (summer 1976): 875–93. Copyright ©

1976 by The University of Chicago. All rights reserved. Reprinted by permission of The University of Chicago Press.

Farganis, Sondra. "Postmodernism and Feminism." In *Postmodernism and Social Inquiry,* edited by David R. Dickens and Andrea Fontana, 101–126. New York: Guilford Press, 1994. Reprinted by permission of Guilford Press.

Haraway, Donna. "A Manifesto for Cyborgs: Science, Technology, and Socialist Feminism in the 1980s." Reprinted from *Feminism/Postmodernism,* edited by Linda Nicholson (1990), 190–233, with permission of the publisher, Routledge: New York, and of the author.

Irigaray, Luce. "The Sex Which Is Not One." In *New French Feminism,* edited by Elaine Marks and Isabelle de Courtivron, 99–106. New York: Schocken Books, 1981. Originally published in *Ce sexe qui n'est pas un.* Copyright © 1977 Éditions de Minuit, Paris. Reprinted by permission of Éditions de Minuit.

Jameson, Fredric. *Postmodernism, or, The Cultural Logic of Late Capitalism,* Copyright 1991, Duke University Press, Durham, N.C. Reprinted with permission.

Jameson, Fredric. "Postmodernism. Or, The Cultural Logic of Late Capitalism." *New Left Review* 146 (1984): 59–92.

Kellner, Douglas. "Introduction: Jameson, Marxism, and Postmodernism." In *Postmodernism: Jameson: Critique,* edited by Douglas Kellner. Washington, D.C.: Maisonneuve Press, 1989. Reprinted by permission of Maisonneuve Press.

Kristeva, Julia. "Oscillation Between Power and Denial." In *New French Feminism,* edited by Elaine Marks and Isabelle de Courtivron, 165–167. New York: Schocken Books, 1981. Originally published in *Tel quel* 58 (summer 1974). Reprinted by permission of Georges Borchardt, Inc.

Chapter 11

Lyotard, Jean-François, *The Postmodern Condition: A Report on Knowledge.* Translated by Geof Bennington and Brian Massumi. Minneapolis: University of Minnesota Press, 1984. English translation and Foreward copyright © 1984 by the University of Minnesota. Original, French-language edition copyright © 1979 by Les Éditions de Minuit. Reprinted by permission of the University of Minnesota Press, and Manchester University Press.

Chapter 12

Bauman, Zygmunt. *Intimations of Postmodernity.* London: Routledge, 1992. Reprinted by permission of Routledge, UK.

Best, Steven. "Jameson, Totality, and the Poststructuralist Critique." In *Postmodernism: Jameson: Critique,* edited by Douglas Kellner, 333–368. Washington, D.C.: Maisonneuve Press, 1989. Reprinted by permission of Maisonneuve Press.

Deleuze, Gilles, and Felix Guattari. *Anti-Oedipus: Capitalism and Schizophrenia.* New York: Viking Penguin, 1972.

Jameson, Fredric. *Postmodernism, or, The Cultural Logic of Late Capitalism.* Copyright 1991, Duke University Press, Durham, N.C. Reprinted with permission.

Kellner, Douglas. "Introduction: Jameson, Marxism, and Postmodernism." In *Postmodernism: Jameson: Critique,* edited by Douglas Kellner. Washington, D.C.: Maisonneuve Press, 1989. Reprinted by permission of Maisonneuve Press.

Lipovestky, Gilles, *The Empire of Fashion: Dressing Modern Democracy.* Copyright ©1987 by Éditions Gallimard (Paris) in L'Empire de l'éphémère. Copyright © 1994 by Princeton University Press. Reprinted by permission of Princeton University Press.

ABOUT
THE AUTHOR

GEORGE RITZER is Professor of Sociology at the University of Maryland. His major areas of interest are sociological theory and the sociology of work. He has served as Chair of the American Sociological Association's Sections on Theoretical Sociology (1989–1990) and Organizations and Occupations (1980–1981). Professor Ritzer has been Distinguished Scholar-Teacher at the University of Maryland and has been awarded a Teaching Excellence award. He has held the UNESCO Chair in Social Theory at the Russian Academy of Sciences and a Fulbright-Hays Fellowship. He has been Scholar-in-Residence at the Netherlands Institute for Advanced Study and the Swedish Collegium for Advanced Study in the Social Sciences.

Dr. Ritzer's main theoretical interests lie in metatheory as well as in the theory of rationalization. In metatheory, his most recent book is *Metatheorizing in Sociology* (Lexington Books, 1991). Earlier books on this topic include *Sociology: A Multiple Paradigm Science* (1975, 1980) and *Toward an Integrated Sociological Paradigm* (1981). He has written a number of essays on rationalization as well as *The McDonaldization of Society* (Pine Forge Press, 1996) and the forthcoming *The McDonaldization Thesis: Explorations and Extensions* (Sage). Professor Ritzer is also the author of another work in applied social theory, *Expressing America: A Critique of the Global Credit Card Society* (Pine Forge Press, 1995). Professor Ritzer's work has been translated into a number of languages, including Chinese, Croatian, Danish, German, Farsi, Italian, Korean, Russian, and Spanish.

In 1996 McGraw-Hill published the fourth edition of Professor Ritzer's basic text *Sociological Theory,* the fourth edition of his *Modern Sociological Theory,* and the second edition of his *Classical Sociological Theory.*

To Sue, with Debts Too Numerous to Mention

CONTENTS

PREFACE

*T*HIS is an effort to offer a readable and coherent introduction to the often self-consciously unreadable and incoherent body of work known as postmodern social theory. It is designed to be an introduction to the fundamental ideas, and most important thinkers, associated with this perspective.

This also involves an attempt to look at this body of theory from the vantage point of the field of sociology. While some postmodern social theorists are sociologists, most are not. Indeed, one of the defining characteristics of postmodern social theory is that it is interdisciplinary. It is certainly possible to look at this theory from a sociological vantage point, but it is also possible to look at it from the point of view of many other fields (literary criticism, anthropology, and so on). Thus, this book will constitute only one of many possible "readings" of postmodern social theory. We will see throughout the book, and especially in Chapters 10 and 11, that postmodern social theory is of great relevance to sociology.

Relatedly, this book undertakes a modern reading of postmodern social theory. That may sound odd, but it is perfectly appropriate given the tenets of postmodernism (and modernism). I accept the view in this book that modernism and postmodernism are not mutually exclusive perspectives but rather alternative ways of looking at the social world. In this light, it is quite acceptable to look at postmodern social theory from a modern point of view. Among other things, a modern viewpoint means that there is an effort here to find some coherence, some underlying order, in the seemingly chaotic world of postmodern social theory.

More generally, this book can be seen as an effort to modernize postmodernism. Some, perhaps most, postmodernists will look askance at such an effort. Most postmodern social theorists are renegades, and they want their theoretical orientation to remain at odds with modernism. Fine! However, it is time for modernists to appropriate some of postmodernism's best ideas and perspectives for their own use. Postmodernists really should have no objection to this since they emphasize the importance of readers rather than authors. Thus, what follows is one modern reading of postmodern social theory.

The most radical of postmodernists not only proclaim the death of modernity but also of modern disciplines like sociology, as well as its subject matter, the social. Such contentions can be rejected out of hand, or they can be taken, as they are in this book, as essentially healthy challenges to sociology. Sociology will be a stronger discipline by understanding and finding ways to respond to these criticisms.

All good postmodernists, radical or moderate, have created perspectives, ideas, and concepts that deserve, nay need, a hearing in sociology. Sociological theory may, in many ways, be quite vibrant, but it seems to lack a plethora of new ideas. What postmodern social theory offers is a storehouse chock full of such ideas. Some will not prove very useful, but my guess is that many will be of great interest and utility to sociologists. In any case, the infusion of so many new ideas cannot help but invigorate sociology and sociological theory.

This is certainly not the first time, nor the last, that sociological theory has turned to other disciplines for new ideas. Since its inception, sociological theory has been the recipient of a steady stream of such ideas from many different fields. It is now time to add postmodern social theory to that list of fields. Of course, the flow has always gone in both directions, and sociological theory has contributed its share of ideas to other disciplines.

Thus, this book comes at an exciting time for sociological theory. There is a brilliant set of new ideas out there, and many of them are beginning to find their way into sociological theory. Sociological theory will never quite be the same. The reader of this book is about to be immersed in that set of ideas as well as in a discussion of what they mean for the revitalization of sociological theory.

Plan of the Book   Chapters 1 and 2 constitute a general introduction to the topics to be covered in this book. Chapter 1 offers an overview of postmodern social theory as well as a discussion of its implications for sociology and sociological theory. Chapter 2 presents a brief description of the development of postmodern social theory. Special attention is devoted to the various theoretical precursors that played central roles in shaping postmodern social theory. With these two chapters as background, we move directly into a discussion of postmodern social theory. Rather than discuss that theory in general terms, the body of the book will focus on the ideas of specific thinkers associated with postmodernism (thereby challenging another tenet of postmodernism—its rejection of a focus on the author). The next five chapters are devoted to the work of French postmodern social theorists; clearly postmodern social theory has been dominated by the French.

In Chapters 3 and 4 we focus on the work of Michel Foucault. As he himself was quick to point out (he died in 1984), Foucault is difficult to categorize. He is sometimes thought of as a poststructuralist and at other times as a postmodernist. We will not dwell on this distinction since many poststructuralists, especially the most radical of them, are also considered postmodernists.

Chapters 5 and 6 deal with another French social thinker, Jean Baudrillard, who is generally considered to be the most important postmodern social theorist. Early in his work, Baudrillard might have been better thought of as a poststructuralist or a post-Marxist, but during the past few decades his work seems clearly postmodern. While this may seem clear to outside observers, it should be pointed out that Baudrillard rarely uses the term and often seeks to dissociate himself from postmodernism.

Chapter 7 deals with the work of other important French postmodernists: Jacques Derrida, Gilles Deleuze, Felix Guattari, Jean-François Lyotard, Jacques Lacan, and Paul Virilio. In other disciplines, several of these thinkers are considered of equal or greater importance than Foucault or Baudrillard. They receive somewhat briefer treatment here because of space constraints and because their work is not quite as important to sociological theory as that of Foucault and Baudrillard. However, that is a judgment call, and I recognize that others would argue that Derrida, Lyotard, and even Lacan are thinkers of prime importance to sociological theory.

Chapter 8 is concerned with other European contributors to the postmodern debate. The work of Anthony Giddens, Ulrich Beck, and Jürgen Habermas represent modern efforts to respond to and critique postmodernism. Zygmunt Bauman is important because he deals with *both* modern and postmodern social issues. While a modernist, Bauman has considerable sympathy for the postmodernist perspective. David Harvey has developed a postmodern orientation heavily shaped by Marxian theory. All in all, Chapter 8 deals more with interventions in postmodern social theory than with contributions to it.

In Chapter 9 we deal with American contributions to the dialogue about postmodernism. The work of Daniel Bell, especially his ideas on the postindustrial society and postmodern culture, is an important precursor to postmodernism. Fredric Jameson is probably the best-known American practitioner of postmodern social theory. We then deal with largely American feminist and multiculturalist perspectives. As we will see, there is a strong, but sometimes contradictory, relationship between these two perspectives and postmodern social theory.

In Chapters 10 and 11 we discuss the implications of the work of the thinkers discussed in this book for contemporary sociological theory. Chapter 10 explores the implications of a variety of epistemological issues raised by postmodernists. The question that orients the discussion in this chapter is: What are the epistemological lessons of postmodern social theory for sociological theory? Chapter 11 employs a postmodernist approach, and many of the most important postmodern concepts, in an analysis of one aspect of our contemporary consumer society—the *new means of consumption*. The goal in this chapter is to move away from abstractions and to use postmodernism in a very concrete way.

Chapter 12 briefly examines two final issues. First, some of the major criticisms of postmodern theory will be reviewed. Second, we will close the chapter and the book with an overview of recent efforts to move beyond postmodern social theory.

I would like to thank an extraordinarily constructive set of reviewers—Bob Antonio, Patricia Clough, Charles Lemert, Mary Rogers, and Steven Seidman—for their insights and thoughts on improving the book. Doug Goodman authored the section on Lacan in Chapter 7 and was helpful on other matters throughout the book. Jan Geesin and Allan Liska were invaluable assistants. Jill Gordon, and in her absence Kathy Blake, helped to move the project along smoothly. As usual, Jeremy Ritzer has been a very perceptive indexer.

George Ritzer

POSTMODERN
SOCIAL
THEORY

1

POSTMODERN SOCIAL THEORY, SOCIOLOGY, AND SOCIOLOGICAL THEORY

SOME FUNDAMENTAL DEFINITIONS
WHAT IS POSTMODERN SOCIAL THEORY?
VULNERABILITY OF SOCIOLOGY AND SOCIOLOGICAL THEORY
INTIMATIONS OF POSTMODERN SOCIAL THEORY IN SOCIOLOGY

SOCIOLOGICAL theory (and, to a lesser extent, sociology more generally) faces a situation today that a number of fields, mainly in the arts, confronted a decade or two ago:[1]

> The postmodern moment had arrived[2] and perplexed intellectuals, artists, and cultural entrepreneurs wondered whether they should get on the bandwagon and join the carnival, or sit on the sidelines until the new fad disappeared into the whirl of cultural fashion.
>
> (Kellner, 1989b:1–2)

While some sociological theorists, and many sociologists, still consider postmodern social theory to be a fad, and it continues to look to some (but not this author) more like a carnival (Norris, 1990) than a serious scholarly endeavor, the simple fact is that sociological theorists[3] can no longer view postmodernism as little more than an interesting side- (if not freak-) show. A good deal of the most interesting and important contemporary social theory swirls in and around the postmodern scene. *Sociological* theory must attend to this growing body of *social* theory.

In fact, this book is premised on the idea that the landscape of sociological theory is being transformed by postmodern social theory. For one thing, the critiques of postmodern social theorists are forcing many sociological theorists to reconsider some of their most basic premises. For another, many of the theoretical ideas created by postmodernists are in the process of being integrated into the mainstream of sociological theory.

---

[1] Other fields that are only recently confronting the postmodern challenge are psychoanalysis (Sass, 1994) and criminology (Schwartz and Friedrichs, 1994).

[2] To at least some observers it has already passed. According to Malcolm Waters (1995:1), "postmodernism was *the* concept of the 1980s." Alexander (1995) argues that a departure from postmodern social theory is already underway. See also Frow (1991), *What Was Postmodernism?*

[3] For a critique of sociological methodology, especially ethnography, from a postmodern perspective, see Clough (1992), *The Ends of Ethnography.*

1

A number of European sociological theorists (e.g., Barry Smart [1993a], Mike Featherstone [1991]) have been on the postmodern bandwagon for some time and they have been joined by a few American sociological theorists (e.g., Charles Lemert [1994], Stjepan Mestrovic [1993], Steven Seidman [1994a], Richard Harvey Brown [1987]). However, almost all of the important postmodern social theorists, virtually all of the people whose work will be treated in detail in this book, are *not* sociologists. Rather, they are most likely to be interdisciplinary social theorists whose work reflects input from a number of different fields. In some cases, their work is a kind of social theory that, in the main, seems very familiar to sociological theorists (Michel Foucault, for example), while in other cases their work appears to represent a profound assault on the basic premises of that theory (for example, Jean Baudrillard). In either case, it is essential that sociological theorists, and students of the field, familiarize themselves with postmodern ideas. At the minimum, those ideas will continue to find their way into sociological discourse; at the maximum they will radically alter the nature of that discourse.

Sociology is a latecomer to postmodernism, but in contemporary social theory postmodernism has been so hot (Kellner, 1989b:2), so debated, so analyzed and re-analyzed that at least one sociological theorist has urged that we stop using the term because it has been "worn frail by overexertion" (Lemert, 1994:142). That is, it has been abused and debased by both supporters and detractors in the course of the overheated debate between them over the merits of postmodern social theory. While that may well be the case, sociological theory still has much to learn from postmodern social theory.

Given its importance and the interest that it has generated, the objective in this book is to offer students of sociology (and other social sciences) an introduction to postmodern social theory. However, it should be pointed out that such an introduction is no easy matter because, among other things, there is great diversity among the generally highly idiosyncratic postmodern social thinkers, and it is difficult, if not impossible, to offer generalizations on which the majority would agree. In addition, it is difficult to tell a coherent story because one of the premises of postmodernism is that distortion often occurs when efforts are made to make the incoherent seem coherent. As Bauman (1992:xxiv) puts it: "any narrative . . . stands a risk of implying more coherence than the postmodern condition could possibly uphold."

In fact, the vast majority of generalizations about postmodernism, whether they stem from supporters or detractors, *are* flawed, usually bearing little or no resemblance to what specific postmodernists have to say. Thus, instead of talking in global terms about postmodernism, the strategy throughout most of this book will be to discuss the ideas of specific thinkers associated in one way or another with postmodernism. (However, because of the need to orient the reader for the specifics to come, we are forced to offer, very cautiously, some generalizations about postmodern social thought as this chapter unfolds.)

Ironically, virtually none of the thinkers discussed in this book would be happy being labeled a postmodernist. Many are avowedly modernists, others better thought of as poststructuralists (more on this below), and still others uncomfortable with, or downright resistant to, any label at all. Whatever they may think of themselves or be thought of by others, the fact remains that their ideas *are* relevant in one way or another to the current literature on postmodern social theory. It is for that reason that their ideas are covered in this book.

Another problem here is that one of the basic tenets of postmodernism is what has been alternately called the death of "man" (including, of course, woman), of the subject, or of the author. While we will return to the meaning(s) of these inter-related ideas at a number of points in this book, for our purposes in this context we can take this to mean that instead of focusing on authors of texts and what they mean by them, postmodernism involves a focus on texts and their relationship to other texts (what the postmodernists call "intertextuality").[4] Here is the way Spivak (1974:liv) puts this issue: "counting the proper names of predecessors must be recognized as a convenient fiction. Each proper name establishes a sovereign self against the anonymity of textuality." While most of this book is devoted to a discussion of texts and how they relate to one another, the discussion is organized under the heading of specific authors. In that sense, and many others, this is distinctly *not* a postmodern undertaking. However, it is my view that it is only by presenting the work of each author independently that we can begin to make any sense at all out of postmodern social theory. It is difficult enough following the intellectual twists and turns in the work of key thinkers like Foucault or Baudrillard, let alone trying to unravel the spider's web of innumerable other texts that surrounds each and every one of their texts. That is not to say that I disagree with the importance of such intertextual analysis, but it is to say that I do not think it an effective way of introducing the basic premises of postmodern social theory.

Some postmodernists would also object to a book devoted to "theory," whether or not it is postmodern. As Best and Kellner (1991:x) put it, "postmodern critiques are directed against the notion of 'theory' itself . . . a systematically developed conceptual structure anchored in the real." That is, there is opposition to the idea that to be considered a theory, a body of systematic ideas must somehow model or represent reality ("representationalism"). Much postmodern theorizing is quite insightful, but it is often quite unsystematic, and very little of it is presented as a model of reality. Indeed, some postmodernists might argue that the effort by traditional sociological theorists to systematically model reality undermines their ability to generate insights. Most sociological theory is guilty of what postmodernists would consider a false separation of the "real" from "theory," as well as of developing theory that purports to represent something—the real—that the postmodernists believe can only be known narrowly and interpretively. What is real cannot be separated from the interpretation of it, and it is impossible to adjudicate conflicts between interpretations.

However, in my view, bodies of ideas do not need to be either systematic or representations of the real to qualify as theories. While postmodernists may reject theory, what most of them in fact do is to theorize, often about the social (or the loss of it). Perhaps they are haphazard at times, but the fact is that these are, at least in part, social theories, and they are relevant to the concerns of sociological theorists.

---

[4] And, as we will see, on "readers" rather than authors.

This book on postmodern social theory employs the same definition of theory that I utilize in *Sociological Theory* (Ritzer, 1996b). That is, theories are sets of ideas that deal with *centrally important social issues,* have *a wide range of application,* and have *stood the test of time* (or promise to). In addition, here as in the other text, I am concerned with theoretical *work done by sociologists,* or with that done in other fields, that has *come to be defined as important in sociology.* The ideas to be discussed throughout this book meet the criteria laid out in this definition of theory. They may not be systematic or represent the real, but that does not prevent them from being considered theories.

To be clear, however, the theories to be discussed in this book are social theories and *not* narrowly sociological theories. Above all, this means that while, like sociological theories, they deal with social issues, they are generally interdisciplinary in nature, drawing on thought from a number of fields, and they are produced by thinkers who defy easy categorization. In fact, sociological theory has always been strongly affected by social theories. For example, Karl Marx was not a sociologist, but he developed a social theory that has had, and continues to have, a powerful impact on sociological theory.

This book flies in the face of another tenet of postmodernism—its skepticism of grand narratives. Grand narratives, such as those offered in textbooks (like this one), which purport to tell *the* story of a field or discipline, are considered by postmodernists to be myths that conceal many dimensions that do not fit into the story being told. A textbook, like this one, implies the privileging of certain ideas over others, valorizing certain perspectives and marginalizing others. Since I am choosing to tell the story of postmodern social theory in one way (out of many possibilities; for others, see Kroker, 1992; Hollinger, 1994; Bertens, 1995), I am valorizing some ideas and thinkers (especially those I choose to discuss in depth) and marginalizing others (those who receive little or no attention in these pages). Furthermore, this is a story told primarily from the perspective of a sociologist; other grand narratives told from other vantage points (literary criticism, linguistics) are not to be found in these pages, even though they might make equally, if not more important, stories.

While I recognize the problems involved in making these kinds of choices and, more generally, in the kind of modernist narrative offered here, such a story needs to be constructed and told to try to give at least some coherence to what is otherwise an admittedly highly incoherent body of thought. An incoherent overview of an incoherent field is in nobody's interest, except perhaps those intellectuals who devote their lives to clarifying incoherent ideas. However, it is important to recognize that I do *not* consider the story to be told in these pages to be *the* story of postmodern social theory. Many such stories are possible, and this is just one of the possible narratives. Thus, it would be better and more accurate to view this book as offering one of many possible narratives and not a grand narrative.

It is also likely that most postmodernists would be appalled at the idea of a text designed to introduce readers systematically to their basic ideas. They would see a textbook as a modern structure that seeks to impose itself on their ideas, attempts to give those ideas a rational ordering, and thereby does grave violence to them.

They would see a textbook as a kind of "prison house" (Jameson, 1972) that confines, and restricts the free play of, those ideas. No doubt violence will be done to postmodern thinking in these pages, but as sensitive as I am to postmodern concerns, I will do my best to limit it as much as possible within the confines of what is, admittedly, a modernist project written by an author who, try as he may, continues to think and write in (mostly) a modern way.[5]

Most postmodernists (and many modernists as well) would undoubtedly argue that instead of reading a text like this one, what readers should do is muck around in the original postmodern texts and make their own sense of that intertextual field. There is no question that they are right in making such an argument. There is also no question that if that was their only option, most readers would know little or nothing about postmodernism. Postmodern social theory is a highly complex, jargonistic, contradictory body of work that would put off all but the most persistent social thinkers. This book is designed for those who really would like to know what the noise surrounding postmodernism is all about but lack the training and/or the time to pore over the innumerable original texts. My hope is that after reading this introduction, the reader will have the background and inspiration to delve into some of the original texts. If not, the reader will at least have some sense of the reasons for all the excitement about postmodern social theory.

SOME FUNDAMENTAL DEFINITIONS

Judith Butler (1995:51) speaks not only for many postmodernists but also most modernists when she announces: "I don't know what postmodernism is." While no concept has greater resonance today among scholars in a wide range of disciplines than "postmodernism," there is enormous ambiguity and controversy over exactly what is meant by that notion and related terms. To add some clarity, it would be useful to distinguish among postmodernity, postmodernism, and postmodern social theory.[6]

• *Postmodernity* refers to a social and political epoch that is generally seen as following the modern era in a historical sense (Kumar, 1995; Crook, Pakulski, and Waters, 1992).
• *Postmodernism* refers to cultural products (in art, movies, architecture, and so on) that are seen as different from modern cultural products (Kumar, 1995; Jameson, 1991).
• *Postmodern social theory* refers to a kind of social theory that is distinct from modern social theory (Best and Kellner, 1991).

---

[5] I am not alone in having this problem; others include Douglas Kellner and Zygmunt Bauman (see Chapter 8). The reader might ponder what it means to have a book about postmodernism written by a modernist; what sorts of distortions are apt to be manifest in such a book? It is also worth thinking about what a postmodernist text on postmodern theory might look like. One possibility is that it might look something like MTV—one fragment after another with little or no connection or coherence.

[6] Here I follow the distinction made by Best and Kellner (1991:5).

Thus, the idea of the postmodern encompasses *a new historical epoch, new cultural products,* and *a new type of theorizing about the social world.* All of these elements of the postmodern, of course, share the perspective that something new and different has occurred (socially, culturally, or intellectually) in recent years, and those new postmodern developments are coming to stand as alternatives to, or perhaps to supplant, modern realities.

The first point is that there is a widespread belief that the era of modernity is ending or has ended, and we have entered a new social epoch—*postmodernity* (Dunn, 1991). As we will see, there are many ways to characterize the difference between the modern and the postmodern world, but as an illustration, one of the best is the difference in viewpoints on whether it is possible to find rational (rationality is a concept closely associated with modernity [Dahrendorf, 1979]) solutions to society's problems. For example, Lyndon Johnson's war on poverty in the 1960s was typical of the way those associated with a modern society believed they could discover and implement rational solutions to its problems. It could be argued that by the 1970s such programs had begun to lose favor, and the transition to a postmodern society was underway (Elazar, 1980). By the 1980s, the Reagan administration and its general unwillingness to develop massive programs to deal with such problems was representative, at least in one sense, of a postmodern society and the belief that there is no single rational answer to various problems.[7] The Reagan administration was known for its postmodern use of the media to communicate using "soundbites," not by its efforts to develop massive programs to solve social problems. Thus, we might conclude that somewhere between the presidential administrations of Lyndon Johnson and Ronald Reagan,[8] the United States began moving from being a modern to a postmodern society. In the mid-1990s, the even more extreme conservative position of Newt Gingrich with his Contract with America makes it clear that we have progressed even further into the postmodern world, in which we are progressively giving up hope of finding grand rational solutions to our most pressing problems. Even a Democratic president, Bill Clinton, was forced to declare in his 1996 State of the Union address that "the era of big government is over."

A word of caution is necessary here. Most postmodernists are uneasy and even unwilling to discuss an historical transition from modernity to postmodernity. For one thing, it constitutes the kind of grand narrative that we have already seen they reject. Second, it involves the kind of linear, chronological thinking that postmodernists associate with modernism and therefore also reject. To postmodernists, things rarely, if ever, progress in a simple, linear manner. Finally, it involves, in their view, far too neat and simplified a distinction between historical epochs. Thus, while it is possible to think of a transition from modernity to postmodernity, and much of this thinking has been given impetus by postmodern social theory, few, if any, postmodern theorists accept such a simple, linear, grand narrative. They

---

[7] Pettegrew (1992) also focuses on the 1980s, but he sees MTV, not the Reagan administration, as the key development.

[8] In using these examples, I am not implying that modernity is necessarily liberal and postmodernity necessarily conservative.

do agree that something has happened; something has changed, but it is not simple and it is not linear (Calhoun, 1993).

Second, *postmodernism* relates to the cultural realm in which it is argued that postmodern products have tended to supplant modern products (Docker, 1994; Strinati, 1995). In architecture, we can, following Jean Baudrillard, the most important postmodern social theorist (see Chapters 5 and 6), contrast the modern and highly rational twin towers in New York City to the more playful, populist, eclectic, and nonrational creations of the postmodern architects. Architect Philip Johnson's AT&T building in New York is often cited as an example of postmodern architecture since it includes both modern and traditional elements. Or, there is the dwelling designed by Frank Gehry that involves a traditional clapboard house surrounded by an industrial-looking corrugated metal wall (Jameson, 1991). In music, classical music would certainly be modern, while Shusterman (1991) sees rap music as postmodern because, among other things, of the fact that it recycles extant styles rather than creating new ones, eclectically mixes styles, and is local (representing primarily the black community) rather than universal. In the realm of television, the highly offbeat show *Twin Peaks* is generally taken to be a good example of postmodernism, while *Father Knows Best,* with its highly rational nuclear family, is a good example of a modern television program. In the movies, *Blade Runner,* showing a Los Angeles of the future combining highly futuristic and highly traditional elements and peopled by "replicants" who often seem more humane than the humans, may be seen as a postmodern work, while the *Ten Commandments* with its biblical grand narrative would certainly qualify as a modern movie.

Third, and of much more direct relevance to us here, is the emergence of *postmodern social theory* and its differences from modern theory. In general, we can say that modern social theory tends to be absolute, rational, and to accept the possibility of discovering truth, whereas postmodern social theory tends to be relativistic and open to the possibility of irrationality. However, as is the case with modern social theory, not all postmodern social theory is of one piece. Smart (1993a) has sought to bring some order to this area by articulating three fundamental positions taken by postmodern social theorists.[9]

• The first, or *extreme postmodernist,* position is that there has been a radical rupture, and modern society has been replaced by a postmodern society. While he is uncomfortable with such labels, it is clear that Jean Baudrillard believes that society has changed radically. Another postmodern thinker who holds such views is Paul Virilio (1991a; 1995); we will discuss his work briefly in Chapter 7.

• The second, or *more moderate,* position is that while a change has taken place, postmodernity grows out of, and is continuous with, modernity. This orientation is adhered to by such postmodern Marxian thinkers as Fredric Jameson (as well as Ernesto Laclau and Chantal Mouffe [1985] and David Harvey [1989]) and

---

[9] Other examples of typologies include Rosenau's (1992) distinction between skeptical and affirmative postmodern thinkers and Kumar's (1995) differentiation between the postmodernism of reaction and resistance.

postmodern feminists such as Nancy Fraser, Donna Haraway, and Linda Nicholson (see Chapter 9).

• Finally, there is the theoretical position adopted by Smart himself that rather than viewing them as epochs, we can see *modernity and postmodernity as engaged in a long-running relationship with one another,* with postmodernity continually pointing out the limitations of modernity. Thus, they can be seen as alternative perspectives, not successive time periods. The most important representative of this point of view is Jean-François Lyotard (Chapter 7); this perspective will also inform the discussion in Chapter 11.

While useful, it should be noted that postmodern social theorists would likely dismiss Smart's typology (they would also reject the distinction among postmodernity, postmodernism, and postmodern social theory [Kumar, 1995]) as greatly simplifying the enormous diversity of their ideas and of distorting each individual's work in the process. In fact, while a useful orienting point for the reader, we will not use Smart's typology any further either. Rather, as pointed out above, we will concentrate (once we get past this introduction) on the ideas of specific thinkers and not on the broad categories of thought into which their ideas might be shoehorned.

WHAT IS POSTMODERN SOCIAL THEORY?

A useful beginning toward gaining a greater understanding of postmodern social theory is provided by Pauline Rosenau (1992) who defines such theory largely in terms of the things to which it is opposed. Above all, and most obviously, postmodernism is critical of modern society and of its failure to deliver on its promises. In light of the horrors of the twentieth century (Auschwitz, the Gulag Archipelago), postmodernists ask how anyone can believe that modernity has brought with it progress and hope for a still brighter future. Postmodernists tend to critique much associated with modernity:

> . . . the accumulated experience of Western civilization, industrialization, urbanization, advanced technology, the nation state, life in the "fast lane." They challenge modern priorities: career, office, individual responsibility, bureaucracy, liberal democracy, tolerance, humanism, egalitarianism, detached experiment, evaluative criteria, neutral procedures, impersonal rules, and rationality.

(Rosenau, 1992:5–6)

Second, as we have already mentioned, postmodern theorists tend to reject what are alternatively called world views, metanarratives, grand narratives, totalizations, and so on. They tend to reject the idea that there is a single grand perspective or answer. As Baudrillard (1990/1993:72), for example, puts it, "The great drives or impulses, with their positive, elective, and attractive powers, are gone." Postmodernists are generally content to live with more limited explanations (local narratives) or with no explanations at all. However, it should be pointed out here that there is often a gap between what postmodernists say and what they do. As we will see, at least some postmodernists do produce grand narratives of their own. Many postmodernists are former Marxian theorists, and as a result they often seek to distance themselves from the grand narratives that characterized that position.

Third, postmodern thinkers tend to accord great importance to more premodern phenomena such as "emotions, feelings, intuition, reflection, speculation, personal experience, custom, violence, metaphysics, tradition, cosmology, magic, myth, religious sentiment, and mystical experience" (Rosenau, 1992:6). As we will see, this is especially true of Jean Baudrillard, chiefly his thoughts on "symbolic exchange."

Fourth, postmodern theorists reject the modern tendency to put boundaries between such things as academic disciplines, "culture and life, fiction and theory, image and reality" (Rosenau, 1992:6). Thus, the work of most postmodern thinkers tends to break through one or more of these boundaries and to suggest that others might want to do the same. For example, we will see Baudrillard describe his social theories as a kind of fiction, science fiction, poetry, and so on.

Fifth, many postmodernists reject the careful, reasoned style of modern academic discourse (Nuyen, 1992). The postmodern author's objective is often more to shock and startle the reader than to win the reader over with a logical, reasoned argument. It also tends to be more literary than academic in style.

Finally, instead of focusing on the core of modern society, postmodern theorists devote their attention to the periphery:

> . . . on what has been taken for granted, what has been neglected, regions of resistance, the forgotten, the irrational, the insignificant, the repressed, the borderline, the classical, the sacred, the traditional, the eccentric, the sublimated, the subjugated, the rejected, the nonessential, the marginal, the peripheral, the excluded, the tenuous, the silenced, the accidental, the dispersed, the disqualified, the deferred, the disjointed.
>
> (Rosenau, 1992:8)

In sum, as Rosenau (1992:8) puts it, the postmodern theorists "offer indeterminacy rather than determinism, diversity rather than unity, difference rather than synthesis, complexity rather than simplification."

VULNERABILITY OF SOCIOLOGY AND SOCIOLOGICAL THEORY

As we have seen, postmodern social theory developed largely outside of sociology and sociological theory. However, the social sciences in general, and sociology in particular, are vulnerable to inroads from postmodern social theory on a variety of grounds. Many of these vulnerabilities are traceable to the wide-scale acceptance of the modern scientific model[10] in the social sciences and in sociology, in particular.

---

[10] Not all postmodern social theorists are opposed to science; see, for example, Latour and Woolgar (1979).

- First, many sociologists are growing impatient with the failure of their scientifically inclined brethren to produce long-promised breakthroughs.
- Second, there is growing awareness that the science that has been produced is most responsive to the needs of those with power and tends to buttress their position in society.
- Third, there is increasing research showing a huge discrepancy between the way science is supposed to operate and the way it actually functions (Knorr-Cetina, 1981; Latour, 1987).
- Fourth, the continuation, even acceleration, of many social problems makes it clear that science is not the answer.
- Fifth, science minimizes, even trivializes, the importance of metaphysical and mystical aspects of social life.
- Finally, science contributes little or nothing to normative or ethical questions or to what we ought to be doing (Rosenau, 1992).

Relatedly, Fuchs and Ward (1994a) argue that sociology is one of a number of fields that is particularly vulnerable to the postmodern critique because it is multi-paradigmatic (Ritzer, 1975), loosely coupled, decentralized, and dominated by texts and "conversations" among scholars. More specifically, Fuchs and Ward argue that fields like sociology are particularly vulnerable to a strong form of *deconstructionism*. Deconstruction is one of postmodernism's key approaches to knowledge, hence theory. (This idea is most often associated with the work of Jacques Derrida; see Chapter 7 for a discussion of his sense of deconstructionism). Briefly, deconstructionists take a text apart to show its basic assumptions and contradictions. Additionally, this "requires that traditional concepts, theory, and understanding surrounding a text be unraveled, including the assumption that an author's intentions and meanings can be easily determined" (Denzin, 1994:185). More generally, deconstructionism "aims to clear away the wreckage of a cluttered theoretical past, which clings to preconceptions that are regarded as no longer workable in the contemporary world" (Denzin, 1994:185). However, the goal of deconstructionism is not then to put it back together in a revised, improved, and truer form. Such a reconstructive task is not undertaken because the deconstructionist rejects the idea that there is some ultimate truth to be discovered. (In fact, the search for truth is seen as concealing a "will to power" [see discussion of this notion and other Nietzschean ideas in Chapter 2], in this case a desire to establish the preeminence of a particular perspective to the detriment of other viewpoints.[11]) There are no ultimate answers; there are only more interpretations, more texts to be "read." In other words, there are only more phenomena to be deconstructed by the deconstructionist.

A textual field like sociology is particularly prone to this strong form of deconstruction. While many postmodernists would disagree, there are, in Fuchs and Ward's (1994a:482) view, other types of fields that in addition to texts "use other means of intellectual production, such as mathematical symbolism, technical de-

---

[11] The will to power can also be viewed in a more positive sense as the capacity for transcendence.

vices, experimental equipment, and the like."[12] Such fields are, in the view of Fuchs and Ward, subject to a much weaker form of deconstruction where, while it is accepted that there is no one truth or privileged epistemological position, science nonetheless proceeds on the basis of ground rules and criteria. In contrast, fields like sociology subject to the strong form of deconstruction tend toward a situation in which "anything goes." Sociologists write texts (books and articles, for example) about other texts (results of surveys or questionnaires) that are about what people say and do (still more texts). Because all are texts, all are subject to deconstruction and reinterpretation. There is no single "true" interpretation of a body of data derived from any of these texts. Here is Fuchs and Ward's description of fields like sociology and why they are particularly prone to deconstructionism and more generally to the postmodern critique:

> Practitioners in textual fields read and write a lot, and they soon start believing that reading and writing is all one can do. They come to see the whole world as text, and whatever doesn't really fit this metaphor becomes to them text-like, or 'semiotic.' After the semiotic transformation of the world is complete, there appears to be nothing beyond the text, and so the universal "crisis of reference and representation" can be proclaimed. When commentaries on commentaries on texts are piled up, anything that is not a text must eventually disappear from sight.
>
> (Fuchs and Ward, 1994b:509)

While this describes the state in sociology, it is not the only field in this category; others include literature, art, and so on—fields in which, as we will see, postmodernism had its beginnings.

Turning from the social sciences and sociology to sociological theory more specifically, Seidman (1991) associates sociological theory with modernism and attributes a number of modern characteristics to it—especially scientism, foundationalism, totalization, essentialism, and insularity—that help make it vulnerable to the attacks of postmodern social theorists. Let us look at each of these briefly.

First, sociological theory is accused of *scientism*. That is, most sociological theorists believe in universal ideas, if not social laws. They adopt the view that there is an accumulating body of theoretical knowledge and that the task of contemporary practitioners is either to add to it or make breakthroughs that move it to a new plateau from which it can once again begin the process of accumulation. However, the absence of laws and the failure to make breakthroughs have opened sociological theory to the attacks of postmodernists.

Second, sociological theory is seen as *foundational*. Foundationalism seeks to base guidelines for social behavior and social analysis on a firm philosophical foundation (Gottdiener, 1993). Relatedly, Seidman (1991:133; italics added) argues that sociological theory "intends to uncover a logic of society; it aims to discover *the one true vocabulary* that mirrors the social universe. . . . Sociological theory aims to denude itself of its contextual embeddedness; to articulate *humanity's universal condition*." It has taken upon itself the responsibility for

---

12 Most postmodernists would also see these as texts and therefore subject to deconstruction.

defining and defending the basic premises, concepts, and explanatory models of sociology. We have assumed the role of resolving disciplinary disputes and conceptual conflicts. . . . Sociological theorists have stepped forward as the virtual police of the sociological mind.

(Seidman, 1991:132)

Sociological theorists see themselves as providing the foundation for the entire discipline of sociology. However, no such single foundation has been uncovered, certainly not one that the discipline as a whole would accept.

Third, sociological theory tends to adopt a *totalizing* view of the world. To Seidman, this means the search for "an overarching totalizing conceptual framework that would be true for all times and all places" (Seidman, 1991:137). On the one hand, this is similar to foundationalism, but on the other to Seidman (1991:139) it means that sociological theorists developed grand narratives of the West's "progress," including "industrialization, modernization, secularization, democratization" and sought to apply them to the world as a whole.[13] The problem with these narratives is that they are unidimensional and ignore many other developments. They have little or nothing to say about many spheres and time periods in the West. As Seidman (1991:140) says, such theories "utterly fail to grasp the multisided, heterogeneous, morally ambiguous social currents and strains that make up the life of any society." Furthermore, such theories completely ignore much of the rest of the world and assume that they have undergone, or would soon undergo, the same progressive developments. For example, a simple model like Durkheim's mechanical-to-organic solidarity tends to "repress important differences between societies" (Seidman, 1991:139). The history of sociological theory has been characterized by conflict among such competing totalizations[14] (for example, Marx's theory of processes leading to the proletarian revolution versus Weber's theory of progressive rationalization) for hegemony, and no single totalization has ever gained preeminence in sociological theory.

Fourth, sociological theories are seen as *essentialist*. That is, they tend to see humans as having basic, fixed, and unchanging characteristics. Social phenomena are viewed as expressions of those essences rather than as products of specific social conditions. A good example is Marx's sense of species being. Such essentialist concepts fail to take into account differences based on "gender, race, ethnicity, class, or sexual orientation" (Seidman, 1991:140). Further, those who adopt one essentialist view tend to disagree with those who adopt other essentialist views.

Finally, sociological theory is viewed as being *insular*, that is, concerned with issues that are of concern only to sociological theorists. To put it another way, the concerns and the disputes of sociological theory have become increasingly metatheoretical, that is in Seidman's (1991:133) terms "self-referential and epistemological." Seidman refers to the debates over micro-macro and agency-structure

---

[13] For a discussion of such a grand narrative in psychology, see Walkerdine (1993).

[14] These might better be seen as grand narratives. In fact, many of the terms associated with postmodern social theory tend to be used inconsistently, and this does not help in trying to gain a clear sense of the perspective.

integration (Ritzer, 1991) as examples of such insular issues that have little or nothing to do with the social world and are of virtually no interest to non-sociologists.

Seidman proceeds to argue that *social* theory represents a viable alternative to sociological theory. Social theories are social stories, or narratives, that are intimately related to the pressing social issues of the day. Furthermore, they are oriented not only to better understanding those issues but also to having an impact on social outcomes. They are not driven by insular theoretical interests but by moral, political, and social concerns.

It is Seidman's thesis that for most of their histories, social and sociological theories have been intertwined. For example, Durkheim did mainly social theory in *The Division of Labor in Society* and primarily sociological theory in *The Rules of Sociological Method.* However, in recent years, and especially after World War II, social theory has been devalued by mainstream sociologists because it is, among other things, ideological and nonscientific. As a result, sociological theory has been ascendant in the discipline. This has had a range of unfortunate consequences, and Seidman wants to see a return to a social theory that would be more consistent with the "postmodern turn" in the social sciences in general.

However, that social theory is not to be the grand social theory of Marx or Durkheim, but it is rather to be "local" and "ethnocentric." There can be no grand social theories because theorists are inevitably embedded in their own particular social circumstances.[15] This prevents them from obtaining the kind of overarching viewpoint they would need to produce grand theories. When they have ventured into producing such grand theories, sociological theorists have constructed what are in Seidman's opinion "myths." For example, a number of theorists have created theories (for example, Marx and a number of neo-Marxists) that depict historical progress toward the salvation and liberation of people from an oppressive society. If sociological theorists are to avoid creating myths, they need to produce theories that are restricted in terms of time and place. Seidman believes that most theories will be local, although it is possible to produce broader theories as long as they are deeply embedded in the context from which they are drawn. In addition, postmodern social theories must not be insular. Rather, they must be practical as well as morally and politically significant. In fact, Seidman urges sociological theorists to take into account the ethical and political implications of their own work and to engage public issues as public defenders and advocates of particular social arrangements.

Even though Seidman urges the creation of postmodern social theories, he does not view these as scientific products. Rather, like the classic social theorists, postmodern social theorists are producing "social narratives," or the even less impressive sounding "stories." To the postmodernist, social theorists are storytellers, and this serves to demystify what theorists do and to eliminate the difference between

---

[15] However, Seidman (1991:136) does not completely rule out the possibility of grand theory: "If a genius comes along tomorrow and proves to the satisfaction of the social scientific community that he or she has succeeded in providing foundations, I will relinquish my standpoint. Until then, however, I propose that we renounce the quest for foundations in favor of local rationales for our conceptual strategies."

their activities and those of laypeople. After all, we are *all* storytellers. Sociological theorists, and sociologists more generally, are seen as having wrapped themselves in a cloak of scientific privilege to distance themselves from those they are analyzing. By viewing the products of social theorists as stories, more people will be able to participate in the public dialogue over these matters.

However, Antonio (1991) argues that from the point of view of postmodernism, or at least the most radical postmodernists, Seidman has not gone nearly far enough. In fact, from that vantage point, Seidman seems to be not so much a critic of the modernist project of sociological and social theory but rather another, albeit slightly different, practitioner of it. For example, "Seidman implies a normative vision emphasizing radically democratic, highly pluralistic, mutually tolerant, and autonomous subcommunities linked by uncoerced communication and cooperation" (Antonio, 1991:157). Furthermore, Seidman's solution—local narratives—does not go nearly far enough from the point of view of the radical postmodernists since even local narratives try to impose coherence on that which is inherently fragmented. As Antonio (1991:157; italics added) puts it, "Worldwide, national, regional, and local portrayals are *all* homogenizing totalizations. A consistent perspectivist method would decompose each into a myriad of inchoate subnarratives."

If Seidman has not gone far enough, and he is already writing the obituary for sociological theory, where does that leave us? First, it still leaves us with need to survey the range of postmodern thinking. After all, postmodernists are saying things, things that sound like theory, and we need to know what they are. This is made even more necessary by the fact that postmodern theory involves a wide range of positions, many of which are in conflict with one another. There is a pressing need to sort out the various ideas that are included under the heading of postmodernism. Second, as pointed out previously, despite all their critiques of grand theories, many postmodernists are producing just that. Here is the way Antonio (1991:161) makes this point: "Regardless of their relentless attacks on the totalizing tendencies of modern theory, postmodernist portrayals of epochal change and sweeping cultural disintegration revive the big discourse of the classical tradition [of sociological theory]."

INTIMATIONS OF POSTMODERN SOCIAL THEORY IN SOCIOLOGY

In fact, postmodern social theory is, at least to some degree, *part* of the classical (and contemporary) sociological tradition. Take, for example, the recent reinterpretation of the work of Georg Simmel entitled *Postmodern(ized) Simmel* (Weinstein and Weinstein, 1993). Weinstein and Weinstein recognize that there is a strong case to be made for Simmel as a liberal modernist (Frisby, 1991) who offers a grand narrative of the historical trend toward the dominance of objective culture or the "tragedy of culture." However, they also argue that an equally strong case can be made for Simmel as a postmodernist. Thus, they acknowledge that both alternatives have validity and, in fact, that one is no more "true" than the other. Weinstein and Weinstein (1993:21) argue: "To our minds 'modernism' and 'postmodernism' are not exclusive alternatives but discursive domains bordering each other." They note they could be doing a modernist interpretation of Simmel but feel that a post-modernist explication is more useful. This leads to the very postmodern view: "There is no essential Simmel, only different Simmels read through the various positions in contemporary discourse formations" (Weinstein and Weinstein, 1993:55).

What sorts of arguments do Weinstein and Weinstein make in defense of a view of Simmel as a postmodernist? For one thing, Simmel is seen as being generally opposed to totalizations; indeed he is inclined to de-totalize modernity. Despite, and aside from, the theory of the "tragedy of culture," Simmel was primarily an essayist and a storyteller, and he dealt primarily with a range of specific issues rather than with the totality of the social world.

Simmel is also described by Weinstein and Weinstein, as he is by others, as a *flaneur,* or someone who is something of an idler. More specifically, Simmel is described as a sociologist who idled away his time analyzing a wide range of social phenomena. He was interested in all of them for their aesthetic qualities; they all existed "to titillate, astonish, please or delight him" (Weinstein and Weinstein, 1993:60). This approach led Simmel away from a totalized view of the world and toward a concern for a number of discrete, but important, elements of that world.

Bricoleur is another term used to describe Simmel (although it is most often associated with the work of the anthropologist, Claude Lévi-Strauss). A *bricoleur* is a kind of intellectual handyman who makes do with whatever happens to be available to him. Available to Simmel was a wide range of fragments of the social world, or "shards of objective culture" as Weinstein and Weinstein (1993:70) describe them in Simmelian terms. As a *bricoleur* Simmel cobbled together whatever ideas he could find to shed meaning on the social world.

There is no need to go too deeply into the details of Weinstein and Weinstein's interpretation of a postmodernized Simmel. The illustrative points made above make it clear that such an interpretation is as reasonable as the modernized vision that is offered far more frequently in sociology. It would be far harder to come up with similar postmodern views of the other major classical theorists, although one could certainly find aspects of their work that is consistent with postmodernism. Thus, as Seidman makes clear, most of sociological theory *is* modernist, but as the case of Simmel illustrates, there are postmodern intimations in even that most modern of traditions.

Another place to look for intimations of postmodernism is among the critics of modern theory *within* sociological theory. As several observers (e.g., Antonio, 1991; Best and Kellner, 1991) have pointed out, a key position is occupied by C. Wright Mills (1959). For one thing, Mills actually used the term "post-modern" to describe the post-Enlightenment era that we were entering: "We are at the ending of what is called The Modern Age . . . The Modern Age is being succeeded by a post-modern period" (Mills, 1959:165–166). Second, he was a severe critic of modern grand theory in sociology, especially as it was practiced by Talcott Parsons. Third, Mills favored a socially and morally engaged sociology. In his terms, he wanted a sociology that linked broad public issues to specific private troubles.

While there are suggestions of postmodernism in Mills's work, it is not there that we find postmodern theory itself. For example, of Mills, Best and Kellner

(1991:8) contend that he "is very much a modernist, given to sweeping sociological generalization, totalizing surveys of sociology and history, and a belief in the power of the sociological imagination to illuminate social reality and to change society." Denzin (1989:279) goes further, calling Mills "America's preeminent 'classical theorist' of the contemporary age." His critiques are "cloaked in the languages and grand 'metanarratives' of the classic age: reason, freedom, democracy, enlightenment and positive knowledge about men and their troubles." Mills is seen by Denzin as a modernist who wrote yet another "totalizing theory of early postmodern American society that would yield yet another version of the gemeinschaft-gesellschaft myth which haunted . . . [modern] theorists" (Denzin, 1989:279). Mills does this because, in part, as Denzin puts it, he kept the wrong sociological company. That is, despite his criticisms of grand theory, Mills is also a part of that theoretical tradition. Even when he turns, as he often does, to Marx he is, in fact, turning to the thinker who is perhaps the premier modern grand theorist; the producer of the preeminent grand narrative.

While there are intimations of postmodernism in the sociologies of Simmel and Mills (and many others; see the discussion of Daniel Bell's work on postindustrial society in Chapter 9), it is not there that we find postmodern theory itself.

SUMMARY

This chapter offers a brief introduction to postmodern social theory and its relationship to sociology and sociological theory. We distinguish between postmodernity (as a social and political epoch), postmodernism (as a separate cultural form), and postmodern social theory (as a distinct kind of social theory). The latter is the focal concern in this book. Three types of positions are adopted by postmodern social theorists: extreme (there is a radical disjunction between modern and postmodern society) and moderate (the postmodern is not discontinuous with the modern) positions as well as one that sees postmodern and modern social theory as alternative ways of looking at the social world.

While one must be wary of generalizing about postmodern social theory since there are major differences among those associated with it, an effort was made to offer a broad portrayal of postmodern social theory. Among other things, it is characterized by its critical approach to the modern world, its opposition to modern grand narratives and totalizations, an emphasis on more pre-modern emotions and feelings, a style that is often more startling than well reasoned, and a tendency to focus on the marginal rather than the central.

Both sociology in general and sociological theory in particular are seen as being vulnerable to the postmodern critique. Much of the vulnerability of sociology is traceable to the failure of the scientific model to deliver on its promises. Postmodern social theory associates science with modernity and is highly critical of both. Sociology is also seen as the kind of multiparadigmatic, textual, conversational field that is most open to postmodern critique and analysis. More particularly, sociological theory is also open to postmodern attack on the basis of its scientism, foundationalism, tendency toward totalization, essentialism, and insularity. Given these weaknesses, postmodern social theory is viewed by its adherents as an alternative to modern sociological theory.

As we will see in the next chapter, the main roots of postmodern social theory lie outside of sociological theory. However, there are some intimations of postmodern social theory within sociology. For example, while there is clearly a strong modernistic dimension to the classical theory of Georg Simmel, it can also be interpreted as presaging many postmodern orientations. One can also find intimations of postmodern social theory in the work of C. Wright Mills (he even employed the term *postmodern* as early as 1959), but Mills is clearly much more a modernist than a postmodernist. Thus, it is outside of sociology that we must look for the main sources of postmodern social theory, and we will concern ourselves with those sources in the following chapter.

2

THE DEVELOPMENT OF POSTMODERN SOCIAL THEORY

*P*OSTMODERN social theory is the product of an extremely diverse and complex set of intellectual and social forces. It would require many volumes to do justice to that rich history. Thus, what follows is little more than a brief sketch offering a few glimpses of that history to orient the reader to the detailed discussions that follow in the rest of this book. It is also a highly selective sketch designed to introduce a few people and ideas with which the reader might not be familiar. Thus, for example, it will be assumed that the reader has some familiarity with the ideas of social theorists who played important roles, positive and negative, in the formation of postmodern social theory (Marx, Durkheim, and Weber). While such thinkers will not be discussed below, other figures less familiar to students of sociology—Sontag, Venturi, Jencks, Nietzsche, Rorty, Freud, Sartre, Saussure, Lévi-Strauss—will be introduced to the reader, at least briefly.

THE ARTS AND LITERARY CRITICISM

While, as we saw in the preceding chapter, there are intimations of postmodernism in sociological theory, the real roots of postmodern thinking lie in literature, architecture, theatre, painting, dance, and related fields. Many of the ideas developed in those fields, in interaction with the development of poststructuralism (to be discussed below), formed the base for the development of what we now know as post-modern social theory. In this section we will give a brief overview of the history of postmodernism in the arts, relying heavily on Hans Bertens (1995), *The Idea of the Postmodern* (see also Huyssen, 1990).

The earliest uses of the term *postmodern* date to the 1870s. The concept made its first appearance in the title of a book in 1926 and surfaced again in the 1930s and 1940s. However, this early and isolated work had little in common with the literature on postmodernism that emerged in the 1960s. A key document is Susan Sontag's (1964/1967) essay, "Against Interpretation," which as the title suggests, viewed interpretation as stifling and oppressive. Instead of the "meanings" derived from interpretations, Sontag underscored the importance of immediate sensations. This essay is also noted for undercutting the distinction between high and low culture.

Another key figure during this period was Leslie Fiedler (1969/1975), a noted critic of modernism with its attendant rationalism and liberal humanism. He felt that we were experiencing the death of modernity and the birth of postmodernity characterized by, among other things, antirationality, romanticism, and sentimentality. Fiedler also emphasized the importance of the local and tribal as opposed to the modernist emphasis on essential, timeless meanings.

In addition to the work of such literary critics, Bertens also sees early manifestations of postmodernism in the music of John Cage, Robert Rauschenberg's collages of found objects, and the novels of Alain Robbe-Grillet, John Barth, and Thomas Pynchon with their distrust of modernist ethics. Overall, Bertens (1995:34) concludes: "It is remarkable how much of what is now broadly seen as the postmodern agenda was already in place by the end of the 1960s."

As the reader will see, this book sees poststructuralism, and its reaction against modernist theory, as the most important and immediate cause of the rise of postmodern social theory. However, Bertens (1955:35) argues "that postmodernist theory arises primarily as a response to contemporary artistic innovation—and not, as is too often thought, to poststructuralist rereadings of the great texts of modernism."

Postmodernism grew more widespread and explicit in the 1970s. A key figure in this period was Inhab Hassan (1971), although his work is now viewed as of more historic importance than it is in terms of its influence on contemporary postmodern thinking. There is, for example, his essay, "POSTmodernISM: A Paracritical Bibliography" in which he underscores the anarchic character of postmodernism. While Hassan focuses on literature, he begins to move in the direction of analyzing the larger culture, the focus of much of later postmodern social theory. The other central figure during this period was William Spanos, especially his journal, *Boundary 2: A Journal of Postmodern Literature and Culture.* However, Spanos was heavily influenced by existentialism, and its foci prevented him from moving in the direction that was to become predominant in postmodern thinking—the focus on language. While existentialism privileged the human subject, the linguistic turn (Brown, 1990) proclaimed the end of such a subject. The more radical political orientation of Spanos's existential postmodernism was also not in tune with the nihilism of much of the postmodernism of the day. By the late 1970s Spanos and his existential brand of postmodernism had been marginalized.

Turning from literary criticism to the field of architecture, Robert Venturi played a key role during the 1960s and 1970s, especially in *Complexity and Contradiction in Architecture* (1966) and *Learning from Las Vegas* (1972), co-authored with Denise Scott Brown and Steven Izenour. In fact, on receiving the prestigious 1991 Pritzker Architecture Prize, Venturi was " 'generally acknowledged to have diverted the mainstream of architecture away from Modernism' " (Bertens, 1995:53). Among other things, Venturi emphasized messiness, complex and contradictory architecture, a both/and rather than an either/or orientation, the importance of an architecture that learns from popular culture and art, the fact that there is not just one but rather multiple languages in architecture, and furthermore that architecture should not be isolated from the other "languages" extant in the environment.

In the mid-1970s, Charles Jencks embarked on a body of work (including "The Rise of Post-Modern Architecture" [Jencks, 1975] and *The Language of Post Modern Architecture* [Jencks, 1977]) that led him to become "the acknowledged guru of Post-Modernism" (Bertens, 1995:57). Among other things, Jencks is known for the idea of "double coding," that is, for example, retaining architecture's elitism and complementing it with the vernacular. Thus, he did not argue for dropping modernistic elements (produced by the field's elites) but rather for extending them to embrace elements not ordinarily included (such as the vernacular). In line with this, Jencks argued for the retention of architecture's representationalism (a view soon to be rejected by postmodernists); in fact, in his view architecture should be a kind of language that represents the tensions of everyday life. Jencks also anticipated the poststructuralist orientation, at least to some degree, by adopting a semiotic view of architecture: seeing architecture as a kind of language. According to Bertens (1995:62), Jencks's perspective encompasses double coding emphasizing plural meanings, the active involvement and participation of the viewer, and a complex mix of representations, ornaments, historical reference, symbolism, and humor.

In the late 1970s, Bertens argued that the center of postmodern developments shifted from the literary field (and architecture) to a variety of other arts including photography, landscape sculpture, and sculpture. However, these developments strongly reflect the theoretical developments to be discussed below and in later chapters, that is, poststructuralism and the work of thinkers like Jacques Derrida, Roland Barthes, and Michel Foucault. Among other things, this means that the focus shifted to signs and their interrelationship rather than the material reality that they were supposed to represent. Involved here is a full-scale assault on the idea of art (and more generally culture) as representing reality; reality comes to be seen as unrepresentable, and signs are viewed as existing free of the real world. Thus, in photography, Douglas Crimp took the position that

> representation has always been an illusion since experience is inevitably mediated by language, and thus always coded . . . all visual perception is coded in one way or the

other, that there is nothing outside precoded representation, that art is therefore always a copy of a copy, and that there is no subject in the traditional sense of the term.

(Bertens, 1995:86–87)

A striking example of this rejection of representing reality is Sherrie Levine's photographs, presented by her as her own, of canonical photographs by such luminaries of the world of photography as Walker Evans. Then there is Richard Prince's rephotographing of advertising images as they appear in glossy magazines.

In addition to their rejection of representationalism, such works reflect a number of basic tenets of postmodernism. For example, they undermine such modern ideas as originality and authenticity; they stand for such postmodern ideas as appropriation and hybridization. Perhaps most importantly, such photography represents the postmodern refusal of authorship—who is *the* photographer in the case of Sherrie Levine's photographs? Clearly, it is difficult to identify the author, the photographer in such cases.

These attacks on authorship, origins, and representation also imply an assault on the traditional practices of art history as well as on the ways in which museums traditionally operate. This is related to a flowering of a more politically conscious postmodernism in the late 1970s and early 1980s. These politically conscious developments offered a way out of the impasses—radical relativism, skepticism— that had been created by poststructuralism. For example, feminist scholars linked authorship to patriarchy (after all, most canonical authors were male), and in refusing and contesting authorship, postmodern feminists are in fact also contesting patriarchy (see Chapter 9). Another example is the more Marxian postmodernists who attacked capitalistic control over art and culture. For example, the work of artist Hans Hacke is designed to show the relationship between art and power in general and, more specifically, of the power of museums and corporate and private collectors of art (Jameson, 1991).

Work in the literature and arts that relates to postmodernism continues to this day, and it continues to evolve. As Bertens (1995:107) concludes, "postmodernity has never stayed long in one particular place." However, we need to shift the discussion, as in fact Bertens does in his own work, to other, more theoretical developments and the role they played in the emergence of postmodern social theory.

PHILOSOPHY, PSYCHOLOGY, AND PSYCHIATRY: NIETZSCHE, RORTY, AND FREUDIAN THEORY

Other fields, especially philosophy, psychology, and psychiatry, must not be left out of this account of the emergence of postmodern social theory, but it is obviously impossible to detail the diversity of their inputs in this introductory chapter. Thus, we will focus in this section on the work of a classical philosopher, Friedrich Nietzsche, who has had a powerful impact on postmodern social theory as well as on that of a particularly important contemporary philosopher, Richard Rorty, especially his book *Philosophy and the Mirror of Nature* (1979). In addition, we will offer a few of the basic premises of Freudian theory.

Friedrich Nietzsche

Friedrich Nietzsche (1992; 1887/1974) is a philosopher whose significance to sociological, and even social, theory has never received the attention it deserves. However, that has changed because of, at least in part, the centrality of many of his ideas to both poststructuralism (Derrida and Foucault, for example) and postmodernism (Baudrillard, for one). It is difficult to summarize his contributions to these perspectives because "His fragmented, contradictory, and 'open' texts welcome diverse interpretations, selective appropriations, and disjunctive fusions" (Antonio, 1995:5). However, Robert J. Antonio (1995; see also Zeitlin, 1994) has recently summarized not only Nietzsche's socially relevant ideas but also his impact on poststructuralism and postmodernism.

Antonio's most basic point is that in contrast to most of the classical sociological theories of modernity, Nietzsche offers an "antisociology" in which he sees decadence, exhaustion, and regimentation where the classical theorists saw progress in the form of greater enlightenment and freedom. It is also an antisociology in another sense—it is presented in a chaotic, aphoristic form rather than the systematic grand narratives produced by the modernists.

Nietzsche takes on two of the most basic assumptions of modern social theory in his rejection of a focus on the "rational subject." First, this means that he rejects the emphasis on, and the positive evaluation of, reason, rationality, and the rationalization process. Instead, Nietzsche praises nonrational and irrational forces and blames the process of rationalization for having a stultifying effect on these impulses. Second, this is linked to Nietzsche's rejection of the modern focus on subjectivity, the soul, and the mind. Instead, Nietzsche concentrates on the body, physiology, and so on. The nonrational impulses controlled and repressed by the rational society are derived from the body. In his view, these forces should be permitted expression, although in a spiritualized way.

A key concept in Nietzsche's work is *ressentiment,* defined by Antonio (1995:7) as "the inclination of the weak to make their suffering meaningful by blaming others and taking 'imaginary revenge'." The main objects of their blame, as well as the objects of control by the larger society, are those who are strong; those whose impulses have not been inhibited and domesticated. As a result of the subordination of such strong individuals, the world has come to be dominated by slaves and their morality rather than by the strong. In Nietzsche's view, Socrates, Catholicism, Protestantism, and the Enlightenment all contributed to the slave morality and even helped to diffuse it more widely. Those who are imbued with the slave mentality are prone to uncertainty and therefore to desperate measures and fanatic prejudices.

These forces have not only served to weaken strong individuals but also the larger culture. The state comes to regiment culture and to be the locus of ressentiment. Nietzsche did not see a socialist revolution as the solution to this problem; in fact, he felt that it would only serve to amplify it. Despite his opposition to socialism, Nietzsche was no advocate of capitalism, which he saw as working against both cultural advancement and strong individuals. Those who participate in the capitalist economy are reduced to "industrious ants" while the capitalist state is staffed by "the flies of the marketplace" (cited in Antonio, 1995:10). Furthermore, the "egalitarianism" that accompanies capitalism serves to reduce everything to the lowest common denominator, thereby contributing to the exhaustion of culture. In the end, the particularities of individuals and cultures are swept away and leveled.

Obviously, Nietzsche prizes those who have escaped these oppressive forces, those he calls "sovereign" individuals. These are unique individuals who react on the basis of their bodily intelligence and their vital instincts rather than conforming totally to roles and to the expectations associated with them. Through dissimulation and self-mastery, they are able to avoid the homogenizing forces of society.

Nietzsche tended to privilege culture and its "will to deception" over science and its "will to truth." Science is associated with rationality and asceticism, while culture is linked to irrationality and uninhibited play. Culture and aesthetics are related to greater freedom, more individuality, greater exuberance, and childishness. Nietzsche favors a world in which culture is dominant and the leaders of that culture will be his sovereign individuals who have "the required strength, creativity and lack of inhibitions . . . capable of resisting rampant demagoguery, chauvinism, toadyism, and coercion" (Antonio, 1995:20). Yet, these leaders had to be careful to avoid excessive moralism and developing an obsession with control.

Antonio demonstrates that Nietzsche's complex and often contradictory ideas have been significant to the development of modern social theory (especially Weber), to left-wing thinkers, to right-wing theorists, and to postmodernists. It is the latter that is of greatest interest to us in this book, and Antonio briefly summarizes Nietzsche's impact on the thinking of several thinkers who will be dealt with in depth in this book—Foucault and his "fundamental Nietzscheanism" (for example, his focus on the diffusion of power; the "micro-physics" of power), Derrida (for example, his attack on cultural homogenization and celebration of difference), and Baudrillard (his focus on simulation, for example). More generally,

> Nietzschean themes are pervasive; postmodernists usually favor innovative, fractal, discordant, aesthetic styles of expression over conventional representation, perspectivist over objectivist theories of knowledge, and nonrational over rational visions of culture. Nietzschean motifs are prominent in their arguments about the role of language in cultural domination, critiques of the therapeutic state, affirmations of multicultural differences, and claims about problematic presuppositions, unexplored areas, and marginalized voices in social theory. Also, their playful attacks on moralistic ideologies, positivism, parochial cultural biases, and intellectual canons have a Nietzschean thrust.
>
> (Antonio, 1995:28)

However, that is not to say that there are not important differences between Nietzsche and postmodern social theory. For one thing, many postmodernists retain a left-leaning, egalitarian, pluralist perspective. Second, their extreme relativism sometimes mirrors that of liberal modernism critiqued by Nietzsche. Third, postmodernists tend to ignore his argument for new forms of authority and cultural domination. Finally, Nietzsche's call for sovereign individuals is often lost as the subject disappears into a postmodern world of signs.

While he subordinated science to culture, Nietzsche accorded importance to the will to truth, especially the willingness to see reality as it really is, "in all its multi-plicity, chaotic uncertainty, and harshness, whatever the costs" (Antonio, 1995:19). Thus, for the sovereign individual "passionate vision and disciplined truthfulness are both needed to face 'open seas' and great tasks" (Antonio, 1995:19).

Richard Rorty

Rorty began *Philosophy and the Mirror of Nature* with a brief overview of West-ern philosophy from the seventeenth through the nineteenth century. Several domi-nant ideas emerged during this period such as a focus on the human as the knower involved in the process of representing the world; a view of philosophy "as a tri-bunal of pure reason, upholding or denying the claims of the rest of culture"; and "as a foundational discipline which 'grounds' knowledge claims" (Rorty, 1979:4). Over the years philosophy grew more and more rigorous, scientific, and self-con-tained. In the process, it came to have less and less to do with all other cultural phenomena.

In the twentieth century a number of philosophers, especially Ludwig Wittgen-stein, Martin Heidegger,[1] and John Dewey, came to question this philosophical ori-entation and to seek a new way of making philosophy foundational. Especially im-portant to Rorty (1979:6) is the fact that, in his view, these thinkers were "in agreement that the notion of knowledge as accurate representation, made possible by special mental processes, and intelligible through a general theory of represen-tation, needs to be abandoned." Given their lead, Rorty (1979:390) adopts the view that what is needed is to deconstruct the theory of representation, or in his terms, "deconstruct the image of the Mirror of Nature." More specifically, what Rorty cri-tiques, and seeks to develop an alternative to, is the following philosophical orien-tation:

> The picture which holds traditional philosophy captive is that of the mind as a great mir-ror, containing various representations—some accurate, some not—and capable of being studied by pure, nonempirical methods. Without the notion of mind as mirror, the notion of knowledge as accuracy of representation would not have suggested itself . . . The story of the domination of the mind of the West by ocular metaphors.
>
> (Rorty, 1979:12–13)

Rorty is not only opposed to a philosophy that accords center stage to representa-tion, but he also attacks the ideas that philosophy should be some sort of ultimate tribunal and that it should be a foundational discipline (for a critique of this, see Norris, 1985).

Rorty associates the ideas to which he is opposed with what he calls *systematic* philosophies. In addition to the ideas rejected above, systematic philosophies in-volve a belief in the human subject as the knower of essences and the search for a single, all-encompassing vocabulary. Instead of systematic philosophies, Rorty is

---

[1] Wittgenstein and Heidegger are also of more direct importance to postmodern social theory.

an advocate of *edifying* philosophies (e.g., Dewey, Heidegger), which are suspicious of all the pretensions of systematic philosophy. Rorty offers a series of contrasts between the two philosophies and in the process gives us a sense of what he means by an edifying philosophy:

> Great edifying philosophies are reactive and offer satires, parodies, aphorisms. They know their work loses its point when the period they were reacting against is over. They are *intentionally* peripheral. Great systematic philosophies, like great scientists, build for eternity. Great edifying philosophies destroy for the sake of their own generation. Systematic philosophers want to put their subject on the secure path of science. Edifying philosophers want to keep space open for the sense of wonder which poets can sometimes cause . . . something which (at least for the moment) cannot be explained and can barely be described.

> (Rorty, 1979:369–370)

Clearly, an edifying philosophy is a far humbler undertaking than systematic philosophy. It not only condemns the idea of having an idea, but it also seeks to avoid taking a position about having views, that is, it is a "nonepistemological sort of philosophy" (Rorty, 1979:381). It does not favor the road taken by science and its research programs because, in its view, there is no one right way of describing reality. (Science is roundly attacked by Rorty [1979:384–385], "So as soon as a program to put philosophy on the secure path of science succeeds, it simply converts philosophy into a boring academic specialty.") The goal is not to discover truth as it is in systematic philosophy (and science), but merely *to continue the conversation.* In contrast, science seeks to close off conversation by finding *the* answer. Lacking final answers, or the truth, edifying philosophies continue to generate new descriptions and to strive toward the truth, a truth that is ever elusive and never attained. As Rorty (1979:373) puts it, "edifying philosophy aims at continuing a conversation rather than at discovering truth." What is needed to keep the conversation going is unconstrained discourse, undertaken at a leisurely pace. It is such discourse that is most apt to generate abnormal discourse, that is, new ideas. The point of edifying philosophy is not to find facts or the truth but to keep the conversation going, and it is through such continual conversations that new insights and perspectives are generated. Thus, edifying philosophy is distant from science, which shuts off such conversations, and is closer to poetry, novels, and most importantly, for our purposes, postmodern social theory. Edification, for Rorty (1979:360), is a "project of finding new, better, more interesting, more fruitful ways of speaking."

Sigmund Freud

Many poststructuralists and postmodernists sought to go beyond the ideas of the creator of psychoanalysis, Sigmund Freud. It is therefore useful to give a brief introduction to at least a few of Freud's ideas that were to prove relevant in a positive or a negative sense in the development of poststructuralism and postmodernism.

In some sense Freud was a structuralist tracing surface-level psychological problems to unconscious processes. Take, for example, the *Oedipus Conflict,* a primordial conflict that must be resolved adequately by the child or else it is destined to produce psychological problems later in life (for a postmodern interpretation of this idea, see the discussion of the work of Deleuze and Guattari in Chapter 7). Freud believed that the four-to-five-year-old male child (the female child is involved in a different dynamic) desires his mother and, as a result, is jealous of, and aggressive toward, his father, who possesses his mother. However, the child fears his father, especially being castrated by him. The resolution of this conflict lies in the child's internalization of the figure of the father, thereby reducing his anxiety. However, if the conflict is not resolved adequately, it represents a deep underlying problem that causes psychological problems in adulthood.

To take one other example, Freud's structuralism is also reflected in his views on things like slips of the tongue and dreams. The meaning of such phenomena does not lie in what is manifest in them but rather in the fact that they are the expression of things that have been repressed by people. Thus, the psychoanalyst must look beneath the surface to discover the underlying, and most important, realities. The logic of the psychoanalyst is, for example, that speakers derive pleasure from slips of the tongue. The latter allow for the release of repressed ideas, but in the process they also serve to disrupt the manifest meaning of what is being said. Thus, the words uttered in slips of the tongue must be interpreted as symptoms of an underlying but unconscious reality.

Some poststructuralists and postmodernists sought to distance themselves from this kind of thinking—for example, Freud's differentiation between pure human needs and actual desires. Baudrillard questioned this distinction as well as what he considered the fallacious idea that pure needs could be separated from desires. More generally, Foucault saw psychoanalysis (and many other "human sciences") as involved in a process of seeking to extend its knowledge of people to enhance its power over them.

Freud produced a theory that was in many ways very modern. He believed that there were essential human characteristics. He adhered, for the most part, to a deterministic, scientific, positivistic perspective. And, in various ways, he adopted a totalistic view of childhood development, of societal repression of human needs and desires, and of the need for patients to solve their problems by talking them through with psychiatrists and allowing expression of their repressed needs, desires, and experiences. Postmodernists are, of course, strongly opposed to such totalizations as being repressive, even terroristic.

However, Freud's theories were, as we will see, instrumental in the development of poststructuralism, and many of the themes of postmodernism can be found in Freud's work. Among the ideas developed by Freud that were to prove relevant to postmodernists were the views that modern society failed to fulfill its promises, that it is impossible to offer an undistorted representation of reality, that the marginal (e.g., dreams, slips of the tongue) are of central importance, and that the process of arriving at a "true" interpretation leads only to other interpretations.

STRUCTURALISM AND POSTSTRUCTURALISM

Following Lash (1991:ix; see also Kurzweil, 1986), we take "the structuralism that swept through French social thought in the 1960s" as the proximate starting point for the emergence of poststructuralism and postmodernism. Structuralism, itself, was a reaction against humanism, especially the existentialism of philosopher and novelist Jean-Paul Sartre, as well as phenomenology.

Sartre's Existentialism

In his early work, Sartre focused on the individual level, especially on individual freedom. He adhered to the view that people are not subject to, or determined by, any social laws. In other words, man "cannot justify his actions by reference to anything outside himself" (Craib, 1976:4).[2]

In *Being and Nothingness,* Sartre (1943) focuses on the free individual and takes the view that "existence is defined by and through one's acts . . . *One is what one does*" (Hayim, 1980:3). At the same time, Sartre attacks the sociologistic view of "objective structures as completely deterministic of behavior" (Hayim, 1980:5). For Sartre, people are free; they are responsible for everything they do; they have no excuses if they do wrong. In some senses, these "staggering responsibilities of freedom" are a tremendous source of anguish to people (Hayim, 1980:17). In other senses, this can be a source of optimism—people hold their fates in their own hands. In his later work—for example, *Critique of Dialectical Reason*—Sartre (1963) devotes more attention to social structures, but even here he emphasizes "the human prerogative for transcendence—the surpassing of the given" (Hayim, 1980:16). In this, Sartre is critical of various Marxists who overemphasize the role and power of social structure. "Dogmatic Marxists have, in Sartre's view, eliminated the humanistic component of Marx's original idea" (Hayim, 1980:72). Sartre was ultimately an existentialist, and as such he always retained the humanism he felt some Marxists had lost.

It is against this kind of humanism, especially as it was manifest in the work of Sartre, who was one of the towering figures of French social thought for decades, that poststructuralists and postmodernists rebelled.[3] They sought to "decenter" social thought, to move it away from a focus on "man" and toward other phenomena, especially language.

Phenomenology

The leading phenomenologist, Edmund Husserl,[4] was interested in the scientific study of the basic structures of human consciousness. He was committed to penetrating the various layers constructed by actors in the real world to get to the essential structure of consciousness. However, this is not easy to do since, while actors are always engaged in the active and highly complex process of ordering the

---

[2] Later in his career, Sartre was drawn more to Marxian theory, but he sought to integrate his early existentialism with his later Marxian approach by focusing on the "*free* individual situated in a *massive and oppressive social structure* which limits and alienates his activities" (Craib, 1976:9; italics added).

[3] McBride (1991) argues that Sartre anticipated many postmodernist ideas.

[4] Husserl had great influence on Derrida, among others.

world, they are most often unaware that they are ordering the world; hence, they do not question it. To Husserl, this is the general thesis of the "natural standpoint." To actors, the social world is naturally ordered, not ordered by them. Thus, the natural standpoint, or the "natural attitude," is an obstacle to the discovery of intentional processes.

Once the natural attitude is disconnected, or bracketed, the phenomenologist can begin to examine the invariant properties of consciousness (Schutz, 1973:103). The phenomenologist must also set aside the incidental experiences of life that tend to dominate consciousness. Husserl's ultimate objective was to look beneath all the layers to see the basic properties of the "transcendental ego" in all its purity. Another way to put this is that Husserl was interested in the pure form of consciousness stripped of all biographical and cultural content.

The idea of the transcendental ego reflects Husserl's interest in the basic and invariant properties of human consciousness. Although he is often misinterpreted on this point, he did not have a mentalistic, metaphysical conception of consciousness. For him, it was not a thing or a place but a process. Consciousness was found not in the head of the actor but in the relationship between the actor and the objects in the world. Husserl expressed this in his notion of *intentionality*. For him, consciousness is always consciousness of something, some object. Consciousness is found in this relationship: consciousness is not interior to the actor; it is relational. Furthermore, meaning does not inhere in consciousness or in objects but in the relationship of actors to objects. This conception of consciousness as a process that gives meaning to objects is at the heart of phenomenology.

Many of the characteristics of Husserlian phenomenology—its humanism, its focus on the subject, its essentialism (the transcendental ego)—came under attack by both structuralists and poststructuralists.

Structuralism

At its most general level, structuralism can be defined as the effort to uncover the general structures that underly human activity. From this point of view, a *structure* may be defined as

> a unit composed of a few elements that are invariably found in the same relationship within the "activity" being described. The unit cannot be broken down into its single elements, for the unity of the structure is defined not so much by the substantive nature of the elements as by their relationship.
>
> (Spivak, 1974:lv)

In addition to this concern for systems and relationships, structuralism is also characterized by its search for the general laws that serve to define such structures.

The structures of concern to structuralism are not in the main the same structures that have been of traditional concern to sociologists (such as those who adopt a structural-functional orientation). While the latter, indeed most sociologists, are concerned with *social* structures (e.g., social class, bureaucracies), what is of primary concern to structuralists are *linguistic* structures (or social structures that can be interpreted as languages). This shift from social to linguistic structures is part of what has come to be known as the *linguistic turn,* which dramatically altered the nature of the social sciences (Lash, 1991:ix). The focus of a good many social scientists shifted from social structure (and from individual human beings) to language,[5] or more generally to signs of various sorts (Gottdiener, 1995).

Structuralism emerged from diverse developments in various fields, but the source of modern structuralism and its strongest bastion to this day is linguistics. The work of Ferdinand de Saussure (1857–1913) stands out in the development of structural linguistics and, ultimately, in various other fields (Saussure, 1966; Culler, 1976). Of particular interest is Saussure's differentiation between *langue* and *parole,* a distinction which was to have enormous significance to the development of not only structuralism but also poststructuralism and postmodernism. *Langue* is the formal, grammatical system of language. It is a system of phonic elements whose relationships are governed, Saussure and his followers believed, by determinate laws. Much of linguistics since Saussure's time has been devoted to the discovery of those laws. The existence of *langue* makes *parole* possible. *Parole* is actual speech, the way that speakers on a day-to-day basis use language to express themselves. Although Saussure recognized the significance of people's use of language in subjective and often idiosyncratic ways, he believed that such day-to-day usage cannot be the concern of the scientifically oriented linguist. Such a linguist must focus on *langue,* the formal system of language, not on the subjective ways in which it is used by actors.

Langue, then, can be viewed as a system of signs. A sign can be seen as a whole, a structure that is composed of a *signifier*—the sound image that the recipient hears when a word is spoken, and a *signified*—what the sound image is used to indicate: the meaning of the word that is called forth in the mind of the recipient. Saussure was interested not only in the signifier and the signified but also in their relationship to one another. Somewhat surprisingly, at least from a sociological point of view, Saussure was little interested in the *referent,* the thing being referred to, because it was extra-linguistic (Genosko, 1994).[6]

To Saussure, language is "a closed system in which all parts are interrelated" (Marks and de Courtivron, 1981:3). Especially important are relations of difference, including binary oppositions. Thus, for example, the meaning of the word *hot* comes not from some intrinsic property of the "real" world but from the word's relationship with, its binary opposition to, the word *cold.* Meanings, the mind, and ultimately the social world are shaped by the structure of language. Thus, instead of an existential world of people shaping their surroundings, we have here a world in which people, as well as other aspects of the social world, are being shaped by the structure of language and its *code,* or the arbitrary rules for combining words.

---

[5] See, for example, Habermas's work on communication or the conversational analyses of some ethnomethodologists.

[6] However, the term *discourse* often came to be used for "the relation between language and the object to which it apparently refers" (Marks and de Courtivron, 1981:3).

Language came to serve as a model for all aspects of human life. In addition, the concern for structure was extended by Saussure, and more importantly by a range of other thinkers, beyond language to the study of all sign systems. This focus on the structure of sign systems has been labeled "semiotics" and has attracted many followers (Eco, 1976; Hawkes, 1977; Gottdiener, 1995). *Semiotics* is broader than structural linguistics because it encompasses not only language but also other sign and symbol systems, such as facial expressions, body language, all forms of communication, and indeed all elements of culture.

Roland Barthes (1964/1967; 1970/1982) is often seen as the true founder of semiotics. Barthes's greatest significance, from the point of view of this discussion, was to extend Saussure's ideas to all areas of social life. As Barthes put it,

> Semiology . . . aims to take in any system of signs, whatever their substance and limits; images, gestures, musical sounds, objects, and the complex associations of all of these, which form the content of ritual, convention or public entertainment: these constitute, if not *languages,* at least systems of signification.

(Barthes, 1964/1967:9)

Or, in more prosaic terms, "Not just language, but wrestling matches are also signifying practices, as are TV shows, fashions, cooking and just about everything else in everyday life" (Lash, 1991:xi). The "linguistic turn" came to encompass all social phenomena, which are now reinterpreted as signs.

Another central figure in French structuralism, indeed Kurzweil (1980:13) calls him "the father of structuralism," is the French anthropologist Claude Lévi-Strauss. Lévi-Strauss extended Saussure's work on language to anthropological issues—for example, to myths in primitive societies. This helped to open the door to the broader application of structuralism to all forms of communication. His major innovation was to reconceptualize a wide array of social phenomena (for instance, kinship systems) as systems of communication and thereby make them amenable to structural analyses (Burris, 1979; Levin, 1981:25). The exchange of spouses, for example, can be analyzed in the same way as the exchange of words. Both are social exchanges that can be studied through the use of structural anthropology.

We can illustrate Lévi-Strauss's (1967) thinking with the example of the similarities between linguistic systems and kinship systems. First, to the structural anthropologist, terms used to describe kinship, like phonemes in language, are basic units of analysis. Second, neither the kinship terms nor the phonemes have meaning in themselves. Instead, like Saussure's *langue,* both acquire meaning only when they are integral parts of a larger system. Lévi-Strauss even used a system of binary oppositions in his anthropology (e.g., the raw and the cooked) much like those employed by Saussure in linguistics. Third, Lévi-Strauss recognized that there is empirical variation from setting to setting in both phonemic and kinship systems, but he argued that even these variations can be traced to the operation of general, although implicit, laws.

All of this is very much in line with the linguistic turn, but Lévi-Strauss ultimately went off in a number of directions that are at odds with that turn. Most important, he argued that both phonemic systems and kinship systems are the products of the structures of the mind. However, they are not the products of a conscious process. Instead, they are the products of the unconscious, logical structure of the mind. These systems, as well as the logical structure of the mind from which they are derived, operate on the basis of general laws. Most of those who have been part of the linguistic turn have not followed Lévi-Strauss in the direction of defining the underlying structure of the mind as the most fundamental structure.

Another variant of structuralism that enjoyed considerable success in France (and many other parts of the world) was structural Marxism, especially the work of Louis Althusser, Nicos Poulantzas, and Maurice Godelier. Although we have made the case that modern structuralism began with Saussure's work in linguistics, there are those who argue that it started with the work of Karl Marx: "When Marx assumes that structure is not to be confused with visible relations and explains their hidden logic, he inaugurates the modern structuralist tradition" (Godelier, 1972b:336). Although structural Marxism and structuralism in general are both interested in "structures," they conceptualize structure differently.

At least some Marxists share with structuralists an interest in the study of structure as a prerequisite to the study of history. As Maurice Godelier said, "The study of the internal functioning of a structure must precede and illuminate the study of its genesis and evolution" (1972b:343). In another work, Godelier (1972a:xxi) said, "The inner *logic* of these systems must be analyzed *before* their *origin*[7] is analyzed." Another view shared by structuralists and structural Marxists is that structuralism should be concerned with the structures, or systems, that are formed out of the interplay of social relations. Both schools see structures as real (albeit invisible), although they differ markedly on the nature of the structures that they consider real. For Lévi-Strauss the real structure is the model, or perhaps the mind, whereas for structural Marxists it is the underlying structure of society.

Perhaps most importantly, both structuralism and structural Marxism reject empiricism and accept a concern for underlying invisible structures. Godelier (1972a:xvii) argued: "What both structuralists and Marxists reject are the empiricist definitions of what constitutes a social structure." Godelier also made this statement:

> For Marx as for Lévi-Strauss a structure is *not* a reality that is *directly* visible, and so directly observable, but a *level of reality* that exists *beyond* the visible relations between men, and the functioning of which constitutes the underlying logic of the system, the subjacent order by which the apparent order is to be explained.
>
> (Godelier, 1972a:xix)

Godelier (1972a:xxiv) went even further and argued that such a pursuit defines all science: "What is visible is a *reality* concealing *another*, deeper reality, which is hidden and the discovery of which is the very purpose of scientific cognition.

Despite these similarities, structural Marxism did not in the main participate in the linguistic turn then taking place in the social sciences. For example, the focal concern continued to be social and economic, not linguistic, structures. Moreover,

---

[7] A concern for origins came to be rejected by postmodernists.

structural Marxism continued to be associated with Marxian theory, and many French social thinkers were becoming at least as impatient with Marxian theory as they were with existentialism.

Poststructuralism

Structuralisms of various types came to dominate social thought, especially in France. However, there soon developed a reaction against structuralism that came to be labeled poststructuralism. We can define poststructuralism as a school of thought that builds upon (Kroker and Levin, 1991), but seeks to distance itself from, the structuralism associated with thinkers like Ferdinand Saussure, Roland Barthes, Claude Lévi-Strauss, Louis Althusser, and so on. Of course, the poststructuralists were also shaped in a positive, but especially a negative, sense by many of the theories discussed above—especially existentialism, phenomenology, and Freudian theory (as well as Marxism).

Poststructuralism is an extremely broad and amorphous school of thought. For example, it encompasses the work of a mainstream sociological theorist,[8] Pierre Bourdieu (1977, 1984), as well as a thinker, Michel Foucault, who is decidedly outside the mainstream. Thus, while Bourdieu's work was dealt with in *Modern Sociological Theory* (Ritzer, 1996c), Foucault's work will be discussed in this book on postmodern social theory. This leads to the issue: What is the difference between poststructuralism and postmodernism? In general, poststructuralism is treated as an intellectual precursor of postmodernism (Bertens, 1995); it is one of the strands of thought that fed into the development of postmodern social theory. In fact, it is *the* most important theoretical source of postmodern social theory. Certainly, the poststructuralist who we will deal with in depth in this book, Michel Foucault, played a key role, positive and negative (see Baudrillard's [1977] *Oublier Foucault* ["Forget Foucault"], for example), in the formation of postmodernism. However, in many senses, as we will see in Chapters 3 and 4, Foucault can also be considered a postmodernist (Best, 1994). Thus, there is a flexible, quite porous, line separating poststructuralism and postmodernism. In fact, in the spirit of postmodernism, we will refuse to draw the line, especially in the rich and diverse work of someone like Foucault.

One general distinction (with many exceptions) is that poststructuralism tends to be more abstract, more philosophical, and less political, than postmodernism. The work of Jacques Derrida (1930–   ), which will be discussed in more detail in Chapter 7, is a good example of poststructural thinking even though he, too, is sometimes thought of as a postmodernist. The latter is the case because, among other things, even in his highly theoretical musings he sees us undergoing a transition from the modern way of thinking to a mode of thought that is beyond modern (Derrida, 1967/1974:87).

However, we can use Derrida here to illustrate what we mean by poststructuralism. A good starting point is Spivak's (1974:lvii) discussion of "Derrida's criticism

---

[8] For a view of Bourdieu as more of a postmodernist, see Harrison (1993).

of 'structuralism,' even as he inhabits it." Thus, the poststructuralists are generally embedded in structuralism at the same time that they are trying to distance themselves from it. To take a specific example, Derrida bases his thinking on Saussure's work on speech at the same time that he critiques Saussure for subordinating and excluding that which was to become of central concern to Derrida—writing.[9] This led Derrida to the creation of a field, "grammatology," or the theoretical science of writing. While Derrida (1967/1974:42) critiques and moves beyond Saussure, he acknowledges the fact that it is Saussure who made the field of grammatology possible. It is the embeddedness in structuralism, as well as the simultaneous critique and movement beyond it, that defines poststructuralism.

Another important body of poststructural work includes that of the French psychoanalyst, Jacques Lacan (1901–   ), as well as the contributions of his followers, disciples, and sometime later critics, especially Julia Kristeva, Luce Irigaray, and Hélène Cixous. Lacan, of course, was building upon Freudian theory and integrating it with other ideas, most notably from our point of view, Saussurian linguistics. Thus, Lacan is noted for statements such as "the unconscious is structured like a language" (in Kurzweil, 1995:98).While psychoanalysts privileged biology, Lacan argued that language and culture were central to the unconscious. More generally, the individual was seen as being formed in language. Further, language is central to the psychoanalytic session.

To Lacan, language always operates on two planes. The task of psychoanalysis is to look for the cause of defective communication. It is the unconscious, and its language, that is the cause of defects in interpersonal communication. There is a structural regularity to these disruptions that makes them amenable to both study and therapy. It is this kind of structural regularity that led Lacan to the later view that it would be possible to mathematize psychoanalysis.

Lacan's ideas were of great influence in a number of fields, including sociology. Many of his disciples, especially Kristeva, Irigaray, and Cixous, have had a powerful impact of their own. In Chapter 9 we will touch on the relationship of their ideas to American feminist postmodern theory. However, they also made contributions to structural analysis. For example, Kristeva created "semanalysis," which is concerned not only with the communicative factors in language but also with such material factors as its sounds, rhythms, and graphability. She also emphasized the importance of poetic language, which defies formalization. In linking linguistics and psychoanalysis, Kristeva saw as paradigmatic the accepting, loving relationship between analyst and patient. For her part, Irigaray argued, for example, that schizophrenia has a language of its own and that its delirium is subject to distinctive linguistic rules, even if they are often broken in practice.

Poststructuralism provides the immediate background to, and in many ways is indistinguishable from, postmodern social theory. Most of the thinkers to be discussed in this book were influenced by structuralism but sought to distance themselves from it. Once in place, poststructuralism itself had an impact on the work of a majority of the theorists covered here. Given this background on structuralism

---

[9] We will explain what Derrida means by writing in Chapter 8.

and poststructuralism, indeed the background provided in these first two chapters, we are now ready to deal with postmodern social theory. However, before we do, there is one final issue that we need to cover.

THE SOCIAL CONTEXT

Up to this point we have, in the main, focused on ideas—structural, poststructural, postmodern, and so on. However, these ideas did not emerge in a social and intellectual vacuum. In this section we need to survey at least a few of the contextual factors involved in the theoretical developments of concern to us here. To keep the discussion manageable, we will focus largely on France, since it is clear that it was the center of the theoretical developments of concern to us in this book.

During and immediately after World War II, French intellectual life was dominated by Marxian theory. However, as many intellectuals began to grow disillusioned with Soviet-style communism, they became attracted to Sartre's existentialism, especially the promise of individual fulfillment in the modern world. But Sartre's ideas began to lose favor because he continued to support the communists despite a growing recognition of the repressiveness of the Soviet Union. In their search for an alternative theoretical perspective, some scholars were drawn to structuralism, which permitted them to remain socialists while giving their work a non-Marxist theoretical underpinning. Structuralism also appealed to those who wanted to develop a science of human subjects.

The radical student revolution of 1968 was a watershed in French intellectual development. The failure of that revolution, and the subsequent disbanding of student groups, led to increasing disillusionment with Marxism and, more generally, to the abandonment of any hope of a grand revolutionary solution to society's problems. Those feelings increased in the next few decades as communism progressively unraveled and then collapsed completely in the Soviet Union and elsewhere. In France, the election of a socialist president, François Mitterand, failed to bring with it the promised reforms. The social democracies throughout Europe that had instituted a variety of well-funded welfare programs began to discover that they could no longer afford such programs. All of these failures brought with them the sense that the old hopes for a grand solution had been illusory. In fact, as the excesses of the Soviet Union came to light, they pointed, as had the Nazi Holocaust, to the fact that such grand solutions could just as easily bring terror as hope.

A wide range of other social changes made it clear that the old theoretical tools no longer sufficed; new theoretical ideas and perspectives were needed. The map of the world was being redrawn as colonial empires were dismantled, decolonialism proceeded apace, and many new and independent nations came into existence. Led by the feminists, a variety of new social movements arose, and many new voices were being heard within France and throughout the world. These groups were clamoring for greater power over their lives as well as in the societies in which they lived.

The economies of the advanced nations, including France, were growing, but poverty and other social ills showed no signs of disappearing. Furthermore, those economies were changing with many industries both retrenching and restructuring.

The result was that many people were out of work who never expected to be un-employed, and many more faced uncertain or disrupted careers. Overall, the econ-omy was moving from the dominance of Fordist production jobs to post-Fordist service-type occupations. Furthermore, the emphasis seemed to be less on produc-tion and more on consumption; we were witnessing the emergence of the "con-sumer society."

Key to the consumer society was the growing importance of the mass media, es-pecially television. The latter not only serves to advertise all of the allures of the consumer society, but it bombards people with a wide array of images that have dramatically altered their lives. Television brought with it an explosion of informa-tion, albeit often in the form of infotainment. More generally, information tech-nologies grew and then exploded with the wide-scale availability of home comput-ers. Seemingly free-floating images, stemming from the television, home computer, and elsewhere, were increasingly omnipresent and exerting great attrac-tion for, and power over, people.

We obviously cannot deal with anything approaching the full range of social changes that affected the theoretical developments of concern to us here. Suffice it to say that there are many of them and that they profoundly shaped the emergence and development of poststructural and especially postmodern thought.

SUMMARY

The roots of postmodern social theory lie in the arts and literary criticism. While postmodernism developed in many different fields, some of the most important work, at least from the point of view of the development of postmodern social the-ory, took place in architecture, especially the ideas of Venturi and Jencks. Postmod-ernism remains a powerful force in art and literary criticism today, but the major inputs into contemporary postmodern social theory are to be found elsewhere.

Three important thinkers in the development of postmodern social theory are the philosophers Friedrich Nietzsche and Richard Rorty and the psychoanalyst Sigmund Freud. Nietzsche has emerged as the dominant philosophical source of postmodern social theory. Theorists associated with the latter are drawn to various aspects of his approach including the aphoristic, unsystematic character of his work, his rejection of reason and rationality, his focus on ressentiment, his interest in the relationship between power and truth, and so on. There are important differ-ences between Nietzsche and postmodern social theorists, but the latter often draw heavily on his work not only for their ideas but even for their style of presentation. Rorty's impact is traceable largely to his rejection of systematic philosophy and his acceptance of edifying philosophy, in which the goal is not to find the answer but merely to keep the scientific conversation going. Freud also had a profound effect on postmodern social theory but more because that theory sought to distance itself from both Freud's modern grand narrative as well as many of his specific ideas.

The humanism of Sartre's existentialism and Husserl's phenomenology serve as a backdrop for the development of structuralism. Of particular importance in the latter is the work of the linguist Ferdinand de Saussure. His distinctions between *langue* and *parole,* and signifier and signified, as well as his thoughts on binary oppositions were to have a profound effect on both poststructuralism and postmodernism. Roland Barthes is important for extending Saussure's ideas on language to the study of signs in general (semiotics). Lévi-Strauss applied these ideas to his anthropological work, demonstrating that social behavior can be analyzed in much the same way as language—another variant of structuralism built on the more structural ideas of Karl Marx.

Poststructuralism may be seen as a school of thought that builds upon, but goes beyond, structuralism. A good example is Derrida's effort to go beyond speech to focus on "writing." Lacan built upon structuralist ideas but sought to integrate them with the psychoanalytic perspective of Freud and others. Poststructuralism provides the immediate background for postmodern social theory and is, in many ways, indistinguishable from it. Many of the thinkers to be discussed in this book as postmodern social theorists are also often labeled "poststructuralists."

The chapter closes with some thoughts on the social changes that were important in the development of poststructuralism and postmodernism.

3

MICHEL FOUCAULT: PART 1: ARCHAEOLOGY OF KNOWLEDGE; GENEALOGY OF POWER

ARCHAEOLOGY OF KNOWLEDGE
GENEALOGY OF POWER
MADNESS AND CIVILIZATION
THE BIRTH OF THE CLINIC
DISCIPLINE AND PUNISH

*M*ICHEL FOUCAULT'S work is dealt with in detail in this book because, depending on one's perspective, it can be seen as either a forerunner to, or as an early example of, postmodern social theory. In either case, subsequent postmodern theorizing has been powerfully affected by Foucault's thinking.

Foucault offers a wide-ranging body of work that will require two chapters to cover adequately. In this chapter we deal with his methodological concerns (Foucault, 1969, 1971/1976) as well as specific empirical studies of the origin of the human sciences (Foucault, 1966/1973), madness and the asylum (Foucault, 1961/1967), medicine and the birth of clinical practice (Foucault, 1963/1975), and crime and the carceral system (Foucault, 1975/1979). In Chapter 4 we will deal with his later work on sexuality, especially the social control of sexuality (Foucault, 1978/1980) and the self and sexuality (Foucault, 1984/1985, 1984/1986).

The wide range of Foucault's work makes it difficult to summarize. In addition, it is also dense and subject to multiple interpretations. Further complicating matters is the fact that Foucault is purposely elusive: "Do not ask who I am and do not ask me to remain the same" (1969, 1971/1976:17). In fact, Foucault did not remain the same; his work shows important shifts over the course of his career.

Foucault's work also shows a variety of theoretical inputs (Smart, 1985). This variety makes it provocative and difficult to handle. Furthermore, the ideas are not simply adopted from other thinkers but transformed as they are integrated into Foucault's innovative theoretical orientations. Thus, Weber's theory of rationalization has an impact, but to Foucault rationalization is found only in certain "key sites," and it is not an "iron cage"; there is always resistance. Marxian ideas (Smart, 1983) are found in Foucault's work, but Foucault does not restrict himself to the economy; he focuses on a range of social institutions. He is more interested in the "micro-politics of power," a multiplicity of minor coercive techniques (Bogard, 1991), than in the traditional Marxian concern with power at the societal level. He practices hermeneutics to better understand the social phenomena of concern to him. However, Foucault has no sense of some deep, ultimate truth; there are simply ever more layers to be peeled away. There is a phenomenological influence, but Foucault rejects the idea of an autonomous, meaning-giving subject. There is a strong element of structuralism but no formal rule-governed model of behavior. Finally, and perhaps most important, Foucault adopts a number of Nietzsche's interests (see Chapter 2), most notably the relationship between power and knowledge (Smith, 1994), but that linkage is analyzed much more sociologically by Foucault. This multitude of theoretical inputs is one of the reasons that Foucault is thought of as a *post*structuralist. As we will see, although he strongly rejected it, structuralism did influence Foucault's early work but tended to recede in importance in the later, even more poststructuralist, work.

In his early writings, Foucault is doing what he calls an "archaeology of knowledge" (Foucault, 1966/1973). However, he quickly not only refines his thinking on an archaeological approach but also lays the groundwork for a dramatic shift toward a "genealogy of power" (Foucault, 1969, 1971/1976). Still later, we witness yet another change to a concern for the "techniques of the self."

Before proceeding, we need to sort out the relationship between his archaeology and genealogy. The two processes are not distinct from one another in his work; rather, they are complementary. Archaeology focuses on a given historical "moment" (which, in fact, can be quite long), while genealogy is concerned with a historical process. More specifically, "Genealogy offers us a processual perspective on the web of discourse, in contrast to an archaeological approach which provides us with a snapshot, a slice through the discursive nexus" (Bevis, Cohen, and Kendall, 1993:194). It is worth underscoring the fact that in both, Foucault remains focused on discourse; the subject matter of concern to him throughout his work is discursive formations.

ARCHAEOLOGY OF KNOWLEDGE

In his archaeology of knowledge, Foucault, reflecting the structuralist focus on language, is interested in studying discursive events, both spoken and written statements. He is particularly interested in early statements in the history of a field. He wants to uncover the basic conditions that make a given discourse possible. The unity of such statements, the way that they come to form a science or a discipline, does not come from the human subject or the author (this rejection of the subject/author is central to Foucault's thinking and in line with later postmodern ideas) but rather from basic discursive rules and practices extant at a given time and place (Flynn, 1978). More specifically, Foucault is interested in the basic discursive practices that formed the base of scientific discourse, particularly in the human sciences.

To Foucault, archaeology is concerned with *objects,* things without context, articles left from the past, silent monuments. (This focus on objects, like the rejection of a spotlight on the subject, is also in line with the later thinking of postmodernists, especially Baudrillard.) In focusing on objects, he wants to move away from the sovereignty of the subject that has reigned, in his view, since the nineteenth century. In other words, the reign of the subject is coterminous with that of modernity (Dean, 1986). This has been manifest especially in the dominance of the *human* subject in anthropology and humanism. Thus, Foucault (1969, 1971/1976:16) takes as his goal the creation of "a method of analysis purged of all anthropologism"; his position is anti-humanistic (Paden, 1987). In fact, even in terms of his own work, Foucault (1969, 1971/1976:17) seeks to avoid the sense of a human subject or author; he writes, he says, "in order to have no face."

Instead of focusing on people and what they say, Foucault (1978) focuses on discourse as *practice*. In looking at discursive practice, Foucault begins with pre-existing unities (psychopathology, for example), but only to break them up, "deconstruct" them,[1] into their component parts. In doing so, he frees up

> the totality of all effective statements (whether spoken or written), in their dispersion as events and in the occurrence that is proper to them . . . a population of events in the space of discourse in general. One is led therefore to the project of a *pure description of discursive events* as the horizon for the search for the unities that form within it.
>
> (Foucault, 1969, 1971/1976:27)

Although he describes discursive events, ultimately Foucault is looking for unities of discourse, but they are not those that have been traditionally defined as the unities (e.g., psychopathology). And, he is looking for those unities in the population of discursive events, *not* in people and what they say. In other words, he has disengaged discursive events (as objects) from the people (subjects) who might engage in them.

Foucault outlines a five-step process for the analysis of a field of discursive events:

1 grasp the statement in the exact specificity of its occurrence
2 determine its conditions of existence
3 fix at least its limits
4 establish its correlates with other statements that may be connected with it
5 show what other forms of statement it excludes.

> (Foucault, 1969, 1971/1976:28)

In this process, Foucault is interested in getting, at least initially, at the regularities that exist within discourse. He traces those regularities to several kinds of *relationships*—relations between statements, between groups of statements, and the "relations between statements and groups of statements and [more sociological] events of a quite different kind (technical, economic, social, political)" (Foucault, 1969, 1971/1976:29).

---

[1] Deconstruction is, as we have seen and will see further, of central concern to postmodern social theory.

Foucault could have examined any body of discourse, but he chose to focus on science, especially sciences of man such as biology (and medicine), economics, and grammar (language). He does so for the tactical reason that he believes that it is easier to study discourse in such well-defined disciplines.

Specifically, he is interested in *discursive formations* where a system of dispersion exists among statements and where there is regularity among elements such as "objects, types of statement, concepts, or thematic choices" (Foucault, 1969, 1971/1976:38; Brown and Cousins, 1980). All of these elements are, in his view, subject to *rules of formation* or the "conditions of existence (but also of coexistence, maintenance, modification, and disappearance) in a given discursive division" (Foucault, 1969, 1971/1976:38). Alan Sheridan contends that Foucault's archaeology of knowledge involves a search for "a set of rules of formation that determine the conditions of possibility of all that can be said within the particular discourse at any given time" (1980:48). Foucault admits that this is a blank, uncharted, indifferent space, but he is prepared to focus on it rather than the foci of most of his predecessors—authors, *oeuvres* (bodies of work), the origin of ideas, influences, traditions, and most generally the history of ideas.

Thus, for example, there are rules for the formation of concepts. The concepts he is examining are not those found in specific individual texts or even in a science at a particular point in time. Rather, he is interested in the anonymous dispersion of concepts through a wide range of books, *oeuvres,* and texts. The rules of formation of these concepts "operate not only in the mind or consciousness of individuals, but in discourse itself, they operate . . . on all individuals who undertake to speak in this discursive field" (Foucault, 1969, 1971/1976:63). He looks at the three major fields mentioned above and is interested in *both* the similarities and differences among concepts (as well as other elements of discourse) in these fields.

Foucault's unit of analysis in such comparative studies is the *statement* (Mahon, 1993). Statements are better thought of as functions than structures (this is another orientation that helps to distance Foucault from structuralism, to help make him a poststructuralist). As a function, a statement "cuts across a domain of structures and possible unities, and . . . reveals them, with concrete contents, in time and space" (Foucault, 1969, 1971/1976:87). He takes as his task to describe this function "as such, that is, in its actual practice, its conditions, the rules that govern it, and the field in which it operates" (Foucault, 1969, 1971/1976:87). In these terms, a *discourse* (or a *discursive formation*) can be defined as "the group of statements that belong to a single system of formation" (Foucault, 1969, 1971/1976:107). In focusing on statements, Foucault is dealing with a different phenomenon than that of concern to those in linguistics, although he makes it clear that his approach is designed to complement, not replace, linguistic analysis.

Foucault takes great pains to differentiate the archaeology of knowledge from the already well-established field known as the history of ideas (Lovejoy, 1936/1940, 1948). In his view, the great themes of the history of ideas are the genesis of ideas, their continuity over time, as well as totalizations such as the spirit of an age. In line with later postmodernists, Foucault rejects the search for the origin, or genesis, of ideas. Similarly, he is at least as interested in differences and contradictions in ideas as he is in continuities. And, he prefers detailed analyses of statements to global generalizations about totalities. (The rejection of totalizations is yet another similarity between Foucault and later postmodernists.) In this context, Foucault articulates four principles that distinguish the archaeology of knowledge from the history of ideas:

1 Archaeology does not focus on the "thoughts, representations, images, themes, preoccupations that are concealed or revealed in discourses." Rather, it is concerned with "those discourses themselves . . . as practices obeying certain rules." To put it another way, archaeology does not treat "discourse as *document,* as a sign of something else," but is rather concerned with discourse itself "as a *monument*." Archaeology "is not an interpretative discipline: it does not seek another, better-hidden discourse"[2] (Foucault, 1969, 1971/1976:138–139).

2 Archaeology does not seek to rediscover the linear and gradual slope that characterizes discourses and their relationship to the other discourses that precede, surround, and succeed them. Rather, the goal "is to define discourses in their specificity . . . a differential analysis of the modalities of discourse" (Foucault, 1969, 1971/1976:139).

3 Archaeology is not concerned with individual bodies of work, or *oeuvres.* Rather it is concerned with the "types of rules for discursive practices that run through individual *oeuvres*"; rules that govern them in whole or in part. It therefore involves a rejection of a focus on the author of the *oeuvre* and does not see the author as the basis of the unity of that work (Foucault, 1969, 1971/1976:139).

4 Finally, archaeology does not involve a search for the origins of discourse, but rather "it is the systematic description of a discourse-object" (Foucault, 1969, 1971/1976:139–140).

In addition to their positive directions, the above can be read as reiterations of orientations Foucault *rejects*—the search for underlying structures, the history of ideas, the focus on the subject, and a concern for origins.

As pointed out above, Foucault is very interested in contradictions within discursive formations, whereas he sees the history of ideas as involved in seeking to suppress contradictions to show coherence and continuity in ideas. To Foucault (1969, 1971/1976:151), a contradiction is "the very law of its [discourses] existence: it is on the basis of such a contradiction that discourse emerges . . . contradiction is ceaselessly reborn through discourse. . . . Contradiction, then, functions throughout discourse, as the principle of its historicity." The goal is not to "uncover" contradictions but to describe them in themselves; they are objects to be described through archaeological analysis. Rather than seeking to eliminate contradictions as does the history of ideas, "archaeology describes the different *spaces of dissension*" (Foucault, 1969, 1971/1976:152). In examining contradictions, the archaeologist is to look at their different types, the different levels at which they occur and can be mapped, and the various functions they can perform. Thus, discourse is a "space of multiple dissensions; a set of different oppositions" and the

---

[2] This is another clear indication of Foucault's *post*structuralism; he is not interested in underlying structures.

task of the archaeologist is to map them, above all, to "maintain discourse in all its many irregularities" (Foucault, 1969, 1971/1976:155–156).

Further, the goal is to compare contradictions; indeed archaeology is inherently comparative. Thus, archaeology is always plural looking at two or more discourses simultaneously. To put this another way, archaeology is inherently interdiscursive. Thus, it looks not for things like the "spirit" of a science, or a *Weltanschauung,* but rather the tangle of contradictions and analogies that make up one discourse in contrast to others.

While Foucault is doing detailed examinations of statements and discourses, he is not unaware of their relationship to the larger social context:

> The archaeological description of discourses is deployed in the dimensions of a general history; it seeks to discover that whole domain of institutions, economic processes, and social relations on which a discursive formation can be articulated.

> (Foucault, 1969, 1971/1976:164)

It is this that makes Foucault's work particularly interesting to sociology.

Similarly, Foucault is interested in the changing nature of discourse, its sequence, and its succession. Unlike the history of ideas, archaeology is willing to acknowledge and study the changes, ruptures, discontinuities, and sudden redistributions that characterize the history of discourse. In fact, the substitution of one discursive formation for another, while rare, is of the utmost importance, and only an archaeology of knowledge can deal adequately with such a dramatic change.

In the end, what Foucault is trying to do is to define a new *domain* of study including objects, statements, rules of formation, discursive formations, and changes in them. He is interested in a "description of statements, of their formation, and of the regularities [as well as irregularities] proper to discourse" (Foucault, 1969, 1971/1976:200).

While it was written prior to *The Archaeology of Knowledge, The Order of Things* can be seen as an effort to apply at least an earlier conception of archaeology to a specific set of intellectual issues (Chua, 1981). Foucault (1966/1973:xi–xii) offers an excellent summary of what he sought to do in this historical study of what we would now call the human sciences (Christie, 1993)—the natural science of biology ("naturalists"), economics, and linguistics ("grammarians"):

> Unknown to themselves, the naturalists, economists, and grammarians employed the same rules to define the objects proper to their own study, to form their concepts, to build their theories. It is these *rules of formation* which were never formulated in their own right, but are to be found only in widely differing theories, concepts, and objects of study, that I have tried to reveal, by isolating, as their specific locus, a level that I have called, somewhat arbitrarily perhaps, *archaeological.* Taking as an example the period covered in this book, I have tried to determine the *basis or archaeological system* common to a whole series of scientific "representations" or "products" dispersed throughout natural history, economics, and philosophy [or linguistics] of the Classical period.

> (Foucault, 1966/1973:xi–xii; italics added).

To put it succinctly and in terms of the title of his work, Foucault is seeking to describe archaeologically the order among (discursive) things in the fields of biology, economics, and linguistics.

The focus in his historical analysis is the two great changes in the *episteme* (a general form of thinking and theorizing establishing ideas, sciences, and so on) of Western culture, the first occurring in the mid-seventeenth century, inaugurating the Classical Age, and the second at the beginning of the nineteenth century, bringing the Modern Age into existence.[3] He is quick to point out that this transition does not necessarily represent progress but merely a change in the way things are ordered.

Here, as in *Archaeology of Knowledge,* Foucault rejects a focus on the subject or the author and, in the process, rejects a phenomenological approach that leads to a concern for transcendental consciousness. As is his pattern, Foucault wants to concern himself with discursive practice and not the knowing subject. Thus, Foucault wants to distance himself from phenomenology, but that is nothing in comparison to his desire to separate his approach from structuralism: ". . . half-witted 'commentators' persist in labelling me a 'structuralist'. I have been unable to get it into their tiny minds that I have used none of the methods, concepts, or key terms that characterize structural analysis" (Foucault, 1966/1973:xiv). Yet, he admits, as is obvious throughout his work, that there "may well be certain similarities between the works of structuralists and my own work" (Foucault, 1966/1973:xiv). This is clear, for example, when he says that in looking for "order in the world" he is looking for "*buried* similitudes [that] must be indicated on the surface of things. . . . A knowledge of similitudes is founded upon the unearthing and deciphering of these signatures" (Foucault, 1966/1973:26; italics added).

Also rejected here is the focus on human beings as the subjects and objects of knowledge. Foucault argues that it was during the period of his study "that the strange figure of knowledge called man first appeared and revealed a space proper to the human sciences" (Foucault, 1966/1973:xxiv). Foucault sees this focus on humans as historically atypical and as distorting. Furthermore, he believes that we are now beginning to witness the end of the dominance of human beings as subjects and objects of scientific study.

In doing this analysis, Foucault (1966/1973:31) makes it clear that he is studying knowledge "at its archaeological level—that is, at the level of what made it possible." He begins with sixteenth-century knowledge, which he sees as limitless but poverty-stricken. However, in the seventeenth century, knowledge began to take a very different form. Without going into a lengthy analysis, Foucault sees sixteenth-century knowledge as characterized by the view that the empirical world is composed of "a complex of kinships, resemblances, and affinities" (Foucault, 1966/1973:54), whereas in the seventeenth century representations replace resemblance: "It is through resemblance that representation can be known, that is, compared with other representations that may be similar to it, analysed into elements

---

[3] In *Archaeology of Knowledge,* Foucault argues that in *The Order of Things* he may have given the mistaken impression that he is analyzing cultural totalities. Thus, he seems to recognize the modern bias in his earlier work, a bias which is also reflected in his periodization of the process under discussion.

(elements common to it and other representations), combined with those representations that may present partial identities, and finally laid out into an *ordered table*" (Foucault, 1966/1973:68; italics added). Foucault proceeds to analyze what were in the Classical Age (the seventeenth century) called natural history, the theory of money and value (economics), and general grammar (linguistics) and concludes that they indicate that the "centre of knowledge, in the seventeenth and eighteenth centuries, is the *table*" (Foucault, 1966/1973:75). In fact, these three fields are little more than sub-regions of the tabular space that represented knowledge in this period.

Looking at specific fields of language during this period, Foucault (1966/1973:120) says, "The fundamental task of Classical 'discourse' is *to ascribe a name to things, and in that name to name their being.*" Of biology (or natural history), he contends that "a grid can be laid out over the entire vegetable or animal kingdom. Each group can be given a name" (Foucault, 1966/1973:141). And, in his view, the "*analysis of wealth* obeys the same configuration as *natural history* and *general grammar*" (Foucault, 1966/1973:200).

However, each of these domains, as well as the entire episteme on which they are based, changes again in the eighteenth century. Within less than twenty years, the classical episteme, with its great emphasis on tables, is toppled. And the effect of this fall is felt in all realms of knowledge. Representation has been displaced, and knowledge has "now escaped from the space of the table" (Foucault, 1966/1973:239). The new basis of knowledge is the "transcendental field of subjectivity" (Foucault, 1966/1973:250). More specifically, "what matters is no longer identities, distinctive characters, permanent tables with all their possible paths and routes, but great *hidden forces* developed on the basis of their primitive and inaccessible *nucleus, origin, causality,* and *history*" (Foucault, 1966/1973:251; italics added). These, of course, are all of the things that Foucault fought against in creating his archaeology of knowledge, especially the emphasis on the human subject. Thus, in the Modern Age, the human being is born and replaces the table as the center of our systems of knowledge.

We are so accustomed to thinking in this modern way that we think human beings have always been the center of thought. However, Foucault makes it clear that man, in this sense, did not exist before the eighteenth century. The classical age has "no epistemological consciousness of man as such . . . [it] absolutely excludes anything that could be a 'science of man' " (Foucault, 1966/1973:309–311). That is, unlike today, man did not occupy the center of the "human sciences"—economics, philosophy (linguistics), and biology. It was the table, and not the human being, that was the center of knowledge. With the eclipse of classical discourse, "man appears in his ambiguous position as an object of knowledge and as a subject that knows: enslaved sovereign, observed spectator, he appears in the place belonging to the king" (Foucault, 1966/1973:312).

Foucault thinks that it is crucial that this anthropological focus, this anthropological prejudice, be recognized *and* destroyed. The focus on the human being has served to warp and distort our thinking. However, in the human sciences we are experiencing yet another epistemic change (with thinkers like Foucault in the forefront), what many have termed the "linguistic turn," and the focus has shifted from human beings to language. Foucault (1966/1973:387) concludes, "As the archaeology of our thought easily shows, man is an invention of recent date. And one perhaps nearing its end." Or, more graphically, "one can certainly wager that man would be erased, like a face drawn in the sand at the edge of the sea" (Foucault, 1966/1973:387).

GENEALOGY OF POWER

Foucault's early archaeological analysis of discourse was later abandoned for an even more poststructuralist approach because Foucault came to realize that his archaeology was silent on the issue of power as well as on the link between knowledge and power. Foucault's genealogy focuses on the origins (in concrete historical conditions) and the (largely discontinuous) development of power/knowledge regimes. The most important source on Foucault's (1969, 1971/1976) thinking on the genealogy of power is his 1971 lecture and essay, "The Discourse on Language." Consistent with the emphasis he places on decentering the subject, Foucault begins by once again seeking to avoid being considered the author or subject of the essay, describing himself as a "nameless voice" and saying "I would really like to have slipped imperceptibly into this lecture" (Foucault, 1969, 1971/1976:215).

A dramatic shift in Foucault's thinking is indicated in this essay. While there certainly was a critical edge to his earlier work, especially aimed at the focus on man and the human sciences, critique now becomes much more central. The key now is power and the way it is exercised over discourse:

> I am supposing that in every society the production of discourse is at once *controlled, selected, organized* and *redistributed* according to a certain number of procedures, whose role is to avert its powers and danger, to cope with chance events, to evade its ponderous, awesome materiality.

> (Foucault, 1969, 1971/1976:216; italics added)

The central point is that discourse is dangerous, and those in power seek to exercise control over those forms of discourse that they consider a potential threat to them.

Foucault identifies four domains in which discourse is considered to be particularly dangerous: politics (or power), sexuality (or desire), madness, and, most generally, what is considered to be true or false. Foucault, following Nietzsche, identifies the latter area as the "will to truth" or "the will to power." In linking these, Foucault (like Nietzsche) is linking knowledge to power; the idea that knowledge is pursued for its own sake, and not to gain power, is rejected by Foucault. Science is an example of a field engaged in an effort to differentiate true from false. In making such a differentiation, a scientific field is implicitly excluding alternative bodies of knowledge as "false." In this way, the will to truth is tied to the will to power; one scientific field seeks to gain hegemony over other fields. Overall, there is a historical trend in the direction of the linkage between the will to power and the will to truth as the central problem confronting discourse in society; it "daily grows in strength, in depth and implacability" (Foucault, 1969, 1971/1976:219).

Discourses on politics, sexuality, and madness are seen as oriented to attaining power and are opposed by those with, or in, power. Despite the growing importance of the will to power and truth, it is largely invisible in society as a whole; "we speak of it least" (Foucault, 1969, 1971/1976:219). Foucault intends to correct that problem by speaking (actually writing) about the will to power and truth.

Foucault (1969, 1971/1976:220) differentiates between systems of exclusion (like those discussed above) and "internal rules, where discourse exercises its own control; rules concerned with the principles of classification, ordering and distribution." That is, disciplines have their own rules that serve to control what is said in them. For example, they often represent closed communities, or fellowships of discourse, that prevent those outside these realms from speaking, at least with any authority. For another, education and credentials are used as mechanisms to appropriate discourse; those with the proper credentials may speak, others may not. Along with other internal mechanisms (e.g., verbal rituals), these devices are generally "linked together, constituting great edifices that distribute speakers among the different types of discourse" (Foucault, 1969, 1971/1976:227).

Thus, Foucault sees himself as undertaking two often (but not always) interrelated tasks. The first is the *critical* task of dealing with "forms of exclusion, limitation and appropriation . . . how they are formed, in answer to which needs, how they are modified and displaced, which constraints they have effectively exercised, to what extent they have been worked on" (Foucault, 1969, 1971/1976:231). The second, or *genealogical,* task is to examine "how series of discourse are formed, through, in spite of, or with the aid of these systems of constraint: what were the specific norms for each, and what were the conditions of appearance, growth and variation" (Foucault, 1969, 1971/1976:232). On the relationship between critical and genealogical analysis, Foucault says,

> The genealogical aspect concerns the effective formation of discourse, whether within the limits of control, or outside of them, or as is most frequent, on both sides of the delimitation. Criticism analyses the processes of *rarefaction, consolidation and unification* in discourse, genealogy studies their *formation,* at once scattered, discontinuous and regular.

> (Foucault, 1969, 1971/1976:233; italics added)

Thus, genealogy is a historical analysis of the relationship between power and discourse, while criticism is aimed at the processes involved in the control of discourse.

Overall, Foucault is concerned with how people regulate themselves and others through the production and control of knowledge. Among other things, he sees knowledge generating power by constituting people as subjects and knowledge being used to govern the subjects. He is critical of the hierarchization of knowledge. Because the highest-ranking forms of knowledge (the sciences) have the greatest power, they are singled out for the most severe critique. Foucault is interested in techniques, the technologies that are derived from knowledge (especially scientific knowledge), and how they are used by various institutions to exert power over people. Although he sees links between knowledge and power, Foucault does not see a conspiracy by elite members of society. Such a conspiracy would imply conscious actors, whereas Foucault is more inclined to see structural relationships, especially between knowledge and power. Looking over the sweep of history, Foucault does not see progress from primitive brutishness to more modern humaneness based on more sophisticated knowledge systems. Instead, Foucault sees history lurching from one system of domination (based on knowledge) to another. Although this is a generally bleak image, on the positive side Foucault believes that knowledge-power is always contested; there is always ongoing resistance to it. Foucault looks at historical examples, but he is primarily interested in knowledge-power relations in the modern world (Donnelly, 1982). As he puts it, he is "writing the history of the present" (Foucault, 1975/1979:31).

With this background on the archaeology of knowledge and the genealogy of power, let us look at some of Foucault's specific substantive works.

MADNESS AND CIVILIZATION

In *Madness and Civilization* (1961/1967), Foucault is doing, at least in part, an archaeology of knowledge, specifically of psychiatry or psychiatric knowledge. He makes it clear that he is not doing a history (or a history of ideas) but rather one of his archaeologies of knowledge. He says, "I have not tried to write the history of that language [psychiatry], but rather the archaeology of that silence" (Foucault, 1961/1967:xi). In such an archaeology, while he is ultimately concerned with the present, he is examining the past ostensibly as it must have existed in its time.

He begins with the Renaissance, when madness and reason were not separated, when there was an incessant dialogue between madness and reason, when they both spoke the same language. However, in the Classical Age (between 1650 and 1800), distance between them was established, the dialogue began to be silenced, they began to speak different languages, and, ultimately, reason came to subjugate madness. In other words, one form of knowledge came to exert power over another (madness). Foucault is describing "a broken dialogue" between reason and madness (Foucault, 1961/1967:x), one with the following end result:

> Here reason reigned in the pure state, in a triumph arranged for it in advance over a frenzied unreason. Madness was thus torn from that imaginary freedom which still allowed it to flourish on the Renaissance horizon. Not so long ago, it had floundered about in broad daylight, in *King Lear,* in *Don Quixote.* But in less than a half-century, it had been sequestered and, in the fortress of confinement, bound to Reason, to the rules of morality and to their monotonous nights.

(Foucault, 1961/1967:64)[4]

While the Renaissance is a period of a comparative lack of silence, today, the mad and the sane live in worlds of total silence (at least vis-à-vis one another); there is

---

[4] There is a clear Weberian, iron-cage imagery here—the "monotonous nights" to be spent by the "mad" (the irrational) in the iron cage constructed by those with reason (rationality).

no dialogue between them. Foucault is interested in what led not only to this separation of sanity and madness but also to the subjugation of madness by the sane.[5]

Foucault does not see what has happened to the mad as an isolated process. The same kind of thing was happening to others, including the poor, the unemployed, and prisoners. Thus, the Renaissance is the period of the founding of houses of confinement—madhouses, workhouses, and prisons. Just as the insane were relegated during this period to the madhouse, the unemployed and poor were sent to workhouses and the prisoners to prison cells. Foucault (1961/1967:39–41) takes as a landmark in this overall process the founding of the Hôpital Général in 1656 which he sees, not as a medical establishment, but as a "semijudicial structure"; a third-order of oppression (others were the police and the courts) that soon spread "its network over the whole of France." Hospitals, madhouses, workhouses, and prisons are not to Foucault what they purport to be but rather part of a broad system put in place during the Renaissance to judge and to oppress people.

The rise of this system, and each of its components, is linked by Foucault to the economic crises of the day. To forestall agitation and uprisings, people were put to work. Those that could not be put to work were confined in places like hospitals, prisons, and mental institutions. In other words, these served as mechanisms of social control.

While this system may not have succeeded in terms of its original purposes (after all, uprisings and even revolutions did occur), it did serve to define the lack of work, that is, idleness (later extended to all types of social uselessness), as an ethical and moral problem. And from the beginning the mad were linked to the poor and the idle. For the first time in history, institutions of morality were formed combining moral obligation and civil law. More generally, things like morality, virtue, and goodness became concerns of the state.

Until the seventeenth century, what was considered to be evil was dealt with in public. The seventeenth century witnessed the beginnings of the rise of confinement for those who were considered "evil." By the eighteenth century the process had reached such an extreme that it was believed that only oblivion, like that associated with confinement, could suppress evil. Shame had come to be associated with that which was inhuman. There was one important difference, however, between the insane and the others who were confined. The insane were shown, displayed, and made a spectacle of even after confinement. One explanation for this difference is that during this period the mad came to be thought of as animals. This permitted those in charge to exert discipline over them, even to brutalize them (we have not yet reached the stage of the medicalization of the treatment of the insane). More important, at least for the purposes of this discussion, this helps to account for why the insane were displayed. That is, their display showed the population how close they were to animals and, implicitly, how close they were to being confined if they stepped out of line. Despite the spectacles, the mad were still behind

---

[5] It should be borne in mind that Foucault can be interpreted as not only writing about the madness of the insane but also of the "madness" of creative individuals like himself.

bars, separated from reason and those who were considered to possess it. It should be recalled that this situation stood in contrast to the Renaissance in which madness was everywhere; it mingled with everything.

The scientific psychology and psychiatry of the nineteenth century eventually arose out of the separation of the mad from the sane, the "invention" of madness, in the eighteenth century. In line with his ideas on the end of the dialogue between the mad and the sane, psychiatry is described as a "monologue of reason about madness" (Foucault, 1961/1967:xi). At first, medicine was in charge of the physical and moral treatment of the mad, but later scientific psychological medicine took over the moral treatment. It was the definition of madness as a moral problem that made psychology possible. "A purely psychological medicine was made possible only when madness was alienated in guilt" (Foucault, 1961/1967:182–183). Later, Foucault says, "What we call psychiatric practice is a certain moral tactic contemporary with the end of the eighteenth century, preserved in the rites of asylum life, and overlaid by the myths of positivism" (1961/1967:276). Thus, for Foucault, psychology (and psychiatry) is a moral enterprise, not a scientific endeavor, aimed against the mad who are progressively unable to protect themselves from this "help." He sees the mad as being sentenced by so-called scientific advancement to a "gigantic moral imprisonment."

A change in perceptual structure took place in the seventeenth and eighteenth centuries. Diseases that at one time were thought to be illnesses of the body (e.g., hysteria, hypochondria) came to be viewed as diseases of the mind. What was once thought to be corporeal was now thought to be mental and therefore associated with immorality. Blame came to fall on those with these illnesses; the illnesses were now seen as the psychological effects of moral faults. This laid the groundwork for nineteenth-century scientific psychiatry and its moral methods. However, we are not yet at that stage. Medicine continued to be content with curing these problems with the physical means (purification, immersion, regulation of movement) that had been used to exorcise sin. However, medicine was soon to recognize the difference between physical medicaments and moral treatment. In later years, psychological attacks on mental problems and physical intervention were juxtaposed; they complemented one another, but never again interpenetrated.

With this clear distinction there arose nineteenth-century psychiatry and its moral methods, which "brought madness and its cure into the domain of guilt" (Foucault, 1961/1967:182). The focus shifted to the interrogation of the subject responsible for the "insane" thoughts or actions. With the separation of the psychological and the organic, and the delegation (usurpation) of unreason by psychology, modern psychology came into being.

Unreason had emerged from confinement in the eighteenth century because of a fear that mental disease was spreading in the houses of confinement. It was as if "maleficent vapors" were pervading the institutions. While this new fear was put in medical terms, it was "animated, basically, by a moral myth" (Foucault, 1961/1967:202). In any case, "unreason was once more present; but marked now by an imaginary stigma of disease, which added its powers of terror" (Foucault,

1961/1967:205). Here Foucault once again attacks the idea of progress. This "new" view of the insane combined the fear of unreason with old spectres of disease. This wasn't progress but a regression involving the reactivation of images of impurity. It was this, more than improved knowledge, that led medicine to deal with mental illness.

One example of such an "advance" was the great reform movement of the second half of the eighteenth century in which houses of confinement were more completely isolated so that they could be surrounded by purer air. Such isolation was also designed to allow "evil" to vegetate in the asylums without spreading to the larger community. This served to eliminate, in the view of the day, the risk of contagion while at the same time retaining the asylum, and the mad contained in it, as an example for the spectators. It remained "a spectacle conclusively proving the drawbacks of immorality" (Foucault, 1961/1967:207).

At the beginning of the nineteenth century the positivists claimed to have been the first to have freed the mad from being confused with criminals. However, Foucault rejects this as he does most claims by the medical establishment. Rather than being brought about by advances in the humanitarianism of the medical profession, Foucault traces it to the mad themselves and their protests against their treatment. It was the mad themselves who succesfully resisted the power of the confinements and those who supported them. In fact, in Foucault's view, the actions of the positivists did more to link madness to confinement than to separate the two.

Needless to say, Foucault rejects the idea that over the years we have seen scientific, medical, and humanitarian advances in the treatment of the mad. What he sees, instead, are increases in the ability of the sane and their agents (physicians, psychologists, psychiatrists) to oppress and repress the mad who, we should not forget, had been on equal footing with the sane before the Renaissance. More recently, the mad have come to be less judged by these external agents and more by themselves; "madness is ceaselessly called upon to judge itself" (Foucault, 1961/1967:265). In many senses such internalized control is the most repressive form of control.

In this context, Foucault looks at the work of those, like William Tuke (1732–1822) and Philippe Pinel (1754–1826), who are generally considered to be the great reformers in the history of mental illness. He argues that we need to look beyond their self-serving justifications. Of Tuke, for example, Foucault (1961/1967:243) says that his action "was regarded as an act of 'liberation.' The truth was quite different." The result of Tuke's actions was that madmen came to be aware of, to feel guilty about, their own madness. Madmen were sentenced to a lifetime of anguish of responsibility and conscience. As a result, the mad were forever vulnerable to punishment not only by others but also by themselves. Thus, madness came to be "ceaselessly called upon to judge itself . . . [and it also came to be judged] by a sort of invisible tribunal in permanent session" (Foucault, 1961/1967:265).

Madmen were also forced to objectify themselves both in work and in observation, an observation that was, by the way, a one-way process. The madman is now piteously observed by himself. And "in the silence of those who represent reason, and who have done nothing but hold up the perilous mirror, he recognizes himself as objectively mad" (Foucault, 1961/1967:264). Thus was born a science of mental illness that involved observation and classification without a dialogue with the mad. It is a world of absolute silence between the mad and those with reason since they no longer have a common language. Thus, Foucault (1961/1967:266) concludes that rather than being therapeutic or humanitarian, Pinel's asylum was involved in the "conversion of medicine into justice, of therapeutics into repression." Everything is now set up so that the madman now recognizes that he is enveloped on all sides by a world of judgment; he is constantly being watched, judged, condemned. In addition, the guilt is internalized and becomes part of the inmate's conscience. Most generally, the inmate is "imprisoned in a moral world" (Foucault, 1961/1967:269). Foucault (1961/1967:278) concludes by describing "that gigantic moral imprisonment which we are in the habit of calling, doubtless by antiphrasis, the liberation of the insane by Pinel and Tuke."

Foucault sees all of this manifest in the modern practice of medicine in its treatment of the mentally ill. The physician plays a central role in the asylum and elsewhere, not as a scientist but "as a juridical and moral guarantee" (Foucault, 1961/1967:270). Science is little more than a disguise, a justification for the moral role played by medical practitioners. In an excellent summation of his position, Foucault (1961/1967:276) argues, "what we call psychiatric practice is a certain moral tactic contemporary with the end of the eighteenth century, preserved in the rites of asylum life, and overlaid by the myths of positivism."

Interestingly, Foucault gives Freud some credit for restoring the dialogue between the mad and the sane:

Freud went back to madness at the level of its *language* . . . he restored in medical thought, the possibility of a dialogue with unreason . . . It is not psychology that is involved in psychoanalysis: but precisely an experience of unreason that it has been psychology's meaning, in the modern world, to mask.

(Foucault, 1961/1967:198)

But, more important, Foucault was also critical of Freud for continuing many of the trends discussed in this section. Thus, he saw Freud's psychoanalysis[6] as becoming pure observation, pure and circumspect silence, and adopting a juridical position. Most important, Freud is seen as having transferred to the physician all of the structures that Pinel, Tuke, and others had set up within the mental institution. As a result, Freud helped the psychoanalyst, as well as the physician, become the powerful force that they have become in psychiatry and more generally in medicine.

Clearly, Foucault's archaeology of knowledge leads him to very different conclusions from those of traditional historians about the history and current status of the mad and their relationship to the sane (and their agents). In addition, it should

---

[6] For a discussion of the influence of psychoanalysis on Foucault's work, see Derrida, Brault, and Naas (1994).

be noted that in this analysis he is examining the roots of the human sciences (especially psychology and psychiatry) in the distinction between the mad and the sane and the exertion of moral control over the mad (Christie, 1993). This is part of his more general thesis about the role of the human sciences in the moral control of people.

As for Foucault's structuralism in this early work, he argues that madness occurs at two "levels," and at "a deeper level madness is a form of discourse" (1961/1967:96). Specifically, madness, at least in the Classical Age, is not mental or physical changes; instead, "delirious language is the ultimate truth of madness" (Foucault, 1961/1967:97). Or, later, "Madness, in the Classical sense, does not designate so much a specific change in the mind or in the body, as the existence, under the body's alterations, under the oddity of conduct and conversation, of *a delirious discourse. . . . Language is the first and last structure of madness*" (Foucault, 1961/1967:99–100).

But there is an even broader structuralism operating in this early work:

> Let classical culture formulate, *in its general structure,* the experience it had of madness, an experience which crops up with the same meanings, in the identical order of its inner logic, in both the order of speculation and in the order of institutions, in *both discourse and decree,* in both word and watchword—wherever, in fact, a signifying element can assume for us the value of a language.
>
> (Foucault, 1961/1967:116; italics added)

THE BIRTH OF THE CLINIC

As the subtitle suggests, in *The Birth of the Clinic: An Archaeology of Medical Perception,* Foucault continues to do an archaeology of knowledge. He is interested in studying a change in the basic structure of experience, and the change in medicine analyzed in this book is but one example of such a change.

He also continues to utilize, at least in part, a structuralist approach focusing on medical discourse and its underlying structure. He argues that in doing history, we are doomed "to the patient reconstruction of discourses about discourse, and to the task of hearing what has already been said" (Foucault, 1963/1975:xvi). In the structural analysis of discourse, the meaning of a statement is derived not from the intentions of the person uttering it but from its relationship to other statements in the system of discourse. Also on structural analysis, Foucault says, "What counts in the things said by men is not so much what they may have thought or the extent to which these things represent their thoughts, as *that which systematizes them from the outset,* thus making them thereafter endlessly accessible to new discourse and open to the task of transforming them" (Foucault, 1963/1975:xiv; italics added).

Of great importance to Foucault in this analysis, as we will see, is perception, or the crucial concept of the *gaze* (Denzin, 1993). It is a historical shift in the gaze of medicine that is the focus of Foucault's archaeology. Furthermore, Foucault sees an analogy between seeing and speaking (to see is to say), and this serves to make the gaze subject to the same kind of structural analysis as the spoken language. As a structuralist, at least in part, Foucault saw the gaze as a kind of language, "a language without words" (1963/1975:68), and he was interested in the deep structure of that "language." Thus, the gaze is the subject of both Foucault's archaeological and structural analyses.

In the eighteenth century, medicine was largely a classificatory science. The focus was on the classificatory system (the "table" discussed above) and the class, genus, or species of a given disease. As yet, there was no clinical structure in medicine. However, in the nineteenth century the gaze of the medical practitioner shifted from the classificatory system, from the "table," to the patient and the patient's body. The key was the development of the clinic where patients were observed in bed (Long, 1992). Here the gaze of the physician on the body "was at the same time knowledge" (Foucault, 1963/1975:81). In other words, knowledge was derived from what physicians could see in contrast to the classificatory systems they read about in books. Physicians were looking at patients and not some system of classification, or table.

The ability to see and touch sick people was a crucial change in medicine and an important source of knowledge (and ultimately power). Of special importance was the ability to examine, or gaze upon, dead bodies in autopsies. Foucault says of the autopsy, "The living night is dissipated in the brightness of death" (1963/1975:146). In other words, the ability to study the dead illuminated many things about health, disease, and death. With the advent of the autopsy and the clinical gaze, death took center stage. "Death left its old tragic heaven and became the lyrical core of man: his invisible truth, his visible secret" (Foucault, 1963/1975:172). Because of the autopsy and its focus on things like diseased organs, the "being," the "essence," of disease disappears. We are left with the realization that all that exists is a series of diseases caused by "a certain complex movement of tissues in reaction to an irritating cause" (Foucault, 1963/1975:189). In addition to the deromanticization of human life (and death), with this, the medicine of diseases ends and the medicine of pathological reactions begins.

From the point of view of the archaeology of knowledge, Foucault sees the anatomo-clinical gaze as the "great break" in Western medicine. Thus, there was no gradual evolution of knowledge leading up to the gaze. Rather, anatomo-clinical gaze represented a fundamental epistemic change, a revolutionary development. After the change in the gaze, doctors were no longer playing the same game; it was a different game with different rules. In the new game, people (patients), and not the disease as part of a broader classification system, had become the object of scientific knowledge and practice. In terms of a more typical structuralist analysis, what had changed was the nature of discourse, things like the names and groups of diseases, the field of objects, and so forth (Foucault, 1963/1975:54).

As was the case with mental illness, Foucault rejects medicine's own history as an exercise in mythology. The gaze did not evolve, as medicine argued, peacefully and effortlessly from prior developments in the field. What really happened was that the clinical relationship, once a universal relationship of humankind with itself, came to be radically restructured and redefined in the last years of the eighteenth century as the province of the medical profession. Once this occurred, a radical change in medical knowledge took place: "A way of teaching and *saying* became a way of learning and *seeing*" (Foucault, 1963/1975:64). Clinical practice made possible "the immediate communication of teaching within the concrete field of experience" (Foucault, 1963/1975:68). Seeing replaced dogmatic language as a way of learning the truth. The clinical gaze was seen, in good structuralist terms, as "a language without words . . . a language that did not owe its truth to speech but to the gaze alone" (Foucault, 1963/1975:68–69). More generally, the structuralist needed to focus on the codes of knowledge in which field and gaze were intertwined.

In *Madness and Civilization,* medicine was an important precursor of the human sciences, and that is an even more central theme in *The Birth of the Clinic.* As Foucault clearly put it, "The science of man . . . was medically . . . based" (1963/1975:36). Up until the end of the eighteenth century, medicine was concerned with the issue of health, but from the nineteenth century, the focus of medicine shifted more to the issue of normality and that which varies from it (the pathological). To put it another way, prior to the nineteenth century, as we have seen, medicine was a classificatory science, and the focus was on a clearly ordered system of diseases. But in the nineteenth century, medicine came to focus on diseases as they existed in individuals and the larger society (epidemics). Medicine came to be extended to healthy people (preventive care), and it adopted a normative posture distinguishing between healthy and unhealthy and, later, normal and pathological states.

> Clinical experience sees a new space opening up before it: the tangible space of the body, which at the same time is that opaque mass in which secrets, invisible lesions, and the very mystery of origins lie hidden. The medicine of symptoms will gradually recede, until it finally disappears before the medicine of organs, sites, causes, before a clinic wholly ordered in accordance with *pathological* anatomy.
>
> (Foucault, 1963/1975:122; italics added)

Medicine had become, again, a forerunner of the human sciences that were to adopt this normal-pathological stance toward people.

Medicine takes on the role of forerunner to the human sciences for another, more general reason: "It is understandable, then, that medicine should have had such importance in the constitution of the sciences of man—an importance that is not only methodological, but ontological, in that it concerns man's being an object of positive knowledge" (Foucault, 1963/1975:197). The shift in medicine to the individual as subject and object of his own knowledge is but one "of the more visible witnesses to these changes in the fundamental structure of experiences" (1963/1975:199). Clearly, the individual was to become the subject and object of the human sciences.

DISCIPLINE AND PUNISH

Many of the themes discussed previously reappear in *Discipline and Punish: The Birth of the Prison* (Foucault, 1975/1979; Foucault and Simon, 1991; for a critique see Garland, 1990:131–175). However, now the genealogy of power (Wickham, 1983) takes more of center stage, and much less attention is devoted to the archaeology of knowledge, structuralism, discourse, and the like. Foucault explains his goal:

> This book is intended as a correlative history of the modern soul and of a new power to judge; a *genealogy* of the present scientifico-legal complex from which the power to punish derives its bases, justifications and rules, from which it extends its effects and by which it masks its exorbitant singularity.

(Foucault, 1975/1979:23; italics added)

In the specific terms of the genealogy of power, Foucault (1975/1979:27) makes it clear here that "power and knowledge directly imply one another; that there is no power relation without the correlative constitution of a field of knowledge, nor any knowledge that does not presuppose and constitute at the same time power relations."

The focus here shifts away from those who created, or were subjected to, the power-knowledge nexus and toward that nexus itself: "it is *not* the activity of the *subject* of knowledge that produces a corpus of knowledge, useful or resistant to power, but *power-knowledge,* the *processes and struggles that traverse it* and of which it is made up, that determines the forms and possible domains of knowledge" (Foucault, 1975/1979:28).[7]

Discipline and Punish is concerned with the period between 1757 and the 1830s, a period during which the torture of prisoners was replaced by control over them by prison rules. Characteristically, Foucault sees this change developing in an irregular way; it does not evolve rationally or in a smooth, evolutionary fashion. The book opens in 1757 with an excruciating portrait of a prisoner who is publicly executed by being "torn," "burnt," and "quartered." The prisoner's body is the object of officials. The state of the body, after punishment is inflicted, demonstrates that a crime has taken place and that the accused is guilty. The public ceremonies involved in such torture are judicial and political rituals that demonstrate both that a crime has taken place and that power is being manifest in an effort to control it. Public ceremonies such as executions were great spectacles, "magnificent theatre," designed to demonstrate publicly that power existed. Executions and torture not only showed the operation of power but also revealed the "truth" of that power.

However, while the public torture and execution of prisoners may have made for good public displays, it was "a bad economy of power" because, for example, it tended to incite unrest among the viewers of the spectacle (Foucault, 1975/1979:79). Spectacles like executions also tended to lead to "centres of illegality" (Foucault, 1975/1979:63). The taverns were full, stones were thrown at executioners, fights erupted, and spectators grabbed at the victims. Furthermore, over time, protests against public executions increased. For all of these reasons officials needed to end public confrontations with the condemned.

---

[7] Foucault is indicating a shift away from the focus on the human subject, a shift that will grow even more dramatic with later postmodernists, especially Baudrillard (see Chapters 5 and 6).

Within less than a century a new system of punishment was in place. Torture disappeared as a public spectacle. Punishment became less physical and much more subtle. The body ceased to be the major target of punishment. Instead of imposing "unbearable sensations" on prisoners, the focus was on things like suspending their rights. Punishment came to be rationalized and bureaucratized. Bureaucratic restraint and control was reflected in the fact that "a whole army of technicians took over for the executioner, the immediate anatomist of pain: warders, doctors, chaplains, psychiatrists, psychologists, educationalists" (Foucault, 1975/1979:11). Instead of the earlier vagaries, punishment became far more predictable. Technologically, the far more efficient guillotine replaced the "hanging machine." This led to greater efficiency; instead of a long, cruel process, death came in a single blow from the blade of the guillotine. Anger and passion were removed from the process; "the executioner need be no more than a meticulous watchmaker" (Foucault, 1975/1979:13). The law was applied, and people acted, impersonally. Even the condemned wore veils to conceal who they were. "The age of sobriety in punishment had begun" (Foucault, 1975/1979:14).

As in the case of madness, the general and accepted view is that all of the changes described above represented a humanization of the treatment of criminals; punishment had grown more kind, less painful, and less cruel. The reality, from Foucault's point of view, was that punishment had grown more rationalized and in many ways impinged more on prisoners as well as on the larger society. Punishment may have grown less intense, but it was at the expense of greater intervention into peoples' lives. Foucault (1975/1979:78) describes "a tendency towards a more finely tuned justice, towards a closer penal mapping of the social body . . . controls become more premature and more numerous." While the link between knowledge and power was clear in the case of torture and public executions, with the development of a more rational system, that link became far less clear. The new system of rules was "more regular, more effective, more constant, and more detailed in its effects; in short, which increased its effects while diminishing its economic cost" (Foucault, 1975/1979:80–81). The new system was not designed to be more humane, "not to punish less, but to punish better; to punish with an attenuated severity perhaps, but in order to punish with more universality and necessity; to insert the power to punish more deeply into the social body" (Foucault, 1975/1979:82). In contrast to torture, this new technology of the power to punish occurred earlier in the deviance process, was more numerous, more bureaucratized, more efficient, more impersonal, more invariable, and more sober, and involved the surveillance not just of criminals but of the entire society. Thus, penal systems did not seek to eliminate punishments but simply to administer them differently.

The criminal, and what is done to him, is a source of knowledge and information for the larger public. As Foucault (1975/1979:112) puts it, the punishment of the criminal is "a living lesson in the museum of order." Thus, the new forms of punishment were less ceremonies and spectacles and more schools for the larger population. "Long before he was regarded as an object of science, the criminal was imagined as a source of instruction" (Foucault, 1975/1979:112). While in an earlier time there were huge ceremonies involving torture and execution, in the modern world we have instead "hundreds of tiny theatres of punishment" (Foucault,

1975/1979:113).[8] More generally, the prison had replaced the scaffold, and this signified, among other things, that power was inscribed into the very heart of the state since the penal system was run by the state.

Foucault relates this to the broader development of what he calls the *disciplines,* which, in the seventeenth and eighteenth centuries, became the general mechanism for exercising domination. The disciplines involve a series of exercises designed to exert meticulous control over the body; "discipline produces subjected and practised bodies, 'docile' bodies" (Foucault, 1975/1979:138). The disciplines not only occurred in prisons but also in public education (the Lancaster schools, for example), hospitals, the workplace (especially Taylorism), and the military. Discipline involves the distribution of individuals in space including the enclosure and partitioning of individuals and the development of functional sites and ranks. "In organizing 'cells', 'places' and 'ranks', the disciplines create complex spaces that are at once architectural, functional and hierarchical" (Foucault, 1975/1979:148).

This new technology, the technology of disciplinary power, was based on the military model:

> Historians of ideas usually attribute the dream of a perfect society to the philosophers and jurists of the eighteenth century; but there was also a military dream of society; its fundamental reference was not to the state of nature, but to the meticulously subordinated cogs of a machine, not to the primal social contract, but to permanent coercions, not to fundamental rights, but to indefinitely progressive forms of training, not to the general will, but to automatic docility.

> (Foucault, 1975/1979:169)

Foucault identifies three instruments of disciplinary power, derived in large part from the military model. First is *hierarchical observation,* or the ability of officials to oversee all they control with a single *gaze.* The military camp is here seen as a model (another is the Panopticon discussed below). The goal is observation that is discreet, largely silent, and permanent. Here is Foucault's "physics of power" involving things like lines of sight and control over various spaces.

Second is the ability to make *normalizing judgments* and to punish those who violate the norms. Thus, one might be negatively judged and subjected to micro-penalties for violations relating to such things as time (for being late), activity (for being inattentive), behavior (for being impolite), and body (adopting the incorrect attitude). Such normalizing judgments serve to compare, differentiate, hierarchicalize, homogenize, and where necessary, exclude people.

Third is the use of *examination* to observe subjects and to make normalizing judgments about them (Meadmore, 1993). This third instrument of disciplinary power involves the other two. That is, examinations involve hierarchical observation and normalizing judgments; they involve, in other words, "a normalizing gaze" (Foucault, 1975/1979:184). An examination "establishes over individuals a visibility through which one differentiates them and judges them" (Foucault,

---

[8] This idea is part of Foucault's thinking on the micro-politics of power; see below.

1975/1979:184). An examination is a wonderful example of the power-knowledge linkage; those who have the power to give examinations gain additional knowledge and thereby more power through the imposition of examinations on subjects. As Foucault (1975/1979:185) puts it, "The superimposition of the power relations and knowledge relations assumes in the examination all its visible brilliance." While we usually associate the examination with schools, it is also manifest in psychiatry, medicine, personnel administration, and so on.

Foucault offers several other important generalizations about the examination:

- First, it *"transformed the economy of visibility into the exercise of power"* (Foucault, 1975/1979:187).
- Second, it *"introduces individuality into the field of documentation"* (Foucault, 1975/1979:189). As a result of its focus on the individual, Foucault (1975/1979:191) wonders "is this [the examination] the birth of the sciences of man?"
- Third, *"the examination, surrounded by all documentary techniques, makes each individual a 'case'"* (Foucault, 1975/1979:191). As a case, the individual becomes both an object of knowledge *and* an object of control. And, of course, the two are linked in the power-knowledge nexus.

By way of summary, we can say that disciplines involve a series of procedures for distributing individuals, fixing them in space, classifying them, extracting from them maximum time and energy, training their bodies, coding their continuous behavior, maintaining them in perfect visibility, surrounding them with mechanisms of observation, registering and recording them, and constituting in them a body of knowledge that is accumulated and centralized.

Foucault does not simply adopt a negative view toward the growth of the disciplinary society; he recognizes that it has positive consequences as well. For example, he sees discipline as functioning well within the military and industrial factories. However, Foucault communicates a genuine fear of the spread of discipline, especially as it moves into the state-police network for which the entire society becomes a field of perception and an object of discipline.

Foucault does not see discipline sweeping uniformly through society. Instead, he sees elements of it "swarming" through society and affecting bits and pieces of society as it goes. Eventually, however, most major institutions are affected. Foucault asks rhetorically, "Is it surprising that prisons resemble factories, schools, barracks, hospitals, which all resemble prisons?" (1975/1979:228). In the end, Foucault sees the development of a *carceral archipelago* in which discipline is transported "from the penal institution to the entire social body" (1975/1979:298; Dutton, 1992; Sewell and Wilkinson, 1992). Although there is an iron-cage image here, as usual Foucault sees the operation of forces in opposition to the carceral system; there is an ongoing structural dialectic in Foucault's work.

Although Foucault's greater emphasis on power in *Discipline and Punish* is evident in the discussion to this point, he is also concerned in this work with his usual theme of the emergence of the human sciences. The transition from torture to prison rules constituted a switch in the object of punishment from the body to the soul or the will. This, in turn, brought with it considerations of normality and morality. Judgment came to be passed "on the passions, instincts, anomalies, infirmities, maladjustments . . . aggressivity . . . perversions . . . drives and desires" (Foucault, 1975/1979:17). Even the subject's will came to be judged. Science entered the process, and this helped give officials greater control over not only offensive acts but over people, "not only on what they do, but also on what they are, will be, may be" (Foucault, 1975/1979:18). In other words, officials came to have the right to judge people as a whole. In Foucault's (1975/1979:18) terms, the judicial system had gotten hold of the "offender's soul." And it is its effort to control the souls of people that is one of the defining characteristics of the human sciences.

More generally, the modern human sciences have their roots in the development of penal law; the human sciences and penal law have their roots in the same "epistemological-juridical" formation. Here is how Foucault bitterly depicts the roots of the human sciences in the "disciplines": "These sciences, which have so delighted our 'humanity' for over a century, have their technical matrix in the petty, malicious minutiae of the disciplines and their investigations" (1975/1979:226). The "humanization" of the penal system and the growth of the human sciences stem from the same sources and both serve to extend discipline and punishment more deeply into the social fabric.

The effort to control the soul also represented the base for a massive expansion of the penal system. Those in power took to "judging something other than crimes, namely the 'soul' of the criminal" (Foucault, 1975/1979:19). Things like insanity and madness came to be associated with crime with the result that officials were now in the position to judge "normality" as well as to prescribe actions that would help bring about the normalization of those who were judged to be abnormal. Thus, one way that expansion took place in the penal system is that what came to be judged was defined far more widely going to the very soul of the "defendant."

Expansion also took place in another sense; more people acquired the right to render these kinds of judgments. Prison officials and the police came to judge the normality and morality of the prisoner. Eventually, the ability to make this kind of judgment was extended to other "small-scale judges" such as psychiatrists and educators. As a result, "the whole penal operation has taken on extra-juridical elements and personnel" (Foucault, 1975/1979:22). The power and ability to judge, especially normality and abnormality, has been generalized and is no longer restricted to the penal system. Out of this emerged new bodies of scientific penal knowledge, and these served as the base of the modern "scientific-legal complex." "A corpus of knowledge, techniques, 'scientific' discourse is formed and becomes entangled with the practice of the power to punish" (Foucault, 1975/1979:23). The new mode of subjugation was that people were defined as the objects of knowledge, of scientific discourse. Power now had a new body of knowledge attached to it. New personnel were in possession of this power, and they adopted a new set of tactics for using it.

In the penal system, its extensions, and in the human sciences, the focus is on the subject in general, and specifically on the body. Human beings became the objects of punishment and of scientific discourse. Scientific knowledge helped make the body a political field and gave birth to political technologies designed to control the body. However, these technologies, and control more generally, were not centralized in the state or in any other structure or institution. Rather, they were diffused in bits and pieces, in a series of tools and methods, throughout society. Thus, rather than deal with power macroscopically as is usually the case in the (modern) social sciences, Foucault (1975/1979:26) is concerned with the "micro-physics of power." As a result, he makes it abundantly clear that there are innumerable points of contact and confrontation between those with power and those on whom they seek to exercise that power.

A focus on the micro-physics of power has several important implications. For one thing, it poses a major problem for the Marxian grand narrative of a revolution that would overthrow the entire power structure. Innumerable micro-centers of power do not lend themselves easily to destruction in a single stroke by a massive revolution. As Foucault (1975/1979:27) puts it, "The overthrow of these 'micro-powers' does not, then, obey the law of all or nothing; it is not acquired once and for all by a new control of the apparatuses nor by a new functioning or a destruction of the institutions." For another, the operation of innumerable micro-sites of power may easily avoid scrutiny or a general sense of their overall impact on society. Thus, it is necessary to examine each of them in the context of the entire network that they form. Even so, it is difficult to assess the overall impact of a large number of micro-sites of power.

One other point, mentioned above, about *Discipline and Punish* is worth special attention. Foucault is generally interested in the way that knowledge gives rise to technologies that exert power. It is in this context that he deals with the Panopticon (Crossley, 1993; Lyon, 1991). A *Panopticon* is a structure that allows officials the possibility of complete observation of criminals; in other words, it permits a certain kind of gaze. With the Panopticon, officials are able to see constantly and to recognize immediately. Constant visibility traps the subjects in "so many cages, so many small theatres, in which each actor is alone, perfectly individualized and constantly visible" (Foucault, 1975/1979:200). In fact, officials need not always be present in the Panopticon; the mere existence of the structure (and the mere possibility that officials *might* be there) constrains criminals. Power functions in the Panopticon nearly automatically. Power here is visible, but it is also unverifiable in that the subjects never know at any given moment whether or not they are actually being observed by officials.

The Panopticon helps to perfect the exercise of power. It reduces the number of people needed to exercise power, while at the same time it increases the number of people over whom power is exercised. Constant pressure is exerted on those observed, even before an act is committed, and officials have the ability to intervene at any point in the process. The Panopticon itself is noiseless and unobtrusive. Using just architecture and geometry (physics, again), the Panopticon acts directly on the subjects; it actually involves the power of one mind (the designer of the Panopticon; the official) over another (the prisoner).

One of the specific forms that the Panopticon can take is that of a tower in the center of a circular prison from which guards are able to see into all cells. More generally, it is an architectural apparatus that permits officials to gather information and exercise power. Thus, the power lies more in the structure, and in the system of which it is part, than in the person who designs or occupies it. The Panopticon is a tremendous source of power for prison officials because it gives them the possibility of total surveillance. Among other things, it is certain and efficient and virtually eliminates the possibility of physical confrontation between officials and inmates. More important, its power is enhanced because the prisoners come to control themselves; they stop themselves from doing various things because they fear that they *might* be seen by the officials who *might* be in the Panopticon. There is a clear linkage here among knowledge, technology, and power.

Furthermore, Foucault returns again to his concern for the human sciences, for he sees the Panopticon as a kind of laboratory (a laboratory of power) for the gathering of information about people. It was the forerunner of the social-scientific laboratory and other social-science techniques for gathering information about people. This is true, at least in part, because the Panopticon came to be used not just with a criminal but more generally with a "madman, a patient, a condemned man, a worker or a schoolboy" (Foucault, 1975/1979:200).

At still another level, Foucault sees the Panopticon, or the panoptic principle, as the base of "a whole type of society" (1975/1979:216), the disciplinary society,[9] a society based on surveillance. It can be used not only to neutralize dangerous behaviors but also to play a more useful role in places like factories and the military, as well as in helping to make people contributing members of society. The mechanisms of the disciplinary society can also be disassociated from specific institutions and broken down so that their component parts can be employed in virtually any social setting. Finally, and most globally, in the hands of the state and the police, the whole social body becomes the object of the disciplinary society.

Discipline may be found in such a wide array of settings because it "may be identified neither with an institution nor with an apparatus; it is a type of power, a modality for its exercise, comprising a whole set of instruments, techniques, procedures, levels of application, targets; it is a 'physics' or an 'anatomy' of power, a technology" (Foucault, 1975/1979:215). Thus, the disciplinary system does not supplant existing systems; rather it infiltrates all of them. The disciplines involve a series of minute technical mechanisms that help to create micro-mechanisms of power in whatever settings they infiltrate.

The development of the disciplinary society corresponded with other historical changes such as large increases in population; increased numbers of people in schools, hospitals, and the military; and the growth in the capitalist economy. These increasingly large systems required cheaper, more efficient, and more effective means of control, and those means were derived from the panoptic principle. These new means of control were, in turn, applied to the production of goods in the factories, the production of knowledge and skills in the schools, the production of health in the hospitals, and the production of destructive force in the military.

The prison is Foucault's paradigm for what is happening throughout society. The prison is an "exhaustive disciplinary apparatus," on which all other systems are modeled to one degree or another (Foucault, 1975/1979:235). The prison is a

---

[9] For an interesting use of this idea, see Zuboff (1988), who views the computer as a modern Panopticon that gives superiors virtually unlimited surveillance over subordinates.

carceral system that sets the stage for society as a whole to become such a system. Processes begun in the prison, and more generally in the judicial system, spread throughout society producing a "carceral net" or a "carceral archipelago" that came to encompass the "entire social body" (Foucault, 1975/1979:298). The power to punish came to operate at every point within society. All sorts of positions have now acquired the capacity to judge us including physicians, teachers, social workers, and the like. While he recognizes that there are forces operating against the carceral system (for example, illegalities on an international scale that are beyond the scope of current judges), the thrust of this work is to leave us with a sense that the carceral system is a Weberian iron cage (O'Neill, 1986). Actually, given Foucault's commitment to the analysis of the micro-politics of power, the image is more of an enormous number of mini-cages in which our lives are even more controlled and even more insufferable than they would be in Weber's society-wide iron cage.

SUMMARY

In this chapter we have examined the bulk of Foucault's published work. We began with his ideas on doing an archaeology of knowledge and then discussed how he did such an archaeology in his studies of several human sciences—biology, economics, and linguistics. Foucault's work then shifted from an analysis of the archaeology of knowledge to the much more critical genealogy of power. Here, he is interested not only in the formation of knowledge but also in the role that power plays in that formation. The majority of the chapter was devoted to three case studies of the archaeology of knowledge and the genealogy of power—the separation and subordination of the mad by the sane (especially in psychiatry), the birth of the medical clinic as well as of the focus on (and control over) the human body through the autopsy, and the end of the torture of prisoners and the beginning of the carceral system of control and the panoptic principle. Running through much of this work is Foucault's interest in the role played by all of these developments in the birth of the human sciences and the power that they exert over people.

As we will see in the next chapter, in his later work, Foucault shifted to a focus on sexuality. While we began with an interest in the relationship between power and sexuality, he soon moved to a concern for the self.

4

MICHEL FOUCAULT: PART 2: SEXUALITY, POWER, AND SELF

POWER AND SEXUALITY
SELF AND SEXUALITY

$\mathbf{W}$E pick up the overview of Foucault's work here with a discussion of his last three major works on sexuality. They begin with Foucault's long-running interest in the power-knowledge nexus in the West, but in the last two works there is a dramatic shift to ancient Greece and Rome and to a concern for the relationship between self and sexuality or, more generally, "the genealogy of the modern subject" (Foucault, cited in Miller, 1993:321).

POWER AND SEXUALITY

The emphasis in the first volume of *The History of Sexuality* is on the genealogy of power (Foucault, 1978/1980). To Foucault sexuality is "an especially dense transfer point for relations of power" (1978/1980:103). His major objective is to "define the regime of power-knowledge-pleasure that *sustains* the discourse on human sexuality in our part of the world" (Foucault, 1978/1980:11). He examines the way that sex is put into discourse and the way that power permeates that discourse as, in fact, it permeates all discourse (Flynn, 1981).

At the beginning of the seventeenth century, sex was largely out in the open. The conventional view is that Victorianism closed off sex and confined it to the home, the conjugal family, and ultimately to silence (much as the mad had been silenced). Foucault takes issue with the view that Victorianism had led to the repression of sexuality in general and of sexual discourse in particular. In fact, he argues the opposite position—that Victorianism led to an *explosion* in discourses on sexuality. As he puts it, "since the end of the sixteenth century, the 'putting into discourse of sex,' far from undergoing a process of restriction, on the contrary has been subjected to a mechanism of increasing incitement" (Foucault, 1978/1980:12). There were undoubtedly efforts in the seventeenth century to subjugate sex at the level of language, to expunge it from things that people said, to eliminate words that made sex too visible. However, instead of elimination, over the last three centuries "one sees a veritable discursive explosion" on the topic of sex. As a result of Victorianism, there was more analysis, stocktaking, classification, specification, and quantitative/causal study of sexuality. Said Foucault, "People will ask themselves why we were so bent on ending the rule of silence regarding what was the noisiest of our preoccupations" (1978/1980:158). Sex was talked about in confessionals, and literature dealt increasingly, and increasingly explicitly, with sex. This increase was especially notable in schools, where instead of the repression of sexuality, "the question of sex was a constant preoccupation" (1978/1980:27). Here is the way Foucault sums up the Victorian hypothesis and his alternative view:

> We must therefore abandon the hypothesis that modern industrial societies ushered in an age of increased sexual repression. We have not only witnessed a visible explosion of unorthodox sexualities . . . never have there existed more centers of power; never more attention manifested and verbalized . . . never more sites where the intensity of pleasures and the persistency of power catch hold, only to spread elsewhere.

> (Foucault, 1978/1980:49)

Contrary to received wisdom, Foucault sees those in power as deeply implicated in the overall tendency to incite discourse about sexuality. Using his now familiar concept, Foucault (1978/1980:24) argues that following the advent of Victorianism those in power devoted "a steady gaze to these [sexual] objects." Not only did those in power seek to analyze and study sex, they also sought to gain control over sex and sexual discourse by making it something to be administered, something to be policed. The policing of sex, and discourses about it, were certainly not taboo; indeed they seemed to escalate dramatically.

For example, those in power were faced with a series of economic and political problems caused by population growth. At the heart of these problems was sex, specifically things like the birth rate, age of marriage, legitimacy, and contraception. It became clear to those in power that the future of society depended on the sexuality of individuals and the ability of the powerful to control it. There resulted studies of, and efforts to intervene in, population growth. Sex became a public issue. More generally, "through the political economy of population there was formed a whole grid of observations regarding sex" (Foucault, 1978/1980:26). As more and more attention was devoted to sex, "a whole web of discourse, special knowledges, analyses, and injunctions settled upon it" (Foucault, 1978/1980:26).

Another example of increasing discourse about sex related to the sexuality of children. More and more was being "said" about this issue, although the "talk" took a variety of different forms. The statements and the documents on this issue were there, but there were also many other signs that needed to be read semiotically—for example, the architectural design of schools reflected the preoccupation of those in power with children's sexuality. One had to study the meaning and intent of that architecture (for example, structures that separated boys and girls) to understand what it was "saying." More and more people—educators, physicians, administrators, and others—became involved in the sexuality of children and the discourse about it. Foucault makes similar specific points about sexuality in medicine, psychiatry, and criminal justice, but his overarching point is that in all of these realms discourse on sexuality had become rampant. Furthermore, there was a dispersion of the centers of sexual discourse. Thus, Foucault concludes, "What is peculiar to modern societies, in fact, is not that they consigned sex to a shadow existence, but that they dedicated themselves to speaking of it *ad infinitum,* while exploiting it as *the secret*" (1978/1980:35).

Those in power concentrated more and more of their gaze on sex. However, it wasn't suppression that resulted from the increased gaze but rather the intertwining of power and sexual pleasure. In fact, Foucault (1978/1980:44) describes, in highly erotic terms, the way those in power approached the issue of sex: "The power which thus took charge of sexuality set about *contacting* bodies, *caressing* them with its eyes, *intensifying* areas, *electrifying* surfaces, *dramatizing* troubled moments. It *wrapped* the sexual body in its *embrace*" (Foucault, 1978/1980:44; italics added). A dialectic emerged between power and pleasure: "Pleasure spread to the power that harried it; power anchored the pleasure it uncovered" (Foucault, 1978/1980:45). Medical exams, psychiatric investigations, pedagogical reports, and family controls can all be seen as exertions of power that are dialectically linked to pleasure, a "pleasure that comes of exercising a power that questions, monitors, watches, spies, searches out, palpates, brings to light; and on the other hand, the pleasure that kindles at having to evade this power, flee from it, fool it, or travesty it" (Foucault, 1978/1980:45). Thus, Foucault sees perpetual spirals of power-pleasure enveloping parents-children, adults-adolescents, educators-students, doctors-patients, and psychiatrists-patients. The combination of power and pleasure virtually guaranteed that there would be more sex and more officials gazing at it.

Once again, Foucault devotes special attention to medicine, this time its discourses on sexuality. It is clear above that medicine is deeply implicated in the power-pleasure nexus. In addition, Foucault challenges the generally accepted idea that medicine is oriented to the scientific analysis of sexuality. For his part, Foucault sees much more morality than science in the sexual concerns of medicine. Foucault is characteristically hard on medicine, seeing the aim of its discourses on sex "not to state the truth, but to prevent its very emergence" (1978/1980:55). He accuses medicine of a "will to nonknowledge" (Foucault, 1978/1980:55). Medicine is indicted for its systematic blindness, for its refusal to see and understand sex.

Also involved in the morality of sexuality is religion, especially Western Christianity, the confession (a kind of discourse), and the need for the subject to tell the truth, especially about sexuality. In fact, as a result and more generally, "We have since become a singularly confessing society" (Foucault, 1978/1980:59). Confession about sex, and most other things, has found its way into medicine, education, family relationships, love relationships, and so on. Power flows to those who are in a position to receive the information divulged in a confession, specifically to receive knowledge about individual sexuality. To Foucault, the wide-scale use of the confession comes down to the extortion of sexual knowledge from people. This was made peculiarly possible in the Occident because science became implicated in the sexual confession; those who received confessions were often scientists.

They wrapped themselves in the cloak of science and came to see sex, and the dangers flowing from it, everywhere. Because the dangers posed by sex were so ubiquitous and because they were generally hidden, they had to be hunted down ruthlessly and tirelessly through such mechanisms as the confession. Further, those who listened to the confessions were supposed to be peculiarly endowed with the ability to interpret them. Therefore, it was the listener who "was the master of truth" (Foucault, 1978/1980:67). Once again, knowledge and power interpenetrate.

Since it was deemed to be the possessor of the truth, science was in a position to determine what was normal and what was pathological sexuality. The sources of the pathologies were hidden, and they needed to be ferreted out by the scientist (especially psychoanalyst) empowered to listen to sexual confessions. Once the sources of the sexual pathologies were uncovered, they were to be treated therapeutically by those very same scientists.

All of this is related to the human sciences and their interest in gaining knowledge of the subject. Subjects are asked to "confess" to social scientists in interviews and in their responses to questionnaires. Social scientists have power over subjects, and the knowledge they obtain furthers that power. Based on their knowledge, and the statistics they use to analyze it, the human sciences acquire the ability to distinguish between the normal and the pathological (or deviant). Thus, the human sciences can be traced in a variety of direct ways to the methods used by those in power to exercise control over sex.

Foucault outlines a number of more general relations of power to sex that have a deleterious effect on sexuality. (However, Foucault recognizes that power also has a positive, constitutive effect on sexuality.) Power can insist on rules that limit sexuality by, for example, prescribing a specific order for sex. Power can prohibit sex and seek to have it renounce itself. Power can engage in censorship thereby silencing sex. Finally, the power apparatus operates in the same way at all levels and does not adapt itself to important differences in sexuality. Thus, even if it operates appropriately in one setting, the power apparatus will inevitably operate poorly in other settings.

It is in this context that Foucault begins to clarify exactly what he means by power, or the "multiplicity of force relations imminent in the sphere in which they operate" (1978/1980:92). Thus, contrary to most established definitions, power is *not* an institution, a structure, a superstructure, or even a strength that people are endowed with. Power is omnipresent

> not because it has the privilege of consolidating everything under its invincible unity, but because it is produced from one moment to the next, at every point, or rather in every relation from one point to another. Power is everywhere; not because it embraces everything, but because it comes from everywhere.

(Foucault, 1978/1980:93)

However, power does sometimes form comprehensive systems that can be analyzed and understood more or less independently, although it is often the case that no one planned them to operate in that way.

Just as power is everywhere, the points of resistance to it are everywhere. Thus, we are back again to the micro-politics of power. It is here that Foucault (1978/1980:95–96) directly challenges Marx and the grand narrative once again: "Hence there is no single locus of great Refusal, no soul of revolt, source of all rebellions, or pure law of the revolutionary. Instead there is a plurality of resistances, each of them a special case." He is willing to admit that there are occasional radical ruptures, but it is the small-scale eruptions that are much more common and likely. Sex is an especially important area for the exercise of power and for outbursts of resistance to it.

Starting in the seventeenth century, the power over life took two basic forms. The first, the *anatomo-politics of the human body,* involved the discipline of the body to optimize its capabilities and increase its use *and* its docility. The second, the *bio-politics of population,* involved the regulation of the population as a whole and utilized controls to regulate births, mortality, level of health, and so on (Hewitt, 1983). These two forms of control, taken together, represented a major change in that the sovereign powers switched from control through death (and the threat of it) to control through life. And, "it was taking charge of life, more than the threat of death, that gave power its access even to the body" (Foucault, 1978/1980:143). Those in power sought the administration of bodies, the management of life. Overall, "methods of power and knowledge assumed responsibility for the life processes and undertook to control and modify them" (Foucault, 1978/1980:142). In other words, life itself had become an object of political control. Thus, "sex was a means of access both to the life of the body and the life of the species" (Foucault, 1978/1980:146). But consistent with his micro-political orientation, Foucault argued that the control over sex and life was the result of a whole series of specific tactics.

Is there any hope of emancipation? Foucault seems to think so, but it lies not in one great revolutionary force but rather in a multiplicity of micro-forces emphasizing the importance of bodies and pleasure, rather than sex:

> It is the agency of sex that we must break away from, if we aim—through a tactical reversal of the various mechanisms of sexuality—to counter the grips of power with the claims of bodies, pleasures, and knowledges, in their multiplicity and their possibility of resistance. The rallying point for the counterattack against the deployment of sexuality ought not to be sex-desire, but bodies and pleasures.

(Foucault, 1978/1980:157)

In the West, "the project of a science of the subject has gravitated, in ever-narrowing circles, around the question of sex" (Foucault, 1978/1980:70). Questions aimed at ascertaining who we are have come to be increasingly directed to sex. Foucault sums this all up: "Sex, the explanation of everything" (1978/1980:78).

SELF AND SEXUALITY

Between the publication of the first volume of the history of sexuality in 1980 and the publication of the later two volumes, *The Use of Pleasure* (1984/1985) and *The*

Care of the Self (1984/1986), Foucault's substantive focus and theoretical orientation underwent another important shift (Bevis, Cohen, and Kendall, 1993; Harrison, 1987).[1] Substantively, Foucault shifted from the modern West to Greco-Roman culture between the fourth century B.C. and the second century A.D. Theoretically, Foucault (1984/1985:12) moved from a genealogy of power to a genealogy of self-awareness, self-control, self-practices—as he puts it, a "genealogy of desiring man." He had grown afraid that had he stayed with the same period, he would have once again found a pattern of control and coercion, this time in the realm of sexuality. He concluded: "Rather than placing myself at the formation of the experience of sexuality, I tried to analyze the formation of a certain mode of relation to the self in the experience of the flesh" (Foucault, in Miller, 1993:320). Here is the way Foucault describes his shift:

> I insisted maybe too much . . . on techniques of domination . . . other techniques [are important] . . . techniques which permit individuals to effect a certain number of operations on their own bodies, on their souls, on their own thoughts, on their own conduct, and this in a manner so as to transform themselves, modify themselves, or to act in a certain state of perfection, of happiness, of purity, of supernatural power, and so on.
>
> (Foucault, in Miller, 1993:321–322)

Before one could do a full-scale study of power in the later period, "it was essential first to determine how, for centuries, Western man had been brought to recognize himself as a subject of desire" (Foucault, 1984/1985:6). As Foucault (1984/1985:13; italics added) describes it, he was led "to substitute a history of ethical problematizations based on *practices of the self,* for a history of systems of morality based, hypothetically, on *interdictions.*" Foucault also sees himself continuing to do an archaeology, this time of the problematization of sexuality, on how sexuality came to be a subject of concern.

He makes it clear that his original plan was to study sexuality in modern Western societies and to focus, among other things, on the "various mechanisms of *repression* to which it [sexuality] was bound to be subjected in every society" (Foucault, 1984/1985:4; italics added). He outlines three concerns in his overall study of sexuality: the formation of the sciences of sexuality, the power systems that regulate sexuality,[2] and his focus in this later work, "the forms within which individuals are able, are obliged, to recognize themselves as subjects of this sexuality" (Foucault, 1984/1985:4).

Thus, Foucault (1984/1985:6) changed his focus to "the slow formation, in antiquity, of a hermeneutics of the self." He saw this as consistent with his long-term interest in the history of the truth, not "what might be true in the fields of learning, but an analysis of the 'games of truth' " (Foucault, 1984/1985:6). In fact, he claims that all his studies have been concerned with such "games."

---

[1] A proposed fourth volume, *The Confessions of the Flesh,* concerned with the "formation of the doctrine and ministry concerning the flesh" (Foucault, 1984/1985:12), was never to be published.

[2] Although, Foucault always recognizes that power is not simply one-way domination; it involves a variety of open strategies.

He takes as the key question in this research, "why is sexual conduct, why are the activities and pleasures that attach to it, an object of moral solicitude?" (Foucault, 1984/1985:10). To put it another way, why has sexuality become a "moral problematic"? In raising this question, Foucault makes it clear that sexuality is not only a matter of power or of interdiction, but also a moral matter.

The problematicization of sexuality is related to what Foucault calls the "arts of existence," or the "techniques of the self":

> those intentional and voluntary actions by which men *not only* set themselves *rules of conduct,* but also seek to *transform themselves,* to *change themselves* in their singular being, and to make their life into an *oeuvre* that carries certain *aesthetic* values and meets certain *stylistic criteria.* These "arts of existence," these "techniques of the self," no doubt lost some of their importance and autonomy when they were assimilated into the exercise of priestly power in early Christianity, and later into educative, medical and psychological types of practice.

> (Foucault, 1984/1985:10–11; italics added, except for *oeuvre*)

Thus, Foucault sees himself as writing a first chapter in the history of techniques of the self.

Methodologically, Foucault focuses not on theoretical texts but rather on prescriptive, practical texts of the historical periods he is analyzing. Such texts "enable individuals to question their own conduct, to *watch over* and give shape to it, and to *shape themselves* as ethical subjects" (Foucault, 1984/1985:13; italics added).

Foucault often acknowledges continuity between the classical world and the modern, Christian world. However, a key difference lies in the fact that while in the modern world there is great compulsion surrounding sexual behavior, in the classical world there was far less coercion. The classical world lacked a "unified, coherent, authoritarian moral system that was imposed on everyone in the same manner" (Foucault, 1984/1985:21). Instead of focusing on the "interdictions" demanding sexual austerity, the focus instead in the classical world should be on the way sexual behavior came to be reflected on and became a subject of "stylization."

To Foucault, morality has two basic elements that can be disassociated from one another. The first are *codes of behavior* in which those in authority enforce the dictates of the code. The second are *forms of subjectivation,* or practices of the self. It is the latter that is focal in the classical world and of focal concern to Foucault. "Here the emphasis is on the forms of relations with the self, in the methods and techniques by which he works them out, on the exercises by which he makes of himself an object to be known, and on the practices that enable him to transform his own mode of being" (Foucault, 1984/1985:30).

Foucault identifies four central domains, four major areas of experience: the relationship to one's body, one's wife or marriage, boys, and the truth. Four types of "stylization" are related to each of these focal concerns: body-dietetics, marriage-economics, boys-erotics, truth-philosophy. More generally, Foucault (1984/1985:91) is concerned with *aphrodisia,* or "acts intended by nature, associated by nature with intense pleasure, and naturally motivated by a force that was always liable to excess and rebellion."

Two major variables are associated with *aphrodisia* in the classical world. First, there is a *quantitative* emphasis on things like moderation and excess and *not* a qualitative focus on the nature of the act. The issue was extent of involvement and not whether an act was good or bad. Excess was identified as a problem, and it was traced to a lack of self-restraint. Second, there is focus on *role-polarity,* especially active-passive, subject-object. The passive and object poles, identified with women, boys, and slaves, were more likely to be defined as problems. Men who were prone to excess and passivity were seen as immoral.

Thus, sexual activity, and *aphrodisia* more generally, were *not* seen as problems in themselves. Indeed, they were viewed as natural and therefore incapable of being bad (this stood in stark contrast to the way sexuality came to be viewed in the modern Christian world). But while it was not condemned, sexuality was nonetheless a subject of moral concern. The moral concern, however, was the proper use of sexuality and *not* the sexual act per se. Thus, the focus was not on a moral code to prohibit certain actions but rather "to work out the conditions and modalities of a 'use,' that is, to define a *style* for . . . the use of pleasures . . . his way of conducting himself in such matters" (Foucault, 1984/1985:53; italics added). The issue was to carefully distribute and control one's acts; to be prudent, reflective, and calculating in how one behaved.

Three issues were central in reflecting on the use of pleasure. The first was the individual's *need.* However, since individual needs vary, it was impossible to come up with a code or a law that applied to everyone, everywhere. Rather than being amenable to codification, moderation required "an *art,* a practice of pleasures that was capable of *self-limitation*" (Foucault, 1984/1985:57; italics added). The second was *timeliness,* practices that took place at the right time and involved the right amount. The third was *status*; the proper use of pleasure varied with the user's social status. Again, it is clear that no code could be developed to handle dimensions with such a high degree of variation.

Instead of the code, the focus in classical society was on one's *attitude,* especially the "domination of oneself by oneself" (Foucault, 1984/1985:65). This was perceived as a constant struggle. Foucault (1984/1985:73) also uses another concept in this context, "care of the self," meaning the ability "to attend effectively to the self, and to exercise and transform oneself." This self-mastery was not only important to the individual but also the state. One who showed power over oneself, self-restraint, was seen as possessing the ability needed to rule over others. How could one rule others if one could not rule oneself? Such restraint was also seen as being "manly" or "virile," while immoderation was associated with femininity. However, the dividing line between manliness and femininity did *not* coincide, as it later came to, with the distinction between heterosexuality and homosexuality.

Foucault offers a succinct contrast between classical and modern society. In the classical world, the control of *aphrodisia* was

> not defined by a universal legislation determining permitted and forbidden acts, but rather by a *savoir-faire,* an art that prescribed the modalities of a use that depended on different variables (need, time, status) . . . In the Christian morality of sexual behavior

. . . Subjection was to take the form not of a *savoir-faire,* but of a recognition of the law and an obedience to pastoral authority.

(Foucault, 1984/1985:91, 92)

The way in which the classical Greeks handled dietetics (another *aphrodisia*) is closely tied to the way they dealt with sexuality. Especially important is the development of a diet, a regimen that ultimately led to "a whole art of living" (Foucault, 1984/1985:101). Dietetics served to problematize the body and helped give rise to medicine. Importance was given to both care of the body and soul; in fact, care of the body (with medicines) was seen as necessary for care of the soul (through regimens). Regimens required vigilance vis-à-vis the self and led to "a whole manner of forming oneself as a subject" (Foucault, 1984/1985:108). Moderation was the key to a regimen, and sex acts eventually came to be seen as a proper domain for a regimen and moderation.

Two basic reasons were behind the vigilance associated with sexuality. The first was concern over deleterious effects of excess on the body; less was always considered better than more. (This is one of the places where the classical world anticipates the modern: "In this dietetics . . . one perceives the emergence of a general tendency toward a restrictive economy" [Foucault, 1984/1985:118].) The second was concern about the well-being of the progeny. For example, if parents were too old, or had poor diets, their offspring might suffer.

Other anxieties were associated with the sex act. First, the form of the act (for example, the violence of it) could be a problem. Second, there was concern about cost, especially the expenditure of bodily fluids. Finally, there was an association with death, at least as contrasted to the life giving of procreation. However, it is important to reiterate that anxiety existed not because sex was seen as evil,

> but because it disturbed and threatened the individual's relationship with himself and his integrity as an ethical subject in the making; it was not properly measured and distributed, it carried the threat of a breaking forth of involuntary forces, a lessening of energy, and death without honourable descendants.

(Foucault, 1984/1985:136–137)

Foucault (1984/1985:153) also relates this to economics, which he defines as "the practice of commanding." The economic art was practiced not only in business but also in managing the city, the household, and even one's marriage. Self-mastery was demonstrated, perhaps most elegantly, in having sexual relations only with one's wife. This kind of self-mastery was seen as a moral precondition for managing others. But again this was a matter of style, and Foucault (1984/1985:181) does *not* "see in this the first outlines of an ethics of reciprocal conjugal fidelity, or the beginnings of a codification of married life in which Christianity was to give a universal form, an imperative value, and the support of a whole institutional system."

In his discussion of erotics, defined as the "purposeful art of love," Foucault (1984/1985:229) focuses on relations with boys (with men), relations that in the

Classical Age were *not* seen as the opposite of heterosexual relations. Thus, the moral issue was excess, whether it involved homosexual *or* heterosexual relationships. Self-control involves the ability to abstain from either homosexual or heterosexual relations.

Nevertheless, the relationship between men did come to be defined as problematic. It became a moral preoccupation, and a special style came to surround it, but it did *not* come to be prohibited. An issue was likely to arise when there was a great disparity in the ages of the participants. The passivity of at least one of the partners was also considered problematic. After all, a passive boy might well become "a free man, master of himself and capable of prevailing over others" (Foucault, 1984/1985:221). Boys were likely to be condemned if their style was bad; for example, if they yielded too easily. Thus, homosexuality was accepted, but it certainly was not a matter of indifference. The concern that existed was for the object of pleasure, the boys. This was to stand in contrast to Christian society where the concern would focus on the subject and the question: How could a man desire a boy or another man?

Finally, Foucault turns to the issue of truth. He argues that it was around the love of boys "that the question of the relations between the use of pleasures and access to the truth was developed, in the form of an inquiry into the nature of true love" (Foucault, 1984/1985:229). Again, Foucault here sees a forerunner to modern Christian society in which questions of truth, love, and pleasure will come to be raised in the context of male-female relationships.

It is with the issue of truth that Foucault begins *The Care of the Self.* Specifically, he undertakes a discursive analysis of Artemidorius's treatise on how to interpret dreams, that is, on finding the truth that the dream reveals. More generally, we have here the beginnings of the search for truth within oneself.

In those dream analyses, Foucault sees much consistency in the first two centuries A.D. with what he found in the earlier time period (roughly the four centuries B.C.) analyzed in *The Use of Pleasure.* For example, the code and its prohibitions are of negligible importance in sexuality. There is also a focus not on the act but the actor (who dreams), the subject, and his style.

As before, Foucault focuses on practical advice texts, and while there are revisions in the doctrine of austerity from the earlier period, these are not radical changes; they do not represent a new way of experiencing pleasure. But there is a change in inflection, "a closer attention, an increased anxiety concerning sexual conduct, a greater importance accorded to marriage and its demands, and less value given to the love of boys: in short, a more rigorous style" (Foucault, 1984/1986:36). Furthermore, there is a change in "the way in which ethical thought defines the relation of the subject to his sexual activity" (Foucault, 1984/1986:36). The literature of the first two centuries A.D. seemed to adopt a more severe attitude toward sexuality, and there was a more intense problematization of it. And it was from this that later, modern, Christian authors borrowed heavily.

While there were changes, they did not represent a dramatic shift to a focus on interdictions, or a tightening of the code, but rather "an intensification of the relation to oneself by which one constituted oneself as the subject of one's acts" (Foucault, 1984/1986:41). This, in turn, was to have a wide-ranging series of effects:

It also took the form of an attitude, a mode of behavior; it became instilled in ways of living; it evolved into procedures, practices and formulas that people reflected on, developed, perfected and taught. It thus came to constitute a social practice giving rise to relationships between individuals, to exchanges and communications, and at times even institutions. And it gave rise, finally, to a *certain mode of knowledge and to elaboration of a science.*

(Foucault, 1984/1986:45; italics added)

Force is now required to deal with sexual pleasure, but it is in this epoch a force that comes from within, through self-mastery, rather than from without. A new art of living is required. And this requires a greater importance be placed on self-knowledge:

The task of testing oneself, examining oneself, monitoring oneself in a series of clearly defined exercise, makes the question of *truth*—the *truth* concerning what one is, what one does, and what one is capable of doing—central to the formation of the ethical subject. Lastly, the end result of this elaboration is still and always defined by the rule of the individual over himself. But this rule broadens into an experience in which the relation to self takes the form not only of a domination but also of an enjoyment without desire and without disturbance.

(Foucault, 1984/1986:68; italics added)

While this is different from the earlier period studied by Foucault, it is also different from what is to come:

One is still far from an experience of sexual pleasure where the latter will be associated with evil, where behavior will have to submit to the universal form of law, and where the deciphering of desire will be a necessary condition for acceding to a purified existence. Yet one can already see how the question of evil begins to work upon the ancient theme of force, how the question of law begins to modify the theme of art and *techne,* and how the question of truth and the principle of self-knowledge evolve within the ascetic practices.

(Foucault, 1984/1986:68)

The emergence of the new stylistics of existence, the cult of the self, can be traced to changes in marriage and politics. Politics came to be seen as a life practice, and hence a linkage was established between oneself and politics. The rational government of others was equated with the rational government of oneself. The ability to govern oneself, to exercise self-restraint, came to be seen as a prerequisite for a good politician.

In the domestic relationship, Foucault sees a change toward greater reciprocity and equality in husband-wife relationships. In fact, a more intense concern for the self is closely tied to the increased valorization of the other. More generally, "attention to oneself and devotion to conjugal life could be closely associated" (Foucault, 1984/1986:163). Marriage becomes more of an art and less an exercise in power or mastery. In this art, sexual relations take on a greater role (although the

Greeks were comparatively silent on sex, especially in comparison to the "meticulous attentiveness" of later Christians who "will then attempt to regulate everything: positions, frequency" [Foucault, 1984/1986:165]). The Greeks did have principles related to matrimonial sexuality, but they did little to regulate and control those behaviors or to distinguish permitted from forbidden forms of sexuality. Overall, Foucault sees an increase in the value accorded to sexual relations in marriage, and this helps to contribute to an increased questioning of the love of boys. In this, *power over oneself* is dissociated from *power over others*. This helped lead to a similar dissociation in social, civic, and political life.

Medicine, with its focus on illness and the body, led to a way of living, to a way of reflecting upon oneself. People were urged to care for themselves, to follow a regimen in order to avoid needing to see a physician about illness. This led to a problematization of the body and its relationship to the environment. One was led to devote constant attention to oneself and one's body.

It is in the context of the notion of a regimen that medicine framed the issue of sexual pleasure. Sexual abstinence and self-restraint, as far as sex is concerned (especially with other men), were considered to be desirable. There was an ambivalent attitude toward sex since it was seen as both therapeutic and potentially pathological. Care of one's body was seen as essential to avoiding the pathologies. Among the regimens to which sex was subjected were the ideas that there was an "auspicious occasion for procreation," that there was a proper "age of the subject" (not too old, for example), and that "individual temperament" was important (Foucault, 1984/1986:125). However, not just the body, but also the soul was to be subjected to a regimen. Thus, people were to avoid being carried beyond the needs of the organism. For example, sex was never to be forced, and certain images were to be avoided. Foucault sees in this the beginning of the "pathologization" of sex, but again it was radically different from what was to take place later. For example, unlike in modern times, sex was not regarded as an "evil" in Greco-Roman culture.

In the first two centuries of our era, the love of boys continued to be seen as natural, although reflection on it lost some intensity, seriousness, vitality, and topicality. What changed was not the taste for boys, or the value judgments aimed at those with such tastes, but rather "the way in which one questioned oneself about it" (Foucault, 1984/1986:189). Most generally, the love of boys came to be seen as "incapable of defining a style of living, an aesthetics of behavior, and a whole modality of relation to oneself, to others, and to *truth*" (Foucault, 1984/1986:192; italics added). A boundary emerged between the two types of sex, a boundary that persists to this day. However, there was, as yet, no rigid line dividing heterosexual and homosexual acts.

Love of boys and love of one's wife continued to exist as two different styles of life. In addition, different philosophies, or means of searching for the truth, accompanied them. Thus, "in the pederastic argumentation, pleasure with a woman cannot be reciprocal because it is accompanied by too much falseness . . . In contrast, pleasure with boys is placed under the sign of *truth*" (Foucault, 1984/1986:223–224; italics added).

Overall, Foucault sees a strengthening of austerity themes around the first centuries of our era, although in his earlier book he detailed similar themes in the four centuries B.C. Again, however, such tightening does *not* stand at the base of later Christian ethics

> when the sexual act itself will be considered evil, when it will no longer be granted legitimacy except within the conjugal relationship, and when the love of boys will be condemned as unnatural.

(Foucault, 1984/1986:235)

Instead of increasing prohibitions, what marked this early era was increased self-preoccupation. Foucault closes with a view of what is to come in the modern Christian world:

> Those moral systems will define other modalities of the relation to self: a characterization of the ethical substance based on finitude, the Fall, and evil; a mode of subjection in the form of obedience to a general law that is at the same time the will of a personal god; a type of work on oneself that implies a decipherment of the soul and a purificatory hermeneutics of the desires; and a mode of ethical fulfillment that tend toward self-renunciation . . . a profoundly altered ethics and . . . a different way of constituting oneself as the ethical subject of one's sexual behavior.

(Foucault, 1984/1986:239–240)

SUMMARY

In this chapter we have examined Foucault's later work on sexuality. In the first of three works, he continues his interest in the relationship between power and knowledge, this time in the realm of sexuality. Contrary to popular belief, he finds an explosion of interest in sexuality in seventeenth-century Victorian society. Those in power sought to incite such interest and in the process to gain control over sexuality. Foucault does not see a single source of such power. Rather, there is micro-politics of power, which is often met with resistance at many points of contact.

In his last two books, Foucault's work underwent a dramatic shift. Instead of looking at the West in the seventeenth to nineteenth centuries, Foucault turned his attention to Greece and Rome in the centuries immediately before and after the birth of Christ. Instead of a genealogy of power, he sought to do a genealogy of self-awareness, self-practices, and self-control in the realm of sexuality. In a sense, he saw the need to discover how people came to see themselves as desiring, as subjects of sexuality, before undertaking (although he obviously had already begun such work) a study of how that desire was the subject of the exercise of power by external agencies. Another way of putting Foucault's focal interest was a concern for how sexuality came to be considered a moral issue. Over the period of his study, Foucault sees the emergence of the care of the self as far as sexuality is concerned, but this is very different from the external and coercive control that was to emerge with the rise of Christianity. While there is some increase in the severeness of attitudes toward sexuality in the Greco-Roman periods examined by Foucault, control still stemmed from the self rather than from external sources. In a sense, Foucault's last two books on sexuality constitute a "prequel" to the first, *The History of Sexuality, Part 1.*

5

JEAN BAUDRILLARD: PART 1: THE BASIC THEORETICAL IDEAS

CONSUMER SOCIETY

THE BREAK WITH MARX AND MARXISM

SYMBOLIC EXCHANGE

ALTHOUGH there are difficulties involved in categorizing Michel Foucault, Jean Baudrillard must surely and unequivocally be a postmodernist. After all, his work has had a profound effect on postmodern social theory, and it has influenced postmodernists in a wide range of fields (Bertens, 1995). In fact, most observers regard him as not only a postmodernist but the most important representative of that approach (e.g., Kellner, 1994). However, Baudrillard's status as a social thinker is *not* as clear-cut as many believe. Baudrillard himself rarely[1] uses the term *postmodern* and is sometimes even hostile to it as a description of his orientation (Gane, 1993). For example, Baudrillard says the following:

> there is no such thing as postmodernism. If you interpret it this way, it is obvious that I do not represent this emptiness . . . It doesn't have anything to do with me . . . I don't recognize myself in all this.

(Baudrillard, in Gane, 1933:22–23)

In fact, Gane (1991b:55) goes even further and argues that "Baudrillard's whole effort is to combat [postmodernism]." For example, Baudrillard (1980–1985/1990:150) sees postmodernity as the "most degraded" historical phase. Postmodern society is viewed as having closed off opportunities opened by the end of modernism. Thus, in Gane's view, Baudrillard is opposed to *both* modernism and postmodernism. To further complicate matters, Kellner (1994:14; italics added) says, "Gane is *completely wrong* to claim that Baudrillard's problematic should not be interpreted as concerned with the postmodern." And, as if the situation is not already confusing enough, according to Zurbrugg (1993), Baudrillard combines modern and postmodern approaches.

While the debate over whether Baudrillard is, or is not, a postmodernist is interesting, it raises perhaps the wrong question. After all, putting Baudrillard (or Fou-

---

[1] Although, as we will see in Chapter 6, it does appear more often in his later work.

cault) into a box, or according him a nice, comfortable label, is a very modern thing to do and flies in the face of much that postmodern social theory stands for. In fact, as we have seen, Foucault fought strenuously against efforts to categorize him and his ideas. Much more important questions are: Has Baudrillard's work influenced the thinking of those who regard themselves as postmodern theorists? Are Baudrillard's ideas useful in thinking about postmodern society? The answer to both of these questions is an unequivocal "yes," and it is for that reason that we can consider Baudrillard to be a postmodern social theorist.

Similarly, and perhaps equally wrongheadedly, others have wondered: Is Baudrillard a sociologist? While Baudrillard taught sociology and sometimes identifies himself with sociology, he generally distances himself from the discipline:[2]

> I prefer singularities, exceptional events. Sociology is, I think, a reductive discipline. . . . I don't consider myself to be deeply sociological. I work more on symbolic effects than on sociological data.

> (Baudrillard, in Gane, 1993:68).

> I'm neither a sociologist nor an anti-sociologist. Sociology was where I landed in the university, certainly. But from the point of view of a discipline, I left it during the sixties, going into semiology, psychoanalysis, Marxism.

> (Baudrillard, in Gane, 1993:81)

Baudrillard's best-known statement on this issue is the following:

> My point of view is completely metaphysical. If anything, I'm a metaphysician, perhaps a moralist, but certainly *not* a sociologist. The only "sociological" work I can claim is my effort to put an end to the social, to the concept of the social.

> (in Gane, 1993:106; italics added)

Despite the unequivocal character of this declaration, if we examine the totality of Baudrillard's statements on this issue, there is at least as much ambiguity over whether or not he is a sociologist as there is over whether or not it is appropriate to think of him as a postmodernist. However, again we are probably asking the wrong question. The real issue is: Have Baudrillard's ideas influenced the thinking of sociologists? The fact is that while the thinking of many social theorists, some of whom are sociologists, has been influenced by Baudrillard's work, most

---

[2] He also distances himself from academia in general. Note the following acid observation: "One could also analyze the academic congress (of scholars, of intellectuals, of sociologists) as places of transmission [of knowledge], of hereditary reproduction of the intelligentsia and of a privileged community on the basis of an agonistic debauch of signs. Conferences are almost as useful to the advancement of knowledge as horse races and parimutuels to the advancement of the equine race" (Baudrillard, 1972/1981:122).

mainstream sociologists are more or less oblivious to his ideas.[3] However, it is possible, even likely, that Baudrillard's influence on sociology will grow in the coming years.

It would be useful to pause here and attempt to deal with another question: What does Baudrillard mean in the quotation in the preceding paragraph by the end of the social? Fundamentally, he means that the social has dissolved, "imploded," into the mass. That is, key social factors like class and ethnic differences have disappeared with the creation of a huge, undifferentiated mass. We will have more to say about his ideas on the mass, especially in the next chapter, but at this juncture it is important to point out that to Baudrillard the mass is to be thought of as a statistical category and *not* as a social collectivity. Since the mass is a nonsocial (rather, a statistical) category, and since the social has imploded into it, the social is dead. If the social is dead, then sociology, which takes the social as its subject matter, must be dead from Baudrillard's point of view. Thus, we need a new way of thinking about the world and a whole new vocabulary to think about it. As we will see, Baudrillard goes a long way toward creating such a new way of thinking and such a new vocabulary (mass, for example, takes on a whole new [nonsocial] meaning in his work).

Another, perhaps misguided, question: Is Baudrillard a theorist? On the surface it seems abundantly clear that he is. After all, he is offering a series of general, abstract ideas about the nature of society. However, there are problems involved in thinking about Baudrillard as a theorist.

- For example, since theory is usually oriented to ascertaining truth, and Baudrillard makes it plain that truth does not exist, can we really think of him as a theorist? Rather than seek truth, "the only thing you can do [with theory] is play with some kind of provocative logic" (Baudrillard, in Gane, 1993:124).
- Similarly, because he rejects the real, Baudrillard's approach is really an "antisocial theory"[4] in the sense that he has rejected the traditional end of social theory "to represent or reflect the real, or to critically engage with the real" (Smart, 1993b:52).
- Baudrillard (1990/1993:110) also believes that it is impossible to predict what will happen with the result that "theory can be no more than this: a trap set in the hope that reality [which, contradictorily, Baudrillard has rejected] will be naive enough to fall into it."

Baudrillard pushes theory to such an extreme, to pataphysics (an idea developed by Alfred Jarry), that many do not consider it to be theory. Baudrillard (1976/1993:5) sees great importance in pataphysics, or " 'a science of imaginary solutions'; that is, a science-fiction of the system's reversal against itself at the extreme limit of simulation." He argues that pataphysics is the only way to combat the more real than real (the "hyperreal") system in which we live. Thus,

---

[3] A few have been negatively affected by Baudrillard's assault on many of sociology's most basic beliefs.

[4] As we saw in Chapter 1, Antonio (1995) has recently depicted Nietzsche, a powerful influence on Baudrillard, as doing an "antisociology."

> I'm not interested in realism . . . My books are scenarios. I *play out* the end of things. . . . It's a game, a provocation. Not in order to put a full stop to everything but, on the contrary, to make everything begin again. So you see, I'm far from being a pessimist.
>
> (Baudrillard, in Gane, 1993:132–133)

Or, "What I try to do is to issue a challenge to meaning and to reality, to seduce them and to play with them" (Baudrillard, in Gane, 1993:137). To Baudrillard, writing is a "fatal strategy,"[5] which impels him to go to extremes. He sees the extremity of his positions as a political act: "Indeed, writing is the only political act that I am capable of" (Baudrillard, in Gane, 1993:181). In the view of Rojek and Turner (1993:xi), Baudrillard's pataphysical work is "closer to the conventions of sci-fi than those of sociology [and sociological theory]." Similarly, Kellner (1994:13) says, "I prefer to read Baudrillard's work as a science fiction, which anticipates the future by exaggerating present tendencies and thus provides early warnings about what might happen if present trends continue."

Or, is Baudrillard better thought of as a poet? (He did, in fact, write poetry.) He admitted that,

> behind all my theoretical and analytical formulations, there are always traces of the aphorism, the anecdote and the fragment. One could call that poetry.
>
> (Baudrillard, in Gane, 1993:166)

But, if he is at times a poet, at other times he is more of a theorist.

Thus, it is clearly hard to pin Baudrillard down. Postmodernist? Sociologist? Theorist? Science fiction writer? Poet? Baudrillard is all of those, and he is none of those. How postmodern!

It should come as no surprise that it is, if anything, even *more* difficult to clarify the nature of the work than it is to unambiguously identify the author. There are at least two reasons for this. First, Baudrillard often resists being lucid by, among other things, refusing to clearly define even his most fundamental concepts. Second, over the years, Baudrillard's work has undergone many significant changes. Thus, there are a number of different theoretical perspectives developed by Baudrillard over the course of his career. While there is some continuity in this body of work, there is also much change.

CONSUMER SOCIETY

Baudrillard's (1968, 1970; Wernick, 1991) early work is heavily influenced by the Marxian perspective and its focus on the economy. However, while Marx and most traditional Marxists focused on production, Baudrillard concerned himself with consumption. By focusing on consumption, Baudrillard joined many Marxists of his day, critical theorists in particular, in moving in the direction of a more cultural analysis. However, early in his career Baudrillard was more Marxian than many of his peers: "Baudrillard remains in many senses on the ground of Marxist theory,

---

[5] See the next chapter for much more on what Baudrillard means by a fatal strategy.

giving more weight to economic and material processes in cultural analysis than other Marxists of this period" (Gane, 1991a:70–71).

Foreshadowing a lifelong interest, even preoccupation, with America as a paradigm for the rest of the world (one of his later books was entitled *America*; see the following chapter), Baudrillard sees America as the home of the consumer society. However, Europe is viewed as witnessing an "irreversible trend towards the American model" (Baudrillard, in Poster, 1988:11). Once Europe adopted the American consumption model, there would be a consolidation of consumption that would "harmoniously conform to the complete consolidation and control of production" (Baudrillard, in Poster, 1988:12). Thus, despite his focus on consumption, in the early stages of his career Baudrillard took a traditional Marxist position and continued to accord ultimate primacy to production. In fact, he sees the objects of consumption as being "orchestrated by the order of production" (Baudrillard, in Poster, 1988:22). Or, in other words, "needs and consumption are in fact an *organized extension of productive forces*" (Baudrillard, in Poster, 1988:43). Despite this apparent acceptance of a simple base-superstructure model (at least in this early stage of his work), Baudrillard accords considerable importance to consumption. As Gane (1991a:57) argues, consumption is not "some slight addition to the circuit of capital . . . but [i]s a crucial productive force for capital itself."

The young Baudrillard was also influenced by the structuralists, including the structural linguists. As a result, he sees the system of consumer objects and the communication system at the base of advertising as forming "a code of significa- tion," which exerts control over both objects and individuals in society. As Genosko (1994:xiii) puts it, "Baudrillard's central claim is that objects have become signs whose value is determined by a disciplinary code." This is our first encounter with the central, slippery, and changing concept of the "code" in Baudrillard's work. We will have much more to say about this concept throughout this chapter and the next, but for now we can, following Genosko, define it as a controlling system of signs. To put it another way, "The *code* in its most general sense is a system of rules for the combination of stable sets of terms into messages" (Genosko, 1994:36). Objects, in this case objects of consumption, are part of this sign system. Thus, we can think in terms of a "discourse of objects," and, as a result, everyone is able to "read" and comprehend such communication (Baudrillard, 1972/1981:37).

When we consume objects, we are consuming signs, and in the process are defining ourselves. Thus, categories of objects are seen as producing categories of persons. "Through objects, each individual and each group searches out his or her place in an order, all the while trying to jostle this order according to a personal trajectory. Through objects a stratified society speaks . . . in order to keep everyone in a certain place" (Baudrillard, 1972/1981:38). In other words, people are (to a large extent) what they consume and are differentiated from other types of people on the basis of consumed objects. Counterintuitively, what we consume is not so much objects, but signs. "Consumption . . . is a *systematic act of the manipulation of signs. . . . In order to become object of consumption, the object must become sign*" (Baudrillard, in Poster, 1988:22). In consuming certain objects we are signifying (although not consciously) that we are similar to those who also consume those objects and that we are different from those who consume other objects. It is the code, then, that controls what we do, and do not, consume.

To the layperson, the world of consumption seems, on the surface, to be quite free. After all, if we have the money (or better yet today, the credit card), we seem to be free to buy whatever we want. But in fact we are free to consume only marginally different objects and signs. Further, in consumption we all feel quite unique, but in fact we closely resemble everyone else in our social group; members of that group consume much the same thing. Thus, it is clear that we are not nearly as free as we think we are.

In another counterintuitive idea, Baudrillard argues that in a world controlled by the code, consumption ceases to have anything to do with the satisfaction of what we conventionally think of as "needs." The idea of needs is derived from the false separation of subject and object; the idea of needs is created to connect them. The end result is a tautology with subjects and objects defined in terms of each other (subjects need objects; objects are what subjects need). Baudrillard seeks to deconstruct the subject-object dichotomy and, more generally, the notion of needs. We do not buy what we need, but rather what the code tells us we should buy. Further, needs themselves are determined by the code so that we end up "needing" what the code tells us we need; "there are only needs because the system needs them" (Baudrillard, 1972/1981:82).

Consumption also does not have anything to do with what we conventionally think of as "reality." Instead, consumption is about "the systematic and indefinite possession of object-signs of consumption" (Baudrillard, in Poster, 1988:25). These object-signs, and the code of which they are part, are not "real." From this point of view, when we purchase a Big Mac at McDonald's we are not (just, mainly) buying food, but rather we are procuring what a Big Mac signifies about us (for example, that we are part of the fast-paced, mobile society or that we cannot afford to eat filet mignon).

In the consumer society controlled by the code, human relationships have been transformed into relationships with objects, especially the consumption of those objects. Says Baudrillard (in Poster, 1988:29), "we are living the period of the objects." These objects no longer have meaning because of their usefulness, their utility (or their "use value," in Marx's terms[6]); nor do they acquire meaning any longer from concrete relationships between people. Rather, the meaning of any object comes from its relationship to, and/or difference from, other objects. This collection, or network, of objects comes to have a meaning and logic of its own. The objects are signs (they have sign value rather than use or exchange value), and the consumption of those object-signs constitutes a language that we can seek to understand. Commodities are purchased as an "expression and mark of style, prestige, luxury, power, and so on" (Kellner, 1994:4). Thus, we all know (because we

---

[6] Marx privileges use value in comparison to exchange value, which is abstract, general, and fetishistic. Baudrillard argues that use value has similar characteristics and therefore must be critiqued by political economists. He goes further to argue that because it is based on an ahistorical, idealist anthropology, "use value fetishism is indeed more profound, more mysterious than the fetishism of exchange value" (Baudrillard, 1972/1981:139). As a result, use value cannot be posited (as Marx does) as an alternative to exchange value, as a revolutionary hope.

all know the "code") that a BMW is preferred to a Hyundai not because it is more useful but rather because in the system of car objects the BMW has far higher status than the Hyundai. To Baudrillard (in Poster, 1988:29), following Thorstein Veblen, we have become a society characterized by "conspicuousness of consumption and affluence."

Again, we seek to align ourselves with some and differentiate ourselves from others on the basis of the object-signs we consume. What we come to need in capitalism is not a particular object (say a BMW) but rather we seek *difference,* and by being different we acquire social status and social meaning. In consumption in modern capitalist society, it is *not* pleasure, not the pleasure of obtaining and using an object that we seek, but rather difference. This also leads to the view that when they are defined in this way, needs can never be satisfied; we have a continuing, lifelong need to differentiate ourselves from those who occupy other positions in society.

Baudrillard (in Poster, 1988:46) concludes, "consumption is a system which assures the regulation of signs and the integration of the group: it is simultaneously a morality (a system of ideological values) and a system of communication, a structure of exchange . . . this structural organization by far transcends individuals and [is] imposed on them." While there are a number of noteworthy aspects of this statement, the idea that consumption is a form of communication is worth underscoring. That is, when we consume something, we are communicating a number of things to others, including what groups we do and do not belong to. Others know the "language" with the result that they understand what we are saying when we purchase a BMW rather than a Hyundai.

In these views on consumption, Baudrillard's (in Poster, 1988:46) linkages to structuralism are clear: "consumption is a system of meaning like language [Saussure], or like the kinship system in primitive societies [Lévi-Strauss]." The following is an even clearer articulation of Baudrillard's structuralism:

> Marketing, purchasing, sales, the acquisition of differentiated commodities and object/signs—all of these presently constitute our language, a code with which our entire society *communicates* and speaks of and to itself. Such is the present day structure of communication: a language (*langue*) in opposition to which individual needs and pleasures are but the *effects of speech (parole).*

(in Poster, 1988:48)

While in this and many other ways Baudrillard uses structuralism, it should be made clear that in many more ways, especially in his later work, he is critical of, if not downright hostile, to it.

The central importance of consumption indicates a profound change in capitalism. In the nineteenth century capitalists concentrated on regulating workers and left consumers largely on their own. In the twentieth century the focus shifted to consumers who could no longer be allowed to decide whether or not to consume or how much or what to consume. Capitalism has come to need to be sure that people participate, and participate actively and in particular ways, in the consumer society. Baudrillard goes so far as to view consumption as "social labor" and to compare its control and exploitation to that of productive labor in the workplace. To put it another way, capitalism has created an exploitable "consuming mass" (Gane, 1991a:65). Not only is the system of consumption controlling, but it also helps to prevent the kind of collective revolutionary action hoped for by Marx. Consumers are assigned collectively to a place in relationship to the code, "without so much as giving rise to any *collective solidarity* (but quite the opposite)" (Baudrillard, in Poster, 1988:55). Thus, it is difficult to envision a social revolution undertaken by those busy trying to acquire the money needed to be the consumers of, for example, BMWs rather than Hyundais. As a result, it is worth noting that Baudrillard has launched a critical analysis of, and assault on, consumer society, without having a revolutionary subject like Marx's proletariat to overthrow it.

In this early work, Baudrillard still thinks in terms of social classes. The elites are defined not by objects or consumption but by their economic and political power and in their ability to manipulate signs and people. The middle and lower classes lack these powers with the result that they are left to dwell on objects and consumption. Furthermore, the code is not yet autonomous from class and class conflict. The code works to the advantage of the ruling class; indeed, Baudrillard (1972/1981:119) sees the code as "the keystone of domination." In his later work, the code will become increasingly autonomous and, if anything, even more controlling. In fact, he concludes early on that class domination may have only been a historical interlude and that society is coming again, as it was previously, to be dominated by signs and the code.

Yet even at this early stage Baudrillard clearly wants to broaden Marxian political economy and to integrate the consumption of signs, and more generally the code, into it. He contrasts this to the vulgar Marxian position that culture (including signs and the code) is an epiphenomenon controlled and manipulated by the dominant class. Thus, in contrast to the vulgar Marxian view, to Baudrillard a revolution in the realm of production would not mean the downfall of culture and the code.

Baudrillard also uses the idea of "means of consumption" as a parallel to the Marxian concept of the means of production. While he has been influenced by structuralism, it is once again clear that at least in his early work Baudrillard remains embedded, at least in part, in a Marxian material base. His paradigm for the new means of consumption seems to be the distinctively French drugstore,[7] although he immediately offers the far more general and significant shopping mall as an alternative model.

To Baudrillard, the (French) drugstore (and the mall) is a synthesis of "profusion and calculation . . . mak[ing] possible the synthesis of all consumer activities, not [the] least of which are shopping, flirting with objects, idle wandering, and all the permutations of these" (Baudrillard, in Poster, 1988:31). The key here seems to be "idle exploration," and in this sense the drugstore (and shopping mall) is more suited, in Baudrillard's view, to modern consumption than the supermarket in which people are more likely to be task oriented and to shop for the specific items that they need.

---

[7] The French drugstore is more like a miniature department store than what Americans think of as a drugstore (or pharmacy).

However, in this analysis of the drugstore, Baudrillard not only retains some of his Marxian materialism, he also combines it with elements of his structuralist position. He does this by arguing that the function of the drugstore is different from that of the supermarket, where the objective is to allow the customer easy access to everyday consumables. Instead, the drugstore "practices an *amalgamation of signs* where all categories of goods are considered a partial field in a general consumerism of signs" (Baudrillard, in Poster, 1988:32). Thus, already the focus is on the system of signs, the code, and not the specific commodity or the particular setting in which the commodity is marketed and purchased.

Baudrillard goes on to discuss the shopping mall more directly. While the contemporary terminology was not yet available to him, Baudrillard recognizes the importance of what the shopping center does to time and space (Giddens, 1984; Harvey, 1989). In terms of time, the mall is "completely indifferent to seasonal changes . . . creat[ing] a perpetual springtime . . . one need not be the slave of time. The mall, like every city street, is accessible seven days a week, day or night" (Baudrillard, in Poster, 1988:34). The mall also eliminates space restrictions by offering for sale a wide array of goods from virtually any place in the world. Baudrillard concludes, "Here we are at the heart of consumption as the total organization of everyday life, as a complete homogenization . . . perpetual shopping . . . the super shopping center, our new pantheon, our pandemonium, brings together all the gods, or demons, of consumption" (Baudrillard, in Poster, 1988:34–35). In this nearly hysterical world of consumerism, what is lost in the process is the possibility of obtaining any sort of meaning from consumption.

Baudrillard recognizes at this early stage the importance of the credit card to the shopping mall, and more generally to the consumer society (Ritzer, 1995). As he puts it, "The card frees us from checks, cash, and even from financial difficulties at the end of the month" (Baudrillard, in Poster, 1988:34).

Consumer society is a place where everything is for sale. Not only are all commodities signs, but all signs are commodities. Given the latter, all "objects, services, bodies, sex, culture, knowledge, etc." are produced and exchanged (Baudrillard, 1972/1981:147–148). Signs, commodities, and culture are indissolubly intertwined. High art, corn flakes, the human body, sex acts, and abstract theory are all signs, and they are all for sale.

Baudrillard is clearly critical of the consumer society, viewing it as creating a series of perverse desires and a generalized hysteria (Gane, 1991a). However, one is forced to wonder about the basis for such a critique. Without an "Archimedean point," how can Baudrillard make these kinds of negative judgments about the consumer society? Bauman makes this point, at least in terms of changing the world, in reference to Baudrillard's work:

> With all solid ground flushed away by the effluvia of decomposing reality, there is *no Archimedes' point* left, either accessible or at least imaginable, on which one could pivot the lever needed to force the derailed world back on track.

(Bauman, 1992:152)

This is a pressing issue because Baudrillard has rejected, especially later in his work, "essentialist" theories (like Marxism) that would have given him such an Archimedean point. Such theories are based on the idea that the current system is a distortion "of a real, and genuine, human form of consumption" (Gane, 1991a:69). For example, following Marx, Marcuse is seen as someone who "postulates an identifiable set of essential, innocent, human needs which can be thrown as a challenge against the modern system" (Gane, 1991b:87).

Baudrillard (in Gane, 1993:193) is left without any "criteria for judging whether the things people do are good or bad." As we will see, Baudrillard attempts to address this issue with his concept of "symbolic exchange." As Gane (1991b:81) puts it, symbolic exchange is "adopted as a basic universal, a kind of substructural necessity, and therefore as a position from which a new challenge can be made to contemporary society." However, this raises the question: Doesn't Baudrillard end up creating the kind of essentialist theory he was so critical of when it was adopted by Marcuse and other Marxists? This is lent credence by the fact that Gane (1991a:76) describes symbolic exchange as a kind of "cultural communism."

That the idea of symbolic exchange becomes Baudrillard's Archimedean point, at least for a time, is made clear by Gane (1991b:7) who sees all of Baudrillard's work as based on his ideas on symbolic exchange: "His project must be regarded as an assault on the 'disenchanted' world [the modern world has lost its enchantment] from the point of view of a militant of the symbolic (enchanted but cruel) cultures." More specifically, Baudrillard is engaged in a "general examination of the differences between symbolic and semiological order" (Gane, 1991a:75). Putting it in more aggressive terms, we can say that Baudrillard's work involves a struggle against the dominance of signs in the name of symbolic exchange (Genosko, 1994).

THE BREAK WITH MARX AND MARXISM

The Mirror of Production (Baudrillard, 1973/1975) is notable because in it Baudrillard makes a radical break with Marx and Marxian theory.[8] That is not to say, as we have seen, that Baudrillard had not critiqued the Marxists earlier; for example, in a slightly earlier work he talks of "the Marxist vulgate" (Baudrillard, 1972/1981:145). However, it is in the *Mirror* that we find a full-blown critique.

The title of this work is of great significance. Baudrillard argues that Marx, in his theory of capitalism, had created a mirror image of theories of production in capitalist society. While Marx may have produced an inverted image of capitalism, it was nonetheless an image that was profoundly shaped and distorted by capitalism. Thus, Baudrillard accuses Marx (and implicitly himself in his earlier work) of not making a sufficiently radical break with capitalism and the theories of capitalism produced by the political economists and others: "Marx made a radical critique of political economy, but still in the form of political economy" (Baudrillard,

---

[8] Baudrillard seeks a similar break with Freud and the psychoanalysts and Saussure and the linguists.

1973/1975:50). Marx is viewed as accepting the fundamental concepts and tenets of the supporters and theorists of capitalism; he is seen as having "changed nothing basic" in that set of ideas (Baudrillard, 1973/1975:33). Thus, one of the most radical of thinkers is now seen as not being radical enough for Baudrillard's tastes.

More generally, Marxism, as a school of thought, is seen as being infected by the "virus of bourgeois thought" (Baudrillard, 1973/1975:39). Furthermore, in continuing to mirror capitalism, later Marxists are accused of aiding and abetting that system: "*Marxism assists the cunning of capital*" (Baudrillard, 1973/1975:31). As a result of this unconscious complicity, Baudrillard (1973/1975:50) concludes that he wants to be "finished with a Marxism that has become more of a specialist in the impasses of capitalism than in the roads to revolution." In other words, his objective is to do what Marx and the Marxists failed to do—break the mirror of production to open up new, truly revolutionary possibilities (although, as we will see in the next chapter, Baudrillard ultimately comes to have no faith in a social revolution).

Baudrillard argues that Marx could not have come up with a fully adequate critique because capitalism, and all its contradictions, was not yet fully developed. This reality served to weaken Marx's historical analyses, his analysis of the capitalism of his day, and his projections for the future of society. Above all, to Baudrillard (1973/1975:36), Marx is guilty (as he is to Habermas) of the "aberrant sanctification of work." That is, Marx bought into the political economists' ideas on the central importance of work, especially creative work. Given the blinders derived from the political economists, Marx was *unable* to think about a number of other things including "discharge, waste, sacrifice, prodigality, play and symbolism . . . the gratuitous festive energizing of the body's powers, a game with death, or the acting out of desire" (Baudrillard, 1973/1975:42, 44). All of the latter are included within what is, as we will see below, Baudrillard's central concept, *symbolic exchange*. To put the issue succinctly and directly, Marx's focus on economic exchange blinded him to the importance of symbolic exchange. The real problem in the social world, for Baudrillard, is the rupture between symbolic exchange and work and not, as Marx would have it, the split between "abstract" and concrete labor. That is, to Baudrillard work (and much else) in contemporary society has ceased to be a form of symbolic exchange. Such work has lost its symbolic, its enchanted, qualities.

Baudrillard identifies three phases in the history of political economy. In the first stage, involving archaic and feudal societies, only the surplus of material production is exchanged. In the second, capitalistic stage, the one of central importance to Marx, the entire value of industrial production is exchanged. In the third stage, even that which was once thought to be inalienable is exchanged: "virtue, love, knowledge, consciousness" (Baudrillard, 1973/1975:119). However, as is the case with economic exchanges, all such exchanges have lost their symbolic qualities. In Baudrillard's view this third phase is at least as distinctive and as revolutionary as the second phase, but it has been ignored by Marxists and political economists who continue to be obsessed with, and blinded by, the economic exchange predominant in the second phase.

Baudrillard also argues that we have moved beyond a society characterized by alienation (he sometimes also uses the Durkheimian term "anomie"[9] in the same context). He labels the era of alienation and anomie the political era and sees it as one characterized by crisis, violence, and revolution. (There was no alienation in primitive societies, which were characterized by symbolic exchange.) However, we have moved beyond the political era and its alienation and now live in a trans-political era characterized by anomalies that he sees as aberrations lacking in any consequence (Baudrillard, 1983/1990:26). (Alienation and anomie, in contrast, had substantial and significant consequences.) As an example of such anomalies, he uses the hostages taken by terrorists. Hostage taking is an aberration that rarely, if ever, has any larger consequences. The terrorists are not apt to achieve their objectives in taking the hostages. Furthermore, since the status of the hostage is absolutely arbitrary and random (anyone in the wrong place at the wrong time could become a hostage), his existence indicates that there are "no longer even any rules for the game of his life or death . . . he [the hostage] is beyond alienation" (Baudrillard, 1983/1990:35). However, Baudrillard (1983/1990:35) goes further to argue: "We are all hostages." Hence, we are all beyond alienation; we are merely aberrations lacking in any meaning or consequence. Baudrillard places this view in his broader theoretical perspective:

> We are all hostages, and we are all terrorists. This circuit has replaced that other one of master and slaves, the dominating and the dominated, the exploiters and the exploited. Gone is the constellation of the slave and the proletarian: from now on it is the hostage and the terrorist. Gone is the constellation of alienation; from now on it is that of terror. It is *worse* than the one it replaces, but at least it liberates us from the liberal nostalgia and the ruses of history. It is the era of the transpolitical that is beginning.

(Baudrillard, 1983/1990:39; italics added)

Thus, the era of the meaningful capitalist-proletariat relationship is over, and it has been replaced by the utterly meaningless relationship between terrorist and hostage. And, to Baudrillard, the latter is far "worse" than its predecessors.

It is worth noting that even though Baudrillard radically separated himself from Marx, Kroker (in Featherstone, 1991:85) describes Baudrillard as "the last and the best of the Marxists." Nevertheless, Baudrillard leaves no doubt, even in his early work, that he feels it necessary to move beyond Marx's theory: "the *mirror of production* in which all Western metaphysics is reflected, must be broken" (Baudrillard, 1973/1975:47). While Marxian concepts sought to destroy the imperialism of bourgeois concepts, Marxism did much the same thing as bourgeois thinking in creating "trans-historical" ideas and concepts. Thus, Marxian thinking, just like bourgeois thinking, needs to be shattered.

Having begun the process of shattering Marxian theory and its attendant concepts, Baudrillard is confronted with the issue of finding an alternative perspective. That alternative begins to emerge more clearly in *Symbolic Exchange and Death*.

---

[9] This alternation of Marxian and Durkheimian terms reflects the fact, to be discussed later in the chapter, that Baudrillard's thinking is affected by the ideas of these two very different social theorists.

SYMBOLIC EXCHANGE

We have already seen the importance of Marx to Baudrillard's work, but with the concept of symbolic exchange we begin to see the powerful influence of the thinking of Émile Durkheim[10] (as well as that of his disciple and nephew, Marcel Mauss, and his thinking on the gift and Georges Bataille's [Richardson, 1994] thoughts on the relationship between excess, expenditure, and sovereignty as well as his effort to connect the gift to the larger society). Gane (1991a, 1991b) argues that *both* Marx and Durkheim were strong influences on Baudrillard's thinking with the result that there was a powerful and unresolved tension in his thinking.

Most generally, of course, the symbolic was of great importance to Durkheim and clearly to Baudrillard in his concept of symbolic exchange. More specifically, Baudrillard and Durkheim "adopt a two-phase world history: segmental (symbolic) societies, superseded by organic (simulation) societies" (Gane, 1991b:200). Further, both have a strong sense of pathologies (e.g., Durkheim's anomie and Baudrillard's consumerism, hostage taking, terrorism, and so on) in the modern world. There are certainly many differences between Baudrillard and Durkheim (Baudrillard's anti-rationalism versus Durkheim's rationalism, for example), but it is clear that Baudrillard's thinking on symbolic exchange is indebted to Durkheim's work on the symbolic and, more specifically, Mauss's and Bataille's work on the gift.

While we have already encountered the concept of symbolic exchange, it is important that we discuss it in some depth before we proceed much further. Most generally, symbolic exchange involves the general and reversible processes of "taking and returning, giving and receiving . . . [the] *cycle* of gifts and countergifts" (Baudrillard, 1973/1975:83; see also Baudrillard, 1976/1993:136). Symbolic exchange is based on a series of principles that stand in opposition to economic exchange in capitalism:

• symbolic exchange is nonproductive in contrast to the productive exchange found in the capitalist economy;[11]
• it is aimed at its own destruction rather than creating a perpetual cycle of commodity exchanges;
• reciprocity is continuous and unlimited rather than limited to a specific exchange of goods;
• and there is strict limitation on the exchange of goods rather than the unlimited production and exchange of goods.

Baudrillard (1980–1985/1990:127) privileges primitive societies in terms of symbolic exchange; such exchange is a primordial process (thus he is accused of having a "noble savage theme" [Levin, 1981:24]). In fact, he refuses to separate primitive society from the symbolic exchanges that occur within them: "Primitive 'society' does not exist as an instance apart from symbolic exchange" (Baudrillard,

---

[10] Interestingly, Baudrillard rarely refers to Durkheim directly.
[11] Lyotard (cited in Genosko, 1994:89) sees symbolic exchange (as well as seduction, to be discussed in Chapter 6) as part of Baudrillard's "hippie anthropology."

1973/1975:78). For the primitives, acts such as eating, drinking, and living are instances of symbolic exchange. As a result, Baudrillard (1973/1975:96) argues that such societies can serve as laboratories that can "teach us about the symbolic operation of social relations." (This is another similarity with Durkheim who used primitive tribes as his laboratory for the study of the social origins of religion.)

It is worth noting that Baudrillard's praise for symbolic exchange and the primitive societies in which it occurs in its purest form is part of his broader advocacy of nonrationality. As such, it forms the base for his critique of our rational world in general and especially the rationality of capitalists, consumers, bureaucrats, scientists, linguists, and Marxists.

When we look at primitive societies we find that production and work are, themselves, acts of symbolic exchange. For example, of artisans, Baudrillard (1973/1975:98–99) says that they live their "work as a relation of symbolic exchange." Baudrillard uses the idea of symbolic exchange to generalize about work as it *should be* (this is Baudrillard's Archimedean point, at least at this stage in his work) rather than as it exists in its distorted form in capitalist societies:

> Work is a process of destruction as well as of "production," and in this way work is symbolic. Death, loss and absence are inscribed in it through this dispossession of the subject, this loss of the subject and the object in the scansion of the exchange.

> (Baudrillard, 1973/1975:99)

Given his concentration on production, Marx was unable to see that destruction, dispossession, loss, and death are also integral parts of work.

However, today we live in a world in which such work, and more generally symbolic exchange, appear to be at an end. "In the immense polymorphous machine of contemporary capital, the symbolic (gift and countergift, reciprocity and reversal, expenditure and sacrifice) no longer counts for anything" (Baudrillard, 1976/1993:35). To take a specific example from contemporary society, one that will be discussed in further detail in the next chapter, we no longer engage in symbolic exchange with the dead. In primitive societies death, as well as the rituals surrounding it, was an integral part of life. Today, however, we have segregated death from life. This inability to engage in (symbolic) exchange flies in the face of the fact that, according to Baudrillard (1983/1990:47), "Exchange is our law." Baudrillard (1983/1990:47) concludes, "We are living at the end of exchange. However, only exchange protects us from destiny. Where exchange is no longer possible, we find ourselves in a fatal situation, a situation of destiny." Instead of exchange, what we have today is "mad speculation" (Baudrillard, 1983/1990:50). Taking hostages is for Baudrillard one example of such a mad speculation.

To put this change another way, to Baudrillard, we have moved from the political economy of the commodity (although commodities are signs) to the political economy of the sign. "The commodity form has given way to the sign form. This means the *code* of equivalence has become more significant than the exchange of commodities" (Gane, 1991b:111). That is, all values have become signs dominated by the code, and the code offers "a structure of control and of power much more subtle and more totalitarian than that of exploitation" (Baudrillard, 1973/1975:121). The problem now, and it is a more radical one, is the structural manipulation of the sign, not the domination and exploitation of labor power. Thus, we are witnessing "the symbolic destruction of all social relations not so much by the ownership of the means of production but by *the control of the code*. Here there is a revolution of the capitalist system equal in importance to the industrial revolution" (Baudrillard, 1973/1975:122). Further, Gane (1991a:72) argues that because the code is a structure that is free of doctrine, "no revolution against it can be mobilized."

Thus, the contemporary, simulated world is destroying symbolic exchange. Yet, in the face of that, Baudrillard adheres "to the superiority of the symbolic cultures and the inevitable frailty and vulnerability of the orders of simulation found in the West . . . The symbolic orders have a primordial nature which ultimately, according to Baudrillard, will be revealed as a higher order" (Gane, 1991b:14). Thus, Baudrillard critiques capitalism from the outside, from the vantage point of symbolic exchange. Marxism, on the other hand, can be seen as critiquing capitalism from within, from the vantage point of the exploited and alienated proletariat.[12]

We could say, following Baudrillard, that symbolic exchange haunts the dominance of signs and the code. Baudrillard recognizes that there is no returning to primitive society and its symbolic exchange. However, he does see it as a radical theoretical alternative to the contemporary world. In fact, he sees it as sufficiently radical to ultimately destroy the contemporary semiocracy, at least in theory (Genosko, 1994).[13]

As we have seen, in his earliest work Baudrillard was affected positively by Saussure's structural linguistics, but he later came to distance himself from much of that. Baudrillard discovered in that work a radical element that Saussure himself could not have seen. That is, a model of symbolic exchange can be found in language itself, especially poetry, which is the rebellion of language against its own laws. There is nothing left over in poetry and therefore no possibility of accumulation; there is just incessant give and take (symbolic exchange). "The poetic recreates the situation of primitive societies in linguistic material: a restricted corpus of objects whose uninterrupted circulation in the gift-exchange creates an inexhaustible wealth, a feast of exchange. . . . The poetic is the restitution of symbolic exchange in the very heart of words" (Baudrillard, 1976/1993:203, 205).

In contrast to poetry where signs are generally highly limited, in language more generally we are suffering from an excess of signs, from sign pollution. Here we find a body of unexchanged language, and it is this that is studied by the traditional field of linguistics. Indeed, Baudrillard equates this body of language with the code. Thus, Saussure found both "the structural operation of representation by signs, but [also] exactly the opposite, the deconstruction of the sign and representation" (Baudrillard, 1976/1993:195). As a result, Saussure may have laid the groundwork not only for linguistics but also "for a decentring of all linguistics" (Baudrillard, 1976/1993:195).

---

[12] However, in another sense Marxism also involves an external critique; a critique from the point of view of the yet-to-be-created world of communism and species being.

[13] Of course, theoretical destruction is a long way from destruction in practice; see the discussion of the "strength of the weak" in the following chapter.

SUMMARY

This chapter has been devoted to a discussion of some of Baudrillard's early theoretical roots and ideas. Many of the early ideas—his focus on the consumer society; objects, signs, and the code; symbolic exchange—had a powerful impact on his later work. The same is true of his intellectual roots in, and differences with, Marxian, Durkheimian, and Saussurian theory. Certainly there are ideas (for example, the means of consumption) that do not resurface much, if at all, in the later work. However, even the ideas that have been jettisoned by Baudrillard himself continue to be important to contemporary analysts of the social world. However, for our purposes, what is important is the continuity between these early ideas and the later ones to be discussed in the following chapter. To take just one example, the idea of symbolic exchange will resurface as at least partly coterminous with Baudrillard's later concept of "seduction."

6

JEAN BAUDRILLARD: PART 2: PROBLEMS IN THE CONTEMPORARY WORLD AND THE POSSIBILITY OF DEALING WITH THEM

WE now turn to a discussion of Baudrillard's analysis of contemporary society as well as his thoughts on responses to the problems associated with it.

CONTEMPORARY SOCIETY: ITS NATURE AND PROBLEMS

The Code

As indicated in Chapter 5, Baudrillard sees us moving from a society dominated by signs and codes associated with commodities to one dominated by more general signs and codes; he sees us moving toward the universal "establishment of an abstract and model system of signs" (Baudrillard, 1983:65). All exchanges, not just those associated with consumption, have come to be dominated by the code. It is now primarily the semiotic world of the code that is destroying symbolic exchange and engaging in symbolic violence aimed at those areas in which symbolic exchange still survives. This abstract code is a much more effective method of dominance than the exploitative capitalist economic system. It is also much more subtle and has far greater totalitarian implications. The structural manipulation of signs and the code is of far more radical significance than was the control of labor power in capitalism. This is the case, if for no other reason, because *all* of our thoughts and actions are affected by signs and the code, not just those associated with our labor. It is those who control the code (a key role is played by the media in general and television in particular), and the code itself, that are destroying the symbolic aspects of social relations, not the capitalists who own the means of production. It is this change from the control of the means of production to the control of the code that Baudrillard sees as a great social revolution, equal in magnitude to the industrial revolution.

At one time, signs related to objects, but now that linkage has been abolished; signs no longer designate any reality. What we have now is simply the "play of signifiers . . . in which the code no longer refers back to any subjective or objective 'reality', but to its own logic" (Baudrillard, 1973/1975:127). Signs relate only to other signs, and their meaning is found in that relationship. Signs are now free, indifferent, totally indeterminate, and totally relativistic.

It is the existence of such a code that neither Marx nor even Saussure anticipated. They both still operated under the assumption that there was a dialectic between signs and reality. However, to Baudrillard (1976/1993:7) that "dialectic is now in shreds, and the real has died." With reality dead, all there are are signs. In this world, signs exchange against other signs rather than against the real. With the death of the dialectic and the real has come the demise of the great humanistic hopes. It is impossible to have such dreams in a relativistic world in which everything is undecidable and substitutable for everything else.

Thus, for example, in contrast to the Marxian position, money and labor now float as signs rather than being material realities. Baudrillard (1976/1993:9) describes modern capitalism as a "generalised brothel of capital, a brothel not for prostitution, but for substitution and commutation." Labor is no longer a power but simply one sign among many. Labor is no longer productive but merely reproductive (of signs, the code). Labor and the factory have disappeared because they are everywhere (as we discussed in Chapter 5, even consumers can be seen as laborers, and, therefore, shopping malls can be viewed as factories). As a result, labor can no longer be a revolutionary force.

While we no longer have the material, economic crises of interest to the Marxists, the capitalists create a "perpetual simulacrum of a crises" (Baudrillard, 1976/1993:32). Their objective in creating such simulated crises (for example, the economic "war" with Japan) is to conceal the fact that the real problem in society now resides in the code and not in the economic system. To put it another way, the capitalists simulate problems in production to conceal the fact that the real problem lies in reproduction. In fact, Baudrillard (1976/1993:33) prefers the "*economic atrocities of capital*—profit, exploitation—than to face up to the situation we are in, where everything operates or breaks down with the effects of the code."

It could be argued that the code becomes modernity in Baudrillard's work. Thus, a critique of the code is a critique of modern society. However, Baudrillard can be criticized for isolating the code and, more importantly, for hypostatizing, or reifying, it (Genosko, 1994).

Fashion

Baudrillard's concern with fashion is part of his broader switch from a focus on economic, social, and political issues to a concern for culture (the media are another of Baudrillard's cultural concerns). Thus, Baudrillard is part of the broad "cultural turn" taking place in the social sciences.

Baudrillard examines the world of fashion as a paradigm of the dominance of the code. In fashion, all we see is the "simple play of signifiers" and, as a result, "the loss of every system of reference" (Baudrillard, 1976/1993:87). Not only does fashion not refer to anything real, but it doesn't lead anywhere either. Fashion does not produce anything, but merely reproduces the code. That is, fashion is produced not "according to its own determinations, but *from the model itself*—that is to say, that it is never produced, but always and immediately *reproduced*. The model itself has become the only system of reference" (Baudrillard, 1976/1993:92). Fashion is, in a sense, the ultimate stage of the commodity form: "With the acceleration and proliferation of messages, information, signs and models, it is in *fashion* as a total cycle that the linear world of the commodity will reach completion" (Baudrillard, 1976/1993:115). Fashion is also without values and morality. It tends to spread like a virus or a cancer. Fashion produces what postmodernists like to call a "pastiche": "Fashion cobbles together, from one year to the next, what 'has been', exercising an enormous combinatory freedom" (Baudrillard, 1976/1993:89).

Given all of these characteristics, it would seem clear that fashion is part of the postmodern world. But, despite fashion's many affinities with postmodernism, here as in many other places, Baudrillard (1976/1993:90) says he is dealing with modernity, *not* postmodernity: "For binary logic is the essence of modernity . . . Modernity is not the transmutation but commutation of all values, their combination and their ambiguity. Modernity is a code and fashion is its emblem."

Fashion exists in the world of "light signs," while "politics, morals, economics, science, culture, sexuality" are "heavy signs" (Baudrillard, 1976/1993:87). But light or heavy, all of these worlds are dominated by signs. Further, light or heavy, these signs are all part of the code that serves to constrain people.

While fashion reflects the dominance of the code, as well as of commodities and simulations, it also in a sense poses a threat to the system. Fashion is one of those areas characterized by "play" rather than "work"; it is a world of illusion. It plays with things like good and evil, rationality and irrationality. "This fashion is taken on by contemporary youth, as a resistance to every imperative, a resistance without an ideology, without objectives" (Baudrillard, 1976/1993:98). Nevertheless, those in power at times feel compelled to crush this play with signs to maintain the predominance of their own signs.

In the end, however, fashion is seen as immune to subversion as the code:

> there is no possible subversion of fashion since it has no system of reference to contradict (it is its own system of reference). We cannot escape fashion (since fashion itself

makes the refusal of fashion into a fashion feature—blue jeans are an historical example of this) . . . one can never escape the reality principle of the code. Even when rebelling against the content, one more and more closely obeys the logic of the code.

(Baudrillard, 1976/1993:98)

The only real answer to the problem of fashion, and most other problems in the contemporary world, lies in the deconstruction of the code.

Simulacra

We have already mentioned the centrally important ideas of simulation and simulacra[1] in Chapter 5, but it is now time to deal with them more systematically. Baudrillard (1983:4) argues that we live in "the age of simulation." The "genuine" and fast-disappearing cultural worlds (symbolic exchange, seduction[2]) that Baudrillard tends to prefer are enchanted worlds. However, a world of simulations "is totally disenchanted and . . . almost shameful" (Baudrillard, in Gane, 1993:143).

Baudrillard offers a wide array of examples of simulations:

• He regards the primitive Indian tribe, the Tasaday, at least as it exists today, as a simulation since the tribe has been "frozen, cryogenized, sterilized, protected *to death*" (Baudrillard, 1983:15). It may at one time have been a "real" primitive tribe, but today what exists is nothing more than a simulation of what the tribe once was.
• A 1987 European Cup soccer match between Real-Madrid and Naples took place at night in a completely empty stadium. Fans were barred because of unruly behavior by Madrid fans at an earlier match. No one (or almost no one) directly experienced the match, but millions saw its televised (therefore simulated) image (Baudrillard, 1990/1993:79–80).
• The caves of Lescaux have been closed, and an exact replica, a simulation, of the caves has been opened to the public.
• Watergate is described as "a simulation of a scandal" (Baudrillard, 1983:30).
• The Gulf War with Iraq is viewed as a simulation of the nuclear war between the United States and the Soviet Union that never occurred (Baudrillard, 1992/1994).
• Then there is Disneyland, "a perfect model of all the entangled orders of simulation" (Baudrillard, 1983:23). Take, for example, the simulated submarine ride to which people flock to see simulated undersea life. Strikingly, many go there rather than the more "genuine" aquarium (itself, however, a simulation of the sea) just down the road.

The widespread existence of simulations is a major reason for the erosion of the distinction between the real and the imaginary, the true and the false. It is increasingly difficult to distinguish the real from the fake; every contemporary event is a mixture of the real and the imaginary. In fact, to Baudrillard, as we have mentioned

---

[1] These are not new ideas; they are traceable to Plato, among others.
[2] Gane (1991b:58) argues that within contemporary culture, seduction is "a resource very similar to symbolic exchange processes."

before, the true and the real have ceased to exist, disappearing in an avalanche of simulations. This makes it dangerous to attempt to unmask simulations since what we are apt to find is that there is nothing to be uncovered, or what is there is undecipherable; there is no "reality" or "truth" behind the simulated exterior.

Since there is no longer any truth or reality, signs no longer stand for anything. Thus, we can be said to live in one "gigantic simulacrum—not unreal, but a simulacrum, never again exchanging for what is real, but exchanging in itself, in an uninterrupted circuit without reference or circumference" (Baudrillard, 1983:11). As a result, among other things, simulations put "an end to meaning absolutely" (Baudrillard, in Gane, 1993:105). To give a specific example, Baudrillard argues that "all of Los Angeles and America surrounding it are no longer real, but of the order of the hyperreal and of simulation" (Baudrillard, 1983:25).

Since the term "hyperreal" has already been used, we need to pause and clarify its meaning. The hyperreal involves simulations and is sometimes used coterminously with this concept; "the hyperreal is . . . entirely within simulation" (Baudrillard, 1976/1993:73). The hyperreal is not produced but is *that which is always already reproduced*" (Baudrillard, 1976/1993:73). More specifically, it is a simulation that is more real than real, more beautiful than beautiful, truer than true. In a hyperreal world there is no way of getting at the source, the original reality. A good example, one used frequently by Baudrillard, is pornography, which he views as "more sexual than sex . . . hypersexuality" (Baudrillard, 1983/1990:11). Rojek and Turner offer the following example of hyperreality:

> Scientists alleged that NASA's pictures of other worlds were being touched up. For example, the drab colours of the planet Mars and the asteroid Gaspara had been enhanced to become more vivid and spectacular.
>
> (Rojek and Turner, 1993:xi)

More generally, and extremely, "*today reality itself is hyperrealist*" (Baudrillard, 1976/1993:74); in other words, there is no more reality; all we are left with is hyperreality. Disneyland is often used by Baudrillard as an example of hyperreality (for example, it is cleaner than the world outside its gates; its personnel friendlier than those in the "real" world). Many parts of the outside world are emulating Disneyland (and other hyperreal institutions like fast-food restaurants) in a variety of ways and in that sense (and others) are growing increasingly hyperreal.

Baudrillard sees the era of simulations and hyperreality as part of a series of successive phases of images (thereby, seeming to contradict the promise of postmodernists not to offer grand narratives):

1 –it [the image] is the reflection of a basic reality
2 –it masks and perverts a basic reality
3 –it masks the *absence* of a basic reality
4 –it bears no relation to any reality whatever: it is its own pure simulacrum.

(Baudrillard, 1983:11)

Of these, the transition from the second to the third stage is crucial. Marxists operated in the second phase, Baudrillard in the third and fourth phases. Thus, Baudrillard (1983:48) contrasts his position to that of the Marxists doing ideological analysis (in the second stage): "It is always the aim of ideological analysis to restore the objective process," but in his own analyses in the third and fourth stages "it is always a false problem to want to restore the truth[3] beneath the simulacrum."

In still another historical model (and yet another seeming grand narrative[4] from a postmodernist ostensibly opposed to such narratives), Baudrillard differentiates among three orders of simulacra, with each order submitting to the one that follows (we will discuss the later addition of a new, fourth order in the next section). In the first order, roughly from the Renaissance to the beginning of the Industrial Revolution, only first-order simulations—counterfeits of originals—were possible. Baudrillard (1976/1993:52) gives as an example stucco imitations of "velvet curtains, wooden cornices, and fleshy curves of the body." Counterfeits do not offer the possibilities of control over society that exist in simulacra, but that control is foreshadowed in counterfeits (Baudrillard, 1976/1993:53).

The second order is the industrial era characterized by production and a pure series of reproductions of identical objects (automobiles, refrigerators), "the serial repetition of the same object" (Baudrillard, 1976/1993:56). Unlike the previous stage, there is no original to be counterfeited; "objects become indistinct simulacra of one another and, along with objects, of the men that produce them" (Baudrillard, 1976/1993:55). Furthermore, there is no need to counterfeit in the industrial era since the products are made on a massive scale and there is no issue of their origin or specificity. "In a series, objects become undefined simulacra one of the other" (Baudrillard, 1983:97).

The third order, one that we have been discussing throughout much of these two chapters, is dominated by the code and the generation of simulations by models rather than the industrial system. This era is characterized by reproduction, not the production which dominated the industrial era. Baudrillard concludes,

> We know that now it is on the level of reproduction (fashion, media, publicity, information and communication networks), on the level which Marx negligently called the nonessential sectors of capital . . . that is to say in the sphere of simulacra and of the code, that the global process of capital is founded.
>
> (Baudrillard, 1983:99)

We have moved "from a capitalist-productivist society to a neo-capitalist cybernetic order that aims now at total control" (Baudrillard, 1983:111).

Baudrillard describes this reality in various ways. For example, he contends that we now live at the end of the age of interpretation, in "the black box of the code" (Baudrillard, 1976/1993:58). Thus, we can never truly understand what is transpiring in contemporary society. He also sees us as living at the "end of dialectical evolution . . . there is no more finality, nor any determinacy" (Baudrillard,

---

[3] And, if we want to seek out the truth, or something approximating it, we cannot go about it directly by "simply looking for it. The only strategy is the reverse one! . . . illusion is the sole route to get somewhere if something is to be found—but 'found' without being searched for" (Baudrillard, in Gane, 1993:61).

[4] Genosko argues that this should not be seen as a neat, unilinear historical model.

1976/1993:59). Since there is no more positivity in the world, negativity is no longer an option. To put it another way, there are no more adversaries to react against. We are in a black box. We may not understand or like it, but there is no other reality to hope for, no other place to which we can hope to go. This leads Baudrillard (in Gane, 1993:95) to an explicitly postmodern position: "So, all that are left are pieces. All that remains to be done is to play with the pieces. Playing with the pieces—that is postmodern."

One means of control in this new world is the referendum. In fact, to Baudrillard since there is no longer any truth, no longer any referential, we live in the age of the referendum. Referenda, and tests more generally, are perfect simulations because, as mentioned before, the answers are designated in advance by the questions. "The irruption of the binary question/answer schema is of incalculable importance. Dislocating all discourse in a now bygone golden age, this schema short-circuits every dialectic of the signifier and the signified, a representative and a represented" (Baudrillard, 1976/1993:64). Furthermore, all alternatives are reduced to a binary code, with DNA serving as the prototype of this, indeed all, simulation. The model for today's world is DNA: "it is in the genetic code that the genesis of simulacra today finds its completed form" (Baudrillard, 1976/1993:57).

People are controlled by referenda (a referendum is to Baudrillard a kind of ultimatum) in the sense that they must respond in ways predetermined by those who construct them. Referenda serve to short circuit genuine discourse.[5] The public opinion that emerges from such referenda is a simulation and is hyperreal, more real than peoples' beliefs. Those who respond often try to reproduce the question; "the ones questioned always pretend to be as the question imagines and solicits them to be" (Baudrillard, 1983:130).

Thus, Baudrillard (1983:128) describes political polls as "the political class' burlesque spectacle, hyper-representative of nothing at all." Polls represent nothing because, as we've seen, the masses respond with simulated replies:

> We record everything, but we don't believe it, because we have become screens ourselves, and who can ask a screen to believe what it records? To simulation we reply by simulation; we have ourselves become systems of simulation. . . . It is this that makes good old critical and ironical judgment no longer possible . . . there is no longer a universe of reference . . . polls will never represent anything.
>
> (Baudrillard, 1983/1990:87, 88)

The distortions associated with polls are part of a broader set of distortions, which means that even with non-stop polling total uncertainty "will never be lifted" (Baudrillard, 1983/1990:90).

---

[5] Here, as elsewhere, Baudrillard is following Marshall McLuhan and his idea that the medium (the referendum in this case) controls the message. However, while McLuhan is ultimately optimistic about a future of a global village in which people are more in touch with one another, Baudrillard remains pessimistic about the media because they engage in one-way communication that is not reversible (it is not symbolic exchange). Nonetheless, McLuhan was "a decisive influence on Baudrillard" (Gane, 1991a:48). On the more general relationship between McLuhan and postmodernism, see Ferguson (1991).

Public opinion is also a simulacra. Public opinion polls lead respondents to re-produce what the pollsters are seeking; respondents do not produce opinions of their own.[6] Thus, public opinion polls are *both* the medium and the message. In this, they resemble television and electronic media, which also involve, explicitly or implicitly, a perpetual questioning and answering, a perpetual polling. "It is im-possible to obtain a *non-simulated response* to a direct question, apart from merely reproducing the question . . . there is total circularity in every case; those ques-tioned always behave as the questioner imagines they will and solicits them to . . . just hot air" (Baudrillard, 1976/1993:67). Thus, Baudrillard concludes, the prob-lem with opinion polls is not, as most believe, their objective influence. Rather, such polls are a problem because they help lead to "operational simulation . . . across the entire range of social practices." In one of his favorite metaphors, polls are a kind of "leukaemia infecting all social substance" (Baudrillard, 1976/1993:67).

Politics and elections follow the same model. An election elicits the desired re-sponse from the electorate. Parties do not stand for anything. Nevertheless, party leaders oppose one another "creating a simulated opposition between the two par-ties" (Baudrillard, 1976/1993:68).

Baudrillard sees referenda, polls, and elections as examples of the new "soft technologies" of control. As Gane (1993:7) puts it, Western society is becoming "repressively tolerant." In the specific case of referenda and polls, the nature of the answer is gently controlled by the nature of the question. More generally, the sin-gle, totalitarian, bureaucratic system of control is an

> archaic rationality compared to simulation, in which it is no longer a single general equivalent but a diffraction of models that plays the regulative role: no longer the form of the general equivalent, but the form of distinct oppositions. We pass from injunction to disjunction through the code, from ultimatum to solicitation, from obligatory passiv-ity to models constructed from the outset on the basis of the subject's "active response", and this subject's involvement and "ludic" participation, towards a total environment model made up of incessant spontaneous responses, joyous feedback and irradiated contacts.

(Baudrillard, 1976/1993:70–71)

Baudrillard goes beyond referenda and polls to argue that the binary system (e.g., the two-party system in politics) is always the most effective system of con-trol. He argues (writing during the Cold War with the Soviet Union) that the binary system of competing superpowers is a more effective device for controlling the world than a single superpower. (With the end of the Cold War and the Soviet Union we will be in a position to see whether or not Baudrillard is right. So far, wars like those in Bosnia seem to support his view.) Similarly, the two-party politi-cal system is a more effective means of control than totalitarianism. Again, the demise of the Soviet Union and its one-party system and the continued vitality of the United States and its two-party system seem to support his position.

---

[6] For a discussion of public opinion polls from a Foucauldian perspective, see Peer (1992).

Baudrillard takes the identical twin towers in New York City as a symbol of the centrality of the binary in the contemporary world. He argues that the twin towers superseded the earlier system of different and competing skyscrapers (the Chrysler Building and the Empire State Building, for example). The twin towers mark the end of the world of competition and of a world in which it is possible to represent some original phenomenon. Since the twin towers are identical, there is no original tower.

In the contemporary simulated world everything is collapsing into everything else; everything is *imploding*. Baudrillard (1983:57) defines implosion as "contraction into each other, a fantastic telescoping, a collapsing of the two traditional poles into one another." Since everything is simulation, everything can dissolve into a single huge simulated mass. For example, in the case of contemporary talk shows, TV is dissolving into life and life is dissolving into TV. What happens on the TV shows is clearly a simulation, but life itself comes to be a simulation, often of what is seen on television. And, in a world of total simulation, "absolute manipulation" becomes possible.

The contemporary hyperreal world of signs that no longer refer to anything, in which the distinction between the real and the imaginary is effaced, in which "reality is immediately contaminated by its simulacrum" (Baudrillard, 1983:149), produces a kind of hysteria. For example, in the contemporary capitalist economy (politics offers another example) there is a hysterical effort to produce and reproduce the real through production, even overproduction. The latter leads to a hyperreal capitalistic system which, through overproduction, is seeking desperately and ultimately unsuccessfully to deny its own dissolution into the code and the world of signs.

The Fractal Order

In the *Transparency of Evil,* Baudrillard (1990/1993) adds a fourth order of simulacra. He labels it the fractal, viral, or cancerous stage; "the current pattern of our culture" (Baudrillard, 1990/1993:6). There is no transcendence here, or even hope of it, merely endless proliferation. Everything, from DNA to AIDS to television images, follows this pattern. More generally, the code is endlessly proliferating as is its hold on the social world.

At the fractal stage we are at the end of difference; everything interpenetrates. We are in the era of the transpolitical, transsexual, transaesthetic. Thus, everything is political, sexual, and aesthetic, and, as a result, nothing is political, sexual, and aesthetic. A major force in this interpenetration in all realms is the media and communication more generally.[7]

For example, art is proliferating, but in the process it is losing its distinctive qualities, especially its capacity to negate and oppose reality. Then there is transsexuality, involving the elimination of sexual difference, our new model of sexuality. Transsexuality can be achieved surgically, but more importantly it can be

---

[7] Thus, Baudrillard (1990/1993:12) opposes Habermas, arguing that "there is no such thing as a communicational utopia."

achieved semiotically. Examples include Madonna and, especially, Michael Jackson, the latter losing (abandoning) his sexual specificity *both* surgically and semiotically. In the sexual realm we have ended up, after the sexual revolution, with a confusion of categories. In fact, Baudrillard (1990/1993:24) sees such confusion as "the problematic fate of all revolutions." Rather than providing grand solutions as the modernists believed, "revolution opens the door to indeterminacy, anxiety and confusion," or "the revolution of our time is the uncertainty revolution" (Baudrillard, 1990/1993:24, 43). In the end, we become not only undifferentiated but also indifferent.

This lack of differentiation is reflected in the fact that our simulations are entirely positive; all negativity has been banished. Take the example of cosmetic surgery, which is aimed at eliminating all offensive characteristics, leaving us all "beautiful." Now we are developing a variety of genetic tests and technologies so that we can eliminate all undesirable characteristics before they come into existence. All of this positivity, all of this elimination of negativity, leaves us in a world resembling "the smile of a corpse in a funeral home" (Baudrillard, 1990/1993:45). We all may look good, but we are dead. Death, in this case, is a world with all positivity and no negativity.

To help us achieve full positivity and eliminate negativity, we engage in such activities as jogging. Jogging, to Baudrillard, is one of those processes of endless proliferation. Like cancer, viruses, and communication, it is obsessional, interminable, and ultimately vacuous.

Our efforts to eliminate all negativity have left us with a declining ability to defend ourselves. We are as vulnerable as the "boy in the bubble" was to germs. In fact, Baudrillard (1990/1993:61) argues that "the extermination of man begins with the extermination of man's germs." Like the AIDS patient, we are all becoming immunodeficient. Because our defenses have disappeared, we are coming to be destroyed by our own antibodies, by the leukemia of the organism. (Computers are similarly vulnerable to their own information, their viruses.) Thus, to Baudrillard (1990/1993:64), "Total prophylaxis is lethal."

The turning of viruses against people and machines is one aspect (see below for others) of what Baudrillard calls the "principle of evil." Evil, to Baudrillard, does not imply good and bad, morality or guilt. Here, the principle of evil is synonymous with reversibility, the turns of fate that, for example, turn bodies against themselves in autoimmunological diseases. The principle of evil encompasses both the best (the body, in this case) and the worst (the immune system turning on the body). In the main, however, Baudrillard (1990/1993:109) privileges evil, which he associates with things he prizes—instability, seduction, ambivalence, "the natural disorder of the world."[8]

---

[8] Another way of looking at evil is as the existence of others and the eternal antagonism between self and other. We can never understand the other; the other is mysterious. Thus, it is the other who is the object of a process that, as we will see, Baudrillard values—seduction. In addition, another valued process, play, is only possible with the other. Alienation is only possible when there is an other. However, with the end of difference, subjects are "doomed to self-metastases, to pure repetition"; we face a future which no longer involves "the hell of other people, but the hell of the Same" (Baudrillard, 1990/1993:122).

These virulent, epidemic processes are capable of getting out of hand and leading us to catastrophe. We are threatened by excess: "runaway energy flows, chain reactions, or frenzied autonomous developments . . . A full-blown and planet-wide schizophrenia now rules" (Baudrillard, 1990/1993:103, 104).

The lack of differentiation is also reflected in our relations with television and computer screens. It is increasingly unclear where we end and such machines begin. This heralds the end of anthropology. It also marks the end of the alienation of people from machines. We now form integrated circuits with those machines, and "runaway energy flows" characterize those circuits.

We have covered a wide range of issues, as does Baudrillard, under the heading of simulacra. Before we leave this topic, however, it should be mentioned that in his most recent book, *The Illusion of the End,* Baudrillard (1992/1994:54) offers us the concept of *desimulation.* That is, we may be tiring of at least some of the simulations he associates with modernity. Baudrillard (1992/1994:54) contends that there is evidence that we are ending "things which long ago ceased to have meaning." One of his major examples is the end of the simulated form of communism that existed in eastern Europe. While there may be some examples of desimulation, it seems unlikely the world as a whole is surrendering the simulacra that, in Baudrillard's view, go to its essence.

Ecstasy

Baudrillard also sees the contemporary world as being *ecstatic.* Ecstasy implies unconditional metamorphosis, escalation for escalation's sake, a continuing process of spinning out of control until all senses are lost. Ultimately, this out-of-control system reveals its emptiness and meaninglessness; it "shines forth in its pure and empty form" (Baudrillard, 1983/1990:9).

Baudrillard offers a number of examples of ecstatic phenomena.

- Fashion, discussed above, can be viewed as the ecstasy of the beautiful; a "pure and empty form of an esthetic spinning about itself" (Baudrillard, 1983/1990:9).
- Advertising is described as "spinning of use-value and exchange-value into annihilation in the pure and empty form of the brandname" (Baudrillard, 1983/1990:10).
- Art is viewed as going beyond itself; "the more hyperreal it becomes and the more it transcends itself towards its empty essence" (Baudrillard, 1983/1990:10).
- Most important, the masses are seen as "the ecstasy of the social, the ecstatic form of the social" (Baudrillard, 1983/1990:11).

The masses, then, can be seen as a pure and empty form that is spinning out of control and in the process of reaching the limit of the social. In this ecstasy, the masses offer hope of overturning the system. However, this is not a Marxian hope that the masses will ultimately come to understand and act on their historic role. Rather, as the masses roll blindly ahead doing what they do, they may well cause the system to fall. He concludes, "this revolution in things . . . lies no longer in their dialectical transcendence (*Aufhebung*) but rather in their potentialization

(*Steigerung*), in their elevation to the second power, to the nth power" (Baudrillard, 1983/1990:34). Dialectics no longer describes the situation, rather it is ecstasy that is in process.

Baudrillard sees cancer and obesity as ecstatic systems. That is, they are *hyper-telic* systems, having "no other end than limitless increase, without any consideration of limits" (Baudrillard, 1983/1990:31). Of obesity, he argues that it displays "something of the system, of its empty inflation . . . its nihilist expression, that of the general incoherence of signs" (Baudrillard, 1983/1990:27). Simulations are seen as being obese, and contemporary systems are viewed as being "bloated with information" (Baudrillard, 1983/1990:28). By overcoming the laws of its own growth, the system has grown obese, obscene. In sum, "obesity no longer has any meaning or direction either, it goes nowhere and no longer has anything to do with movement: it is the ecstasy of movement" (Baudrillard, 1983/1990:34).

Obesity without end resembles the metastases of cancer. Present-day information systems can be seen as cancerous; metastases "producing too much meaning, a production of superfluous meaning" (Baudrillard, 1983/1990:32). Like cancer and obesity, our current world is in a state of total delirium.

Baudrillard (1983) describes discourse in similar terms as being circular, ceaselessly going round and round. He sees discourse as resembling a Möbius strip; if you cut it in two, an additional spiral results. More specifically, Baudrillard (1983/1990:44, 45) sees not only the political as hostages to the media but the media as hostages to the polity. They are in a state of "circular blackmail"; "There is no end to this chain of blackmail."

The media play a key role in this kind of thinking. We are bombarded by ceaseless information from the media; floating signifiers circulate endlessly. In fact, as we have seen, we have become part of the media circuit representing little more than networks, or nodes, in the media system. Furthermore, the media play a key role in the creation of a depthless, superficial world.[9] All things, great and small, are part of it, and it is impossible to differentiate among them. "In the end it makes everything circulate in one space, without depth, where all the objects must be able to follow one after the other without slowing down or stopping the circuit" (Baudrillard, in Gane, 1993:147). Everything is available for communication, banalization, commercialization, and consumption.

Baudrillard is fascinated with double spirals (like DNA) for this reason: "There is nothing to discover, there is a spiralling . . . and regeneration." Things go round and round, but beneath it all there is no essential meaning to be discovered.

Death

We live in a world in which we exclude minorities, and the paradigm for that is the exclusion of the dead and the dying; it is the model for all other exclusions. Thus, "death exists when *society* [e.g., church, state] discriminates against the dead"

---

[9] Rojek (1993:117) offers the following quotation from Andy Warhol: " 'If you want to know all about Andy Warhol . . . just look at the surface of my paintings and films and me, there I am. There's nothing behind it'."

(Baudrillard, 1976/1993:144). In a sense, cemeteries were our first ghettos. Baudrillard sees a historical process here (another seeming grand narrative). In primitive societies the dying and dead were part of society; they were involved in the process of symbolic exchange (during ceremonies, for example) and its reversibility. "*Symbolic* death . . . is exchanged in a social ritual of feasting" (Baudrillard, 1976/1993:147). Exchange does not come to an end just because life has stopped. However, over time the dead have been progressively excluded (the Enlightenment and the rise of capitalism play crucial roles here) until now where they have ceased to exist; the symbolic exchange with the dead has been ruptured; we've ended "the symbolic reversibility of death" (Baudrillard, 1976/1993:147). To be dead is no longer normal; indeed, it is an anomaly and nothing is more unthinkable than death. But our society is atypical: "Every other culture says that death begins before death, that life goes on after life, and that it is impossible to distinguish life from death" (Baudrillard, 1976/1993:159). It is we (Westerners) who are the "primitives" when it comes to dealing with death.

Baudrillard also sees the treatment of death as anticipating the way in which life will be treated. That is, death is controlled "in anticipation of the future confinement of life in its entirety" (Baudrillard, 1976/1993:130). The separation of the dead from the living anticipates a variety of other dichotomous separations ("The dead were the first to play this role" [Baudrillard, 1976/1993:169])—subject/object, conscious/unconscious, individual/social body, man/labor. Just as we have separated the dead, we have segregated the aged into ghettos (homes for old people, retirement communities). We have segregated them to colonize and control them. In contrast, "In other social formations, old age actually exists as the symbolic pivot of the group" (Baudrillard, 1976/1993:163). Because we are separating the old, we are suffering an "early social death" (Baudrillard, 1976/1993:163). In sum, contemporary society excludes rather than engages in symbolic exchange.

Baudrillard also links the contemporary exclusion of death to capitalism. (Communist societies are also indicted for seeking to abolish death.) At least in part because death was excluded, people in capitalism have become obsessed with death. In an effort to cope with this, they shifted their focus to the accumulation of money and goods.

The contemporary treatment of death is also linked to rationalized, bureaucratized societies. Baudrillard's (1976/1993:177) critique of the rational treatment of death is part of a broader critique of "a meticulously regulated universe." Life (and death) "is no longer anything but a doleful, defensive bookkeeping, locking every risk into its sarcophagus" (Baudrillard, 1976/1993:178). All rational interventions in individual lives, by the state, medicine, reason, science, can be seen as terrorist acts. In fact, people seem to recognize this by engaging in such symbolic acts as refusing to wear seat belts (a fatal strategy [see below] undertaken by the object). But always, the contemporary world remains vulnerable to symbolic exchange in general, and death in particular: "*An infinitesimal injection of death would immediately create such excess and ambivalence that the play of values would completely collapse*" (Baudrillard, 1976/1993:154).

The denial of death has not eliminated death; on the contrary, Baudrillard believes that ours has become a death culture: "the law of symbolic exchange has not changed one iota. We continue to exchange with the dead, even those denied rest, those for whom rest is prohibited. We simply pay with our own death and our anxiety about death for the rupture of symbolic exchanges with them" (Baudrillard, 1976/1993:134). Instead of symbolic exchange with the dead, we now face death alone. As a result, we've created "an anguish concerning death . . . psychological hell" (Baudrillard, 1976/1993:146).

Instead of dealing with the dead, we make the dead appear alive through the funereal arts. The dead therefore become a "stuffed simulacrum of life" (Baudrillard, 1976/1993:181). Made into simulated life forms, the dead lose their right (a right we all have) to difference.

We have created the notion of "natural death," but this is a concept that is devoid of meaning and leaves the social group without a role to play. Death has become banal, commonplace, and policed. (In contrast, to "the primitives, there is no 'natural' death: every death is social, public and collective" [Baudrillard, 1976/1993:164].) Each of us buries our dead alone. "To us, the dead have just passed away and no longer have anything to exchange . . . the dead are subtracted from the total in an economic operation . . . What banality!" (Baudrillard, 1976/1993:164). Because we have made everyday death banal, we focus instead on violent death. In it, we see something like the primitive sacrifice: "The chance accident or catastrophe, which we therefore experience as *socially* symbolic events of the highest importance, as sacrifices" (Baudrillard, 1976/1993:165).

While Baudrillard is critical of the modern treatment of death, he seems to praise cannibalism as a model of symbolic exchange: "This devouring is a social act, a *symbolic* act, that aims to maintain a tissue of bonds with dead men or the very thing they devour. . . . Devouring . . . is a *social* act . . . the transformation of the flesh into a symbolic relation, the transmutation of the body in social exchange" (Baudrillard, 1976/1993:138).

In segregating death, contemporary society has robbed us of our last chance to engage in symbolic exchange with the system: "It is necesssary to rob everyone of the last possibility of *giving* themselves their own death as the last 'great escape' from a life laid down by the system" (Baudrillard, 1976/1993:177).

America

As pointed out earlier, America is for Baudrillard a model of the kind of contemporary world he is describing.[10] Baudrillard (1986/1989:9) sees an analogy between the deserts of America's west and its western cities; the cities have an "equally desert-like banality." Thus, America is characterized by both natural and social deserts:

• Most generally, "America is a desert" (Baudrillard, 1986/1989:99) and that is true of it culturally, intellectually, and aesthetically.

• Los Angeles is described as "an inhabited fragment of the desert" (Baudrillard, 1986/1989:53).

---

[10] For a critique of *America,* see Vidich (1991).

- California is described as "the world centre of the simulacrum and the inauthentic" (Baudrillard, 1986/1989:102).
- Californian "culture itself is a desert" (Baudrillard, 1986/1989:126).

America, its states, its cities, and its deserts seem to be devoid of meaning; they are all sites in which meaning has been exterminated. Baudrillard even finds a process of the "desertification of signs and men" (Baudrillard, 1986/1989:63). Thus, in his travels in America, Baudrillard (1986/1989:5) "sought the finished form of the future catastrophe."

Specifically, in the case of the New York marathon, Baudrillard finds a race that has lost the meaning of the original marathon; people are (ecstatically) running the race merely to do it; to feel alive; to say that they did it. He finds the same meaninglessness[11] in the graffiti that defaces New York and many other cities. Graffiti artists seem to be doing little more than proving that they can do what they do. All of these signs are being produced by the graffiti artist, but there is no essence beneath the signs.

As Baudrillard (1986/1989:27) puts it more generally, "For me there is no truth of America." Later, Baudrillard says:

> America is the original version of modernity . . . no past and no founding truth . . . it lives in a perpetual present. Having seen no slow, centuries-long accumulation of a principle of truth, it lives in perpetual simulation, in a perpetual present of signs.

> (Baudrillard, 1986/1989:76)

Not only are there no truths in America, there are no lies either; all there are are simulations. The real and the imaginary have come to an end in America, and it is this fate that awaits European societies. America is a paradise, albeit a "mournful, monotonous and superficial" paradise (Baudrillard, 1986/1989:98).

America has all the characteristics Baudrillard associates with the contemporary (postmodern?) world:

- "It is hyperreality" (Baudrillard, 1986/1989:28);
- it is "the perfect simulacrum" (Baudrillard, 1986/1989:28);
- it has depthless, empty emotion such as the smile of Ronald Reagan;
- it is a world of superficial images seemingly "invented with the screen in mind" (Baudrillard, 1986/1989:55), where "life is cinema" (Baudrillard, 1986/1989:101);
- the "authentic" are things like Disneyland and TV (Kroker, 1985);
- it possesses decentered cities where we can see "the whole of life as a drive-in" (Baudrillard, 1986/1989:66);
- it is characterized by an absence of difference (the androgyny of Michael Jackson is used, again, as an example);
- it is a world of kitsch in which the aesthetic and higher values have disappeared;

---

[11] As we will see, Baudrillard also has a more positive view of graffiti and graffiti artists.

• it is a world of meaningless movement with traffic on America's freeways "coming from nowhere, going nowhere" (Baudrillard, 1986/1989:125).

These are America's problems, but because of the influence of America they are becoming everyone's problems, and they will eventually be found throughout the rest of the world.

Baudrillard closes by wondering whether the United States is as powerful as is often assumed. He asks, "is it still really powerful or merely simulating power?" (Baudrillard, 1986/1989:115). He gives the example of the invasion of Grenada and describes it as a "risk-free scenario, calculated production, artificial event— success ensured" (Baudrillard, 1986/1989:109). He concludes that the United States is no longer a world power but merely a simulation of such a power.

If you think some or all of what Baudrillard has to say about America (and many other things) is outrageous, you may not be far wrong. In a reflection on *America,* Baudrillard (in Gane, 1993:132) says the following: "Let me specify that *America* should not be read as a realist text. Its subject matter being a fiction itself, I've exaggerated this quality, without actually entering into science fiction." To put it another way, since America is a hyperreal society, it takes a hyperreal work to analyze it critically.[12]

Other Issues

There are many other issues that could be discussed in this section, but let us make do with a few more derived from Baudrillard's (1992/1994) most recent work, *The Illusion of the End.* One is his argument that we have become obsessed with "useless perfection." He gives as an example what he calls the "stereophonic effect"; that is, as our stereo equipment grows increasingly sophisticated, the music we listen to has fewer and fewer flaws. However, we are led to wonder: Is this really music? This is nowhere clearer than in the case of the compact disc, which, while it eliminates the flaws associated with audio tapes or records, produces sound that in the view of many experts is not "really" music.

Baudrillard sees this as but an illustration of the general principle that the closer we seem to get to the heart of things, the more those things seem to disappear:

Right at the heart of news, history threatens to disappear. At the heart of hi-fi, music threatens to disappear. At the heart of experimentation, the object of science threatens to disappear. At the heart of pornography, sexuality threatens to disappear. Everywhere we find the same stereophonic effect, the same effect of absolute proximity to the real, the same effect of simulation.

(Baudrillard, 1992/1994:6)

---

[12] Paradoxically, in another work, Baudrillard (1980–1985/1990:209) says, "I shall never forgive anyone who passes a condescending or contemptuous judgment on America."

It is clear that Baudrillard links this general principle to his key concept of a simulation. Thus, for example, a compact disc is a simulation, an increasingly perfect simulation (compared, say, to an LP, another simulation) in which the "real" grows even more remote.

This leads Baudrillard to argue that we need to resist calling upon, and using, all of our resources. Great resources were brought to bear in the creation of CDs, but the net result was more and greater simulation. More generally, Baudrillard (1992/1994:102) argues that when we draw upon and use all of our resources, the results kill "metaphors, dreams, illusions and utopias by their absolute realization."

In another line of argument, Baudrillard sees us living in an era of nonevents; the age of epic events has passed. The irony is that while things no longer really occur, they still seem to happen (the Gulf War as a simulated nuclear war would be an example). Part of the reason for the dominance of nonevents is that we now live in an age of deterrence (Bogard, 1991). Rather than seeking to produce events, we are devoting increasing time and energy to causing a variety of things *not* to occur. For example, we engage in a wide range of activities (jogging, for one) to ward off death by making ourselves more perfect, more immortal.

We are also depicted as living in a nostalgic age, interested in reviving many things from our past. Instead of fomenting revolution, or creating grand new ideas, we focus on reanalyzing and reinterpreting the past. It is in the context of this issue that Baudrillard engages in one of his most sustained analyses of postmodernity, which he associates with this recycling of the past. Postmodernity involves repentenance for the sins of modernity and "the recycling of past forms, the exalting of residues, rehabilitation by *bricolage,* eclectic sentimentality" (Baudrillard, 1992/1994:35). Beyond that, we are deconstructing our past in "almost a viral, epidemic form" (Baudrillard, 1992/1994:33). Thus, whereas modernity was concerned with "the market, ideology, profit and utopia," postmodernity is "unreal and speculative, lacking even the notion of production, profit and progress" (Baudrillard, 1992/1994:36).

Baudrillard is also led to reflect on postmodern individualism, which he gloomily associates with increased penetration and control of the individual at the micro-level:

> This "post-modern" individualism arises . . . out of a *liberalization* of slave networks and circuits, that is, an individual diffraction of programmed ensembles, a metamorphosis of the macro-structures into innumerable particles which bear within them all the stigmata of the networks and circuits—each one forming its own micro-network and micro-circuit, each one reviving for itself, in its micro-universe, the now useless totalitarianism of the whole.

(Baudrillard, 1992/1994:107)

Now little more than a node in a broader system, the individual can no longer be alienated from herself, can no longer even differ from herself. No longer different from other or self, the individual grows indifferent to time, space, politics, sex, and so on. We live in the age of terminal boredom.

ARE THERE ANY GROUNDS FOR HOPE?

Chastened by the failures of revolutionary movements, Baudrillard offers little, or nothing, in the way of hope for a revolutionary solution to the problems he associates with contemporary society. One place in his early work in which he seems to come close is equating signification with terrorism against symbolic exchange and concluding: "only total revolution, theoretical and practical, can restore the symbolic in the demise of the sign and of value. Even signs must burn" (Baudrillard, 1972/1981:163). In his later work, however, Baudrillard (in Gane, 1993:123) not only rejects social revolution but comes to believe that "we can no longer [even] fix the way things are going." Thus, even social reform seems to be out of the question. Not only that, the reader gets the clear sense that the efforts to respond to contemporary problems are as dangerous as the problems themselves. If anything at all is to be done, it should not be rationally planned and organized. As Baudrillard (1990/1993:105) puts it, "we should entertain no illusion about the effectiveness of any kind of rational intervention."

Why does Baudrillard hold out no hope for revolution, reform, or any kind of rational intervention? The answer, at least in part, is traceable to his views on the code. That is, because the code is omnipresent it will inform, constrain, and ultimately undermine any efforts to deal with current problems. In effect, Baudrillard concludes that the code cannot be dealt with because it is everywhere, including the efforts to deal with it.

However, even if there are no rational responses, are there any nonrational or irrational responses to our contemporary problems? As we will see in this section, Baudrillard does offer a number of such ideas on responding to the problems he has described. Thus, we agree with Genosko (1944:103): "To conclude [as most observers have] that Baudrillard's vision is dark, nihilistic and hopeless is unwarranted."

Seduction

The concept of seduction is a close relative to the idea of symbolic exchange. Indeed, Genosko argues that it is with this concept that Baudrillard gives symbolic exchange a new face. As was pointed out earlier, symbolic exchange "haunts" the contemporary world as the nonrational alternative to it. In effect, symbolic exchange plays much the same role in Baudrillard's work as does species-being in Marx's work. That is, it is not only the base of Baudrillard's critique of the contemporary world but also at the root of his image of an alternative to it. While symbolic exchange plays these (and other) roles in Baudrillard's theory, seduction can be seen, at least in part, as a way of responding to the problems associated with that world.

We ordinarily think that what we want is to attain complete clarity. However, Baudrillard rejects this, arguing that complete clarity is *obscene,* leaving everything exhibited and visible. Rather, Baudrillard prefers the *scene* that involves absence and illusion. "For something to be meaningful, there has to be a scene, and for there to be a scene, there has to be an illusion, a minimum of illusion, of imaginary moment, of defiance to the real, which carries you off, seduces or revolts you" (Baudrillard, 1983/1990:65). The scene can also be described as "enchanted space." Scenes are arenas of free play without the usual ludicrous restraints, but "with the irruption of obscenity, this scene is lost . . . everything has its reasons. . . . There is no longer . . . play" (Baudrillard, in Gane, 1993:61). While scenes may be visible, the *obscene* is hypervisible. Pornography in general is a good example of the obscene; a more specific instance offered by Baudrillard is the pornographic effort to show close-ups of the female orgasm. Passion is characteristic of a scene, but it disappears in the obscene, which is cool, white.

Most generally, "obscenity takes on all the semblances of modernity" (Baudrillard, 1983/1990:58). Seemingly everything in the modern world is visible; everything is filmed, broadcast, videotaped, and so on. We have become voyeurists, obsessed with ourselves. We are subjected to "the rampant obscenity of uninterrupted social commentary" (Baundrillard, 1983/1990:59). And then, with "everything oversignified, meaning itself becomes impossible to grasp" (Baudrillard, 1983/1990:60). The social world has become promiscuous; social prostitution is rampant. Polls, talk shows, and the media more generally force us to tell our secrets, even when there are none to tell. Baudrillard (1983/1990:68) talks of the "pornography of information and communication." We have become over-informed; "buried alive under information" (Baudrillard, 1980–1985/1990:90).

Instead, and as a response to the obscene contemporary world, Baudrillard advocates the "play and power of illusion" (Baudrillard, 1983/1990:51). Illusion lies at the base of seduction, and for Baudrillard (1983/1990:51) the choice is between seduction and terror: "that which is no longer illusion is dead and inspires terror." Examples of things without illusion (in addition to pornography) are cadavers, clones, and, increasingly, much of the contemporary world. To ward off terror and death, we must rediscover and remake illusion.

We ordinarily associate seduction with women (and Baudrillard has been criticized for this[13]), but it is better to think of seduction as "games with signs" (Kellner, 1994:14). We tend to think of seduction and illusion as false and therefore to be rejected in our search for the "truth." However, to Baudrillard illusion is not false and does not involve false signs; rather it is senseless, involving senseless signs. "There is no real, there never was a real. Seduction knows this, and preserves its enigma" (Baudrillard, 1983/1990:108). More concretely, Baudrillard (1983/1990:175) argues: "Our fundamental destiny is not to exist and survive, as we think: it is to appear and disappear. That alone seduces and fascinates us. That alone is scene and ceremony."

Baudrillard's focus on seduction is derived, at least in part, from a rejection of Freud and his focus on the desire of the subject. (Just as he sought to liberate Marx from the mirror of production, as pointed out earlier, he seeks to liberate Freud

---

[13] Baudrillard (in Gane, 1993:86) says that there is a "privileged relation between femininity and seduction." However, he does make it clear that femininity is not restricted to women: "Femininity appears in certain individuals, men or women" (Baudrillard, in Gane, 1993:111). For some of the controversy surrounding this, see Plant (1993).

from the "mirror of desire.") Rather than the desire of the subject, Baudrillard (1983/1990:139) offers a focus on the seductive power of the object: "What makes you exist is not the force of your desire (wholly a nineteenth-century imaginary of energy and economy), but the play of the world and seduction; it is the passion of playing and being played, it is the passion of illusion and appearance."

The power (and the hope) of the masses (and more generally the subject) comes from their ability to seduce the elites; "only the object is seductive . . . all initiative and power are on the other side, the side of the object" (Baudrillard, 1983/1990:119). Further,

> Is it not rather the seducer who is seduced, and does the initiative not revert secretly to the object? The seducer believes he envelopes it in his strategy, but he is caught by the lure of his banal strategy and it is rather the object that envelopes him in its fatal strategy.

> (Baudrillard, 1983/1990:120)

Baudrillard (1983/1990:148) offers a fatal theory (more on this below) of "the world prey to the law of things, that is, to total predestination." Further,

> this is a world where there is no such thing as chance. Nothing is dead, nothing is inert, nothing is disconnnected, uncorrelated or aleatory. Everything, on the contrary, is fatally, admirably connected—not at all according to rational relations (which are neither fatal nor admirable), but according to an incessant cycle of metamorphoses.

> (Baudrillard, 1983/1950:150)

More specifically, Baudrillard (1983/1990:181) associates fatality with the object, the masses: "the object is considered more cunning, cynical, talented than the subject, for which it lies in wait. The metamorphoses, the ruses, the strategies of the object surpass the subject's understanding." Fatality is the strategy of objects, the masses.

Baudrillard sees the world ruled by destiny, magic, seduction; these provide its secret organization. The enemy of all of this is rationality. The effort to understand and deal with the world rationally will end in catastrophe—"resolving all totality into causality or probability. That is true entropy" (Baudrillard, 1983/1990:155). Instead, "Incalculable connections are the stuff of our dreams, but also of our daily bread" (Baudrillard, 1983/1990:155). The power of seduction lies in its reversibility. That is, in seduction signs are received, and they, in turn, are immediately sent back. To put this another way, seduction involves symbolic exchange.

A good example of seduction and what has happened to it in the modern world is art. To Baudrillard (in Gane, 1993:144), the goal of art is to "posit the power of illusion against reality . . . it was always trying to *seduce* the reality of things." However, art in the modern world is no longer involved in illusion and seduction but rather in simulation. More generally, in the hyperreal world of simulation it is more and more difficult to find any illusion or seduction.

Baudrillard (1983/1990:156) argues that we all welcome catastrophe: "The only real pleasure in the world is watching things 'turn' into catastrophe, to emerge finally from determinacy and indeterminacy, from chance and necessity, and enter the realm of vertiginous connections." We want not the assurance of predictability but the lack of assurrance associated with vertigo. Seduction is one way of achieving vertiginous-ness and thereby counteracting the numbing control of contemporary society.

Fatal Strategies

As is clear above, seduction is one example of what Baudrillard describes as a se-ries of fatal strategies. His thinking on such strategies is linked to his view that the social sciences have traditionally focused on the subject. Postmodern social theory in general, and Baudrillard in particular, seek to "decenter" the social sciences by focusing on the object. The social sciences have always seen the subject as essen-tial, "the royal road of subjectivity" (Baudrillard, 1983/1990:111), but to Bau-drillard it is the object, and its fate, that is essential. While we usually think of sub-jects as active and objects as passive, to Baudrillard the object "isn't passive and yet it isn't a subject" (Baudrillard, in Gane, 1993:51). The object can be almost anything (the consumer goods discussed in the previous chapter are objects), al-though from a variety of sociological points of view, it is most often the "mass" that is considered the object. The masses do not want to be, and cannot be, liber-ated. Their power lies in their silence, their absence of desire:

> atonal, amorphous, abysmal, they exercise a passive and opaque sovereignty; they say nothing, but subtly, perhaps like animals in their brute indifference (although the masses are "essentially" rather hormonic or endocronic—that is, antibodies), they neutralize the whole political scene and discourse.

(Baudrillard,1983/1990:94)

The masses absorb, feed off, the accelerating power of the system. Baudrillard (1983/1990:95) describes "the stupefying power of the mass-as-object . . . an absolute power, a power of death over the social body." The masses are dangerous, dragging "power down to its fall" (Baudrillard, 1983/1990:95). Thus, objects possess fatal strategies, and these stand in contrast to the banal strategies of the subject. In describ-ing what he means by a fatal strategy, Baudrillard (in Gane, 1993:50) says, "some-thing responds of its own accord, something from which it is impossible to escape."

The power of the masses comes, ironically, from their lack of knowledge. For example, they leave it to advertising and information systems to persuade them, to make choices for them. But who has the power here? While we usually think the power resides with the systems, it could be argued that it is the masses who have the power. One can even view the masses as snobs delegating annoying choices to others; the elites in charge of advertising and other systems relieve the masses of the tiresome process of needing to make choices. The masses have "the ironic power of withdrawal, of non-desire, non-knowledge, silence, absorption then ex-pulsion of all powers, wills, of all enlightenment and depths of meaning" (Bau-drillard, 1983/1990:99). Instead of looking at the masses as alienated, unconscious, and repressed, Baudrillard (1983/1990:99) argues that we can look at the masses "as possessing a delusive, illusive, allusive strategy, corresponding to an uncon-scious that is finally ironic, joyous and seductive."

The silence of the masses is not a sign of their alienation but of their power: "the silence was a massive reply through withdrawal, that the silence was a strategy . . . they [the masses] *nullify* meaning. And this is truly a power. . . . Basically they absorb all systems and they refract them in emptiness" (Baudrillard, in Gane, 1993:87–88). In other words, the masses are the "black hole" of the social world. The masses are silent because they are overwhelmed with information and, in any case, there is no way of reversing the flow of that information from the media. (In fact, we are not to think of the masses as a social phenomenon [after all, the social is dead] involving millions of people but rather an inertial "form" created by the overwhelming flood of information.) Thus, a strategy of silence, of inertia, develops among the masses. The silence of the masses is fatal. It is one of their fatal strategies, strategies that indicate that the "object is more subtle, more ingenious, than the subject" (Gane, 1991b:174). Ultimately, these fatal strategies lead the world in the direction of a "downward spiral of the worst outcomes into catastrophic outcomes" (Gane, 1991b:207).

Baudrillard has called the revenge of the masses, and of objects in general, the "revenge of the crystal." Of the crystal, Baudrillard says, it is

> the object, the pure object, the pure event, something which no longer really has an origin or an end . . . There is today a possibility that the object will say something to us, but there is also above all the possibility that it will take its revenge!
>
> (Baudrillard, in Gane, 1993:51)

Baudrillard sees objects in general, and the masses in particular, as "evil genies." And these evil genies are, in Baudrillard's (1983/1990:7) view, likely to be "victorious over . . . the subject." The masses (and subjects) are "evil"[14] because they are unreasonable: "Unreason is victorious in every sense, which is the very principle of Evil" (Baudrillard, 1983/1990:7). According to the principle of evil, "any order exists only to be disobeyed, attacked, exceeded, and dismantled" (Baudrillard, 1983/1990:77). The mass is a "genie" in the sense that, magically, it is the mass and not those who supposedly dominate it who are likely to emerge victorious. How are they going to win out?

> Things have found a way of avoiding a dialectics of meaning that was beginning to bore them: by proliferating indefinitely, increasing their potential, outbidding themselves in an ascension to the limit, an obscenity that henceforth becomes their immanent finality and senseless reason.
>
> (Baudrillard, 1983/1990:7)

The victory of the masses will not be a dazzling revolution "but obscure and ironic; It won't be dialectical, it will be fatal" (Baudrillard, 1983/1990:96). It will not be a

---

[14] As we have seen in this chapter, Baudrillard uses the concept "evil" in a variety of different ways and he does not take the time to reconcile these differences.

revolution, "but . . . massive *devolution,* . . . a massive delegation of power and re-sponsibility. . . . massive *de-volition* and withdrawal of the will" (Baudrillard, 1983/1990:97).

More specifically, the masses are evil genies because, as we saw previously, they respond to the simulations of the polls with simulations of their own. "This is what we could call the evil genie of the object, the evil genie of the masses, eter-nally blocking the truth of the social and its analyses" (Baudrillard, 1983/1990:93). Because of the irony involved in this, Baudrillard sees hope in ironic theory rather than the critical theory that has been relied upon by Marxists.

The answer to the ecstatic "acceleration of networks" characteristic of contem-porary society is not to try to be "faster" than them but to turn instead to the tor-toise-like masses characterized by "insoluble immobility, the slower than slow: in-ertia and silence, inertia insoluble by effort, silence insoluble by dialogue" (Baudrillard, 1983/1990:8). The masses are always underestimated, but their "deep instinct remains the symbolic murder of the political class" (Baudrillard, 1983/1990:94). One of the ways in which the masses do this is by challenging the subject and pushing "it back upon its own impossible position" (Baudrillard, 1983/1990:113). The mass is also seen as a mirror, "that which returns the subject to its mortal transparency" (Baudrillard, 1983/1990:113).

For example, as we have seen, the general view is that the masses are being se-duced by the media, but Baudrillard argues that it may well be the masses that are seducing the media. Further, the media may provide "the surface which the masses take advantage of to remain silent" (Baudrillard, 1983/1990:80).

While Baudrillard sees hope in the masses, he rejects the grand narrative of the Marxists (and others) who envisioned a grand conclusion culminating in the over-throw of the capitalist system. More generally, "it is the end of linearity, the end of finality . . . it is also the end of the origin, of the possibility of going back, in a lin-ear fashion, to the origin" (Baudrillard, in Gane, 1993:175). Baudrillard (1983/1990:24) concludes, "we are no longer in the age of grandiose collapses and resurrections, of games of death and eternity, but of little fractal events, smooth an-nihilations and gradual slides." Thus, the current social world will end not with a bang but with a series of whimpers.

The revolt of the masses will be much like the victory of cancer cells (another object) over the body. Both the masses and cancer cells can be seen as uncontrol-lable, undisciplined, nondialectial, and subliminal. Both cancer and the masses are hypertelic. In their mindless, limitless increase the masses will destroy the social body in the same way that cancer cells destroy the physical body.

Baudrillard believes that groups, even revolutionary groups, can attain their ends, but they cannot attain them directly. Rather, he argues that groups must aim "to the side, beyond, off center"; in this way, "duplicity is strategic and fatal" (Baudrillard, 1983/1990:77, 78).

More generally, Baudrillard (in Gane, 1993:169) announces, "I'm on the side of the principle of evil." This is based on the premise that we live in a world of end-less and hopeless repetition. In such a world, "We must ourselves inject some evil, or at least some decay, some virulence, and forge another type of discourse, per-haps to awaken all that a bit" (Baudrillard, in Gane, 1993:176).

Other Ways Out

Given the dominance of the code, revolutionary potential is seen, at least in Bau-drillard's early work, as lying among those who are excluded from the code—stu-dents, blacks, females, and so on. They take as their objective the abolition of the code. Given this new objective and the new revolutionary forces, "the working class is no longer the gold standard of revolts and contradictions" (Baudrillard, 1973/1975:140).

Intellectuals need to adopt an ironic stance toward the contemporary world. This means that they should "embrace contradictions, to exercise irony, to take the opposite tack, to exploit rifts and reversibility, even to fly in the face of the lawful and the factual" (Baudrillard, 1990/1993:39). The latter is related to pataphysics and using science fiction to turn the system against itself. Obviously there is no concrete revolutionary strategy here; theoretical rather than practical violence is involved. Thus, there is no actual impact, but could we expect any in a world with-out reality?

Baudrillard seems to hold out hope in speech as contrasted to discourse that is controlled by the code. Those excluded by the code, such as the groups mentioned above, can rebel through their use of speech. But, he is not arguing for some ulti-mate massive outpouring against the code. We ought not to wait for such a future; "Each man is totally there at each instant. . . . The utopia is here in all the energies that are raised against political economy. . . . Utopia . . . wants only the spoken word; and it wants to lose itself in it" (Baudrillard, 1973/1975:166–167).

Baudrillard also sees another fatal problem (other fatal problems were discussed in the preceding section) within modern society dominated by the code. That is, such societies are destined to symbolic disintegration; they are unable to reproduce themselves symbolically. Once again, Baudrillard (1973/1975:147) sees modern society as being haunted by the spectre of symbolic exchange, where "nothing can be given without being returned, nothing is ever won without something being lost, nothing is ever produced without something being destroyed, nothing is ever spo-ken without being answered." In contrast, the power of the code is traceable to the fact that it is capable of giving a variety of things but is incapable of receiving any-thing; it allows no possibility of return. The gift (in this case, from the code) is the source of power, and the only way to undermine it is through a countergift that is unable to be returned. Thus, instead of "direct, dialectical revolution" against a "real" infrastructure, Baudrillard (1976/1993:36) urges the "reversal, the incessant reversibility of the counter-gift and, conversely, the seizing of power by unilateral exercise of the gift." In sum,

> the only solution is to turn the principle of its power back against the system itself: the impossibility of responding or returning. To *defy the system with a gift to which it cannot*

respond save by its own collapse and death. Nothing, not even the system, can avoid the symbolic obligation, and it is in this trap that the only chance of a catastrophe for capital remains. . . . The system must *itself commit suicide in response to the multiplied challenge of death and suicide.*

(Baudrillard, 1976/1993:36–37)

Baudrillard sees the code as growing increasingly coherent, but as it does it simultaneously (dialectically?) grows progressively unstable. Thus, he sees a fatal, catastrophic flaw in the seemingly unassailable code:

Every system that approaches perfect operativity simultaneously approaches its downfall. . . . A gentle push in the right place is enough to bring it crashing down. . . . They collapse under the weight of their own monstrosity, like fossilized dinosaurs, and immediately decompose. This is the *fatality* [italics added] of every system committed by its own logic to total perfection and therefore to total defectiveness, to absolute infallibility and therefore irrevocable breakdown: the aim of all bound energies is their own death. This is why the only strategy is *catastrophic,* and not dialectical at all. Things must be pushed to the limit, where quite naturally they collapse and are inverted.

(Baudrillard, 1976/1993:4)

Given the transition from the dominance of capitalism to the dominance of the code, the latter cannot be destroyed by a direct dialectical revolution. The system cannot be confronted in the realm of the real but rather must be confronted in the symbolic realm. "The revolution is everywhere where an exchange crops up . . . that shatters the finality of the models, the mediation of the code . . . the revolution is symbolic or it is not a revolution at all" (Baudrillard, 1976/1993:205). In that realm, the answer lies in "reversal, the incessant reversibility of the counter-gift and, conversely, the seizing of power by unilateral exercise of the gift. . . . We must therefore displace everything into the sphere of the symbolic, where challenge, reversal and overbidding are the law, *so that we can respond to death only by an equal or superior death*" (Baudrillard, 1976/1993:36). We are, in a sense, reversing the power of the system, which is the fact that it gives gifts without the possibility of return. The objective is to "*defy the system with a gift to which it cannot respond save its own collapse and death.* Nothing, not even the system, can avoid the symbolic obligation, and it is in this trap that the only chance of a catastrophe for capital remains" (Baudrillard, 1976/1993:36–37). The only option open to the system in such a situation is to commit suicide. Power comes from unilateral giving; the abolition of power comes from the counter-gift, which cannot be returned.

Reckless squandering, like the counter-gift, poses a threat to the system: "We would like to see a functional squandering everywhere so as to bring about symbolic destruction. . . . Only sumptuous and useless expenditure has meaning" (Baudrillard, 1976/1993:94, 155–156).

We can gain another sense of responses to contemporary realities in Baudrillard's thinking on the contemporary city and the graffiti artists it has spawned (although, as we saw above, Baudrillard appears to give up on them later in his work). We have gone from the urban/industrial society to a society and its cities characterized by "a riot of signs." In other words, in one of Baudrillard's more quotable (and famous) quotations, "metallurgy has become semiurgy" (Baudrillard, 1976/1993:77, 79). Similarly, the "city is no longer the politico-industrial zone that it was in the nineteenth century, it is the zone of signs, the media and the code" (Baudrillard, 1976/1993:77). Based on signs, the city is vulnerable on the level of signs. In this sense, graffitists represent a threat to the city since they reverse the process of signs emanating from the city and respond with signs of their own. Furthermore, they are revolutionary not because their signs or slogans are revolutionary but because their "message is zero" (Baudrillard, 1976/1993:83). More generally, Baudrillard (1976/1993:80) argues that we must "attack by means of difference, dismantling the network of codes, attacking coded differences by means of an uncodeable absolute difference, over which the system will stumble and disintegrate." There is no need for organized masses and raised political consciousness; what we need are graffitists "to scramble the signals of urbania" (Baudrillard, 1976/1993:80).

Death takes on particular importance to Baudrillard (1976/1993:4) in his thinking about an alternative to the dominance of the code: "Perhaps death and death alone, the reversibility of death, belongs to a higher order than the code. Only symbolic disorder can bring about an interruption in the code." Here, Baudrillard does not mean by death a real event that marks the end of a subject or a body. Rather, death is "a *form* in which the determinacy of the subject and of value is lost" (Baudrillard, 1976/1993:5). Thus, death is not only something awaiting us at the end of the system but is always stalking the code and threatening it with indeterminacy and symbolic extermination. As a system of symbols, the code can only be combatted by symbols, specifically the reversed symbols of death. Thus, symbolic death in general poses a threat to the system. For example, in terms of capitalism, "If political economy is the most rigorous attempt to put an end to death, it is clear that only death can put an end to political economy" (Baudrillard, 1976/1993:187). More specifically, suicide, because it is a form of nonrational death, a way of giving our lives away (a gift) with no possibility of return, also threatens the system.

One way of summing up much of what Baudrillard has to say about responding to the problems of the modern world is caught by the concept, "the strength of the weak" (Genosko, 1994:72; Genosko, 1992). All of the possibilities outlined above derive their strength from their weakness—objects, the masses, seducers, graffiti artists, the dead, and so on. This is a striking idea that, while not original to Baudrillard, reaches its apogee in his work. Here is what Baudrillard has to say about the strength of another weak group—children:

> Whereas adults make children believe that they, the adults, are adults, children for their part *let* adults believe that they, the children, are children. Of these two strategies the second is the subtler . . . their [children's] vitality and development announce the eventual destruction of the superior-adult-world that surrounds them. Childhood haunts the adult universe as a subtle and deadly presence.

> (Baudrillard, 1990/1993:168–169)

In a world in which it is no longer possible to believe in the powerful, Baudrillard sees hope in children, indeed all of those who are weak.

In *The Illusion of the End,* Baudrillard (1992/1994:120) discusses the possibility of a *"poetic reversibility of events."* Thus, there is hope in the weak poet and the enchantment of poetry:

> Against the simulation of a linear history "in progress," we have to accord a privileged status to these backfires, these malign deviations, these *lightweight catastrophes* which cripple an empire much more effectively than any great upheavals.

(Baudrillard, 1992/1994:121; italics added)

SUMMARY

In this chapter, we picked up the review of Baudrillard's work by focusing on some of his major analyses and critiques of contemporary society as well as some of his thoughts on responding to those problems. Much attention was devoted to the code and its control over what transpires in society. Similarly important are Baudrillard's thoughts on the simulated, hyperreal character of society. One of Baudrillard's more recent views is that we have entered a new, fractal order characterized by meaningless and endless proliferation. This is a world that is ecstatic and resembles the hypertelic growth of cancer, AIDS, obesity, and the like. The way in which death has come to be treated can be seen as emblematic of the way in which many other matters are handled in contemporary society.

Then we turned our attention to some of Baudrillard's thoughts on responses to the problems he has described. It is important to reiterate that while Baudrillard is often thought of as a nihilist, he does have much to say about such coping methods. In this regard, Baudrillard accords great importance to seduction, which is closely related in his thinking on symbolic exchange. In a world in which signs are destroying symbols, Baudrillard sees great need for more symbolic behavior like seduction. Then there are a number of fatal strategies open to a wide range of objects. These are not rational in character, but they are likely to bring the system ever closer to catastrophe. A number of other responses are detailed such as giving gifts to the system and the reckless expenditure of resources. Thus, there are things to be done, or that are being done unknown to those doing them, but it remains unclear whether the system will devolve as a result or whether the code will grow ever more powerful.

OTHER FRENCH POSTMODERN THINKERS: DERRIDA, DELEUZE AND GUATTARI, LYOTARD, LACAN, VIRILIO

JACQUES DERRIDA: GRAMMATOLOGY AND WRITING

GILLES DELEUZE AND FELIX GUATTARI: TOWARD SCHIZOANALYSIS

JEAN-FRANÇOIS LYOTARD: THE DEATH OF THE GRAND NARRATIVE

JACQUES LACAN: THE IMAGINARY, THE SYMBOLIC, THE REAL

PAUL VIRILIO: DROMOLOGY

*T*HE last four chapters have been devoted to the work of two French thinkers—Michel Foucault and Jean Baudrillard—whose work is central to our understanding of the development of postmodern social theory. In this chapter we deal, in much less depth, with several other thinkers associated with French postmodern social theory. Although they are dealt with in less detail, that is not to say that they are of less importance to our understanding of postmodernism.

In previous chapters we have surveyed a wide range, even the entire corpus, of a theorist's work. To make this book manageable, in this chapter we will not allow ourselves that luxury. In the main, we will need to settle for a discussion of centrally important pieces of work rather than an entire *oeuvre*. In this chapter we will deal with key ideas associated with important French poststructuralists/postmodernists—Jacques Derrida's work, especially his ideas on "grammatology" and "writing," Gilles Deleuze and Felix Guattari's work on "schizoanalysis," Jean-François Lyotard's attack on the "grand narrative," Jacques Lacan's structural psychoanalysis, and Paul Virilio's "dromology," or theory of speed.

JACQUES DERRIDA: GRAMMATOLOGY AND WRITING

Charles Lemert (1990) traces the beginning of poststructuralism (and ultimately postmodern social theory) to a 1966 speech by Jacques Derrida, one of the acknowledged leaders of this approach (Lamont, 1987), in which he proclaimed the dawn of a new, poststructuralist age. In contrast to the structuralists, especially those who were involved in and followed the linguistic turn and focused on speech, Derrida focuses on writing. In fact, he created a "science" of writing that he called *grammatology* (Derrida, 1967/1974:4). While he thinks of grammatology as a science (in part to distinguish it from historical studies of writing), it is clearly not a positivistic science. In fact, it might be better to think of it as a type of knowledge rather than a science.

This brings us immediately to the difficult issue of what Derrida means by *writing*. In one sense, as we saw in Chapter 2, the term is used to distinguish his post-structuralist approach from that of Saussure and his focus on speech. To Derrida, not only is writing of great importance, but it is more general than, it encompasses, speech.

Although there are no hard and clear dividing lines between them, Derrida distinguishes between two types of writing. The first, the one with which we are most familiar, is the narrow sense of "graphic notation on tangible material" (Spivak, 1974:lxix). The second, and the one of concern to Derrida, is what might be termed "living," or "natural" writing. This type of writing "carries within itself the trace of a perennial alterity"; it is a gesture that is "effacing the presence of a thing and yet keeping it legible" (Spivak, 1974:xxxix, xli). Thus, writing is a sign "sous rature" (i.e., under erasure); a process where the sign is both conserved and effaced.[1] This is exemplified by the use of a word that is crossed out in such a way that the word is still legible to the reader. Both the original word and the fact that it has been crossed out are important to writing.

Perhaps we can get a better handle on what Derrida means by writing by looking at several closely related terms. A *trace,* for example, can be defined as "the absence of a presence" (Spivak, 1974:xvii). Thus, a trace is like the word under erasure in writing. The trace is the role played by the radical other within the sign. The trace determines the sign even as it is radically absent from the sign. Because signs always have traces of other signs, they must be studied under erasure. Writing, therefore, always reflects these traces, this radical alterity. Writing is about signs, the radical alternative to those signs, and their relationship to one another.

Another key term to Derrida (and postmodernism), one with a similar meaning, is *differance* (Jones, 1992). This concept implies the radically other (as well as perennial postponement). The structure of presence is seen as being constituted by difference (as well as by deferment). Instead of simply concentrating on the presence, the focus in the study of a text is on "a play of presence and absence," which is also the "place of the effaced trace" (Spivak, 1974:lvii). (Linking two of the concepts being discussed here, Derrida [1967/1974:57] says that "difference cannot be thought without the *trace.*") There is a sense here of continual process, of continual movement that will never reach stasis, rather than the lawlike behaviors characteristic of a structuralist perspective (Jameson, 1972:174).

Yet another related concept employed by Derrida, *arche-writing,* conveys an even more processual, even revolutionary image. One of the ways that Derrida (1967/1974:60) defines arche-writing is as a "movement of *differance.*" That *differance* was violated originally by language which sought to inscribe, classify, or

---

[1]Here is one of the places where Derrida distinguishes his position from Saussure (and indicates why he is considered a poststructuralist): "Saussure was not a grammatologist because, having launched the binary sign, he did not proceed to put it under erasure" (Spivak, 1974:lviii).

otherwise do violence to writing. Arche-writing stands as a threat to that which did violence to writing:

> To think the unique *within* the system, to inscribe it there, such is the gesture of the arche-writing; arche-violence, loss of the proper, of absolute proximity, of self-presence, in truth the loss of what has never taken place, of a self-presence which has never been given but only dreamed of and always already split, repeated, incapable of appearing to itself except in its own disappearance.

(Derrida, 1967/1974:112)

In sum, with all of these ideas—writing, trace, *differance,* arche-writing (and a number of others; play, for example)—Derrida is communicating the sense that there is always an alterity lurking behind the sign; always something hiding behind that which is present. It is that reality and the relationships that are involved in it that are the foci of Derrida's work. Rather than the image communicated by a positivistic science, grammatology leaves us with a sense of a radically different type of knowledge and, indirectly, a very different kind of world.

We could say, overall, that Derrida (1967/1974:73) is meditating on writing, *differance,* and so on to deconstruct structuralism. For example, rather than separating signifier and signified as Saussure does, Derrida sees them as interchangeable; one being the difference of the other. The sign in Derrida's work is reduced to "no more than a legible yet effaced, unavoidable tool" (Spivak, 1974:lxv).

The term *deconstruction* is not only used here but in a general sense at several points in this book (Denzin, 1994; Pecora, 1992).[2] However, the concept takes on a more specific meaning in Derrida's work, one intimately linked to the ideas already discussed in this section. Here is the way Spivak defines it:

> To locate the promising marginal text, to disclose the undecidable moment, to pry it loose with the positive lever of the signifier; to reverse the resident hierarchy, only to displace it; to dismantle in order to reconstitute what is always already inscribed.

(Spivak, 1974:lxxvii)

Thus, in doing deconstruction, Derrida often focuses on the small, tell-tale moments in a text. The goal is to locate the key moment, the key contradiction. It involves working with the point in the text where things (and being) are concealed, covered up. However, such a deconstruction is never oriented to ascertaining the truth. It is deconstructing in order to deconstruct endlessly again and again; there is no sense of ever hitting bottom, of ever finding the truth. While reconstruction may take place along the way, it will only give way to further deconstruction.

This leads to another key term in postmodernism: *decentering*. In various ways, Derrida is engaged in the process of decentering. For example, he wants to move structuralism away from its focus on the sign and to a concern for the "becoming sign"; away from objective structures to a concern for the relationship between

---

[2]Derrida [1967/1974:70], himself, uses the term in a general way in, for example, arguing that to deconstruct is to "make enigmatic."

subjective and objective structures. For another, he expresses an interest in focusing not on the core of a text, but its margins, even its blank spaces (Derrida, 1967/1974:68).

Derrida also has broader goals in this process of decentering. For one thing, he seeks to move structuralism away from its focus on speech, its phonocentrism, and toward a concern for writing. For another, Derrida links phonocentrism to logocentrism (the search for a universal answer [Logos, God, creative subjectivity, full self-consciousness] to what is true, right, beautiful, and so on) and in critiquing phonocentrism, he wants to move us away from our traditional logocentrism within which is produced "without ever posing the radical question of writing, all the Western methods of analysis, explication, reading, or interpretation" (Derrida, 1967/1974:46). An apt phrase to describe what Derrida (1978:230) is about is "the deconstruction of logocentrism." Logocentrism has contributed to what Derrida (1978:196) describes as the "historical repression and suppression of writing since Plato." It has led to the closure of not only philosophy but also the human sciences. Quite pointedly, Derrida (1978:199) sees logocentrism as inhibiting the development of structuralism, or what he calls "a certain linguistics." In urging us not to abandon ourselves to this kind of "structural formalism," in other words in seeking to go beyond structuralism, Derrida (1978:28) gives us yet another reason why he is to be considered a poststructuralist.

In its broadest terms, decentering is aimed at dealing with what Derrida considers to be the problem of centrism, or "the human desire to posit a 'central' presence at beginning . . . and end" (Spivak, 1974:lxviii).

Thus Derrida's work is a treasure trove of concepts that have become central to poststructuralism and postmodernism. There are others that we can only mention briefly. For example, Derrida rejects linearity, which he associates with modernity. For another, he also rejects the search for origins. These ideas, too, stand at the heart of poststructural/postmodern thinking.

In one of his later works, *Writing and Difference,* Derrida grew less conceptual and more sociological, more political. He also made it even clearer why he was to be considered a *post*structuralist. For example, in contrast to those theorists who saw people constrained by the structure of language, Derrida reduced language to writing that does not constrain its subjects. Furthermore, Derrida also saw social institutions as nothing more than writing and therefore incapable of constraining people. Derrida deconstructed language and social institutions, and when he finished all that remained was writing. While there is still a focus here on language, it is *not* as a structure that constrains people.

Derrida's work is poststructuralist in another sense. While the structuralists saw order and stability in the language system, Derrida sees language as disorderly and unstable; different contexts give words different meanings. As a result, the language system cannot have the constraining power over people that the structuralists think it does. Furthermore, this view of language makes it impossible for scientists to search for the underlying laws of language. And, most generally, difference in meanings calls into question any type of meaning or knowledge (Ross, 1983).

Derrida was one of Foucault's students, and like his mentor, Derrida wanted to write a history of madness. However, he did not want to write "a history of madness described from within the language of reason, the language of psychiatry *on* madness . . . on madness already crushed beneath psychiatry" (Derrida, 1978:34). Instead, he wanted to allow madness, in its vibrant state before it was crushed by psychiatry, to speak for itself. Thus, Foucault is seen as not having gone far enough; as conducting a revolution against reason within reason. In other words, from Derrida's perspective, Foucault's work continued to be logocentric. In contrast, Derrida (1978:62) argues that "reason is madder than madness—for reason is non-meaning and oblivion . . . madness is more rational than reason, for it is closer to the wellspring of sense, however silent or murmuring." Given this valorization of madness, and implicitly and more generally of nonrationality and even irrationality, Derrida (1978:84) contends that "we will be incoherent, but without systematically resigning ourselves to incoherence. The possibility of the impossible system will be on the horizon."

More specifically, Derrida wants to go beyond the rational structure to get at the writing that goes on, that is the "game," within it. Writing is "inaugural," that is, it is "dangerous and anguishing. It does not know where it is going, no knowledge can keep it from the essential precipitation toward the meaning that it constitutes and that is, primarily, its future" (Derrida, 1978:11).

A good example of Derrida's thinking is his discussion of what Antonin Artaud (1976) calls the "theatre of cruelty." Derrida contrasts the latter to the traditional theatre, which he sees as dominated by a philosophizing logic. Instead, he wants to see the theatre "[l]iberated from diction, withdrawn from the dictatorship of the text," although he is careful to point out that he is not arguing for "improvisational anarchy" (Derrida, 1978:190). Philosophizing logic is the theatre's god, and it renders the traditional theatre theological. A theological theatre is a controlled, enslaved theatre:

> The stage is theological for as long as its structure, following the entirety of tradition, comports the following elements: an author-creator who, absent and from afar, is armed with a text and keeps watch over, assembles, regulates the time or the meaning of representation . . . He lets representation represent him through representatives, directors or actors, *enslaved* interpreters . . . who . . . more or less directly represent the thought of the "creator." *Interpretive slaves* who faithfully execute the providential designs of the "master." . . . Finally, the theological stage comports a *passive,* seated public, a public of spectators, of consumers, of enjoyers.

> (Derrida, 1978:235; italics added)

Clearly, Derrida is critiquing authors and the traditional theatre for its control over, its enslavement of, theatrical personnel, actors, and audiences.

Derrida (1978:239) envisions an alternative stage (perhaps, implicitly, an alternative society) in which "Speech will cease to govern the stage." Such an alternative stage will, among other things, no longer be governed by authors and their texts. The actors will no longer take dictation; the authors will no longer be the dictators of what transpires on the stage. However, this does not mean that the stage will become anarchic. What Derrida (1978:240) is not crystal clear about is the alternative stage he is espousing. However, we do get a hint when he discusses the construction of a stage "whose clamor has not yet been pacified into words." Or, when he discusses a theatre of cruelty that "would be the art of difference and of expenditure without economy, without reserve, without return, without history" (Derrida, 1978:247). Derrida's (1978:250) theatre would be marked by difference; it would be characterized by what Artaud called "passionate overflowing."

It is clear that Derrida is calling for a radical deconstruction of the traditional theatre. More generally, he is implying a critique of society in general, which is in the thrall of logocentrism. Just as he wants to free the theatre from the dictatorship of the writer, he wants to see society free of the ideas of all of those authors, the intellectual authorities, who have created the dominant discourse. In a sense, Derrida wants the theatre to move away from its traditional center—its focus on the writer (the authority)—and give the actors more free play. And, this point too is generalizable to society as a whole. Derrida associates the center with *the* answer, with a lack of different answers, and ultimately with finality and therefore with death. The center is linked with the absence of that which is essential to Derrida (1978:297)—"play and difference." A theatre, and a world, without a center would be one which is infinitely open, ongoing, and self-reflexive.

Derrida (1978:300) concludes that the future decentered theatre and world "is neither to be awaited nor to be refound." His point is that we are not going to find the future in the past, nor should we passively wait for our fate to unfold. Rather, the future is to be found, is being made, in what we are doing. We are all currently in the process of writing the future, but we do not know, cannot know, what that future will be.

Having debunked Western logocentrism and its intellectual authority, in the end Derrida leaves us without an answer; in fact, of course, there is *no* answer. The search for the answer, the search for the logos, has been destructive and enslaving. All we are left with is the process of doing, we are left with play and with difference. Writing is, once again, central here because it is both decentering and an affirmation of play and difference.

GILLES DELEUZE AND FELIX GUATTARI: TOWARD SCHIZOANALYSIS

One of the best-known works in poststructuralism and postmodernism is Gilles Deleuze and Felix Guattari's (1972/1983) *Anti-Oedipus: Capitalism and Schizophrenia*. The intellectual context of the book is well expressed by Michel Foucault in his preface to it:

> During the years 1945–1965 (I am referring to Europe), there was a certain way of thinking correctly, a certain style of political discourse, a certain ethics of the intellectual. One had to be on familiar terms with Marx, not let one's dreams stray too far from Freud. And one had to treat sign-systems—the signifier—with the greatest respect.
>
> (Foucault, 1983:xi)

Like Foucault, Deleuze and Guattari sought to fashion their theoretical perspective in reaction to the dominance of Marxian, Freudian psychoanalytic, and Saussurian structuralist thinking. Foucault labels those who follow Freudian and Saussurian perspectives "poor technicians of desire" who, given their focus on "every sign and symptom," "would subjugate the multiplicity of desire to the twofold law of structure and lack" (Foucault, 1983:xiii).

Foucault also saw fascism as an enemy of the kind of work undertaken by Deleuze and Guattari. In fact, he thought that their book could have been entitled "*Introduction to the Non-Fascist Life*" (Foucault, 1983:xiii). However, it is not just fascist political regimes that are opposed but also "the fascism in us all, in our heads and in our everyday behavior, the fascism that causes us to love power, to desire the very thing that dominates and exploits us" (Foucault, 1983:xiii). *Anti-Oedipus* is both an effort by the authors to liberate themselves from the then-dominant modes of thinking *and* to help free people from fascistic constraints, both external and internal.

The book's title and its focus on the Oedipus complex, of course, represents the centrality of Freud and psychoanalysis, at least as a person and a perspective, as well as the authors' desire to distance themselves from them. Of the psychoanalyst's famous couch, Deleuze and Guattari (1972/1983:334) pungently argue that it "smells bad. . . . It reeks of the great death and the little ego." Indeed, the book represents an attack on the idea of the Oedipus complex and its focus on the "holy family" of "daddy-mommy-me" (Deleuze and Guattari, 1972/1983:51). In addition to its specific problems, the Oedipus complex is seen as but one example of the kind of totalizing idea from which people should be freed. Further, Deleuze and Guattari linked the Oedipus complex to capitalism and thus were launching an attack on the latter as well.

At the heart of all of this is the idea that we have all been oedipalized and made neurotic by our families during the socialization process and, as a result, have come to want fascism. The goal is to free us from this yoke and to allow our desires to run free; the goal is a "desiring revolution." The model of someone who is free of the oedipal yoke, whose desires are running free, is the schizophrenic. As Deleuze and Guattari (1972/1983:2) put it, "A schizophrenic out for a walk is a better model than a neurotic lying on the analyst's couch." However, it should be pointed out that it is more the schizophrenic process than the schizophrenic (whose development has been arrested) that is the model for Deleuze and Guattari. More generally, what Deleuze and Guattari seek is "a collective subjectivity, a nonfascist subject—anti-oedipus" (Seem, 1983:xxiii). Such a subject, with desire allowed to run free, would be an explosive, even a revolutionary, force.

As pointed out above, Deleuze and Guattari valorize schizophrenia. This stands in contrast to Freud who, in their view, disliked schizophrenics because they resisted being oedipalized. More generally, the psychoanalysts had discovered the production of desire, but then they had turned around and sought to repress it. To Deleuze and Guattari people are inherently desiring machines as well as producing machines. They see these two types of "machines," as well as the "schizophrenic machine" as part of "species life": "Schizophrenia is the universe of productive and reproductive desiring-machines, universal primary production as the 'essential reality of man and nature' " (Deleuze and Guattari, 1972/1983:5). Thus, schizophrenia is seen as an inherent part of species life. Schizophrenics live intensely; they come closer than most to being desiring-machines. However, psychoanalysts have opposed them, and by implication all of humanity, and have sought to repress their lives, their desires.

Machine imagery runs through *Anti-Oedipus.* "Desire is a machine, and the object of desire is another machine connected to it" (Deleuze and Guattari, 1972/1983:26). Another major machine is capitalism, and Deleuze and Guattari see it as an effort to repress the desiring machine:

> capitalism, through its process of production, produces an awesome schizophrenic accumulation of energy or charge, against which it brings all its vast powers of represssion to bear, but which nonetheless continues to act as capitalism's limits . . . it continually seeks to avoid reaching its limit while simultaneously tending toward that limit.

> (Deleuze and Guattari, 1972/1983:34; see also 266)

Schizophrenia is capitalism's limit, and the schizophrenic is Deleuze and Guattari's revolutionary agent:

> The schizophrenic deliberately seeks out the very limit of capitalism: he is its inherent tendency brought to fulfillment, its surplus product, its proletariat, and its exterminating angel. He scrambles all the codes and is the transmitter of the decoded flows of desire.

> (Deleuze and Guattari, 1972/1983:35)

Currently, the desiring machine is forced to fit the "restricted code of Oedipus" (Deleuze and Guattari, 1972/1983:47). What we need to do is to "schizophrenize" both society as a whole and the individual unconscious. Such a "schizophrenization" would allow us "to shatter the iron collar of Oedipus and rediscover everywhere the force of desiring-production" (Deleuze and Guattari, 1972/1983:53). Through schizophrenization, we would be cured of the cure; that is, we would be freed from the oppression of psychoanalysis. We would also, in the process, be freed of capitalism, "[f]or what is schizo, if not first of all the one who can no longer bear 'all that': money, the stock market, the death forces" (Deleuze and Guattari, 1972/1983:341).

We need to replace psychoanalysis, with all of its exclusions and restrictions (Deleuze and Guattari see the psychoanalyst in league with such social control agents as the police), with schizoanalysis. The goal of schizoanalysis is to undo the harm done by psychoanalysis; to de-oedipalize the unconscious or undo the "daddy-mommy spider web" (Deleuze and Guattari, 1972/1983:112). (Thus, in poststructural/postmodern terms Deleuze and Guattari are interested in deconstructing the oedipal complex.) In so doing, schizoanalysis would be better able to get at peoples' real problems. And at least one of those real problems is the desire of people for their own represssion.

Schizoanalysis, as a process, would help free the desiring-machine, and desire is seen as a revolutionary force. It is an explosive force that calls into question the established order. Snidely, Deleuze and Guattari (1972/1983:116) argue that "desire, not left-wing holidays," is the true revolutionary force. In fact, desire is seen as an inherently revolutionary force.

As is true of much of poststructuralism and postmodernism, the code is of central importance to Deleuze and Guattari. The code is viewed as being oppressive and in need of disruption, and it is the role of the schizophrenic to disrupt the code, especially one aspect of the code—Oedipus, that "despotic signifier" (Deleuze and Guattari, 1972/1983:54). The schizophrenic flow is "a violence against syntax, a concerted destruction of the signifier, non-sense erected as a flow, polyvocity that returns to haunt all relations" (Deleuze and Guattari, 1972/1983:133).

Of course, it is not only the code that needs to be undermined, but it is also capitalism and the family system (daddy-mommy-me) that was brought into being to help support it. Deleuze and Guattari clearly link capitalism and the family:

> families . . . *play at Oedipus*. . . . But behind all this, there is an economic situation: the mother reduced to housework, or to a difficult and uninteresting job on the outside; children whose future remains uncertain; the father who has had it with feeding all those mouths—in short, a fundamental relation to the outside of which the psychoanalyst washes his hands, too attentive to seeing that his clients play nice games.
>
> Deleuze and Guattari, 1972/1983:356)

Oedipus is also seen as being more directly a product of the capitalist system. As Deleuze and Guattari (1972/1983:267) graphically put it, "it is not via a flow of shit or a wave of incest that Oedipus arrives, but via the decoded flows of capital—money." Oedipus is used in capitalism to colonize our families and ultimately ourselves. It also helps the family play its essential role in capitalism as "a unit of production and of reproduction" (Deleuze and Guattari, 1972/1983:265).

Yet we need to be cautious here because Deleuze and Guattari, like most poststructuralists and postmodernists, reject the idea of a grand narrative and of a revolutionary subject that will solve all of our problems once and for all. They offer a vivid image of our fragmented world: "We live today in the age of partial objects, bricks that have been shattered to bits, and leftovers" (Deleuze and Guattari, 1972/1983:42). In a fragmented world it is impossible to generate a grand narrative about it or about overcoming it: "We no longer believe in a primordial totality that once existed, or in a final totality that awaits us at some future date" (Deleuze and Guattari, 1972/1983:42). Instead of a single grand revolution, they think, like Foucault, in terms of microphysics and "infinitesimal lines of escape" (Deleuze and Guattari, 1972/1983:280). Eschewing the Enlightenment, its problem and its solutions, Deleuze and Guattari refuse to offer a clear political program. Had they offered one, it would have been "grotesque and disquieting at the same time" (Deleuze and Guattari, 1972/1983:380).

They are content to remain with schizoanalysis in which the objective is not the construction of a new world but rather deconstruction:

> Destroy, destroy. The task of schizoanalysis goes by way of destruction—a whole scouring of the unconscious, a complete curettage. Destroy Oedipus, the illusion of the ego, the puppet of the superego, guilt, the law, castration.
>
> (Deleuze and Guattari, 1972/1983:311; see also 381)

The goal of such destruction is to liberate schizoid flows that are inherent to desiring-machines.

In the end, Deleuze and Guattari oppose all grand narratives—capitalism, Marxism, psychoanalysis—based on rational principles. Instead, they end up favoring the irrationality of schizophrenia and of desire. The solution to the problems posed by the rational systems put in place by the grand narratives lies in irrationality.

JEAN-FRANÇOIS LYOTARD: THE DEATH OF THE GRAND NARRATIVE

"Simplifying to the extreme, I define *postmodern* as incredulity toward metanarratives" (Lyotard, 1979/1984:xxiv). To put it another way, postmodernity involves making "war on totality" (Lyotard, 1988/1993:16). Since the major metanarratives that Lyotard attacks are the emancipatory and scientific grand narratives associated with the Enlightenment, postmodernism involves a "severe reexamination . . . [of] the thought of the Enlightenment" (Lyotard, 1988/1993:3). Lyotard (1988/1993:82) is especially critical of the Enlightenment's emancipatory grand narratives, which "created the possibility of total war, totalitarianisms, the growing gap between the wealth of the North and the impoverished South, unemployment and the 'new poor,' general deculturation and the crisis in education . . . and the isolation of the artistic avant-gardes."

Deferring, at least for the moment, the meaning of this position, it seems clear here (and elsewhere) that Lyotard sees himself as a postmodernist. Yet, as Jameson points out, it is a limited postmodern vision:

> although he has polemically endorsed the slogan of a "postmodernism" and has been involved in the defense of some of its more controversial productions, Lyotard is in reality quite unwilling to posit a postmodernist stage radically different from the period of high modernism and involving a fundamental historical and cultural break with this last. Rather, seeing postmodernism as a discontent with an[d] disintegration of this or that high modernist style—a moment in the perpetual "revolution" and innovation of high modernism, to be succeeded by a fresh burst of formal invention—in a striking formula he has characterized postmodernism, not as that which follows modernism and its particular legitimation crisis, but rather as a cyclical moment that returns before the emergence of ever new modernisms in the stricter sense.
>
> (Jameson, 1984b:xvi)

Thus, to Lyotard postmodernism is not a new historical epoch but a recurrent historical phase within modernism. As he puts it, the postmodern is "undoubtedly part of the modern" (Lyotard, 1988/1993:12). We have had postmodern phases before within modernism, and we will have them again. "A work can become modern only if it is first postmodern. Thus understood, postmodernism is not modernism at its end, but in a nascent state, and this state is recurrent" (Lyotard, 1988/1993:13).

Given this rather conservative view of postmodernism, Lyotard explicitly rejects the extreme postmodern position (while simultaneously continuing to contribute to postmodern social theory). For example, Lyotard disassociates himself from the Baudrillardian position on "the dissolution of the social bond and the disintegration of social aggregates into a mass of individual atoms thrown into the absurdity of Brownian motion" (Lyotard, 1979/1984:15). Rather, to Lyotard, we all exist as "nodal points" in the fabric of social relationships.

The heart of Lyotard's views on postmodernism lie, as we have seen, in his thoughts on narratives, especially grand narratives. Modernity, to Lyotard, has been characterized by the preeminence of grand narratives. However, with the failure of most of the projects derived from those grand narratives (communism, for example), Lyotard feels that it is time to make "war" on such totalistic perspectives. His paradigm of this failure, as it is for Zygmunt Bauman (see Chapter 8), is Auschwitz. In light of the attempted destruction of the Jews by the Nazis operating with a very modern grand narrative (the ultimate triumph of the Aryan race), he asks: "How could the grand narratives of legitimation still have credibility in these circumstances?" (Lyotard, 1988/1993:19). He goes so far as to say, "One is then tempted to give credence to a grand narrative of the decline of the grand narratives" (Lyotard, 1988/1993:29).

An understanding of Lyotard's thinking on grand narratives is based on his ideas on the relationship between narratives and science, but both are seen as Wittgensteinian "language games." Social relationships are viewed as games that require language in order to participate. Such "language games are the minimum relation required for society to exist" (Lyotard, 1979/1984:15). Language games are, from Lyotard's point of view, the social bond.

Both narratives and science, of course, are forms of knowledge. Knowledge is defined broadly to include denotative statements—know-how, knowing how to live, how to listen, and so on. A narrative is the preeminent form of traditional, customary knowledge. It is through narratives that the pragmatic rules that are the bond that holds society together are transmitted. That bond is created not only by the meaning of the narratives but also by the sheer act of reciting them. The legitimation for such narratives does not come from some external source; rather, they come from "the simple fact that they do what they do" (Lyotard, 1979/1984:23).

Science, in contrast, accepts only denotative statements. In other words, it is only "truth value" that determines the acceptability of scientific statements. Unlike narratives, science is not a direct and shared component of the social bond. Although there are these and other differences between narratives and science, the fact is that they are both language games, and one is no more or less necessary than the other:

Both are composed of sets of statements; the statements are "moves" made by the players within the framework of generally applicable rules; these rules are specific to each particular kind of knowledge, and the "moves" judged to be "good" in one cannot be of the same type as those judged "good" in another, unless it happens that way by chance.

(Lyotard, 1979/1984:26)

Those operating within a narrative framework see both narratives and science as variants of narrative cultures. Thus, they accept the fact that one narrative cannot judge another. They also accept the idea that narratives are no better or no worse than science. Problems arise, in their view, because science does not accept this point of view. Those working from a scientific perspective have a negative view of narratives and question the validity of statements derived from them. From the point of view of science, narratives are seen as "savage, primitive, underdeveloped, backward, alienated, composed of opinions, customs, authority, prejudice, ignorance, ideology. Narratives are fables, myths, legends, fit only for women and children" (Lyotard, 1979/1984:27). In other words, science questions the legitimacy of narratives and, in the process, helps to legitimate "legitimation" as a problem. Science wants everyone to believe that it offers legitimate, "true" knowledge and it critiques narratives for being illegitimate and "untrue."

However, in various ways science has helped to lead to a questioning of its own legitimacy. First, it has done so, as pointed out above, simply by raising the issue of legitimacy. As a result, it becomes possible, as the postmodernists have done, to question the legitimacy of science. Second, scientists themselves often resort to narratives (for example, when they appear on television to discuss issues of general interest) and in so doing raise questions of their own legitimacy. When they do this, what makes what they have to say any more legitimate than what announcers or even actors have to say? Finally, science has come to be closely linked to the state (through state-supported research funding, for example), and a questioning of the state's legitimacy inevitably extends to science.

Lyotard identifies two grand narratives of legitimation. The first is speculative, cognitive-theoretical, scientific and the second is emancipatory, practical, and humanistic. Today, in the postmodern world, *both* grand narratives have lost their credibility. People have clearly lost faith in the great emancipatory narratives such as those associated with Marxism and communism. Similarly, speculative-scientific grand narratives have given way to technoscience (and the dysfunctions and risks associated with technologies such as nuclear reactors [see Chapter 8]) where the focus is on maximally efficient performance and useful results rather than "truth," or the ultimate solution to all of society's problems. This has helped lead at least some to the realization that science is nothing more than another narrative, a game like all other games. While the two types of grand narratives have suffered irreparable harm, Lyotard does not see this as a bad thing. With the decline of the grand narratives, "legitimation becomes plural, local and immanent . . . there will necessarily be many discourses of legitimation . . . legitimation descends to the level of practice. . . . There are no special tribunals set apart" (Fraser and Nicholson, 1990:23).

One might think that Lyotard has given up on science, but he does see a role for postmodern science, a science in which the focus is not on performativity and determinism. Rather, postmodern science involves what Lyotard calls *paralogy,* or the "searching for and 'inventing' counterexamples, in other words, the unintelligible, supporting an argument means looking for a 'paradox' and legitimating it with new rules in games of reasoning" (Lyotard, 1979/1984:54). In other words, Lyotard sees a place for a science that is constantly undermining itself and its own legitimacy (paralogy) (Lyotard, 1979/1984:60).[3]

The key to postmodern science is the generation of new ideas. There is no distinctive scientific method or scientific narrative; scientists tell stories just like everyone else. There is no grand narrative associated with science, just a series of little narratives involving the generation and attempted verification of new ideas. There is no grand consensus but simply a consensus on the rules of a series of local games and the moves to be made in them. Thus, postmodern science is a series of local language games with heterogeneous rules involving the search for dissent in which the objective is the generation of new ideas. Instead of consensus, there is the search for dissensus, for *differend.*

While Lyotard rejects a search for consensus such as that advocated by Habermas, he does not reject the idea of justice. For one thing, to Lyotard, justice involves a renunciation of terror, especially the terroristic effort to impose a single grand narrative on all. The problem with grand narratives is that they inevitably leave some groups out and that narrative is then imposed on them, often with disastrous results. Graphically, and more specifically, Lyotard (1988/1993:77–78) argues, "Neither liberalism (economic and political) nor the various Marxisms have emerged from these bloodstained centuries without attracting accusations of having perpetrated crimes against humanity." To forestall the development and terroristic imposition of grand narratives in the computerized world that he sees as emerging, he urges that everyone be given "free access to the memory and data banks" (Lyotard, 1979/1984:67). In the end, Lyotard is arguing for a system that respects "both the desire for justice and the desire for the unknown" (Lyotard, 1979/1984:67). Any new grand narrative would be unjust to some and would prematurely cut off the search for the unknown.

More concretely, Lyotard (1988/1993:80) argues that the "post" in postmodernism means "a procedure of analysis, anamnesis, anagogy, and anamorphosis that elaborates an 'initial forgetting'." Anamnesis involves remembering, especially life before this one. Anamorphosis involves the making of a distorted image. Anagogy involves mystical interpretations. Clearly, all of these fly in the face of the rationality associated with modern grand narratives.

Writing is key to Lyotard (as it was to Derrida) and to opposition to grand narratives. Obviously, language is intimately associated with writing, but it can be both adversary and accomplice. The key to writing is not to be overly constrained by extant knowledge but to oppose it with something singular, unique: "To say what it already knows how to say is not writing. One wants to say what it does not know

---

[3]For a discussion of paralogy and its relationship to Rorty's pluralism, see Fritzman (1990).

how to say, but what one imagines it should be able to say" (Lyotard, 1988/ 1993:89). He associates his view with Theodor Adorno's notion of "micrologies," which "capture the childhood of the event and inscribe what is uncapturable about it" (Lyotard, 1988/1993:90). More generally, Lyotard (1988/1993:100) seeks "renewing ties with the season of childhood, the season of the mind's possibilities."[4] Thus, he defines a "new task for didactic thought: to search out its childhood anywhere and everywhere, even outside childhood" (Lyotard, 1988/1993:107). We need to be patient in our thinking; we do not need to be making progress; we need to do no more than continually starting.

JACQUES LACAN: THE IMAGINARY, THE SYMBOLIC, THE REAL[5]

Although Lacan (1966/1977) considered himself to be a structural psychoanalyst, in many ways his ideas initiated the end of structuralism and, in the view of some, began poststructuralism. One of the central tenets of structuralism is the death of the subject, but, for a psychoanalyst such as Lacan, it is not easy to dispose of the subject. Lacan accepted the structuralist belief that the meaning of a word is determined only by its difference from other words and not by its relationship to the thing that it supposedly represents. Lacan even accepted that the subject was also, in some sense, a product of this differential structure. Nevertheless, psychoanalytic patients are more than structures made up of words, even if they are not some type of pure Cartesian subjects who think and therefore are. Human subjectivity is not eternal or natural, but neither is it simply socially constructed. Rather, the subject is *both* socially determined and self-constituting. This is the problem that Lacan's theories attempt to address. Such an effort is of great interest to the social sciences given their historic concern with the relationship between individuals and social structures.

When first approaching Lacan's texts one is reminded of C. Wright Mills' (1959) critique of Talcott Parsons: If someone only translated Parsons's writings into plain English, they would be quite unremarkable. In Lacan's case, one wonders whether any significant ideas would be left after the removal of all of the puns, literary references, flippant etymologies, long digressions and so on. Such word play seems to be at the heart of many of Lacan's arguments. At times Lacan brilliantly makes his point in one disturbing sentence, at other times his parenthetical expressions take up pages. He mixes allusion to grade-B movies with insightful explorations of classic poetry. Most often he is ironic, sardonic, and caustic, but there are also moments of truly human expression.

To begin to get a sense of Lacan's ideas, we need to understand the relationship between his thinking and that of the founder of psychoanalysis, Sigmund Freud (Lacan, 1973/1978). This is important because of the influence that certain interpretations of Freud have had in the social sciences. Lacan often claimed that his

---

[4]As we have seen, Baudrillard also valorizes children.
[5]This section was written by Doug Goodman, University of Maryland.

ideas were a "return to Freud," but, as Malcolm Bowie points out, the relationship is much more complex.

> He could be a grateful disciple, annotating and elucidating the Freudian texts, but not seeking to make an original contribution of his own; or a defender of Freud against misrepresentation and attack coming from outside the profession of psychoanalysis; or an apologist for the earlier against the later Freud; or the proponent of a "pure" Freudian message in the face of those colleagues who have tamed and institutionalized his teaching; or a continuator of Freud who brings the whole doctrine to its point of consummation. Lacan adopts each of these roles in turn, and seldom pauses to announce or explain his switches of position. And occasionally a new master appears: Freud may become the mere harbinger of the Lacanian word, or the originator of a theory now eclipsed and made obsolete by Lacan's own.

(Bowie, 1991:45)

The social sciences have interpreted and used Freud's ideas in three ways. First, Freud's theory of drives has been understood as representing an essential instinctual level that society should attempt to satisfy or, at least, recognize. Lacan rejects this interpretation of Freud. For Lacan, it is a fantasy to think of drives as biological. It is a dream of a primal identity before culture and language.

A second way in which Freud has been used in sociology (for example, by both Parsons and his arch-critic Mills) has been to argue for the necessity of a social order that strengthens the ego. Lacan also rejects this interpretation of Freud. According to Lacan, Freud mistakenly relied on the Western overvaluation of the rational, independent self. However, it was to Freud's credit that he introduced a theory that was able to correct this mistake by emphasizing the importance of the nonrational.

Finally, sociologists have relied upon Freud's theory of internalization to explain how individuals are affected by cultural structures. While sociologists have seen internalization as the straightforward incorporation of cultural values into the individual psyche, Freud described a much more ambivalent process. For him, internalization was as likely to result in violent rejection of social values as passive acceptance. Lacan would agree with this critique and, in fact, sees the process of internalization of culture as much more complex than even Freud described.

Three concepts lie at the core of Lacan's thinking: the *imaginary,* the *symbolic,* and the *real.* It is important for the reader to realize that Lacan does not use these words in the ordinary sense. They are not clearly demarcated stages nor, as Bowie (1991:91) points out, are they mental forces. Instead they are "orders each of which serves to position the individual within a force-field that traverses him."

For Lacan, psychoanalysis is intimately related to Saussure's ideas about language (*langue*). Psychoanalysis is, after all, "the talking cure." The symptoms that it uncovers are primarily verbal or at least symbolic. Lacan (1966/1977:59) tells us that "the symptom is itself structured like a language," and "it is a language from which speech must be delivered." In other words, the bodily symptom must be translated into speech.

He agrees with Saussure's division between signifier (the sound of the word) and signified (the meaning of the word), but he sees the two separated by a "bar," or a barrier, which creates two parallel and irreducible worlds. The world of material sounds is connected in a limitless "chain" of language. The world of meaning arbitrarily "slides below" this chain of signifiers. That is, meaning is fluid and separated from sounds. The material words (sounds) can only be connected to a precise meaning (their signified) retrospectively. Even then, as we approach that meaning, it dissolves into a structure of signifiers—a structure of intrinsically meaningless sounds. This is the recurrent experience in psychoanalysis. As the analyst approaches the heart of the symptom, it dissolves into a fantastic chain of imaginary memories and arbitrary symbols.

Lacan, however, believed that *langue* only represents the symbolic domain. However, as we have seen, there are also the imaginary order and the real. The self-constitution of human subjectivity can only be understood as a relationship among these three orders.

The imaginary is that order in which the individual experiences herself as a whole and complete subject. It is the realm in which the rational ego develops through an identification with the images of wholeness that the individual perceives around her. According to Lacan, this is an illusion and a misrecognition. Lacan uses the metaphor of a toddler seeing herself in a mirror. The toddler actually experiences her own body as a fragmented collection of drives and body parts. However, she is seduced into believing she is a unity by the unitary image that is seen in the mirror. Later, the adult comes to believe that she is a whole and unfragmented subject who is (or should be) in control of herself. This image, according to Lacan, is a deception, and the ego upon which it is modeled is grounded in falseness. Because of this, the subject desperately tries to stabilize her identity by accumulating roles and positions with which she can identify. Society itself can be seen as part of this frantic attempt to create a structure in which the subject can finally find a stable place, a role, an identity.

This attempt, however, is doomed to failure because this wholeness can only be represented within the symbolic order—an order of difference and not of identity. No matter how hard we try to stabilize our identity of wholeness and unity, the social world where we must seek this identity always subverts our endeavor because this order is created by others and escapes our control.

The symbolic order is a supra-personal structure of preexisting social determinations. It is the sphere of culture and language. We are born into it, and it gives us our name and tells us what race, class, gender, and other social categories we are. In the imaginary, egos are defined by their identifications. In the symbolic, subjects are defined by their individuality—their difference from others and even their difference from themselves. There is always a *gap* between the social categories and our selves. In the symbolic we *lack* the ability to completely and permanently identify with our social position. Bowie describes it as follows:

> It is the realm of movement rather than fixity and of heterogeneity rather than similarity. It is the realm of language, the unconscious and an otherness that remains other. This is the order in which the subject as distinct from the ego comes into being, and into a manner of being that is always disjointed and intermittent. . . . Whereas the inhabitant of the

imaginary ventures into the world of others only to freeze, foreshorten and incorporate it, the symbolic is inveterately intersubjective and social.

(Bowie, 1991:93)

For Lacan, humanity begins as such only when we enter the symbolic. This occurs when the needs that we have—both biological, such as food, and social, such as identification with the mother—are replaced by symbols. These symbols are not of our own creation but are part of what Lacan calls the *discourse of the Other.*

In the symbolic, the signifier dominates over the signified. It is full of sound . . . signifying nothing. Whatever meaning the word expresses does not come from the subject but rather from the social order. In the symbolic it is the intersubjective rather than the subjective which is in control. This order has only an arbitrary relationship to the human subject.

It is at this level that the unconscious emerges. The unconscious is not the instinctive; instead it represents the absences, gaps, and lacks which structure language. For Lacan, there are not two languages, an unconscious and a conscious. There is only one language that always exceeds our conscious understanding. It is there, in that excess, that the subject of the unconscious is found. "I think where I am not, therefore I am where I do not think" (Lacan, 1966/1977:166).

Rather than seeing the social world as distorting or draining the ego, Lacan sees it as constructing the place of the symbolic subject. This symbolic subject replaces the imaginary ego as the heart of the individual. The symbolic is a world of publicly available words, roles, and institutions. The subject takes her place in that world, but it is a place that is marked by absence and difference. It is a place that is external to the rational ego; therefore the subject is forever threatened by her own otherness. According to Lacan, there is an insoluble contradiction in the symbolic. We only become independent, self-constituting human beings within the symbolic, but the symbolic is always beyond our control and never provides us with a stable subjectivity without a gap between our identity and our self.

The Other is one of Lacan's names for that which introduces lack and gap into the heart of subjectivity. The Other is the symbolic order which exists outside of us and prior to us and yet which represents the only place where the subject can emerge. Because the subject is outside of herself, we can say that the self is decentered. The imaginary tries to dissolve otherness through identification, but the symbolic reveals it to be the core of our self.

Nevertheless, the imaginary and the symbolic are not in opposition. For there to be meaning, the symbolic requires the imaginary. The movement of signifiers along the signifying "chain" in the symbolic order disrupts all meaning. Like looking up a word in the dictionary of a language that we do not know, one word leads to other words but meaning remains elusive. All words tend toward meaninglessness. For there to be meaning, some signifiers must have their relation to a signified frozen. This is the role that identification within the imaginary performs.

The symbolic subject can never completely identify with its social designation (gender, class, and so on). She always feels alienated. The subject as such—the subject as a unity—can only be experienced through an imaginary identification. We imagine that we are an unfragmented identity that is in control of our desires, our ideas, our self. It is this primary narcissism that unifies the symbolic subjectivity and structures meaning. From this vantage point, the imaginary is revealed to be a creation of the symbolic, a "myth" that the symbolic needs to stabilize itself.

An imaginary figure is at the center of the symbolic and provides it with its stability. Lacan calls this figure the *phallus*. The phallus is the symbolic representation of that which cannot be represented symbolically. It is a *simulacrum*—a copy of something that never existed. It is the idea of the mother's penis. Since the mother's penis never existed, the phallus is the pure representation of absence. It is this pure absence that provides the center around which the symbolic can form. It represents within the symbolic that which made the symbolic possible. Above all the phallus represents castration (Lacan, 1966–1982/1985).

Castration is not the cutting off of the material penis. Nor does castration simply represent the cutting off of the individual from his or her own body. It is first of all the cutting off of all possibility of a stable identification, of all unmediated relationships with other people. Beyond that it represents the individual cut off from the control of language where desire is located.

Although the phallus appears to be the representative of absence itself, its true nature is as an exchange point for the meaningless and arbitrary force of society. Lacan calls this the law of the father or, more often, the *nom-du-père*. He is indicating, with a play on words (*non* and *nom* sound the same in French), both that we are dealing with a name—a symbol for the father rather than the real father—and that this law is a refusal, a "no," to any complete identification with the mother. It forbids the incestuous relationship with the mother and partitions people into those who are accessible for desire and those who are not. It is this "no" that creates that absence and that fundamental difference upon which the symbolic order is founded.

This is not to say that the individual father intervenes to wrest each child from complete identification with the imaginary. Instead, something that can be represented by the father intervenes to direct the infant to what is outside the imaginary, to what has the force of law. Therefore, it is the *figure* of the castrating father that stands at the boundary of the imaginary and the start of the symbolic. And it is here that the arbitrary and meaningless force of society is able to exert its limited, transitory, and ultimately unsuccessful influence over the symbolic order.

At most, society can only create a temporary and precarious meaning by interweaving the signifier and signified so that momentarily their movement is arrested. Lacan refers to these frozen points of meaning as a *point de caption,* or anchoring point. Any attempt, however, to analyze how that meaning is produced will disrupt it. The subject itself is never a *point de caption,* but its designators are. Gender, race, ethnicity, and deviance are all places where a social force interweaves signified and signifier to produce meaning. But in every case when we analyze these points they become unintelligible. And when we approach their meaning it disappears. They all turn out to be arbitrary and contingent social constructions. Try as she might, the subject cannot find a stable and permanent identity within the symbolic. Although doomed to ultimate failure, the subject is always trying to include the symbolic within her imaginary identifications—to become the role, to be a part of fixed and secure society.

Thus, there are two trends traversing the field of meaning. On the one hand, the imaginary tends always to freeze the symbolic into a structure of stable meanings; on the other hand, the symbolic tends to exclude the imaginary and to disperse into the play of difference without meaning. Neither of these actually occurs because of the third order, which Lacan (1986/1992) calls the real. It is the real that governs the relationship between the symbolic and the imaginary. It forces the imaginary to seek its impossible expression within the symbolic, and it forces the symbolic to take the imaginary as its core and to structure its intrinsically meaningless elements around this imaginary identification.

Lacan says very little about the real except to say that it is best understood as that which transforms the random permutations of a meaningless universe into a human trauma. Most important, it is to be distinguished from reality. Reality— what we know, what we perceive, the world we live in—is part of the symbolic order. The real is precisely that which escapes reality.

Bowie (1991:112) offers a set of alternative terms for the three orders that sums up the preceding discussion. "The would-be-truth-seeker will find that the imaginary, the symbolic and the real are an unholy trinity whose members could as easily be called Fraud, Absence and Impossibility."

Lacan was primarily interested in psychoanalysis, and all his references to a social theory are peripheral and open to interpretation. This, however, has not kept his work from having an influence upon social theorists. The Lacanian approach has reintroduced problems and concepts that the social sciences have mistakenly marginalized: the self-constitution of subjectivity, the importance of imaginary identification, and the impossibility of fixed meaning. Lacan's theories suggest that the relation between the subject and the social order is a traumatic one—that the insertion of the individual into the social and symbolic order introduces an impossibility into the center of subjectivity that forever throws the subject off-center in relation to herself. Furthermore, it implies that the social itself is an impossible imaginary identification. The challenge that Lacan's ideas present to the social sciences is this: the social, the central signifier-signified of those sciences, is structured around an impossibility, a lack, and that the history of the social sciences is a succession of hopeless attempts to cover over that lack.

PAUL VIRILIO: DROMOLOGY

Paul Virilio, the final French theorist to be discussed in this chapter, is less well known than the other thinkers discussed above. Nonetheless, he has created an innovative and intriguing body of work that is worthy of broader recognition. The best term to describe his work is *dromology*. This concept is derived from the suffix "drome," referring to running or a racecourse; in Virilio's (1991a:91) work it indicates his focal concern with the "decisive importance of speed."

At a broad level, Virilio is concerned with the breakdown of boundaries brought about by a series of technological changes over time in modes of transportation, communication, telecommunication, computerization, and so forth. The early forms of these changes led to changes in spatial arrangements, especially the breakdown in physical boundaries. Virilio (1991a:13) contends that as a result of the breakdown in spatial arrangements, "distinctions of *here* and *there* no longer mean anything." In other words, it makes little or no difference today whether one lives in the city, the suburbs, or in a rural area. Similarly, it matters little whether one lives in the United States, England, or Japan.

However, Virilio is more interested in the issue of time than space largely because time is more important than space in a postmodern world. In fact, he argues that increases in speed are serving to erode spatial distinctions and to make it increasingly difficult to distinguish space from time. As a result of cathode-ray tubes, whether they are found in our television sets or attached to our computers, "spatial dimensions have become inseparable from their rate of transmission" (Virilio, 1991a:14). In other words, space and time have become progressively indistinguishable from one another. Furthermore, speed has come to overwhelm distance; "acceleration and deceleration, or the movement of movement, are the only true dimensions of space, of speed-space, of dromospheric space" (Virilio, 1991a:102). Thus, Virilio (1991a:18) creates the notion of "speed distance" and argues that it serves to annihilate physical and spatial dimensions. Especially important in this process today are advances in the means of communication and telecommunication.

In addition to obliterating space, speed, especially the speed of the communication of knowledge and information, has created a bewildering world of images and appearances. We are increasingly unable to tell where we are, what time it is, or what we are supposed to do. Virilio (1991a:140) traces this to "the decay of visible markers, the loss of visible referents, the disintegration of various standards." What we are faced with is a crisis of conceptualization and representation. We have gone from a world of stable images to one in which such images are highly unstable:

> aesthetics of accelerated disappearance has displaced that of the progressive emergence of forms and figures in their material support . . . . Where once the aesthetics of the appearance of an analogical, stable image of static nature predominated, we now have the aesthetics of the disappearance of a numerical, unstable image of fleeting nature, whose persistence is exclusively retinal.

> (Virilio, 1991a:36)

Our referents are increasingly less likely to take a material form; they are increasingly little more than fleeting images. We are less and less likely to observe things directly. Rather, we sense things indirectly through mediating technologies like the mass media. While we are able to sense many more things in this way, it is increasingly difficult to make them intelligible since we lack unmediated knowledge of them. As a result, in Virilio's view, we are faced with a crisis of intelligibility, a crisis he links to the issue of postmodernity; in fact, he implies it goes beyond postmodernity:

> The question of *modernity* and *post-modernity* is superseded by that of *reality* and *post-reality:* we are living in a system of technological temporality, in which duration and

material support have been supplanted as criteria by individual retinal and auditory instants.

(Virilio, 1991a:84)

Advanced technologies of all types play a central role here as they mediate between us and the things we see. The cinema played a major role in this development as the movie camera came to come between us and the things we see. This problem also exists, and is greatly extended, with the arrival of television. Technologies like these make it far more difficult for us to truly understand what we are seeing, in part because what we are seeing is filtered through the eyes of the camera-person and the camera. In addition, we become far less active interpreters of what we see and more passive "telespectators." Furthermore, the spatial and temporal lines between us and these media tend to erode; there are no perceptible limits here, no clear line between where the television image ends and we begin. Furthermore, with the coming of the computer, this is increasingly a problem both at home and on the job.

One of the recurrent themes in Virilio's work is the relationship between the kinds of changes discussed above and the changing nature of war (Virilio, 1983). To Virilio (1991b:94), "in the technical domain," war is always the best model. The development of the various technologies of concern to Virilio (e.g., the computer) is closely linked to military research and technological development. The increased speed that results from these technological advances is affecting all sectors of society, including the military. As in the rest of society, speed leads to the destruction of time for reflection. The rapidity with which weapons can be launched makes it impossible for military officers to reflect on their actions. Rather, the launching of enemy missiles, for example, leads automatically to the launching of retaliatory weapons. What results is a "totally involuntary war" (Virilio, 1991a:136). Furthermore, instead of direct encounters between armies, we now have instantaneous interface mediated through computers and television screens. These and other things are associated with what Virilio calls "pure war."

Technology, or what Virilio (1995) sometimes calls the "art of the motor," clearly plays a central role in his work. As we've seen, the movie camera and its successor, the television camera, play a central role in mediating experiences and disseminating images. In his most recent book, Virilio explores a new role for technology under the heading of "endocolonization." That is, instead of a focus on colonizing the world, technology is coming to be used to colonize the human body; that is, the focus has shifted from the territorial body to the animal body. Endocolonization is concerned with the "*intraorganic intrusion of technology and its micromachines into the heart of the living*" (Virilio, 1995:100). The focus has shifted from the creating of megamachines to colonize the world to micromachines (e.g., pacemakers) to colonize the body. Thus, he sees a transplant revolution succeeding the communication revolution.

Previously, we mentioned the sedentariness that has resulted from the substitution of "teleaction" for immediate action. This sedentariness is a product of the creators of postmodern technology who have, in turn, come up with a new set of technologies to counter it. Slowed down to a state of near-inertia by the media, people can now be simultaneously speeded up through the implantation of various microtechnologies that can help them to think and act more quickly.

> remote-control teletechnology . . . will be driven to try to get rid of the dissatisfaction and frustration that result from the growing passivity and inertia of the individual dispossessed of immediate physical activity. Whence the desire to *overstimulate* the patient's organism at the same time as *tranquilizing;* in other words, to "program" the very intensity of the patient's nervous and intellectual activities just as the motor function of a machine is now already programmed.

> (Virilio, 1995:124)

The focus is shifting to doing to the human body what has been done to everything else in postmodern society. In a sense, the human body has to be brought up to speed; the speed that characterizes the rest of society now must be brought into human beings.

The implantation of various technologies also raises another familiar issue to Virilio, and other postmodernists, the elimination of the distinction between inside and outside. If there are technologies outside of us, and inside of us, and those outside stimulate those inside us, then where do we as humans end and nonhuman technologies begin? In this way, Virilio is dealing with the issue of the death of the subject within his novel ideas on speed and motors.

Another of Virilio's consistent concerns is the issue of control. With endocolonization, control over people is being taken to a whole new level. In the past, control has been exercised almost exclusively from the outside. The prison, and especially Foucault's Panopticon, would be good examples. However, with endocolonization we open up the possibility of control from the inside.[6] Clearly, this brings with it new and frightening possibilities: "For the specialists of neuroscience . . . Internal space lies open like a town about to be destroyed by invaders" (Virilio, 1995:127). (Note, here, the use of the imagery of warfare to describe this "invasion.")

Control is also central to Virilio's analysis of the coming explosion in virtual reality. With global frontiers being eliminated, science has turned to the conquest of internal frontiers like mental images. Virtual technology is an external technology, but its goal is internal control. Virtual reality technology (a *"microchip-based reality engine"* [Virilio, 1995:150]) will seek to channel and control mental images; it will involve "the cybernetic domination of thought" (Virilio, 1995:142). The level of control will, in his view, be unimaginable as people will no longer be free to construct their own mental images. Virtual reality will produce other problems, as well, such as increasing our inability to position ourselves in time and space. We will all find ourselves quite lost in a virtual universe.

I have only been able to touch on a few of Virilio's ideas here, but it is clear that he is in the process of producing a very interesting variant on French postmodern social theory.

---

[6]Of course, sociology has been long concerned with another kind of control from within resulting from socialization and the internalization of norms and values.

SUMMARY

A great deal of ground has been covered in this chapter. We began with Jacques Derrida's ideas on grammatology, or the science of writing. Writing, for Derrida, is processual involving a powerful sense of difference. There is a sense that radical alterity always looms in the background. Implied here is a radically different kind of knowledge and social world. Rather than separating the signifier and the signified as Saussure does, Derrida sees them as interchangeable. Derrida is also most often associated with the very important concept of deconstruction. Among many other things, this means a focus on marginal texts and of continual deconstruction without the illusion that one will ever discover the "truth." Decentering is involved in Derrida's work in various ways, including his effort to move away from a focus on the sign to the "becoming sign" and to move structuralism away from a focus on speech to one on writing. Writing also has a more liberating sense in Derrida's work, freeing us from external constraints; we are all currently involved in "writing" the future.

Deleuze and Guattari seek to liberate us from the interrelated control of the Oedipus complex and of capitalism over our desires. Their goal is a desiring revolution, and their model for such a revolution is the schizophrenic. What they want to do is "schizophrenize" society. Instead of psychoanalysis, Deleuze and Guattari propose schizoanalysis designed to undo the harm of psychoanalysis and to help set desire free. The objectives of such a revolution would be the destruction of the code, capitalism, and the traditional family structure that is so central to psychoanalysis. However, this is not to be a grand revolution but rather a series of microconfrontations. Schizoanalysis is oriented to the deconstruction of the old world rather than the reconstruction of a new one.

Jean-François Lyotard is best known for his critique of, his "war" on, the grand narrative. In this context, he rejects science's effort to distinguish itself from other narratives; all narratives are language games. Science has questioned the legitimacy of other kinds of narratives, but in raising this issue it has helped lead to questions about its own legitimacy. However, Lyotard does see hope for a science oriented toward "paralogy," or searching for paradoxes rather than answers, a science which continually undermines itself and its own legitimacy. The search is for dissensus rather than consensus. Lyotard not only questions science as a grand narrative but also the emancipatory, practical, and humanistic grand narratives associated with movements like Marxism and communism. He is especially critical of the terrorism associated with such perspectives. Focusing on creativity, Lyotard, like Derrida, emphasizes the importance of writing as well as of renewing ties with childhood, with creative possibilities.

Lacan's theories represent a challenge to a modern sociology based upon the idea of rational agents. His structuralist interpretation of Freud contained the beginnings of a postmodern conception of the subject and of a postmodern account of the relationship between social power and knowledge. Lacan rejected the idea of a unitary, rational subject in control of her own thoughts and desires. He suggested instead that the self is made up of imaginary identifications and intrinsically meaningless symbols and that it is haunted by an impossible real.

The final theorist discussed in the chapter is Paul Virilio. He is best known for his work on "dromology," or the study of the importance of speed in the postmodern world. Speed is seen as serving to eliminate spatial boundaries and even making it harder and harder to distinguish time from space. In fact, in his view, speed has come to overwhelm distance. Related to this is the bewildering array of images that bombard us on a daily basis, leading to a crisis of conceptualization and representation, a crisis of intelligibility. Technological changes play a key role here, and many of those developments are related to warfare. Instantaneous wars, wars that are unintelligible even to those who are supposed to be in charge of them, are a product of our increasingly speed-oriented society. In addition to external technological control, Virilio has recently become concerned with endocolonization, or colonization from within through such things as transplants of body parts and the implanting of micromachines. Such actions will allow the body to be brought up to "speed" with the rest of society. They also will lead to the death of the subject since it will be increasingly difficult to distinguish the external technologies from those within the body. Endocolonization as well as virtual reality promise new and unprecedented levels of control.

OTHER EUROPEAN PERSPECTIVES: GIDDENS, BECK, HABERMAS, BAUMAN, AND HARVEY

ANTHONY GIDDENS: THE JUGGERNAUT OF MODERNITY
ULRICH BECK: MODERNITY AND RISK
JÜRGEN HABERMAS: MODERNITY AS AN "UNFINISHED PROJECT"
ZYGMUNT BAUMAN: FROM MODERN TO POSTMODERN
    Legislators and Interpreters
    Toward a Postmodern Way of Thinking
    Postmodern Sociology, Sociology of Postmodernity
    Postmodernity and the (Possible) End of the War Against Ambivalence
    Learning to Live with Ambivalence?
    Postmodern Politics and Ethics
DAVID HARVEY: POSTMODERNISM AND MARXISM

*O*THER European theorists have had to take into account and respond to the poststructuralist and postmodernist theories emanating largely from France. In this chapter we look at the responses of three British (Giddens, Bauman, and Harvey) and two German (Beck and Habermas) social theorists. Three of these thinkers (Giddens, Beck, and Habermas) have responded by continuing the development of their modern orientations and by critiquing postmodern social theory. The fourth, Bauman, started as a modernist but in recent years has developed a number of postmodern ideas of his own. Finally, Harvey has both articulated and critiqued a postmodern orientation from a Marxian perspective. Thus, unlike the last five chapters, and to some degree like the succeeding chapter, this chapter deals not so much with postmodern social theory as with contemporary alternatives to it, as well as reactions to, and interventions in, that theory.

ANTHONY GIDDENS: THE JUGGERNAUT OF MODERNITY

In an effort to not only be consistent with his structuration theory (Giddens, 1984) but also to create an image (and a grand narrative) to rival those of classical thinkers like Weber and his iron cage, Anthony Giddens (1990) has described the modern world (with its origins in seventeenth-century Europe) as a "juggernaut." More specifically, he is using this term to describe an advanced stage of modernity—radical, high, or late modernity. In so doing, Giddens is arguing against those who have contended that we have entered the postmodern age, although he holds out the possibility of some variety of postmodernism in the future.

Here is the way Giddens describes the juggernaut of modernity:

> a runaway engine of enormous power which, collectively as human beings, we can drive to some extent but which also threatens to rush out of our control and which could rend itself asunder. The juggernaut crushes those who resist it, and while it sometimes seems to have a steady path, there are times when it veers away erratically in directions we cannot foresee. The ride is by no means wholly unpleasant or unrewarding; it can often be exhilarating and charged with hopeful anticipation. But, so long as the institutions of modernity endure, we shall never be able to control completely either the path or the pace of the journey. In turn, we shall never be able to feel entirely secure, because the terrain across which it runs is fraught with risks of high consequence.

(Giddens, 1990:139)

Modernity in the form of a juggernaut is extremely dynamic; it is a "'runaway world'" with great increases in the pace, scope, and profoundness of change over prior systems (Giddens, 1991:16).

Giddens is quick to add that this juggernaut does not follow a single path. Furthermore, it is not of one piece but rather is made up of a number of conflicting and contradictory components. Thus, Giddens is telling us that he is not offering us an old-fashioned (modern) grand narrative, or at least not a simple unidirectional grand narrative.

The idea of a juggernaut fits nicely with Giddens's (1984) structuration theory, especially the importance in that theory of time and space. The image of a juggernaut is of something that is moving along *through time* and *over physical space*. However, the juggernaut imagery does *not* fit well with Giddens's emphasis on the power of the agent; the image of a juggernaut seems to accord this modern mechanism far more power than the agents who steer it. This is consistent with the more general critique of Giddens's work that there is a disjunction between the emphasis on agency in his purely theoretical work and the substantive historical analyses that "point to the dominance of system tendencies against our ability to change the world" (Craib, 1992:149).

In his analysis of modernity, at least at the macro level, Giddens focuses on the *nation-state* (rather than the more conventional sociological focus on society), which he sees as radically different from the type of community characteristic of premodern society. Giddens defines modernity in terms of four basic institutions:

• The first is *capitalism* characterized, familiarly, by commodity production, private ownership of capital, propertyless wage labor, and a class system derived from these characteristics.

• The second is *industrialism,* which involves the use of inanimate power sources and machinery to produce goods. Industrialism is not restricted to the workplace, and it affects an array of other settings such as "transportation, communication and domestic life" (Giddens, 1990:56).

- While Giddens's first two characteristics of modernity are hardly novel, the third—*surveillance capacities*—is, although it owes a deep debt to the work of Michel Foucault (see Chapter 3).[1] As Giddens (1990:58) defines it, "Surveillance refers to the supervision of the activities of subject populations [mainly, but not exclusively] in the political sphere."
- The final institutional dimension of modernity is military power, or the *control of the means of violence,* including the industrialization of war.

Modernity is given dynamism by three essential aspects of Giddens's structuration theory. The first is time and space separation, or *distanciation* (although this process of increasing separation, like all aspects of Giddens's work, is not unilinear; it is dialectical). In premodern societies, time was always linked with space, and the measurement of time was imprecise. With modernization, time was standardized, and the close linkage between time and space was broken. In this sense, both time and space were "emptied" of content; no particular time or space was privileged; they became pure forms. In premodern societies, space was defined largely by physical presence and therefore by localized spaces. With the coming of modernity, space is progressively torn from place. Relationships with those who are physically absent and increasingly distant become more and more likely. To Giddens, place becomes increasingly "phantasmagoric," that is, "locales are thoroughly penetrated by and shaped in terms of social influences quite distant from them. . . the 'visible form' of the locale conceals the distanciated relations which determine its nature" (Giddens, 1990:19).

Time and space distanciation is important to modernity for several reasons. For one thing, it makes possible the growth of rationalized organizations like bureaucracies and the state with their inherent dynamism (in comparison to premodern forms) and their ability to link local and global domains. For another, the modern world is positioned within a radical sense of world history, and it is able to draw upon that history to shape the present. Finally, it is a major prerequisite for Giddens's second source of dynamism in modernity—disembedding.

As Giddens (1990:21) defines it, *disembedding* involves "the 'lifting out' of social relations from local contexts of interaction and their restructuring across indefinite spans of time-space." There are two types of disembedding mechanisms that play a key role in modern societies, both of which can be included under the heading of abstract systems. One is symbolic tokens, the best known of which is money. Money allows for time-space distanciation; we can engage in transactions with others who are widely separated from us by time and/or space. The other is expert systems, defined as "systems of technical accomplishment or professional expertise that organise large areas of material and social environments in which we live today" (Giddens, 1990:27). The most obvious expert systems involve professionals like lawyers and physicians, but everyday phenomena like our cars and homes are created and affected by expert systems. Expert systems provide guarantees (but not without risks) of performance across time and space.

---

[1]There is a clear cross-fertilization here and elsewhere between modern and postmodern theories.

Trust is very important in modern societies dominated by abstract systems and with great time-space distanciation. The need for trust is related to distanciation: "We have no need to trust someone who is constantly in view and whose activities can be directly monitored" (Giddens, 1991:19). Trust becomes necessary when we no longer have full information about social phenomena as a result of increasing distanciation in terms of either time or place (Craib, 1992:99). Trust is defined "as confidence in the reliability of a person or systems, regarding a given set of outcomes or events, where that confidence expresses a faith in the probity or love of another, or in the correctness of abstract principles (technical knowledge)" (Giddens, 1990:34). Trust is not only of great importance in modern society in general but also to the symbolic tokens and expert systems that serve to disembed life in the modern world. For example, in order for them to work, people must have trust in the money economy and in the legal system.

The third dynamic characteristic of modernity is its *reflexivity*. While reflexivity is a fundamental feature of Giddens's structuration theory (as well as of human existence, in his view), it takes on special meaning in modernity where "social practices are constantly examined and reformed in the light of incoming information about those very practices, thus constitutively altering their character" (Giddens, 1990:38). Everything is open to reflection in the modern world, and that includes the process of reflection itself. This serves to make everything open to question, to leave us with a pervasive sense of uncertainty. Relatedly, there is the problem of the "double hermeneutic" with the reflection of experts on the social world tending to alter that world.

The disembedded character of modern life raises a number of distinctive issues. One, as we have seen, is the need for trust in abstract systems in general and expert systems in particular. In one of his more questionable metaphors, Giddens sees children as being "inoculated" with a "dosage" of trust during childhood socialization. This serves to provide people with a "protective cocoon," which, as they mature into adulthood, helps to give them a measure of ontological security and trust. This trust tends to be buttressed by a series of predictable routines that we encounter on a day-to-day basis.

However, there is a series of new and dangerous risks associated with modernity that always threatens our trust and threatens to lead to pervasive ontological *insecurity*. As Giddens sees it, while disembedding mechanisms have provided us with security in various areas, they have also created a distinctive "risk profile." Risk is globalized in intensity (for example, nuclear war can kill us all) and in the expansion of contingent events that affect large numbers of people around the world (e.g., changes in the worldwide division of labor). Then there are risks traceable to our efforts to manage our material environment. Risks also stem from the creation of institutional risk environments such as global investment markets. People are increasingly aware of risks, but mystical phenomena like religion are increasingly less important as ways of believing that those risks can be transformed into certainties. A wider range of publics are now likely to know of the risks we all face. Finally, there is a painful awareness that expert systems are limited in their ability to deal with these risks. It is this set of risks that gives modernity the feeling of a runaway juggernaut and fills us with ontological insecurity.

What has happened? Why are we suffering from the negative consequences of being aboard the juggernaut of modernity? Giddens suggests several reasons. The first is *design faults* in the modern world; those who designed elements of the modern world made a series of mistakes. The second is *operator failure;* the problem is traceable not to the designers but to those who run the modern world. Giddens, however, gives prime importance to two other factors: *unintended consequences* and *reflexivity of social knowledge.* That is, the consequences of a system can never be forecast fully, and new knowledge is continually sending systems off in new directions. For all of these reasons, we cannot completely control the juggernaut; that is, we cannot fully manage the modern world.

However, rather than giving up in the face of the juggernaut and its attendant risks, Giddens suggests the seemingly paradoxical course of *utopian realism.* That is, he seeks a balance between utopian ideals and the realities of life in the modern world. He also accords importance to the role that social movements can play in dealing with some of the risks of the modern world and pointing us toward a society in which those risks are ameliorated.

Given his views on modernity, where does Giddens stand on postmodernity? For one thing, he rejects most, if not all, of the tenets we usually associate with postmodernism. For example, of the idea, often associated with postmodernism, that systematic knowledge is impossible, Giddens (1990:47) says that such a view would lead us "to repudiate intellectual activity altogether." For another, although he sees us as living in an era of high modernity, Giddens believes it is possible now to gain a glimpse of postmodernity. Such a world, in his view, would be characterized by a post-scarcity system, increasingly multilayered democratization, demilitarization, and the humanization of technology. (Such positive images stand in stark contrast to the pessimism of a postmodernist like Baudrillard.) However, there are clearly no guarantees that the world will move in the direction of some, to say nothing of all, of these highly positive postmodern characteristics. Yet, reflexively, Giddens believes that writing about such eventualities can play a role in helping them to come to pass.

While *The Consequences of Modernity* is a largely macro-oriented work, *Modernity and Self-Identity: Self and Society in the Late Modern Age* (Giddens, 1991) focuses more on the micro aspects of late modernity, especially the self.[2] While Giddens certainly sees the self as dialectically related to the institutions of modern society, most of his attention here is devoted to the micro end of the continuum. While we, too, will focus on the micro issues, we should not lose sight of the larger dialectic:

> Transformations in self-identity and globalisation . . . are the two poles of the dialectic of the local and the global in conditions of high modernity. Changes in intimate aspects of personal life . . . are directly tied to the establishment of social connections of very wide scope . . . for the first time in human history, "self" and "society" are interrelated in a global milieu.
>
> (Giddens, 1991:32)

---

[2]For a postmodern view of the self, see Gergen (1991).

As we have seen, Giddens (1991:32) defines the modern world as reflexive, and he argues that the "reflexivity of modernity extends into the core of the self . . . the self becomes a *reflexive project.*" That is, the self comes to be something to be reflected upon, altered, even molded. Not only does the individual become responsible for the creation and maintenance of the self, but this responsibility is continuous and all-pervasive. The self is a product of both self-exploration and of the development of intimate social relationships. In the modern world, even the body gets "drawn into the reflexive organisation of social life" (Giddens, 1991:98). We are not only responsible for the design of our selves but also (and relatedly) our bodies. (Giddens shares an interest in the body with Foucault, among others.) Central to the reflexive creation and maintenance of the self is the appearance of the body and its appropriate demeanor in various settings and locales. The body is also subject to various "regimes" (e.g., diet and exercise books) that not only help individuals mold their bodies but also contribute to self-reflexivity as well as to the reflexivity of modernity in general. The result, overall, is an obsession with our bodies and our selves within the modern world.

The modern world brings with it the "*sequestration of experience*" or the "connected processes of concealment which set apart the routines of ordinary life from the following phenomena: madness; criminality; sickness and death; sexuality; and nature" (Giddens, 1991:149, 156).[3] Sequestration occurs as a result of the growing role of abstract systems in everyday life. This sequestration brings us greater ontological security, but it is at the cost of the "exclusion of social life from fundamental existential issues which raise central moral dilemmas for human beings" (Giddens, 1991:156).

While modernity is a double-edged sword, bringing both positive and negative developments, Giddens (1991:201) perceives an underlying "looming threat of *personal meaninglessness.*" All sorts of meaningful things have been sequestered from daily life; they have been repressed. However, dialectically, increasing self-reflexivity leads to the increasing likelihood of the return of that which has been repressed. Giddens (1991:208) sees us moving into a world in which "on a collective level and in day-to-day life moral/existential questions thrust themselves back to centre-stage." The world beyond modernity, for Giddens, is a world characterized by "remoralization." Those key moral and existential issues that have been sequestered will come to occupy center stage in a society that Giddens sees as being foreshadowed, and anticipated, in the self-reflexivity of the late modern age.

Giddens (1992) picks up many of these themes in *The Transformation of Intimacy: Sexuality, Love and Eroticism in Modern Societies.* Here, Giddens focuses on ongoing transformations of intimacy that show movement toward another important concept in Giddens's thinking about the modern world—the *pure relationship,* or "a situation where a social relation is entered into for its own sake, for what can be derived by each person from a sustained association with another; and which is continued only so far as it is thought by both parties to deliver enough satisfactions for each individual to stay within it" (Giddens, 1992:58). In the case of

---

[3]There is a strong linkage here to much of Foucault's work.

intimacy, a pure relationship is characterized by emotional communication with self and other in a context of sexual and emotional equality. The democratization of intimate relationships can lead to not only the democratization of interpersonal relations in general but the macro-institutional order as well. The changing nature of intimate relations, in which women ("the emotional revolutionaries of modernity" [Giddens, 1992:130]) have taken the lead and men have been "laggards," has revolutionary implications for society as a whole.

In the modern world intimacy and sexuality (and as we saw above, much else) has been sequestered. However, while this sequestration was liberating in various senses in comparison to intimacy in traditional societies, it is also a form of repression. The reflexive effort to create purer intimate relationships must be carried out in a context separated from larger moral and ethical issues. However, this modern arrangement comes under pressure as people, especially women, attempt to reflexively construct themselves and others. Thus, Giddens is arguing for not sexual liberation or pluralism but rather for a larger ethical and moral change, a change that he sees already well under way in intimate relationships:

> We have no need to wait around for a sociopolitical revolution to further programmes of emancipation, nor would such a revolution help very much. Revolutionary processes are already well under way in the infrastructure of personal life. The transformation of intimacy presses for psychic as well as social change and such change, going "from the bottom up," could potentially ramify through other, more public, institutions.
>
> Sexual emancipation, I think, can be the medium of a wide-ranging emotional reorganisation of social life.

(Giddens, 1992:182)

Thus, Giddens not only focuses substantively on modernity, but he also sees the possibility of a brighter future for the modern world. Such a grand narrative, with its promise of a happy ending, is, as we have seen, in stark contrast to the perspectives of the postmodern social theorists.

ULRICH BECK: MODERNITY AND RISK

We have already touched on the issue of risk in Giddens's work on modernity. As Giddens says,

> Modernity is a risk culture. I do not mean by this that social life is inherently more risky than it used to be; for most people that is not the case. Rather, the concept of risk becomes fundamental to the way both lay actors and technical specialists organise the social world. Modernity reduces the overall riskiness of certain areas and modes of life, yet at the same time introduces new risk parameters largely or completely unknown to previous eras.

(Giddens, 1991:3–4)

Thus, Giddens (1991:28) describes as "quite accurate" the thesis of the work to be discussed in this section, Ulrich Beck's *Risk Society: Toward a New Modernity*.

1986 *publ.*

In terms of our concerns in this section, the subtitle of Beck's work is of greatest importance since it indicates that he, like Giddens, rejects the notion that we
have moved into a postmodern age. Rather, in Beck's view we continue to exist in
the modern world, albeit a new form of modernity. The prior, "classical" stage of
modernity was associated with industrial society, while the emerging new modernity is associated with the risk society. While we do not yet live in a risk society,
we no longer live only in an industrial society; that is, the contemporary world has
elements of both. In fact, the risk society can be seen as a type of industrial society
since many of those risks are traceable to industry. Beck offers the following
overview of his perspective:

> *Just as modernization dissolved the structure of feudal society in the nineteenth century
> and produced the industrial society, modernization today is dissolving industrial society
> and another modernity is coming into being . . . .* The thesis of this book is: we are wit-
> nessing not the end but the *beginning* of modernity—that is, of a modernity *beyond* its
> classical industrial design.

(Beck, 1992:10)

What, then, is this new modernity? and what is the risk to society that accompanies it?

Beck labels the new, or better yet newly emerging, form *reflexive modernity*. A
process of individualization has taken place in the West. That is, agents are becoming increasingly free of structural constraints and are, as a result, better able to reflexively create not only themselves but also the societies in which they live. For
example, instead of being determined by their class situations, people operate more
or less on their own. Left to their own devices, people have been forced to be more
reflexive. Beck (1992:97) makes the case about the importance of reflexivity in the
example of social relationships in such a world: "The newly formed social relationships and social networks now have to be individually chosen; social ties, too,
are becoming *reflexive,* so that they have to be established, maintained, and constantly renewed by individuals."

Beck sees a break within modernity and a transition from classical industrial society to the risk society, which while it is different from its predecessor continues
to have many of the characteristics of industrial society. The central issue in classical modernity was wealth and how it could be distributed more evenly. In advanced
modernity the central issue is risk and how it can be prevented, minimized, monitored, or managed. In classical modernity the ideal was equality, while in advanced
modernity it is safety. In classical modernity people achieved solidarity in the
search for the positive goal of equality, but in advanced modernity the attempt to
achieve that solidarity is in the search for the largely negative and defensive goal of
being spared from dangers. Of this, Bauman (1995:279) says, "We do not so much
move 'forward', as clear up the mess and seek an exit from the havoc perpetrated
by our own actions yesterday."

The risks are, to a large degree, being produced by the sources of wealth in
modern society. Specifically, it is industry and its side effects that are producing a
wide range of hazardous, even deadly, consequences for society and, as a result of
globalization (Featherstone, 1990; Robertson, 1992), the world. Using the con-

cepts of time and space, Beck makes the point that these modern risks are not restricted to place (a nuclear accident in one geographic locale could affect many other nations) or time (a nuclear accident could have genetic effects that might affect future generations).

While social class is central in industrial society, and risk is central in the risk society, risk and class are not unrelated. As stated by Beck,

> The history of risk distribution shows that, like wealth, risks adhere to the class pattern, only inversely: wealth accumulates at the top, risks at the bottom. To that extent, risks seem to *strengthen,* not to abolish, class society. Poverty attracts an unfortunate abundance of risks. By contrast, the wealthy (in income, power, or education) can *purchase* safety and freedom from risk.

(Beck, 1992:35)

What is true for social classes is also true for nations. That is, to the degree possible, risks are centered in poor nations, while the rich nations are able to push many risks as far away as possible. Further, the rich nations profit from the risks they produce by, for example, producing and selling technologies that help prevent risks from occurring or dealing with their adverse effects once they do occur.

However, neither wealthy individuals nor the nations that produce risks are safe from them. In this context, Beck (1992:37) discusses what he calls the "boomerang effect," whereby the side effects of risk "strike back even at the centers of their production. The agents of modernization themselves are emphatically caught in the maelstrom of hazards that they unleash and profit from."

While advanced modernization produces the risks, it also produces the reflexivity that allows it to question itself and the risks it produces. In fact, it is often the people themselves, the victims of the risks, who begin to reflect on those risks. They begin to observe and to collect data on the risks and their consequences. They become experts who come to question advanced modernity and its risks. They do this, in part, because they can no longer rely on scientists to do it for them. Indeed, Beck (1992:70) is very hard on scientists for their role in the creation and maintenance of the risk society: "Science has *become the protector of a global contamination of people and nature.* In that respect, it is no exaggeration to say that in the way they deal with risks in many areas, the sciences *have squandered until further notice their historic reputation for rationality.*"

While in classical industrial society nature and society were separated, in advanced industrial society nature and society are deeply intertwined. That is, changes in society often affect the natural environment, and those changes, in turn, affect society. Thus, according to Beck (1992:80), today "nature *is* society and society is also *'nature'.*" This also means that nature has been politicized, with the result that natural scientists, like social scientists, have had their work politicized.

The traditional domain of politics, the government, is losing power since the major risks are emanating from what Beck calls "sub politics," for example, large companies, scientific laboratories, and the like. It is in the subpolitical system that "the structures of a new society are being implemented with regard to the ultimate goals of progress in knowledge, outside the parliamentary system, not in opposition to it, but simply ignoring it" (Beck, 1992:223). This is part of what he calls the "unbinding of politics," where politics is no longer left to the central government but is increasingly becoming the province of various subgroups as well as of individuals. These subgroups and individuals can be more reflexive and self-critical than a central government, and they have the capability to reflect on, to better deal with, the array of risks associated with advanced modernity. Thus, dialectically, advanced modernity has generated both unprecedented risks as well as unprecedented reflexive capacities to deal with those risks.

JÜRGEN HABERMAS: MODERNITY AS AN "UNFINISHED PROJECT"

Jürgen Habermas is not only arguably today's leading social theorist, but he is also the leading defender of modernity and rationality in the face of the assault on those ideas by postmodernists (and others). According to Seidman,

> In contrast to many contemporary intellectuals who have opted for an anti- or postmodernist position, Habermas sees in the institutional orders of modernity structures of rationality. Whereas many intellectuals have become cynical about the emancipatory potential of modernity . . . Habermas continues to insist on the utopian potential of modernity. In a social context in which faith in the Enlightenment project of a good society promoted by reason seems a fading hope and spurned idol, Habermas remains one of its strongest defenders.
>
> (Seidman, 1989:2)

Habermas (1987) sees modernity as an "unfinished project," implying that there is far more to be done in the modern world before we can ever begin thinking about the possibility of a postmodern world.

Habermas regards modernity as being at variance with itself. By this he means that the rationality (largely formal rationality) that has come to characterize social systems is different from, and in conflict with, the rationality that characterizes the life-world.[4] Social systems have grown increasingly complex, differentiated, integrated, and characterized by instrumental reason. The life-world, too, has witnessed increasing differentiation and condensation (but of the knowledge bases and value spheres of truth, goodness, and beauty), secularization, and institutionalization of the norms of reflexivity and criticism (Seidman, 1989:24). A truly rational society would be one in which *both* system and life-world were permitted to rationalize in their own way, following their own logics. This would lead to a society with material abundance and control over its environments as a result of rational systems *and* one of truth, goodness, and beauty stemming from a rational life-world. However, in the modern world, system has come to dominate and to colonize the life-world. The result is that while we may be enjoying the fruits of system

---

[4]A similar view pervades Ritzer's (1996a) analysis of McDonaldization as a formally rational system producing irrationalities, in part because its dehumanizing practices are in conflict with the substantive rationality of those who work in, and utilize, such a system.

rationalization, we are being deprived of the enrichment of life that would come from a life-world that was allowed to flourish. Many of the social movements (the "greens," for example) that have arisen at the "borders" between life-world and system in the last few decades are traceable to a resistance against the colonization and impoverishment of the life-world.

In analyzing the way in which system colonizes the life-world, Habermas sees himself in alignment with much of the history of modern social thought:

> The main strand of social theory—from Marx via Spencer and Durkheim to Simmel, Weber and Lukacs—has to be understood as the answer to the entry of system-environment boundaries into society itself [Habermas's life-world], . . . which has been understood as the *hallmark of modernity.*

> (Habermas, 1991:255–256; italics added)

In other words, the "hallmark of modernity" to Habermas, as well as to most of classical social theory, has been, in Habermas's terms, the response to the problem of the colonization of the life-world by the system.

What, then, for Habermas would constitute the completion of modernity's project? It seems clear that it would be a fully rational society in which the rationalities of *both* system and life-world were allowed to fully express themselves without one overwhelming or destroying the other. We currently suffer from an impoverished life-world, and that problem must be overcome. However, the answer does not lie in the destruction of systems (especially economic and administrative systems) since it is they that provide the material prerequisites needed to allow the life-world to rationalize.

One of the issues dealt with by Habermas (1987) is the increasing problems confronted by the modern, bureaucratic social welfare state. Many of those associated with such a state recognize the problems, but their solution is to deal with them at the system level by, for example, simply adding a new subsystem to deal with the problems. However, Habermas does not think the problems can be solved in this way. Rather, they must be solved in the relationship between system and life-world. First, "restraining barriers" must be put in place to reduce the impact of system on life-world. Second, "sensors" must be built to enhance the impact of life-world on system. Habermas (1987:364) concludes that contemporary problems cannot be solved "by systems learning to function better. Rather, impulses from the life-world must be able to enter into the self-steering of functional systems." These would constitute important steps toward the creation of mutually enriching life-world and system. It is here that social movements enter the picture because it is they that represent the hope of a recoupling of system and life-world so that two can rationalize to the highest possible degree.

Given this objective, Habermas sees little hope in the United States, which seems intent on buttressing system rationality at the cost of a continuing impoverishment of the life-world. However, Habermas (1987:366) does see hope in Europe, which has the possibility of putting "an end to the confused idea that the normative content of modernity that is stored in rationalized life-worlds could be set free only by means of ever more complex systems." Thus, Europe has the possibility of assimilating "in a decisive way the legacy of Occidental rationalism" (Habermas, 1987:366). That legacy translates today into restraints on system rationality to allow life-world rationality to flourish to the extent that the two types of rationalities can coexist as equals within the modern world. Such a full partnership between system and life-world rationality would constitute the completion of modernity's project. Since we remain a long way from that goal, we are far from the end of modernity, let alone on the verge, or in the midst, of postmodernity.

Habermas not only makes a case for modernity but also a case against the postmodernists. Habermas (1981) offered some early criticisms of postmodernity[5] in an essay, "Modernity versus Postmodernity," that has achieved wide notoriety. In that essay, Habermas (1981:9) raises the issue of whether, in light of the failures of the twentieth century, we "should try to hold on to the *intentions of the Enlightenment,* feeble as they may be, or should we declare the entire project of modernity a lost cause?" Habermas, of course, is not in favor of giving up on the Enlightenment project or, in other words, giving up on modernity. Rather, he chooses to focus on the "mistakes" of those who do reject modernity. One of the latter's most important mistakes is their willingness to give up on science (he would associate Lyotard [see Chapter 7], among other postmodernists [e.g., Rorty; see Chapter 2], with this point of view), especially as it relates to the life-world. The separation of science from the life-world, and leaving it to experts, would, if done in conjunction with the creation of other autonomous spheres, involve the surrender of "the project of modernity altogether" (Habermas, 1981:14). Habermas refuses to give up on the possibility of a rational (scientific) understanding of the life-world as well as on the possibility of the rationalization of that world.

Holub (1991) has offered an overview of Habermas's most important critiques of the postmodernists. First, Habermas believes that the postmodernists are equivocal about whether they are producing serious theory or literature (Baudrillard is an excellent example of this). If we treat them as producing serious theory, then their work becomes incomprehensible because of "their refusal to engage in the institutionally established vocabularies" (Holub, 1991:158). On the other hand, if we treat the world of the postmodernists as literature, "then their arguments forfeit all logical force" (Holub, 1991:158). In either case, it becomes almost impossible to critically analyze the work of the postmodernists seriously because they can always claim that we do not understand their words or their literary endeavors.

Second, Habermas feels that the postmodernists are animated by normative sentiments, but what those sentiments are is concealed from the reader. Thus, operating with only the postmodernists' stated objectives, readers are unable to truly understand what postmodernists are really up to; why they are critiquing society in the way that they are. Furthermore, while they have hidden normative sentiments, the postmodernists overtly repudiate them. The lack of such overt sentiments prevents postmodernists from developing a self-conscious praxis aimed at overcoming the problems they find in the world. In contrast, the fact that Habermas's nor-

---

[5]See also, Habermas (1986), Freundlieb (1988), Keohane (1993), and Rorty (1984).

mative sentiments (free and open communication) are overt and clearly stated makes the source of his critiques of society clear, and they provide the base for political praxis.

Third, Habermas accuses postmodernism, contrary to its premises, of being a totalizing perspective that fails "to differentiate phenomena and practices that occur within modern society" (Holub, 1991:159). For example, the view of the world as dominated by power and surveillance (Foucault exemplifies this point of view) is not fine-grained enough to allow for meaningful analysis of the real sources of oppression in the modern world.

Finally, the postmodernists are accused of ignoring that which Habermas finds as absolutely central—everyday life and its practices. This constitutes a double loss for postmodernists. On the one hand they are closed off from an important source for the development of normative standards. After all, the rational potential that exists in everyday life is an important source of Habermas's ideas on communicative rationality. Second, the everyday world also constitutes the ultimate goal for work in the social sciences since it is there that theoretical ideas can have an impact on praxis.[6]

ZYGMUNT BAUMAN: FROM MODERN TO POSTMODERN

Zygmunt Bauman has been a perceptive analyst of the modern world *and* he has offered incisive insights into the advent of the postmodern world. Relatedly, he has dealt with the issue of modern sociology as well as what a postmodern sociology and a sociology of postmodernity might look like. Thus, depending on which aspects of his work one wishes to emphasize, he can be thought of as *either* a modern or a postmodern social theorist. For example, *Modernity and Ambivalence* (Bauman, 1991) and *Modernity and the Holocaust* (Bauman, 1989) are modernist works in subject and style, while *Postmodern Ethics* (Bauman, 1993) and *Life in Fragments: Essays in Postmodern Morality* (Bauman, 1995) are postmodernist in orientation. It is the works on postmodernism that will occupy our attention here.

Legislators and Interpreters

Bauman's (1987) thinking on the difference between modern and postmodern sociology is embedded in his broader distinction between the practitioners of two types of intellectual work—*legislators* and *interpreters.* These two types of strategies can be analyzed at a given point in time or processually, over time. When looked at in the latter sense, we can say that legislators are involved in a modern type of intellectual work and are therefore associated with modern sociology, while interpreters are doing a postmodern type of intellectual work and, as a result, are linked to postmodern sociology (Bauman, 1992:23).

Bauman associates a number of characteristics with the *legislator:*

---

[6]Of course, many postmodernists oppose and fear having such an impact.

• The *authoritative statements* of legislators serve to *arbitrate* in cases where there are differences of opinion.

• Such authoritative statements lead people to select opinions which, because of the fact that they have been supported by the legislators, are considered to be *correct* and *binding*.

• The authority to serve as arbitrators stems from the legislators' *superior knowledge base*.

• Intellectuals have *better access* to such knowledge than nonintellectuals.

• That access "is better thanks to *procedural rules* which assure the attainment of truth, the arrival at moral judgement, and the selection of proper artistic taste. Such procedural rules have a *universal validity,* as do the *products* of their application" (Bauman, 1987:4–5).

• Those who employ these rules (those in intellectual professions such as the sciences) become, as a result, the *collective owners* of the knowledge that is produced.

• That knowledge is, as a result, regarded as being "of direct and crucial *relevance* to the *maintenance and perfection* of the social order" (Bauman, 1987:5; italics added).

• This is all dependent on the work of other intellectuals who *formulate* the procedural rules and maintain control over the proper application of those rules.

• Intellectuals, like the knowledge they produce, "are *not* bound by *localized*, communal traditions" (Bauman, 1987:5: italics added).

• Because they are not bound to any specific locale, intellectuals have the right to *validate or invalidate* localized ideas. They are thereby able to falsify local (or weak) ideas.

Largely, but not exclusively, associated with modernity and modern sociology, legislators have enormous power, especially in determining what people know (or think they know).

A very different set of ideas is associated with the *interpreter*:

• Interpreters *translate* the ideas associated with one community tradition so that they can be comprehended by those in other communities.

• Interpreters are not oriented toward selecting the best ideas; the goal is simply to *facilitate* communication among autonomous communities.

• Interpreters seek to *prevent distortions* in communication.

• In order to do so, interpreters must develop a *deep understanding* of the system of knowledge to be translated.

• In addition, interpreters "need to *maintain the delicate balance* between the two conversing traditions necessary for the message to be undistorted (regarding the meaning invested by the sender) and understood (by the recipient)" (Bauman, 1987:5; italics added).

Overall, the interpreters of one community are not in a superior position to those who interpret another community; no one interpreter is inherently superior to any other. Compared to legislators, interpreters have little power, especially to impose their interpretation on community members and other interpreters. Interpreters are associated more with postmodernity than with modernity.

Obviously, the postmodern mode of the interpreter is very different from the modern approach of the legislator. However, Bauman (1987:5) makes it clear that we ought not see the interpreter as superseding the legislator in some sort of unilinear historical development.[7] Rather, what is happening is a change in their relative importance.

Toward a Postmodern Way of Thinking

Bauman recognizes that postmodernism has many different meanings, but for him it is its distinctive state of mind that is the most important meaning of postmodernism.[8] Especially notable is the fact that postmodernists are reflexive; they are far more inclined (than modernists) to critically reflect upon themselves and their ideas. As a result, the postmodernist mindset is "marked above all by its all-deriding, all eroding, all-dissolving *destructiveness*. It seems sometimes that postmodern mind is a critique caught at the moment of its ultimate triumph . . . obsessive self-criticism" (Bauman, 1992:vii–viii; italics added).

In this context, Bauman makes an interesting distinction between modern society and modern culture. To him, the postmodern mind represents an extreme version of modern culture, epitomizing and radicalizing its restlessness and its insatiability. To the degree that such a mindset has become predominant, it represents a triumph of (radical) modern culture over the much more static and conservative character of modern society. In their triumph, radical modern culture and the postmodern mind serve to overthrow the power structures that serve to hold modern society together. Bauman sees promise in this, as he does in much else associated with postmodernism, because it is the overthrow of these social structures that allows modern society to become better able to achieve its potential.

With their ascent, postmodernists do not seek to substitute one set of truths for the set they have succeeded in overthrowing. Rather, postmodernists are content to live without such truths. Postmodernists are relentlessly critical, but they are content not to propose anything new to replace that which they have helped to demolish. There is a sense, though, that in demolishing power structures (and mental blocks), the postmodernist is setting the stage for a new standard of truth (and beauty, etc.) to emerge at some future point in time.

While Bauman links postmodern and modern thinking in various ways, he seems most interested in distinguishing between the two modes of thought. For example, the modernist is characterized by an effort to understand the world rationally, and the process of achieving such an understanding helps to serve to disenchant the world. In contrast, the postmodernist is critical of rational thinking and is involved in an effort to re-enchant the world:

---

[7]Although, as we will see, he seems to change his mind on this in his later work.
[8]Bauman (1992:12) also views modernity as a distinctive (but different) mindset.

> Postmodernity . . . brings "re-enchantment" of the world after the protracted and earnest, though in the end inconclusive, modern struggle to dis-enchant it (or, more exactly, the resistance to dis-enchantment, hardly ever put to sleep, was all along the "postmodern thorn" in the body of modernity). The mistrust of human spontaneity, of drives, impulses and inclinations resistant to prediction and rational justification, has been all but replaced by the mistrust of unemotional, calculating reason. Dignity has been returned to emotions; legitimacy to the "inexplicable," nay *irrational* . . . . The postmodern world is one in which *mystery* is no more a barely tolerated alien awaiting a deportation order. . . . We learn to live with events and acts that are not only not-yet-explained, but (for all we know about what we will ever know) inexplicable. We learn again to respect ambiguity, to feel regard for human emotions, to appreciate actions without purpose and calculable rewards.

> (Bauman, 1993:33)

More important, the modernist is characterized by the effort to legislate, to control the world, to make it more docile, while the postmodernist, as we have seen, is interested in working toward the dismantling of such controls. What modernists seek to do (although often not consciously) and what postmodernists are so adamantly opposed to is caught well by Bauman (1992:xvii) when he argues, "Modernity was a long march to prison. It never arrived there (though in some places, like Stalin's Russia, Hitler's Germany or Mao's China, it came quite close), albeit not for the lack of trying."

Postmodern Sociology, Sociology of Postmodernity

Bauman is generally opposed to the development of what he calls "postmodern sociology." One of the reasons for his opposition is the fear that a radically different postmodern sociology would give up on the formative questions that lay at the foundation of the discipline. Bauman also opposes a postmodern sociology because it would, by its very nature, be in tune with the culture of postmodernity. Since postmodern culture is very different from modern culture, postmodern sociology would have to be very different than modern sociology. For example, the difference between rational modern culture and nonrational postmodern culture would be reflected in the respective sociologies. Bauman is not ready for a nonrational sociology; he wants a sociology that is to a large extent continuous with its origins.

However, there is at least one aspect of postmodern sociology that Bauman does feel comfortable with—its multiparadigmatic status.[9] Postmodern sociology "aims not so much at the *fusion of horizons,* as at the *widening of horizons* through exposition of their inherent plurality and their mutually *supplementary,* rather than mutually *exclusive,* character" (Bauman, 1992:133). While modern sociology is characterized by paradigms seeking to differentiate themselves from alternative approaches and attempting to achieve hegemony within sociology, in the inher-

---

[9]Although, it is the case that modern sociology can also be described as multiparadigmatic (Ritzer, 1975).

ently pluralistic postmodern sociology the multiple paradigms would coexist peacefully and seek to complement one another.[10]

Despite some sympathy for a postmodern sociology, Bauman feels that what we really need to develop is a *sociology of postmodernity*. While postmodern sociology breaks sharply with modern sociology, a sociology of postmodernity is continuous with modern sociology by, for example, "deploying the strategy of systematic rational discourse to the task of constructing a theoretical model of postmodern society as a system in its own right" (Bauman, 1992:65). While it is continuous with modern sociology, the sociology of postmodernity accepts "the distinctiveness of the postmodern figuration, instead of treating it as a diseased or degraded form of modern society" (Bauman, 1992:27). Thus, in the sociology of postmodernity the postmodern society is seen as a unique social form and not merely as an aberrant form of modernity.

Bauman clearly feels that modern sociology, largely as we know it, is up to the task of analyzing postmodern society. Yet modern sociology must adapt to the new realities of such a society. For example, the discipline must abandon its traditional preoccupation with the nation-state because as a framework the nation-state is not "large enough to accommodate the decisive factors in the conduct of interaction and the dynamics of social life" (Bauman, 1992:65). Also to be abandoned is the organismic model that has dominated sociology from its origin. Yet another idea that ought to be jettisoned is the image of progress. Instead, Bauman adopts a favorite idea of postmodernists, *Brownian movement*, where

> each momentary state is neither a necessary effect of the preceding state nor the sufficient cause of the next one. The postmodern condition is *underdetermined* and *underdetermining*. It "unbinds" time; weakens the constraining impact of the past and effectively prevents colonization of the future.
>
> (Bauman, 1992:190)

Finally, Bauman urges the abandonment of the modern focus on constraint. Instead, the sociology of postmodernity should focus on agency as well as the habitat that it produces and in which it operates. Thus while continuous with modern sociology, Bauman's sociology of postmodernity would have some very distinctive characteristics.

More positively, the reality that is to be analyzed by the sociology of postmodernity is "more fluid, heterogeneous and 'under-patterned' than anything the sociologists tried to grasp intellectually in the past" (Bauman, 1992:65). Beyond this, the surface changes that have taken place in the postmodern world are manifestations of a deeper transformation of the social world, changes "in the spheres of systemic reproduction, social integration and the structure of the life-world, as well as in the novel way in which these three spheres are linked and co-ordinated"

---

[10]Again, this is not so different from at least some views of modern sociology, especially Ritzer's (1981) on the need for an integrated sociological paradigm to supplement extant sociological paradigms.

(Bauman, 1992:64). In sum, the sociology of postmodernity involves a "continuation of *modern* concerns under postmodern conditions" and it "would be distinguished not by new procedures and purposes of sociological work . . . but by a new *object* of investigation" (Bauman, 1992:111).[11]

Bauman offers a number of major tenets of a sociological theory of postmodernity, including:

1 The postmodern habitat is a complex and unpredictable system.[12]

2 The postmodern habitat is complex because it lacks a central goal-setting organization and it contains a great many large and small, mainly single-purpose agencies. No one of these agencies is large enough to subsume or control the others, and each is resistant to centralized control. While they may be partially dependent on one another, "the lines of dependence cannot be fixed and thus their actions (and consequences) remain staunchly under-determined, that is autonomous" (Bauman, 1992:192). Thus, agencies are largely free to pursue their own institutionalized purposes.

3 While they are likely to be well-ordered internally, when they operate in the larger habitat, agencies face an arena that

> appears as a space of chaos and chronic *indeterminacy,* a territory subjected to rival and contradictory meaning—bestowing claims and hence perpetually *ambivalent.* All states the habitat may assume appear equally *contingent* (that is, they have no overwhelming reasons for being what they are, and they could be different if any of the participating agencies behaved differently).

> (Bauman, 1992:193)

Agencies need to be cognizant of the fact that what they do affects the habitat in which they are operating.

4 The existential situation of agents is quite fluid (Bauman, 1992:193). The identity of agents needs to be self-constituted continually, largely on the basis of trial and error. Identity is permanently changing but not developing in any clear direction. At any given time, the constitution of identity involves the disassembly of some existing elements and the assembly of new elements.

5 The only constant in all of this is the body, but even here agents devote continual attention to the cultivation of the body. People engage in a series of self-controlling and self-enhancing activities (jogging, dieting) that they would have resented were they imposed on them by some external organization. Thus, these regimens are "not perceived as externally imposed, cumbersome and resented necessities, but as manifestos of the agent's freedom" (Bauman, 1992:194). More generally, we can say that agents are no longer coerced; rather, they are seduced (see Baudrillard, Chapter 6, on seduction).

---

[11]One of the central concerns of postmodern sociology would be the consumer society that Bauman sees as central to postmodernism.

[12]This unpredictability renders useless the current reliance of sociology on statistical analysis.

6 Lacking a predesigned life-project, agents need a series of orientation points to guide their moves throughout their lifespan. These are provided by other agencies (real or imagined). Agents are free to approach or abandon these other agencies. Allegiance to a particular agency is accomplished through the selection of "symbolic tokens" indicating that one belongs to, identifies with, that agency. Agents are free to choose (or not to choose) these tokens as long as they are available and accessible.

7 Symbolic tokens must be visible as well as materially present. They also must have perceived utility to agents in the sense that they are useful in the process of self-constitution and they reassure the agent that "the current results of self-assembly are indeed satisfactory" (Bauman, 1992:195). Lacking certainty in a postmodern world, these reassurances are important to an agent. The ability of tokens to reassure people depends on whether they are vouched for by experts and whether they are of significance to large numbers of people. The need for such sources of authority stems from "the insatiable thirst of the self-constituting agents for reassurance" (Bauman, 1992:195). This leads to the general point that "*freedom* of choice and *dependence* on external agents reinforce each other, and arise and grow together as products of the same process of self-assembly and of the constant demand for reliable orientation points which it cannot but generate" (Bauman, 1992:195).

8 Accessibility to resources varies among agents depending on their personal assets, especially knowledge. Those with more knowledge can choose among a wider range of assembly patterns. Variations in freedom to choose among resources is the main basis of social standing and social inequality in postmodern society. Knowledge is also the main stake in any kind of conflict aimed at the redistribution of resources. This emphasis on knowledge tends to further enhance the status of experts. "Information becomes a major resource, and experts the crucial brokers of all self-assembly" (Bauman, 1992:196).

In terms of his legislator-interpreter distinction, Bauman seems now to be arguing that we may be witnessing the end of legislative sociology. While some may grieve over this loss, others will be liberated by it and free to do new and different types of sociology. No longer able to provide unquestioned foundations, sociology has been liberated to engage in unprecedented self-reflection and to achieve an unprecedented level of critical self-understanding:

> Sociology may then come to fulfill, at long last, the Enlightenment dream of the meeting of rational minds—without recourse to the post-Enlightenment subterfuges of blind alleys or twisted roads to Auschwitz, masquerading as short-cuts to a world without problems, conflicts and change.
>
> (Bauman, 1992:86)

Or,

> Freed from the blackmail of legislative reason, sociology may concentrate on the task for which—due to the nature of its inquiry—it has been always best prepared. It may

"come out"—openly become what it was destined to be all along: the informed, systematic commentary on the knowledge of daily life, a commentary that expands that knowledge while being fed into it and itself transformed in the process.

(Bauman, 1992:144)

The sociology that emerges from this self-reflection will be, not surprisingly, "an *interpretive*, a 'sense-making', a world mapping knowledge, that results in a mental setting in which decisions are taken and freedom of choice is exercised" (Bauman, 1992:90).

Postmodernity and the (Possible) End of the War against Ambivalence

Postmodernity is a perspective that has arisen in the wake of modernity; it is, as indicated earlier, modernism taking a look at itself and assessing its strengths and weaknesses:

Postmodernity does not necessarily mean the end, the discreditation o[r] the rejection of modernity. Postmodernity is no more (but no less either) than the modern mind taking a long, attentive and sober look at itself, at its condition and its past works, not fully liking what it sees and sensing the urge to change. Postmodernity is modernity coming of age: modernity looking at itself at a distance rather than from inside, making a full inventory of its gains and losses, psychoanalysing itself, discovering the intentions it never before spelled out, finding them mutually cancelling and incongruous. Postmodernity is modernity coming to terms with its own impossibility; a self-monitoring modernity, one that consciously discards what it was once unconsciously doing.

(Bauman, 1991:272)

In one of many efforts to offer a sense of postmodernity, Bauman argues that while modernity is characterized by "pilgrims" seeking predefined goals, postmodernity is characterized by a diverse set of "strollers," "vagabonds," "tourists," and "players." Each of the latter types communicates part of what postmodern life is all about, but that life is "too messy and incoherent to be grasped by any one cohesive model" (Bauman, 1995:91). Above all else, Bauman sees fragmentation as defining the postmodern social world. Thus, strollers wander about playfully observing fleeting fragments of the lives of those they encounter. Vagabonds are masterless strangers who roam about with no set destination; even they do not know where they will be going next. Tourists, too, are on the move, and while they may be in many places, they are never of any of them. Finally, players deal with life as a game without lasting consequences; they approach life much like children do. These four types, taken together, communicate some of the transient, fragmentary reality that is postmodernity.

Bauman offers us yet other ways of trying to get a handle on postmodern society. For example, we get another sense of how he views postmodernity in his discussion of contemporary art as a paradigm of the postmodern world. First, contemporary art defies order, either synchronic or diachronic. Second, there are no clearly recognizable dominant artistic schools or styles. Third, art tends to take the form of pastiche. Fourth, it rejects mimesis and tends to be self-referential. Fifth, there is no ultimate truth in contemporary art. And sixth, there is, as well, no ultimate authority in such art.

More generally, Bauman (1992:31) defines postmodern culture (of which contemporary art is a part) as, among other things,

- pluralistic;
- undergoing constant change;
- lacking in a "universally binding authority";
- involving a leveling of hierarchies (a more level playing field);
- subject to "interpretive polyvalence";
- dominated by the media and its messages;
- lacking in ultimate reality since all there is are signs; and
- dominated by the spectacle (from TV, and elsewhere).

Perhaps most striking is Bauman's (1992:31) adoption of Simmel's "tragedy of culture" to describe postmodern culture: "the tragedy of culture . . . has reached its completion; the body of objectively available cultural products is well in excess of the assimilating capacity of any member of society."

Pluralism comes first in the above list because it occupies a central place in Bauman's analysis of postmodern culture. As he puts it, "the main feature ascribed to 'postmodernity' is thus the permanent and irreducible *pluralism* of cultures, communal traditions, ideologies, 'forms of life' or 'language games' . . . or the awareness and recognition of such pluralism" (Bauman, 1992:102). Given such pluralism, the modern goal of securing the global hegemony of a "superior" culture no longer makes sense. Rather, in a postmodern world of cultural pluralism we must focus on how different cultures can communicate with and understand one another.[13] This is another way of restating the thesis of the ascendancy of interpreters over legislators.

From art and culture, Bauman moves to a discussion of postmodern society. To Bauman, postmodernity can also be seen as a social form (or figuration). While he associates the modern social form with work, he links postmodern society with consumption. Like Baudrillard (see Chapter 5), Bauman argues that capitalism, once it has won control over the realm of production, turns its attention to consumption. However, at least superficially, there appears to be a major difference here since while Baudrillard sees control in the realm of consumption, Bauman envisions a consumer whose pleasure principle is permitted free reign in the marketplace. Freedom in the realm of consumption serves as a sort of safety valve that helps to sustain the control that exists in the production sphere.

---

[13]At this point Bauman (1992:103) argues that he tries to define modernity/postmodernity "independent of the 'existential' issue: whether it is the 'actual conditions' which differ, or their perception." However, in discussing culture, as well as in the ensuing discussion of society, Bauman does seem to focus on existential issues.

However, on closer inspection Bauman, like Baudrillard, emphasizes control over consumption: "For the *consumer system,* a spending-happy consumer is a necessity; for the *individual consumer,* spending is a duty—perhaps the most important of duties" (Bauman, 1992:50). There are pressures to consume on both the social and the systemic level. On the *social* level the consumer feels pressure to spend to keep up symbolically with peers, to develop a self-definition that accords distinction as well as differentiation, and to receive social approval. On the *systemic* level, there is pressure to consume from the companies that merchandise consumer goods. These pressures, while powerful, perhaps even overwhelming, are not experienced by consumers as efforts at control but rather as sources of joy and pleasure. Like Pierre Bourdieu, Bauman (1992:51) believes that such seduction[14] is cheaper and more efficient than traditional controls; seduction may be taking "the place of repression as the paramount vehicle of systemic control and social integration." The result of the control of both production and consumption is a strengthened and more secure capitalist system. The capitalist system now reproduces itself by what at least appears to be individual freedom and not through more blatant forms of suppression.

Systemic reproduction and social integration in capitalist society are now on an entirely new footing. Contemporary capitalism "has nothing to gain from those things the rigid and repressive social system of 'classical' capitalism promoted: strict and universal *rules,* unambiguous criteria of *truth, morality and beauty,* indivisible *authority of judgement*" (Bauman, 1992:52). Postmodernity *is,* at least in one sense, this new, seductive form of capitalism that has replaced the coercive system of classical capitalism. This new society, especially in the realm of consumption, needs to be analyzed, in Bauman's view, with new concepts and new intellectual tools.

It is important to reiterate that while Bauman emphasizes consumption and the role played by seduction in it, he is well aware that repression continues to exist in the postmodern world, especially in the realm of production.

While Bauman discusses postmodernity in its artistic, cultural, and social forms, we should not forget that he is also interested in it from the point of view of intellectuals (e.g., legislators versus interpreters) for whom it offers, among other things, the novel experience of a new self-awareness. In fact, Bauman (1992:101; italics added) also looks at postmodernity as a cognitive phenomenon, as the "feeling of anxiety, out-of-placeness, loss of direction which, as I propose, constitutes the *true referent of the concept of 'postmodernity'.*" This cognitive analysis of postmodernity as a whole, and the anxiety that is found in it, is a reflection of the situation in which intellectuals find themselves.

Learning to Live with Ambivalence?

Ambivalence is a distinctive product of modernity, but postmodernism offers at least the possibility of overcoming that problem by simply accepting and learning

---

[14]As we saw in Chapter 6, Baudrillard discusses seduction in a very different way.

to live with ambivalence. In fact, Bauman is able to define postmodernity in opposition to modernity and its need to eliminate ambivalence:

> postmodernity means a resolute emancipation from the characteristically modern urge to overcome ambivalence and promote the monosemic clarity of the sameness . . . . Postmodernity is modernity that has admitted that non-feasibility of its original project. Postmodernity is modernity reconciled to its own impossibility—and determined, for better or worse, to live with it. Modern practice continues—now, however, devoid of the objective [ambivalence] that once triggered it off.

> (Bauman, 1991:98)

However, even if it is successful in learning to live with ambivalence, and thereby eliminating it as a source of problems (and that is by no means assured), postmodernism is fully capable of producing a range of other problems. Thus, Bauman (1991:97) concludes, postmodernity is "worrying yet nevertheless exhilarating." Or, to put it another way, postmodernity is "fraught with antinomies—torn between the chances it opens and the threats that hide behind every chance" (Bauman, 1991:251). (Most postmodernists have, as we will see, a far more pessimistic view of postmodern society; see also Mestrovic's [1993] discussion of the barbarism that he associates with postmodernism.)

Rather than seeking to eliminate ambivalence, postmodernity accepts the messiness of the world; it is not determined to impose order on it. Thus, for example, the postmodern world is more accepting of the stranger. More generally, it is a more tolerant world; it tolerates differences. However, tolerance brings with it even more ambiguity. Thus, the postmodern world is destined to be a far more uncertain world than modernity. "Lacking modernity's iron fist, postmodernity needs nerves of steel" (Bauman, 1991:245).

While Bauman generally sees postmodernity as preferable to modernity, he is, quite characteristically, ambivalent about it. For example, he argues that postmodernity shares with modernity a fear of the void. Postmodernity did not succeed in eliminating those fears, but it did serve to privatize them. Faced with private fears, postmodern individuals are also doomed to try to escape those fears on their own. Not surprisingly, they have been drawn to communities as shelters from these fears. However, this "neotribalism" raises the possibility of conflict between the tribes. Bauman worries about these hostilities and argues that we need to put a brake on them through the development of solidarity.

While the modern world sought to eliminate distinct communities and assimilate them into the whole, "postmodernity . . . is the age of community: of the lust for community, search for community, invention of community, imagining community" (Bauman, 1991:246). Maffesoli (1995) has dubbed this the age of "neotribalism." These new tribes, or communities, are the refuge for strangers and more specifically for a wide range of ethnic, religious, and political groups. These communities, and their groups, are tolerated by the larger society. "Emancipated from modern hubris, the postmodern mind has less need for cruelty and humiliating the other" (Bauman, 1991:257). However, less cruelty and humiliation and more tolerance are not enough as far as Bauman is concerned. Each of these communities needs to be *respected* by all other communities as well as by the society as a whole.

While it offers hope against ambivalence, the latter does not totally disappear in postmodernity. There is still popular disaffection and discontent, but the postmodern state no longer feels the need to control it. Rather, it may be that scattered ambivalence can be used to help society reproduce itself: "Once declared to be a mortal danger to all social and political order, ambivalence is not an 'enemy at the gate' any more. On the contrary: like everything else, it has been made into one of the stage props in the play called postmodernity" (Bauman, 1991:279).

However, the tolerance of postmodernity does not necessarily lead to solidarity. Because it is characterized by a lack of concern, postmodernity could make it easier to engage in acts of cruelty. "Postmodernity is a site of opportunity and a site of danger; and it is both for the same set of reasons [especially tolerance]" (Bauman, 1991:262). Furthermore, Bauman argues that it is quite

> easy for the postmodern tolerance to degenerate into the selfishness of the rich and resourceful . . . . The unfinished business of modern social engineering may well erupt in a new outburst of savage misanthropy, assisted rather than impeded by the newly legalized postmodern self-centredness and indifference. The protective wall of playful unconcern that the postmodern style offers was precisely what the perpetrators of modern mass cruelties missed.
>
> (Bauman, 1991:259–260)

Life in the postmodern "habitat" is not easy. It is a life without clear options and with strategies that are always open to question. However, if there is one thing that is clear in the postmodern world, it is that "freedom confined to consumer choice is blatantly inadequate for the performance of life-tasks that confront a privatized individuality" (Bauman, 1992:185). However, the paradox here is that postmodern society is, above else, a consumer society. Therefore, we seem to be doomed to the knowledge that the world we live in is inadequate to our needs.

Postmodern Politics and Ethics

While modern social theory traditionally separated theory from politics, that cannot be the case in postmodern theory (Bauman, 1992:196). Existentially, in the postmodern situation the power of the nation-state erodes. Instead of the centrality of the state, power devolves to local and partial agencies dealing with a series of local and partial policies. This serves to defuse and dissipate grievances that can no longer be directed to the state. Groups may come together to deal with specific issues, but they are likely to be split internally and to fall apart once the issue in question has been resolved or disappeared. Within this postmodern political world, some modern political problems (e.g., inequality) persist, although they are no longer as central as they once were.

While some forms of modern politics persist, it is the distinctively postmodern forms that move to center stage. Bauman outlines four main forms of postmodern politics.

- First, there are *tribal politics*. Postmodern tribes exist symbolically as imagined communities, and they are constantly renewed by symbolic rituals. Thus, tribes compete with one another by engaging in spectacular, often shocking, rituals to attract public attention and assure their survival.
- Second, there is the *politics of desire*. Here tribes seek to establish "the relevance of certain types of conduct (tribal tokens) for the self-constitution of agents" (Bauman, 1992:199). Once proven, such tokens acquire a seductive power and come to be desired by agents. Politics arises here as agencies compete with one another to have their tokens become the objects of peoples' desires.
- Third, there is the *politics of fear*. In the postmodern world, people are less likely to fear centralized control but more likely to relate to "uncertainty as to the soundness and reliability of advice offered through the politics of desire" (Bauman, 1992:199). People fear that various agencies are harming them, especially bodily.
- Finally, there is the *politics of certainty*. In a world in which people are constantly seeking to constitute themselves, they are always looking for confirmation of the fact that they have made the right choices. Experts are crucial here, and people must come to trust them. However, experts are regularly doing things that lead people to question that trust and ultimately their own self-identity.

Postmodern politics is played out largely on these four stages. Overall, agents are offered more things (consumer goods, symbolic tokens) than they can possibly use. How to decide which offers to accept and which to refuse? Most often it is on the basis of the relative amount of public attention accorded to each offer; the more the attention, the better the offer. Thus, "Postmodern politics is mostly about the reallocation of attention. Public attention is the most important—coveted and struggled for—among the scarce resources in the focus of political struggle" (Bauman, 1992:200).

Bauman (1993:21) is also interested in the status of an ethical code in a postmodern era that is inherently antagonistic to the idea of "a coherent set of precepts that ought to be obeyed by any moral person." In postmodernity the old ethical systems are no longer seen as adequate. This has opened up the possibility of a radical new understanding of moral behavior. Thus, as usual, Bauman sees postmodernity as offering an opportunity, in this case in the realm of ethics. Perhaps in postmodernity the "chances of 'moralization' of social life may—who knows?—be enhanced. It remains to be seen whether the time of postmodernity will go down in history as the twilight, or the renaissance, of morality" (Bauman, 1993:3).

It is clear that a postmodern ethics must reject much of what passed for modern ethics. Postmodern ethics must reject things like coercive normative regulation and the search for things like foundations, universals, and absolutes. Also to be rejected is modernity's search for an ethical code that is nonambivalent and lacking in contradictions. Despite such rejections, it is clear that the great issues in ethics have not lost their importance. Even in a postmodern world we are confronted with such issues as human rights, social justice, the conflict between peaceful cooperation and individual self-assertion, and the confrontation between individual conduct and the collective welfare. These issues persist, but they must be dealt with in a novel manner.

The moral code, looked at from a postmodern perspective, is rife with ambivalence and contradictions. Among the aspects of the moral condition viewed from a postmodern perspective are the following:

1 People are neither good nor bad but "morally ambivalent . . . . No logically coherent ethical code can 'fit' the essentially ambivalent condition of morality" (Bauman, 1993:10).

2 Moral phenomena are not regular and repetitive. Therefore, no ethical code can possibly deal with moral phenomena in an exhaustive fashion.

3 Morality is inherently laden with contradictions that cannot be overcome, with conflicts that cannot be resolved (with *aporia* [perplexities]).

4 There is no such thing as a universal morality.

5 "[F]rom the perspective of the 'rational order,' morality is and is bound to remain *irrational*" (Bauman, 1993:13).

6 Since Bauman rejects coercive ethical systems emanating from society as a whole, he argues for an ethical system that emanates from the self. It is based on the assumption of "being *for* the Other before one can be *with* the Other" (Bauman, 1993:13).

7 While the postmodern perspective on morality rejects the modern, coercive form of morality, it does *not* accept the idea that anything goes, the idea of complete relativism. Among the ideas central to a postmodern orientation to ethics are the following:

a Deconstruction of "the 'without us the deluge' claims of nation-states, nations-in-search-of-the-state, traditional communities and communities-in-search-of-a-tradition, tribes and neo-tribes, as well as their appointed and self-appointed spokesmen and prophets" (Bauman, 1993:14–15).

b "the remote (and, so be it, utopian) prospect of the emancipation of the autonomous moral self and vindication of its moral responsibility" (Bauman, 1993:15).

c "a prospect of the moral self facing up, without being tempted to escape, to the inherent and incurable ambivalence in which that responsibility casts it and which is already its fate, still waiting to be recast into its destiny" (Bauman, 1993:15).

Despite the ideas just discussed, neither Bauman nor postmodernism can offer an ethical code to replace the modern ethical code that is being dismantled. As a result, we are destined to a life of irresolvable moral dilemmas. Bauman (1995:42) argues that it is possible that the end of the "ethical era ushers in the era of morality." That is, without an overarching ethical code, people are left with their own individual moralities. "In a cacophony of moral voices . . . individuals are thrown back on their own subjectivity as the only ultimate ethical authority" (Bauman,

1992:xxii). Thus, the challenge of the postmodern world is how to live morally in the absence of an ethical code and in the presence of a bewildering array of seemingly equal moralities. Without such an overarching code, life in the postmodern world is not likely to grow any easier, although it is at least possible that life will become more moral with the dismantling of the oppressive and coercive ethical code associated with modernity. After all, Bauman associates the most heinous of crimes (e.g., the Holocaust) with the modern ethical code. At the minimum, we will be able to face moral issues directly without the disguises and deformities that came with the modern ethical code (Bauman, 1995:37).

Instead of the coercive and deforming ethical codes of modernity, there is hope in the conscience of the moral self, especially its need to be *for* the Other. The Other is the responsibility of the moral self. Power (as well as freedom) is implied in this relationship: "One is responsible *to* someone stronger than oneself; one is responsible *for* someone weaker than oneself" (Bauman, 1995:64). Being for the other does not determine goodness and evil. That will be worked out in the course of the relationship. It will be worked out in a world devoid of certainty and where there will never be a clear dividing line between good and evil.

Bauman concludes:

> we have little choice but to place our bet on that conscience which, however wan, alone can instil the responsibility for disobeying the command to do evil. Contrary to one of the most uncritically accepted philosophical axioms, there is no contradiction between the rejection of (or scepticism towards) the ethics of socially conventionalized and rationally "founded" norms, and the insistence that it does matter, and *matter morally,* what we do and from what we desist. Far from excluding each other, the two can be accepted or rejected only together. If in doubt—consult your conscience.
>
> Moral responsibility is the most personal and inalienable of human possessions, and the most precious of human rights.
>
> (Bauman, 1993:250)

In this way, Bauman adopts a postmodern position *without* surrendering to relativism and nihilism. Nonetheless, there is a fundamental tension between the unconditional need to be for the other and the "discontinuous, fragmentary, episodic, consequences—avoiding life" that Bauman associates with postmodernity (Bauman, 1995:268).

The postmodern world is simultaneously one of great moral hope and great personal discomfort: "The ethical paradox of the postmodern condition is that it restores to agents the fullness of moral choice and responsibility while simultaneously depriving them of the comfort of the universal guidance that modern self-confidence once promised" (Bauman, 1992:xxii). To put it another way, morality, like much else in the postmodern world, has been privatized. Without a larger ethical system to guide them, ethics for individuals become matters of "individual discretion, risk-taking, chronic uncertainty and never-placated qualms" (Bauman, 1992:xxiii). Postmodernity may be either our "bane" or our "chance" (Bauman, 1995:8). Which it will be is far from determined at this juncture in history.

DAVID HARVEY: POSTMODERNISM AND MARXISM

David Harvey's foray into postmodernist theory from a Marxian perspective (1989; Kamolnick, 1994) not only closes this chapter but anticipates the discussion of Frederic Jameson's work in the next chapter. The collapse of the Soviet Union, and communism more generally, has posed deep threats to all varieties of neo-Marxian social theory (Callari, Cullenberg, and Biewener, 1995). At the same time, postmodernism, with its rejection of such central components of most varieties of neo-Marxian theory as the grand narrative, the revolutionary subject, centralized power, and social class, has created an additional set of threats. But there are also opportunities for Marxian theorists, and some have gravitated toward postmodern social theory as a theoretical orientation to be integrated with their Marxian orientation. In this section we take a brief look at the work of David Harvey, and in the next chapter on American interventions we discuss the Marxian approach of Frederic Jameson.

While Harvey sees much of merit in postmodern thinking, he sees serious weaknesses in it from a Marxian viewpoint. Postmodern theory is accused of overemphasizing the problems of the modern world and of underemphasizing its material achievements. Most important, it seems to accept postmodernity and its associated problems rather than suggesting ways of overcoming these difficulties: "The rhetoric of postmodernism is dangerous for it avoids confronting the realities of political economy and the circumstances of global power" (Harvey, 1989:117). What postmodern theory needs to confront is the source of its ideas—the political and economic transformation of late twentieth-century capitalism.

Central to the political economic system is control over markets and the labor process (these two arenas involve the issue of *accumulation* in capitalism). While the postwar period between 1945 and 1973 was characterized by an inflexible process of accumulation, since 1973 we have moved to a more flexible process. Harvey associates the earlier period with Fordism (as well as Keynesian economics) and the later period with post-Fordism. While Fordism is inflexible, Harvey sees post-Fordism as associated with flexible accumulation resting "on flexibility with respect to labour processes, labour markets, products, and patterns of consumption. It is characterized by the emergence of entirely new sectors of production, new ways of providing financial services, new markets, and, above all, greatly intensified rates of commercial, technological, and organizational innovation" (1989:147).

While Harvey sees great changes and argues that it is these changes that lie at the base of postmodern thinking, he believes that there are many *continuities* between the Fordist and post-Fordist eras. His major conclusion is that while "there has certainly been a sea-change in the surface appearance of capitalism since 1973 . . . the underlying logic of capitalist accumulation and its crisis tendencies remain the same" (Harvey, 1989:189). Thus, Harvey adopts a viewpoint that resembles, at least in the latter respect, that of Jameson.

Central to Harvey's approach is the idea of time-space compression. He believes that modernism served to compress both time and space and that that process has accelerated in the postmodern era, leading to "an intense phase of time-space compression that has a disorienting and disruptive impact upon political-economic practices, the balance of class power, as well as upon cultural and social life" (Harvey, 1989:284). But this is *not* essentially different from earlier epochs in capitalism: "We have, in short, witnessed another fierce round in that process of annihilation of space through time that has always lain at the center of capitalism's dynamic" (Harvey, 1989:293). To give an example of the annihilation of space through time, cheeses once available only in France are now widely sold throughout the United States because of rapid, low-cost transportation. Or, in the 1991 war with Iraq, television transported us instantaneously from air raids in Baghdad to "scud" attacks on Tel Aviv to military briefings in Riyadh.

Thus, to Harvey, postmodernism is *not* discontinuous with modernism; they are reflections of the same underlying capitalist dynamic. Both modernism and postmodernism, Fordism and post-Fordism, coexist in today's world. The emphasis on Fordism and post-Fordism will "vary from time to time and from place to place, depending on which configuration is profitable and which is not" (Harvey, 1989:344). Such a viewpoint serves to bring the issue of postmodernity under the umbrella of neo-Marxian theory, although it is, in turn, modified by developments in postmodern thinking.

Finally, Harvey discerns changes and cracks in postmodernity, indicating that we may already be moving into a new era, an era that neo-Marxian theory must be prepared to theorize, perhaps by integrating still other idea systems.

SUMMARY

This chapter deals with the interventions of five European theorists in the literature on postmodern social theory. We begin with Anthony Giddens's work on the juggernaut of modernity. While Giddens sees us in a late stage of modernity, it is still modernity as far as he is concerned. However, Giddens does hold out the possibility of moving toward a postmodern society. Most notable here, however, is his thinking on modernity as a juggernaut moving through time and space, as well as his ideas on three essential modern processes—distanciation, disembedding, and reflexivity. While he sees many positive byproducts of the juggernaut of modernity, Giddens is also sensitive to the risks associated with it. Giddens not only deals with modernity at the macro level but also at the micro level in terms of its impact on self-identity and intimate relationships.

Beck picks up on one aspect of Giddens's work to emphasize the place of risk in the modern world. Indeed, to Beck, we have moved from classical modernity defined by wealth and how to distribute it more equitably to advanced modernity where the defining issue is risk and how to avoid, or deal with, it.

Habermas sees modernity as an unfinished project. He rejects the postmodern position because he still has faith in the modern project. Rather than jumping to some postmodern alternative, Habermas favors allowing modernity to complete its project by becoming more fully rational at both the life-world and the system levels. We also detail several of Habermas's more specific criticisms of postmodern social theory.

Zygmunt Bauman offers a useful distinction between modern (legislators) and postmodern (interpreters) intellectuals. Among other things, legislators are able to offer authoritative statements, while interpreters are generally restricted to translating ideas from one community to another. The interpreters, and more generally a postmodern mind and way of thinking, are on the ascendancy, while the legislators and modern thought are in decline. While a postmodern way of thinking has its problems, at least it does not lead us to Auschwitz and other notable pathologies associated with the modern mode of thought.

Bauman does not favor postmodern sociology because it would, among other things, be nonrational. However, what Bauman does think we need is a sociology of postmodernity. That is, he wants modern, rational sociology to devote its attention to the postmodern social configuration. However, Bauman does seem to think that we are witnessing the end of foundational legislative sociology and that it is being replaced by a more reflective, interpretive, or sense-making, sociology.

In Bauman's view, postmodernity may bring with it the end of the modern war against ambivalence; postmodernism is defined at least in part by its acceptance of ambivalence. While there are opportunities associated with postmodernity, there are also dangers linked to it (e.g., the selfishness of the "haves"), and, given its inherent ambiguity, life in it will certainly not be easy. Bauman also examines the politics and the morality associated with postmodernity. Politically, postmodernity will, among other things, be characterized by local rather than national politics. Ethically, postmodernity will be defined by individual morality rather than grand ethical systems. In Bauman's view, this postmodern morality must be dominated by a need and a responsibility for the Other.

David Harvey offers a Marxian approach to the postmodern world. While he recognizes that dramatic changes have taken place in recent years, he also sees continuities between modern and postmodern society in the capitalist system that dominates both. Harvey is best known for his ideas on the acceleration of time-space compression in the postmodern world. He also sees the beginning of fractures in the postmodern world giving renewed possibilities to Marxian theory.

9

AMERICAN INTERVENTIONS:
BELL, JAMESON, FEMINISTS,
AND MULTICULTURALISTS

DANIEL BELL: POSTINDUSTRIAL SOCIETY
FREDRIC JAMESON: THE CULTURAL LOGIC OF LATE CAPITALISM
FEMINIST THEORY AND POSTMODERN THEORY
MULTICULTURAL THEORY

*I*n this chapter we examine largely American interventions in the literature on postmodern social theory. We begin with the work of a mainstream sociologist, Daniel Bell, who, while he is certainly not a postmodernist, is widely known for the creation of a concept, "postindustrial society," that is often seen as compatible with postmodern views of the social world. Next, we examine the ideas of a nonsociologist, Fredric Jameson, who, like David Harvey, seeks to contribute to postmodern social theory while remaining within Marxian theory. We will then deal with American contributions to two bodies of literature that are implicated in the debate on postmodern social theory. The first is feminist social theory, which, while it has its postmodern theorists, has a highly ambivalent attitude toward, and relationship with, postmodern social theory. The second is theoretical work on multiculturalism, work which has a series of close affinities with postmodern thinking.

DANIEL BELL: POSTINDUSTRIAL SOCIETY

As we saw in Chapter 1, the concept of postmodernity involves the idea that a new, postmodern society has come into existence and succeeded modern society. While he is clearly a modernist, Daniel Bell (1973, 1976) created the similar idea that we are in the process of evolving from an industrial to a postindustrial society. Given his modern orientation, Bell had no hesitation in offering this as a grand narrative of developments, especially in the United States, Japan, Western Europe, and even the (former) Soviet Union. Also reflective of his modernist perspective is the fact that Bell had some highly critical things to say about postmodernism.

Bell divides society into three realms: social (or techno-economic) structure, polity, and culture. The coming of postindustrial society involves, primarily, changes in social structure, especially the economy, the work world, and science and technology. While they do not cause changes in the other parts of society—polity and culture—changes in social structure clearly have major implications for them. However, Bell's primary focus, at least initially, is on the changing character of social structure.

Bell (1973:14) offers a very parsimonious summary of the elements of the change he envisions. First, within the economy we witness the transition from the predominance of goods production to service. While there are various types of services (e.g., retail, banking), it is health, education, research, and government service that are the most decisive for a postindustrial society.

Second, professional and technical work comes to dominate the occupational realm. Especially important here is the rise of scientists and engineers.

Third, theoretical knowledge is essential to postindustrial society. Such knowledge is viewed as the basic source of innovation and policy formulation. Involved here is an emphasis on theoretical rather than empirical knowledge and the codification of knowledge. It is the growth of this type of knowledge, in all its variety, that is central to the emergence of the postindustrial society:

> the major source of structural change in society—the change in the modes of innovation in the relation of science to technology and in public policy—is the change in the character of knowledge: the exponential growth and branching of science, the rise of a new intellectual technology, the creation of systematic research through R&D budgets, and as a calyx of all of this, the codification of theoretical knowledge.

> (Bell, 1973:44)

Fourth, postindustrial society is oriented toward the assessment and control of technology and its impact. Bell (1973:26) sees much hope here: "The development of new forecasting and 'mapping techniques' makes possible a novel phase in economic history—the conscious, planned advance of technological change, and therefore the reduction of indeterminacy about the economic future."

Finally, decision making involves the creation of a new "intellectual technology." To handle the large-scale complexity of postindustrial society, we witness the emergence and increasing importance of new intellectual technologies such as "information theory, cybernetics, decision theory, game theory, utility theory, stochastic processes" (Bell, 1973:29).

Bell articulates his ideas within the context of a grand narrative, "a general schema of social change" from preindustrial (Asia, Africa, North America), industrial (Western Europe, the [former] Soviet Union and Japan), and postindustrial (with the United States being the sole representative, at least at the time he was writing). There are a number of distinctions among these three types of societies. For example, occupationally, preindustrial society is dominated by farmers, miners, fishermen, and unskilled workers; industrial society by semi-skilled workers and engineers; and postindustrial society by professional and technical scientists.

In design, preindustrial societies involve a "game against nature." That is, people are primarily involved in efforts to extract things from nature in the realm of mining, fishing, forestry, and agriculture. Industrial societies are focused on a "game against fabricated nature"; that is, a society dominated by the machine and the resulting need to coordinate, schedule, program and organize things to a high degree. Because it is dominated by services, postindustrial society is a "game between persons," a game that primarily involves differences in knowledge. As Bell (1973:127) puts it, "What counts is not raw muscle power, or energy, but information."

Also central in the new knowledge-based, postindustrial economy is the development of new technologies and a new relationship between science and technology. Scientific research has been institutionalized, and new science-based industries have come into existence. Overall, the "new fusion of science with innovation, and the possibility of systematic and organized technological growth, is one of the underpinnings of the postindustrial society" (Bell, 1973:197). This leads to the need for more university-trained students and more and better universities. In Bell's (1973:245-246) view, "the university increasingly becomes the primary institution of the postindustrial society." The university is increasingly charged with producing the highly trained experts needed to guide society in this period of dramatic change.

In preindustrial societies, the landowners and the military hold the power, and they exercise it through the direct use of force. In industrial society, the business people have the lion's share of the power, although they exercise it indirectly by influencing politicians. Scientists and researchers come to the fore as the dominant figures in the postindustrial society, and they seek to balance technical and political forces.

While Bell focuses on the social structure (or the techno-economic) in *The Coming of Post-Industrial Society,* it is culture and, to a lesser extent, the polity that take center stage in a later book, *The Cultural Contradictions of Capitalism* (Bell, 1976). The book is premised on the idea that these three focal realms "are ruled by contrary axial principles: for the economy, efficiency; for the polity, equality; and for the culture, self-realization (or self-gratification)" (Bell, 1976:xi-xii). Bell's main focus is on the conflict between the techno-economic and the cultural realms:

> what I find striking today is the radical disjunction between the social structure (the techno-economic order) and the culture. The former is ruled by an economic principle defined in terms of efficiency and functional rationality, the organization of production through the ordering of things, including men as things. The latter is prodigal, promiscuous, dominated by an anti-rational, anti-intellectual temper in which the self is taken as the measure of aesthetic worth of experience.

> (Bell, 1976:37)

Still functioning in the techno-economic realm, the old character traits of self-discipline, restraint, and delayed gratification now come into conflict with the hedonism that characterizes the cultural domain.

Bell sees a long-running conflict between the techno-economic realm and modern culture, but that conflict reached new heights in the 1960s with the rise of postmodernism, which is seen as a logical outgrowth of modernism. Bell does not define postmodern culture, but he associates such terms as "impulse," "pleasure," "liberation," and "eroticism" with it. Clearly, a culture defined in this way is at odds with a techno-economic realm still defined by efficiency and rationality. "What we have today is a radical disjunction of culture and social structure, and it is such disjunctions which historically have paved the way for more direct social revolutions" (Bell, 1976:53). In fact, in some basic ways the revolution has begun as the new hedonism has moved out of the realm of art and culture into life itself, and it creates a life style that is now available to more and more people.

While he may write about postmodernism, at least in a limited sense, Bell does not operate as a postmodern social theorist, in part because he so obviously disapproves of the cultural changes he associates with postmodernism. However, one thing Bell does have in common with postmodern social theorists is the central role he accords to the consumer society. Because of the mass production and sale of goods of all types, prodigality and ostentatious display have replaced frugality and asceticism. This is part of a general trend toward an erosion of traditional cultural values; toward a cultural hedonism "concerned with play, fun, display and pleasure" (Bell, 1976:70). There is, as a result, an enormous disjunction between such a culture and the techno-economic realm still dominated by the Protestant Ethic. "It is this disjunction which is the historic cultural crisis of all Western bourgeois society. This cultural contradiction is, in the longer run, the most fateful division in the society" (Bell, 1976:84).

Bell is writing in the 1970s as a modernist critic of a series of changes, especially cultural changes, that he dimly perceives as being part of some new postmodern development. In retrospect one has to give Bell credit for beginning to piece together a series of developments that we now, two decades later, recognize as postmodern culture. Among the issues that Bell touched on under this heading are changes in time and space, the lack of a center, the dominance of a visual culture, nonrationality and irrationality, anti-intellectualism, the breakdown of the distinction between high and low culture, the loss of the self, the theater of Antonin Artaud, and so on. And Bell was reading, albeit not dispassionately, the work of people like Foucault, Sontag, and McLuhan. While he is best known for his ideas about postindustrial society, in many ways Bell was a more prescient analyst of the then-emerging postmodern culture.

FREDRIC JAMESON: THE CULTURAL LOGIC
OF LATE CAPITALISM

The dominant position among postmodern theorists (one shared by Daniel Bell) is clearly that there is a radical disjunction between modernity and postmodernity. However, there are many postmodernists who argue that while postmodernity has important differences with modernity, there are also significant continuities between them. The best-known thinker associated with the latter position is Fredric Jameson (1984b, 1991). Like many significant postmodernists, Jameson is not a sociologist. He is best known as a literary theorist, although he is also a wide-ranging social theorist.[1]

---

[1]Jameson has been a professor of French and Comparative Literature and is currently the William A. Lane Professor of Comparative Literature and Director of the Graduate Program in Literature and the Duke Center for Critical Theory at Duke University.

Jameson adopts the Marxian position,[2] following Ernest Mandel (1975; Norton, 1995),[3] that capitalism continues to be of central importance, although it is now in its "late" phase. Late capitalism continues to dominate today's world, but it has spawned a new cultural logic—postmodernism. In other words, while the cultural logic may have changed, the underlying economic structure is continuous with earlier forms of capitalism. Furthermore, capitalism continues to be up to its same old tricks of spawning a cultural logic to help maintain itself.

In writing in this vein, Jameson is clearly rejecting the claim made by many postmodernists and poststructuralists (Lyotard, Baudrillard, Foucault) that Marxian theory is perhaps the grand narrative par excellence and therefore has no place in, or relevance to, a postmodern way of thinking and a postmodern world. Jameson is not only rescuing Marxian theory but endeavoring to show that it offers the best theoretical explanation of postmodernity: "The Marxist framework is still indispensable for understanding the new historical content, which demands, not a modification of the Marxist framework, but an expansion of it" (Jameson, in Stephanson, 1989:54). Interestingly, while Jameson is generally praised for his insights into the culture of postmodernism, he is often criticized, especially by Marxists, for offering an inadequate analysis of the economic base of this new cultural world. In fact, Jameson spends very little time analyzing that economic base and devotes virtually all of his attention to the cultural logic.

Also consistent with the work of Marx, and unlike most theorists of postmodernism, Jameson (1984b:86) sees both positive and negative characteristics, "catastrophe and progress all together," associated with postmodern society. Marx, of course, viewed capitalism in this way as productive of liberation and very valuable advancements *as well as* being the height of exploitation and alienation. In fact, Jameson seems ambivalent about postmodernism:

> I want to propose a dialectical view in which we neither see postmodernism as immoral, frivolous or reprehensible because of its lack of high seriousness, nor as good in the McLuhanist, celebratory sense of the emergence of some wonderful new utopia. Features of both are going on at once.

> (Jameson, in Stephanson, 1989:52-53).

He accepts many of its basic tenets such as the death of the subject (including the end of charisma and the genius), the end of entrepreneurialism and inner-directed individuality, the eclipse of subjectivity, and the new anonymity. For example, of the death of the subject, Jameson says

> the extinction of the "great moderns" is not necessarily an occasion for pathos. Our social order is richer in information and more literate, and socially, at least, more "democratic" in the sense of the universalization of wage labor . . . this new order no longer needs prophets and seers and the high modernist and charismatic type, whether among its cultural producers or its politicians. Such figures no longer hold any charm or magic

---

[2]For a critique of Jameson's Marxian orientation, see Ellis (1994).

[3]Jameson's (1981) Marxian orientation predates his effort to use Mandel's (1975) perspective to analyze late capitalism.

for the subjects of a corporate, collectivized, post-individualistic age: in that case, good-bye to them without regrets . . . woe to the country that needs geniuses, prophets, Great Writers, or demiurges!

(Jameson, 1991:306)

However, Jameson rejects some of postmodernism's most extreme views such as the celebration of "schizophrenic flux and nomadic release" (Jameson, 1991:174).

While he is a critic of the postmodern world, Jameson has no nostalgia for modernism. For example, he sees modernism as characterized by uneven development. Thus, while artists may be able to express power and control in that world, the artist's subjects are not similarly endowed. Uneven development is also manifest in the fact that some social structures are more developed than others. He uses, as an example, Kafka's *The Trial,* in which one sees a modern bureaucracy existing side-by-side with an old-fashioned political structure. Postmodernity has succeeded in sweeping away the archaic remnants[4] and is, in a sense, more modern than modern:

In the postmodern, then, the past itself has disappeared (along with the well-known "sense of the past" or historicity and collective memory). Where its buildings still remain, renovation and restoration allow them to be transferred to the present in their entirety as those other, very different and postmodern things called *simulacra.* Everything is now organized and planned; nature has been triumphantly blotted out, along with peasants, petit-bourgeois commerce, handicraft, feudal aristocracies and imperial bureaucracies. Ours is a more homogeneously modernized condition; we no longer are encumbered with the embarrassment of non-simultaneities and non-synchronicities. Everything has reached the same hour on the great clock of development or rationalization (at least from the perspective of the "West").

(Jameson, 1991:309-310)

Jameson (1984b:54) begins his analysis by recognizing that postmodernism is ordinarily associated with a radical break, but then after discussing a number of things usually associated with postmodernism, he asks, "does it imply any more fundamental change or break than the periodic style—and fashion—changes determined by an older high modernist imperative of stylistic innovation?" He responds that while there certainly have been esthetic changes, those changes continue to be a function of underlying economic dynamics:

What has happened is that aesthetic production today has become integrated into commodity production generally: the frantic economic urgency of producing fresh waves of ever more novel-seeming goods (from clothing to airplanes), at ever greater rates of turnover, now assigns an increasingly essential structural function and position to aesthetic innovation and experimentation. Such economic necessities then find recognition

[4]This contradicts the idea of many postmodern theorists that their theories represent a pastiche of the old and the new.

in the institutional support of all kinds available for the newer art, from foundations and grants to museums and other forms of patronage.

(Jameson, 1984b:56)

The continuity with the past is even clearer and more dramatic in the following:

this whole global, yet American, postmodern culture is the internal and superstructural expression of a whole new wave of American military and economic domination throughout the world: in this sense, as throughout class history, the underside of culture is blood, torture, death and horror.

(Jameson, 1984b:57)

Thus, Jameson seeks to embed his analysis in an economic base and to avoid producing "yet another disembodied culture critique or diagnosis of the spirit of the age" (Jameson, 1991:400).

Jameson employs Mandel's (1975) thinking on the three stages in the history of capitalism.[5] The first stage, analyzed by Marx, is market capitalism and the emergence of unified national markets. The second stage, analyzed by Lenin, is the imperialist phase with the emergence of a global capitalist network. The third period, labeled by Mandel (and Jameson, following Mandel) as "late capitalism,"[6] involves "a prodigious expansion of capital into hitherto uncommodified areas" (Jameson, 1984b:78). This expansion, "far from being inconsistent with Marx's great nineteenth-century analysis, constitutes on the contrary the purest form of capital yet to have emerged" (Jameson, 1984b:78). For Jameson, the key to modern capitalism is its multinational character and the fact that it has greatly increased the range of commodification; indeed culture itself has come to be commodified. A number of other things are linked with the stage of multinational capitalism including transnational business, a new international division of labor, production moving to third world areas, a dizzying growth in international banking and the stock market, and new types of interrelationships among the media, computerization, and automation.

Jameson also links this developmental process to changes in signs. Signs came into being in the early stages of capitalism and had an unambiguous relationship to their referents. Later, in modernism, signs were decoupled from referents, although this

disjunction does not completely abolish the referent, or the objective world, or reality, which still continues to entertain a feeble existence on the horizon like a shrunken star or red dwarf. But its great distance from the sign now allows the latter to enter a moment of autonomy, of a relatively free-floating Utopian existence, as over against its for-

---

[5]According to Kellner (1989a:13-14), "Jameson's own thought is relentlessly diachronic and 'history' emerges as his master category . . . he interprets Marxism as *the* theory of history . . . this 'absolute presupposition' of Jameson's project."

[6]Jameson (1991:xviii) uses a number of terms as more or less synonymous with late capitalism including " 'multinational capitalism,' 'spectacle or image society,' 'media capitalism,' 'the world system,' even 'postmodernism' itself."

mer objects. This autonomy of culture, this semiautonomy of language, is the moment of modernism.

(Jameson, 1991:96)

Then there is postmodernism, a heightened later stage characterized by "a kind of reversal of quantity into quality, reification penetrates the sign itself and disjoins the signifier from the signified. Now reference and reality disappear altogether, and even meaning—the signified—is problematized. We are left with that pure and random play of signifiers" (Jameson, 1991:96). This pure play of signifiers is of central importance to Jameson, as it was to Baudrillard, who strongly influenced Jameson's thinking.

More generally, changes in the economic structure have been reflected in cultural changes.[7] Thus, Jameson associates realist culture with market capitalism, modernist culture with monopoly capital, and postmodern culture with multinational capitalism. This seems to be an updated version of Marx's base-superstructure argument, and many have criticized Jameson for taking such a deterministic position. For example, Jameson (1991:301) discusses how analyses of, and comparisons between, modern and postmodern cultural phenomena "are in reality the figuration and the expressive raw material of a deeper comparison between the modes of production themselves." Indeed, he argues that the various postmodernisms share an interest in, if not an exaltation of, the market. However, Jameson has his own misgivings about such an argument (e.g., that it obligates one to talk about culture in economic terms), has tried hard to avoid such a "vulgar" position, and has described a more complex relationship between the economy and culture. To deal with this complex relationship, Jameson has employed concepts "like overdetermination, uneven development, semi-autonomy, and reciprocal interaction" (Kellner, 1989a:18). Nonetheless, even as sympathetic a critic as Featherstone (1989:119) concludes, "it is clear that his view of culture largely works within the confines of a base-superstructure model."

Culture has not only gone from a stage in monopoly capital in which it is, at least to some degree, autonomous to a more tightly integrated state in multinational capitalism, but it has also undergone explosive growth in the latter phase:

a prodigious expansion of culture throughout the social realm, to the point at which everything in our social life—from economic value and state power to practices and to the very structure of the psyche itself—can be said to have become "cultural" in some original and as yet untheorized sense. This proposition is, however, substantively quite consistent with the previous diagnosis of a society of the image or the simulacrum, and a transformation of the "real" into so many pseudo-events.

(Jameson, 1991:48)

Jameson describes culture in this new state as a "cultural dominant." Postmodernism is that cultural dominant, and it is described as a "force field in which very

---

[7]Although Jameson (1991:67) makes it clear that culture, like the economy, is unmistakably material.

different kinds of cultural impulses . . . must make their way" (Jameson, 1984b:57). Thus, while postmodernism is "a new systematic cultural norm," it is made up of a range of quite heterogeneous elements (Jameson, 1984b:57). By using the term "cultural dominant," Jameson also clearly means that while postmodern culture is controlling, there are various other elements that exist within today's culture, especially the heterogeneous and resistant elements that postmodernism is attempting to subdue and dominate. Thus, in discussing a cultural dominant, Jameson is not suggesting an inevitable or uncontested cultural uniformity.

Within postmodern culture, Jameson argues that video (both commercial video and experimental video, or video art) is the most likely candidate for the dominant position. He sees the "total flow," the ceaseless rotation of components, as characteristic of video and, more generally, of postmodern culture. And video, in turn, is closely tied to other elements involving such total flow including computers and information technology. The precursor of video, especially given its total flow, is the cartoon. The implication seems to be that we are increasingly confronting a cartoon-like reality.

Cartoons, like video, can be seen as texts, and like most other poststructuralists and postmodernists, Jameson sees the "text" replacing the "work" (e.g., the masterwork, the work of art produced by a specific author or artist) in postmodern society:

> Everything can now be a text in that sense (daily life, the body, political representations), while objects that were formerly "works" can now be reread as immense ensembles of systems of texts of various kinds, superimposed on each other by way of the various intertextualities, successions of fragments, or, yet again, sheer process . . . the autonomous work of art thereby—along with the old autonomous subject or ego—seems to have vanished, to have been volatilized.
>
> (Jameson, 1991:77)

With the coming of texts, there is no more canon, no more masterpieces or great works. Instead, all we have left are texts, "that is . . . the ephemeral . . . disposable works that wish to fold back immediately into the accumulating detritus of historical time" (Jameson, 1991:78). Unlike works, texts have *no* deeper meaning. Attempts to find meanings, to thematize texts, to interpret them,[8] only serve to interrupt the flow that is essential to them. Thus, "the postmodernist text . . . is . . . a structure of sign flow which resists meaning, whose fundamental inner logic is the exclusion of the emergence of theories as such" (Jameson, 1991:91).

The centrality of texts means that postmodern thinking is opposed to the generation of propositions, even the appearance of making primary statements, the making of statements with positive, affirmative content, the making of statements about being, and, ultimately, the rendering of judgments about truth. All of these oppositions are linked to

---

[8]However, Jameson contradicts himself here since he often does interpretive work. As Kellner (1989b:11; see also, Best, 1989:341) puts it, "Jameson is . . . unabashedly committed to hermeneutics." Contrast this to the following statement by Jameson: "I tried to show how this goes along with a new kind of depth, that is various hermeneutics in which one interprets an appearance in terms of some underlying reality which these philosophies then uncode" (in Stephanson, 1989:44).

the widespread feeling that inasmuch as everything we utter is a moment in a larger chain or context, all statements that seem primary are in fact only links in some larger "text" . . . we can never go back far enough to make primary statements, that there are no conceptual (but only representational) beginnings, and that the doctrine of presuppositions or foundation is somehow intolerable as a testimony to the inadequacies of the human mind.

(Jameson, 1991:392)

However, it is worth noting that while Jameson is willing to admit that there can be no truth, he believes that we *can* (and should) continue to search out that which is false; we can vigilantly search out and destroy ideological illusions.

The emergence of texts and their attendant implied assault on meaning is part of a broader attack on "anything that smacks of 'reality,' 'representation,' 'realism,' and the like—even the word *history* has an *r* in it" (Jameson, 1991:94).[9] Involved in this is a rejection of anything associated with an external real world. Jameson resists going this far, refusing to reject the idea of referent, although he admits to being uncomfortable with older theories of reference.

The heart of Jameson's (1984b) thinking is his comparatively clear image of a postmodern society composed of five major elements:

1. Postmodern society is characterized by superficiality and depthlessness. Tired of the search for meaning associated with the modern world, people in a postmodern world "want to live on the surface for a while" (Jameson, 1991:151). Furthermore, the cultural products of postmodernism are largely surface images that do not delve deeply into underlying meanings. A good example is Andy Warhol's famous painting of Campbell soup cans. Warhol's images appear to be nothing more than perfect representations of those cans. To use a key term associated with postmodern theory (and, as we saw in Chapters 5 and 6, most often associated with the work of Jean Baudrillard), Warhol's painting is a *simulacrum* in which one cannot distinguish the original from the copy. A simulacrum may also be seen as a copy of a copy; Warhol was reputed to have painted his soup cans not from the cans themselves, but from a photograph of them. Jameson (1984b:66) describes a simulacrum as "the identical copy for which no original ever existed." A simulacrum is, by definition, superficial; lacking in depth.

2. Postmodernism is characterized by a waning of emotion or affect. As his example of this, Jameson contrasts another of Warhol's paintings, another near-photographic representation, this time of Marilyn Monroe, to a classic modernist piece of art—Edvard Munch's, *The Scream. The Scream* is a surreal painting of a person expressing the depth of despair or, in sociological terms, anomie or alienation. Warhol's painting of Marilyn Monroe is superficial and expresses no genuine emotion. This is reflective of the fact that to the postmodernists the alienation and anomie that caused the kind of reaction depicted by Munch is part of the now-past modern world. In the postmodern world alienation has been replaced by (psychic) fragmentation. Since the world, and the people in it, have become fragmented, the

---

[9]The contradiction here is that Jameson clearly does historical analyses. This is one of many manifestations of the uncomfortable fit between his Marxism and his postmodernism.

effect that remains is "free-floating and impersonal" (Jameson, 1984b:64). There is a peculiar kind of euphoria, of highs and lows, associated with these postmodern feelings, or what Jameson prefers to call "intensities." These are not feelings that offer clues that tell us something about meaning or the world. Rather, they are more on the order of the reactions of someone on drugs or, reminiscent of Deleuze and Guattari, a schizophrenic. He gives as a more concrete example of intensities, a photorealist cityscape "where even automobile wrecks gleam with some new hallucinatory splendour" (Jameson, 1984b:76). Euphoria based on automobile disasters in the midst of urban squalor is, indeed, a peculiar kind of emotion. Another example of postmodern intensity is "the body . . . plugged into the new electronic media" (Donougho, 1989:85).

3. There is a loss of historicity. In the postmodern world, we recognize that we cannot know the past. All we have access to are texts about the past and all we can do is produce yet other texts about that topic. Since there is no historical continuity, we are free to cannibalize the past as we wish, taking pieces from here and there and stitching them together in a seemingly random manner (Jameson, 1984b:65-66). This leads us to another key term in postmodern thinking: *pastiche*. That is, since it is impossible for historians to find the truth about the past, or even to put together a coherent story about it, they are satisfied with creating pastiches, or hodgepodges of ideas, sometimes contradictory and confused, about the past. Further, there is no clear sense of historical development, of time passing. Past and present are inextricably intertwined. For example, in historical novels such as E. L. Doctorow's *Ragtime*, we see the "disappearance of the historical referent. This historical novel can no longer set out to represent historical past; it can only 'represent' our ideas and stereotypes about that past" (Jameson, 1984b:71). Another example, the movie *Body Heat*, while clearly about the present, creates an atmosphere reminiscent of the 1930s. In order to do this,

> the object world of the present-day—artifacts and appliances, even automobiles, whose styling would serve to date the image—is elaborately edited out. Everything in the film, therefore, conspires to blur its official contemporaneity and to make it possible for you to receive the narrative as though it were set in some eternal Thirties, beyond historical time.

> (Jameson, 1984b:68)

A movie like *Body Heat* or a novel like *Ragtime* is "an elaborated symptom of the waning of our historicity" (Jameson, 1984b:68). This loss of temporality, this inability to distinguish between past, present, and future, is manifest at the individual level in a kind of schizophrenia (see the discussion of the work of Deleuze and Guattari in Chapter 7). For the postmodern individual, events are fragmented and discontinuous.

4. There is a new technology associated with postmodern society. Instead of productive technologies like the automobile assembly line, we have the dominance of *re*productive technologies, especially electronic media like the television set and the computer. Rather than the "exciting" technology of the industrial revolution, we have technology like television "which articulates nothing but rather implodes,

carrying its flattened image surface within itself" (Jameson, 1984b:79). The implosive, flattening technologies of the postmodern era give birth to very different cultural products than the explosive, expanding technologies of the modern era.

5. There is the postmodern multinational capitalistic system which lies at the base of both these technologies and their cultural representations. Thus, Jameson is not a technological determinist but sees technologies as means by which we can begin to grasp the postmodern capitalistic world. Capitalism is not, for Jameson, simply a component of postmodernism, it is the basis of postmodern society.

It is worth noting that in his discussion of culture, Jameson moves back and forth between examples of high (the paintings of van Gogh) and low (the popular movie, *Body Heat*) culture. Thus, Jameson (1991:318) argues that "the cultural and artistic dimension of postmodernism is popular (if not populist), and . . . it dismantles many of the barriers to cultural consumption that seemed implicit in modernism." The obliteration of cultural distinctions, of course, is very characteristic of postmodernism in general.

Thus, Jameson presents us with an image of postmodernity in which people are adrift in, and unable to comprehend, the multinational capitalist system or the explosively growing culture in which they live. As a paradigm of this world, and of one's place in it, Jameson offers the example of Los Angeles' Hotel Bonaventure,[10] designed by a famous postmodern architect, John Portman. One of the points that Jameson makes about the hotel is that people are unable to get their bearings in the lobby. The lobby is an example of what Jameson means by *hyperspace*, an area where modern conceptions of space are useless in helping us orient ourselves. For example, one is no longer able to identify components within hyperspace. In the case of the Hotel Bonaventure, the lobby is surrounded by four absolutely symmetrical towers which contain the rooms. As a result, visitors often found themselves in the wrong tower; they were unable to distinguish one tower from the others. In fact, the hotel had to add color coding and directional signals to allow people to find their way. But the key point is that as designed, people had great difficulty in getting their bearings in the hyperspace of the hotel lobby.

Another interesting analysis of this type is Jameson's interpretation[11] of a house designed by the architect, Frank Gehry. The house not only illustrates the idea of hyperspace, but also the elimination of the distinction between inside and outside in postmodern works, as well as several other postmodern ideas. The Gehry house is an example of "wrapping." What Gehry did was to take an existing two-story clapboard house and wrap it in a kind of corrugated metal fence. Gehry created a pastiche of old and new; "you could look through the new house, and see the old house as though it was now packaged in this new skin" (Jameson, 1991:109). The use of a cheap industrial material like corrugated metal clearly indicates the postmodern wish to eliminate the line between high and low culture. This house within a house seems to lack a center, which Jameson links to the state of multinational capitalism as well as related cultural phenomena:

---

[10]Many postmodernists disagree with Jameson and see this hotel as more modern than postmodern (Shumway, 1989).

[11]In doing such interpretations, Jameson is clearly distancing himself from many postmodernists.

it confronts us with the paradoxical impossibilities (not the least impossibilities of representation) which are inherent in this latest evolutionary mutation of late capitalism toward "something else" which is no longer family or neighborhood, city or state, nor even nation, but as abstract and nonsituated as the placelessness of a room in an international chain of motels or the anonymous space of airport terminals that all run together in your mind.

(Jameson, 1991:116)

The house, like much else in the postmodern world, seems to be characterized by "existential messiness," and to feel like a "bad trip" (Jameson, 1991:117).

Most important, from the point of view of this discussion, there is a loss of spatial orientation in the Gehry house; it is another example of hyperspace. It is symptomatic of

new kinds of space . . . space that includes old and new, inside and outside, the framed platforms of the older house and the reconstituted yet strangely amorphous areas between the frame and the wrapper. It is essentially only this last type of space . . . which can be characterized as postmodern; that is to say, as some radically new spatiality beyond the traditional and the modern alike which seems to make some historical claim for radical difference and originality.

(Jameson, 1991:120)

The spatial characteristics of the Gehry house are such that it is even difficult to photograph. This difficulty is traceable to the fact that it is hard to position oneself (the photographer, in this case) vis-à-vis that house just as it is hard to position oneself in the postmodern world.

More generally, Jameson sees space replacing time as central in a postmodern world; in fact, even time itself has become spatialized. For example, Jameson (1991:299-300) sees MTV "as a spatialization of music . . . . You no longer offer a musical object for contemplation and gustation; you wire up the context and make space musical around the consumer." The "end of time" is also related to the end of the search for origins as well as for a telos toward which the world is headed. This also means, to Jameson (1991:156), that nostalgia for the modern is not the answer to the problems of postmodern society; "the way back to the modern is sealed for good." However, we can still oppose the excesses of today and seek a better future; we still need utopian visions. But art, like Warhol's painting of the soup cans, is not functioning as a political statement helping to move us toward such a future state. Rather, such art seems to be little more than "representations of commodity or consumer fetishism" (Jameson, 1991:158). Jameson is convinced that while spatialization may take away from our ability to think in terms of time and history, it does succeed in opening up new possibilities for utopian thinking, especially the creation of new cognitive maps (see below).

However, both time and space, and how they are lived, depend on the mode of production; neither time nor space is natural. Rather, "both are the consequence and projected afterimages of a certain state or structure of production and appropriation, of the social organization of productivity" (Jameson, 1991:367). More specifically, temporality was central to high modernity and spatiality is key to post-modernity, but *both* are linked to the state of capitalism.

The decline of modern temporality is reflected in postmodern novels and histo-riography. The postmodern historian's reliance on genealogy (see Chapter 3 for a discussion of Foucault's ideas on genealogy) involves the "new free play with the past" (Jameson, 1991:368) This is found in both "wild imaginary genealogies and novels that shuffle historical figures and names like so many cards from 'a finite deck'" (Jameson, 1991:367).

The situations in the lobby of the Bonaventure hotel and in attempting to photo-graph the Gehry house are metaphors for our inability to get our bearings in the multinational economy and cultural explosion of late capitalism.

Unlike many postmodernists, Jameson as a Marxist is unwilling to leave it at that and comes up with at least a partial solution to the problem of living in a post-modern society. This stands in contrast to Lyotard who leaves us to just go on gam-ing and Deleuze and Guattari who leave us to our libidinal pleasures (Best, 1989). What we need, Jameson says, are *cognitive maps* to be able to find our way around in the postmodern world. Yet, these are not, cannot be, the maps of old. Thus, Jameson awaits a

> breakthrough to some as yet unimaginable new mode of representing . . . [late capital-ism], in which we may again begin to grasp our positioning as individual and collective subjects and regain a capacity to act and struggle which is at present neutralized by our spatial as well as our social confusion. The political form of postmodernism, if there ever is any, will have as its vocation the invention and projection of a global cognitive mapping, on a social as well as a spatial scale.
>
> (Jameson, 1984b:92)

These cognitive maps can come from various sources: social theorists (including Jameson himself who can be seen as providing such mapping in his work), artists, novelists, and people on an everyday basis who can map their own spaces. Of course, the maps are not ends in themselves to a Marxist like Jameson but are to be used as the basis for radical political action in postmodern society.

The need for maps is linked to Jameson's view, discussed above, that we have moved from a world that is defined temporally to one that is defined spatially. In-deed, the idea of hyperspace and the example of the lobby of the Hotel Bonaven-ture reflect the dominance of space in the postmodern world. Thus, for Jameson, the central problem today is "the loss of our ability to *position ourselves within this space and to cognitively map it*" (Jameson, in Stephanson, 1989:48).

Interestingly, Jameson (1989:387) links the idea of cognitive maps to Marxian theory, specifically the idea of class consciousness: " 'cognitive mapping' was in reality nothing but a code word for 'class consciousness' . . . only it proposed the need for class consciousness of a new and hitherto undreamed of kind, while it also inflected the account in the direction of that new spatiality implicit in the post-modern." The goal is the mapping of class relations on a global, or multinational, scale and ultimately the mobilization of oppressed groups for social action.

In addition to cognitive mapping, Jameson sees some hope in what he calls "homeopathic" techniques. He means by these techniques attempts at undermining the postmodern system from within with its own elements; pushing it to its limits. This can be done by, for example, combatting images with other images, or, as Jameson puts it more specifically, "dissolving the pastiche by using all the instruments of pastiche itself" (Stephanson, 1989:59). This is the kind of strategy that most postmodernists would be comfortable with, and while Jameson discusses it, it does not seem to have great centrality to him, probably because it is too idealistic, not material enough for his neo-Marxian sensibilities.

Jameson also has great hope for writers and artists:

> Yet in our time, where the claims of the officially political seem extraordinarily enfeebled and where the taking of older kinds of political positions seems to inspire widespread embarrassment, it should also be noted that one finds everywhere today—not least among artists and writers—something like an unacknowledged 'party of Utopia': an underground party whose numbers are difficult to determine, whose program remains unannounced and perhaps even unformulated, whose existence is unknown to the citizenry at large and to the authorities, but whose members seem to recognize one another by means of secret Masonic signals. One even has the feeling that some of the present exhibitors may be among its adherents.
>
> (Jameson, 1991:180)

Scholars are left with several important tasks in Jameson's system. For one thing, he recognizes the importance of *commentary,* or the process by which those using one language comment on another. A second is *transcoding,* or "measuring what is sayable and 'thinkable' in each of these codes or idiolects and compar[ing] that to the conceptual possibilities of its competitors" (Jameson, 1991:394). As Best explains it,

> transcoding involves a trans-positional movement from cause(s) to effect(s), a translation which is always *transformation.* Transcoding allows us to identify "the relationship between the levels or instances [of a social whole], and the possibility of *adapting* analyses and findings from one level [e.g., art] to another [e.g., the economy]" where these levels do not develop in any simple one-to-one correspondence with one another or the economy.
>
> (Best, 1989:350-351)

In addition to transcoding, Jameson holds out the possibility of producing entirely new codes requiring entirely new skills and abilities.

While Jameson's work is vulnerable on a number of counts (see Chapter 12 for a discussion of some of the criticisms of his work), it remains an important American contribution to postmodern theory.

FEMINIST THEORY AND POSTMODERN THEORY

Americans are certainly not the only ones to contribute to the development of feminist theory; it is a truly international theoretical perspective (on, for example,

French feminism, see Spivak, 1992). In addition, and relatedly, feminist theory has been a part of poststructuralism and postmodernism for decades (Spivak and Gross, 1984-1985). Take, for example, the work of the three important French disciples of Jacques Lacan (see Chapter 7): Julia Kristeva, Luce Irigaray, and Helene Cixous. Lacan, heavily influenced by Freud, was highly patriarchal arguing, for example, that woman does not exist, or is not whole. As a result, Kristeva, Irigaray (McDermott, 1987), and Cixous, while strongly affected by Lacan's ideas, sought to distance themselves from his phallocentrism (Kurzweil, 1995:126).

Irigaray, for example, was offended by Lacan's (and Freud's) focus on the penis. As a result, the clitoris is reduced to a "little penis," the vagina is seen as little more than a home for the penis, and women are viewed as being dominated by a drive to possess the equivalent of a penis. In contrast, Irigaray argued that instead of being limited sexually (as are men), *"woman has sex organs just about everywhere.* She experiences pleasure almost everywhere . . . the geography of her pleasure is much more diversified, more multiple in its differences, more complex, more subtle, than is imagined" (Irigaray, 1981:103). Not only does she offer a theoretical critique of the Freudians in general and Lacan in particular, but she also offers a radical feminist political program:

> Let women tacitly go on strike, avoid men long enough to learn to defend their desire notably by their speech, let them discover the love of other women protected from that imperious choice of men which puts them in a position of rival goods, let them forge a social status which demands recognition, let them earn their living in order to leave behind their condition of prostitute.
>
> (Irigaray, 1981:106)

Kristeva takes a similarly revolutionary view, albeit within a more poststructuralist perspective:

> If women have a role to play in this on-going process, it is only in assuming a *negative* function: reject everything finite, definite, structured, loaded with meaning, in the existing state of society. Such an attitude places women on the side of the explosion of social codes: with revolutionary moments.
>
> (Kristeva, 1981:166)

Cixous takes a revolutionary position strongly influenced by Derrida:

> Woman must write her self: must write about women and bring women to writing, from which they have been driven away as violently as from their bodies—for the same reasons, by the same law, with the same fatal goal. Woman must put herself into the text—as into the world and into history—by her own movement . . . . Let the priests tremble, we're going to show them our sexts.
>
> (Cixous, 1981:245, 255)

Clearly, such poststructural/postmodern ideas are, and have been, of relevance to feminist theory and reflect the fact that feminism (and postmodernism) are international in scope. While we recognize this fact, our focus in this section is on American feminist theorists and their relationship to postmodern social theory.

Feminists in general, and American feminists in particular, have generally been deeply ambivalent about postmodernism (Benhabib, 1995; Farganis, 1994:115; Fox-Genovese, 1993; Singer, 1992; Stavro-Pearce, 1994; Warnke, 1993; Wolff, 1990).[12] On the one hand, Flax (1990:40) sees feminism as a "type of postmodern philosophy." On the other, Di Stefano (1990:64; see also Lovibond, 1990) argues, "Contemporary Western feminism is firmly, if ambivalently, located in the modernist ethos." Harding (1990) argues that feminism needs *both* modern and postmodern perspectives, but it doesn't need the same aspects of the two approaches as the majority group does, nor does it need to use them for the same purposes. Then, there are those who see a tension—sometimes helpful, sometimes destructive—between feminism and postmodernism (as well as modernism). Thus, there is obviously no clear and simple relationship between feminism and postmodernism (and modernism).

One clear point of agreement is the fact that both feminists and postmodernists have challenged the modern, Enlightenment idea of " 'a God's eye view' " (Nicholson, 1990:2). In other words, both tend to reject universalizing, totalizing, grand narratives. Fraser and Nicholson (1990:19) outline a number of other similarities between feminism and postmodernism, including their critique of mainstream philosophy and their development of new forms of social criticism. Other commonalities identified by Farganis (1994) include a critique of objectivity and a recognition of the importance of language and discourse.

However, feminist critiques of postmodernism seem to be stronger and more numerous than the arguments for commonalities between them:

• First, feminists tend to reject the postmodern critique of the subject, especially the unified subject. Clearly, despite the rise of third-wave feminism, many feminist theorists continue to see women as just such a unified subject.

• Second, there is a tendency among feminist theorists to reject the postmodern opposition to universal, cross-cultural categories. Clearly, cross-cultural concepts like gender and gender oppression are central to feminist theory.

• Third, while feminists generally accept the postmodern critique of the "view from nowhere," they are not so sure that the postmodern alternative, "the view from everywhere," is the answer. An excessive concern with differences can cause the theorist to lose sight of the transhistorical and centralized sources of female oppression.

• Fourth, feminists commonly question the ability to develop a critical political agenda from a postmodern perspective (Stabile, 1995). Among other things, the poststructural/postmodern tendency is to focus on discourse about women rather than their experiences and, more important, the practical solutions to their problems (Marks and de Courtivron, 1981:3). More sweepingly, Bordo argues:

> The programmatic appropriation of poststructuralist insight, I will argue, in shifting the focus of crucial feminist concerns about the representation of cultural diversity from practical contexts to questions of adequate theory, is highly problematic for feminism.

---

[12]It is hard to generalize here since feminist social theory is at least as diverse as postmodern theory and there is a dense and tangled relationship between the two theoretical orientations.

Not only are we thus diverted from attending to the professional and institutional mechanisms through which the politics of exclusion operate most powerfully in intellectual communities, but we also deprive ourselves of still vital analytical tools for critique of those communities and the hierarchical, dualistic power structures that sustain them.

(Bordo, 1990:136)

Because of the political difficulties posed by postmodern theory for feminism, Farganis (1994:123) argues that "any more sustained liaison with postmodernism is unadvisable."

Perhaps the most interesting criticism of postmodernism from a feminist perspective relates to a striking correspondence in the rise of these two theories (Hartsock, 1987; Di Stefano, 1990). On the one hand, feminist theory enjoyed a powerful renaissance by focusing on women as the subject, by developing a sense of "truth" from their perspective, and by thinking that a liberating world may flow from the discovery of that truth. But just as feminist theory was gaining ground, along came postmodern theory to question the bases of feminist theory—concern for the subject, truth, and liberation. The implication here is the existence of yet another phallocentric perspective capable of perpetuating women's subordination, this time to undermine the nascent feminist theory. Having already undergone their enlightenment, males associated with postmodern social theory were ready to critique and reject such an idea just as women were about to achieve their own enlightenment.

While aware of the "uneasy distance" between feminism and postmodernism, Fraser and Nicholson (1990:19; Nicholson, 1992) argue that the two theories can complement one another. The strength of postmodernism in philosophy complements the strength of feminist theory in social criticism. Further, each is useful for pointing out weaknesses in the other. For example, postmodernism underscores the lingering essentialism in feminism, while the latter points out the androcentrism and political naiveté of postmodernism. While Fraser and Nicholson (1990:26) see things to be gained from postmodernism, they do not think that the "meager critical resources" offered by postmodernism are nearly sufficient to analyze "a phenomenon as pervasive and multifaceted as male dominance." Thus, they see the need for other theoretical resources such as large-scale social and historical theories, interactionist approaches to everyday life, critical-hermeneutic analyses of culture, and more specific sociologies of the historical and cultural forces related to gender.

There is also an uneasy relationship between feminism and postmodernism in Harding's (1986, 1990, 1991; for a critique see McCaughey, 1993) work on feminist science. Arguing that science is gendered, Harding makes the case for a feminist science. Postmodernism is seen as arguing against such a science on several grounds: it is too epistemological, it is excessively foundational, it values science too highly, it is essentialistic (since there is no such thing as the feminine), and it is excessively modernist (Harding, 1991). In response, Harding argues that there are postmodern tendencies in feminist science, and, conversely, there are modern tendencies (e.g., the belief in progress) in postmodernism. She concludes that both feminist science and postmodernism exist with one foot in the Enlightenment and the other in the present (or future). This is not to conclude that they are the same, but it is to say that there are instructive similarities and constructive differences between the two perspectives.

More generally, Farganis offers a useful summary of the dilemmas facing feminist theory in the postmodern age:

> The issue is whether feminist theory, by recognizing differences and privileging multiple voices and sites can (1) protect feminist thought from foundationalism, (2) avoid the cacophony that often accompanies the recognition of knowledge's sociality, (3) nurture a more pluralistic and even tolerant notion of personhood, and (4) write an emancipatory politics from a position that denies privilege.

> (Farganis, 1994:118)

While the main thrust of feminist theory seems to stand opposed to postmodern theory, there are those who are more sympathetic to it.[13] We will examine the work of Judith Butler who has attempted to articulate a sense of the feminist subject in light of the postmodern critique of the subject, as well as Donna Haraway's (1990, 1991) work on cyborgs.

Judith Butler (1990:xi) can be seen as operating, at least in part, from a Foucauldian perspective in a "critical genealogy of gender categories," especially of "woman" as a stable, coherent subject.[14] Elsewhere, she describes herself as doing "a Foucauldian reinscription of the subject" (Butler, 1995:48). Specifically, Butler is addressing the foundationalism of feminism with its focus on woman as the subject. She sees this as part of the Foucauldian juridical power that produces subjects, including women. She seeks to do a genealogy of this that critiques the "categories of identity that contemporary juridical structures engender, naturalize and immobilize" (Butler, 1990:5).

Her central conclusion is that "woman" is not a single given foundation but rather a variable construction. On the one hand, this means that "woman" is a cultural construct and therefore varies from one time or place to another. On the other hand, there is no preexisting agent in feminist theory. The latter position leads immediately to the question: Can there be a feminist politics without a subject or an agent? Butler (1990:142) responds, "My argument is that there need not be a 'doer behind the deed,' but that the 'doer' is variably constructed in and through the deed."

The female subject does not exist outside of discourse; it is not a prediscursive I. Rather, the female subject, female identity, is constituted in and by discourse. Female identity, indeed all identity, is a practice, not a given. The I does not exist prior to discourse, it exists in interlocking discourses. Agency exists not because of a quality of the actor but because there is variation in discourses. Thus, in Butler's view, there can be a nonfoundational feminist subject and agent.

---

[13]A number of feminists have, for example, found great utility in the theories of Michel Foucault (Cooper, 1994; Diamond and Quimby, 1988; Doran, 1994; Morgan, 1991; Phelan, 1990; Still, 1994); for a critique of such an approach, see Lloyd (1993).

[14]For a critique of at least one aspect of Foucault's perspective from a feminist perspective, see Hengehold (1994).

The genealogical problem is that the history of discourse is characterized by repetitive discourses that serve to limit and subvert identity, especially the identity of women. Thus, Butler's goal becomes the deconstruction of these repetitive discourses and gender norms. The result of this deconstruction would be "proliferating gender configurations, destabilizing substantive identity, and depriving the naturalizing narratives of compulsory heterosexuality and their central protagonists: 'man' and 'woman'" (Butler, 1990:146).

Butler recognizes that her position will be considered controversial by feminists, but she argues that identity categories are not needed to mobilize feminism as identity politics. In fact, she argues that the continued existence of such identity categories as "woman" "work[s] to limit and constrain in advance the very cultural possibilities that feminism is supposed to open up" (Butler, 1990:147). The opening up of the category "woman" to multiple meanings makes it possible for identity politics to be inclusionary rather than exclusionary. Because gender is constructed, it is possible to think in terms of a wider array of gender configurations.

Butler concludes a recent essay with the following warning to feminists who insist on adhering to foundationalism:[15]

> If there is a fear that, by no longer being able to take for granted the subject, its gender, its sex, or its materiality, feminism will founder, it might be wise to consider the political consequences of keeping in their place the very premises that have tried to secure our subordination from the start.

(Butler, 1995:54)

Thus, females who have historically been subordinated by male foundationalism would be unwise and misguided to substitute a female foundationalism of their own. In addition to all of its other problems, such foundationalism would enhance the position of some women and subordinate others.

Donna Haraway's cyborg—part machine, part organism—is offered as a paradigm of the modern/postmodern world in general and a postgender world in particular: "By the late twentieth century, our time, a mythic time, we are all chimeras, theorized and fabricated hybrids of machine and organism; in short, we are cyborgs" (Haraway, 1990:191). While the cyborg is a creature of science fiction (shades of Baudrillard's pataphysics), it is also increasingly a creature of the social world. For example, in modern medicine there are innumerable instances of hybrid humans—those with artificial hearts, limbs, or hips, to name just a few.

Haraway relates the rise of cyborgs to the erosion of all sorts of boundaries between humans and nonhumans in, for example, the animal rights movement and the development of lively machines (virtual reality goggles, for example) while people themselves grow increasingly inert. However, her strongest argument deals with the erosion of the boundary between the physical and the nonphysical. For example, we are now able to carry more and more machines with us (the walkman, miniature televisions, cellular phones); they have, in a sense, become part of us.

---

[15]Butler is critical of not just foundationalism but all universalizing tendencies, including patriarchy.

More generally, and important, are the signals, the electromagnetic waves, the floating signifiers that flash back and forth between people and their machines so quickly and frequently that it becomes increasingly impossible to differentiate one from the other. For example, many of us have become cyborgs—half-human, half-television set—for several hours a day. We beam signals to it through our remote controls, and it more than reciprocates by beaming signals to us through advertisements and programs.

A cyborg world is both constraining and enabling. On the positive side, it might be seen as a world "in which people are not afraid of their joint kinship with animals and machines, not afraid of permanently partial identities and contradictory standpoints" (Haraway, 1990:196). However, it is also possible to see that "a cyborg world is about the final imposition of a grid of control on the planet" (Haraway, 1990:196).

Haraway has created a theoretical idea of importance both to society as a whole as well as to women in particular. Thus, she argues that we need to look at women as involved in an "integrated circuit" created by science and technology. There are new sources of technological power here, but there are also new resources developed by people to deal with these new developments. The point is that we need new theoretical ideas (like cyborgs) and new theories (perhaps fusing feminist and postmodern perspectives) to deal with these new realities. In other words, new political forms and political objectives are likely to emerge from such a new way of looking at things. While she recognizes the problems associated with being a cyborg, Haraway (1990:223) concludes by saying, "I would rather be a cyborg than a goddess."

While it may be an important new way of looking at women, Haraway's ideas on a cyborg draw heavily on postmodern theory. For example, she clearly rejects, as does postmodern theory, the kind of dualistic thinking that has dominated modern thinking. For another, the idea of a cyborg is intimately related to central postmodern/poststructural concerns like communication, language, the code, and writing:

> Writing is preeminently the technology of cyborgs, etched surfaces of the late twentieth century. Cyborg politics is the struggle for language and the struggle against perfect communication, against the one code that translates all meaning perfectly, the central dogma of phallogocentrism. That is why cyborg politics insist on noise and advocate pollution, rejoicing in the illegitimate fusions of animal and machine.

(Haraway, 1990:218)

Haraway's ideas on the cyborg are explored briefly here to illustrate the theoretical possibilities that arise when an effort is made to fuse feminist and postmodern theories. It is certainly likely that we will see more such efforts in the future, but the main thrust of this section, and of feminist theory to date, has been the criticisms of, and uneasiness with, postmodern social theory.

MULTICULTURAL THEORY

Like feminist theory, multicultural theory is not restricted to American contributions; however, it is there that its strength lies, at least at this point in its development. According to Rogers (1996b:1) "Multiculturalism as a moment is distinctively, though not exclusively, American. It emerged as the second wave of the civil rights movement that shaped American society during the 1950s and 1960s." However, there are now signs of diversification as "multiculturalism has emerged as a public-policy issue in the Netherlands, England, Canada, and other countries" (Rogers, 1996b:8).

As in the case of feminist theory (which is usually seen as one type of multicultural theory), multiculturalism has a complex relationship with postmodern social theory. Some multiculturalists are postmodernists, others are ambivalent, and still others are critical of this theoretical orientation. However, there is more affinity than hostility between multiculturalism and postmodern social theory. As Rogers (1996b:6) puts it, "Multicultural theorists . . . favor broadly postmodernist stances."

However, there is also another kind of linkage between multiculturalism and postmodernism. Rather than being a direct source of intellectual ideas, postmodernism can be seen as having created the intellectual climate that permitted multiculturalism to develop. Conversely, as multiculturalism took hold, it created a social and political environment that was conducive to the growth and development of postmodern social theory. Thus, it might be best to see the two as mutually enriching products of the late twentieth century and an atmosphere that is conducive to both.

The development of multicultural theory was foreshadowed by the reemergence of feminist sociological theory in the 1970s. The feminists argued that social theory had been largely closed to women's voices; more recently many minority groups have echoed the feminists' complaints. In fact, minority women (e.g., African American, Latina) began to complain that feminist theory was restricted to white middle-class females and had to be receptive to many other voices. Today, feminist theory has become far more diverse (as has social theory) (Clough, 1994). There is, for example, the interest in black feminist theory (Collins, 1990), Chicana feminist discourse (Segura and Pesquera, 1996), queer feminist theory (Butler, 1990), and postcolonial feminism (Minh-ha, 1989).

More generally, a number of other multicultural voices have been added to the feminist perspectives. Examples include an Afrocentric perspective (Asante, 1987, 1996), the Native American point of view (Buffalohead, 1996), the bisexual outlook (Valverde, 1996), the Asian-American viewpoint (Wei, 1996), the male standpoint (Connell, 1996), and even an Appalachian view (Banks, Billings, and Tice, 1996).

The relationship between postmodern social theory and multiculturalism can be clarified by discussing the affinity between at least some of the major concepts we have discussed throughout this book and multiculturalism.

Needless to say, most multiculturalists accept the postmodern opposition to grand narratives. Clearly, grand narratives serve to downplay or to even exclude totally the minority groups and perspectives represented in multiculturalism. By their very nature, grand narratives focus inordinately on the experiences of majority groups and their versions of reality. Multiculturalists want to see emphasis placed on the experiences and the narratives of various minority groups. In their view, the most satisfying story is one that accords a place for a multitude of narratives.

Second, multiculturalists are in full accord with the postmodern rejection of es-sentialism. In this context, essentialism implies "that one dimension of individuals' identities—gender, sexual orientation, or race, for instance—is capable of render-ing their 'situations of experience . . . essentially the same in all social, cultural, and historical contexts" (Rogers, 1996b:2). One example would involve a focus on black I.Q. and to argue that it, and therefore all blacks, would experience the same fate in all situations. Another would be according centrality to female childbearing capacities and arguing that this tends to define women and their place in the social world. Obviously, such essentialistic views have been used for centuries to help oppress blacks, women, and other minority groups. Supporters of multiculturalism clearly accept the postmodern critique and rejection of essentialism.

In a more positive way, the multiculturalists are in accord with the notion of de-centering. Clearly, the social world, and analyses of that world, have all centered on majority groups. Multiculturalists would like to see both decentered. Minority groups should, in their view, occupy a more important position within the social world, and they should be accorded similar significance in social analyses of that world.

Another postmodern concept that obviously resonates with multiculturalists is difference. Among other things, the concept leads to a focus on the radical other, as well as the relationship between that other and that which remains at the cen-ter. In fact, the focus is on the continual interplay between the two, as well as be-tween the groups that make up the radical other. Most of those who support a given multicultural perspective would see themselves as part of the radical other. They would want to emphasize that vantage point as well as the interplay be-tween their groups, other minority groups, and the majority group. A further at-traction of such a perspective is its fluidity. This leads to the view that minority positions are not etched in stone and can be changed, even radically. Such a per-spective is obviously attractive to the kind of politically minded activists often attracted to multiculturalism.

In addition to such general orientations, multiculturalists also find attractive a number of more specific ideas associated with postmodern social theory. Take, for example, the idea of the body generally associated with the work of Michel Fou-cault. Especially attractive are the ideas that bodies are a source of difference and that they are central areas of contestation between majority and minority groups. Among the aspects of the body that are of central importance to multiculturalists are the color of one's skin, the way one uses one's body during sexual relations, the capacity to bear children, and so on. Minority groups often feel that majority groups have seized on aspects of their bodies and oppressed them because they are different in some way. Thus, the sense is that a battle of epic proportions has been waged over the body and the way it looks and is used. This is a battle that minority groups feel that they lost, at least in the past. However, it is an arena which they are prepared to contest again, and this time they intend to win. That is, they intend to defend the beauty of the entire spectrum of skin colors, the glory of childbearing, and the fulfillment associated with the whole panoply of sexual practices.

If the body is a physical manifestation of difference, then identity is its cultural correlate. Thus, a battle has been waged over identity that is similar to the one that has been fought over the body. Minorities feel that the majority has sought to define their identities and, more often than not, to define them in negative terms. Minorities are seeking to gain control over their own identities, to define them themselves, *and*, perhaps most important, to define them in positive terms. Blacks, gays, Chicanas, and many others are actively involved in such efforts.

While there is an affinity between multiculturalism and postmodern social theory, it is certainly not simple or unequivocal. Further complicating the issue of gaining a sense of multiculturalism and its relationship to postmodern social theory is the great diversity of multicultural writings and perspectives. These are, by their very nature, "local" perspectives, and it is impossible to generalize adequately about their relationship to one another and to postmodern social theory. Thus, we can do little more than offer two examples of multiculturalism in this section.

Cornel West, a distinguished professor of African-American studies, is certainly knowledgeable about postmodern social theory. At times it informs his analyses of the plight of black Americans, while at other times he has no compunction about abandoning it and employing a more modern orientation. Let us take a look at West's (1994) *Race Matters* from this perspective.

West links the problems of black Americans to postmodern culture, a culture which for him is increasingly a market (or consumer) culture. He sees this consumer culture as an important cause of what he sees as the most fundamental issue facing black America—"*the nihilistic threat to its very existence*" (West, 1994:19). By nihilism, West (1994:20) does not mean the abstract notion of concern to most postmodern social theorists but rather the far more concrete "profound sense of psychological depression, personal worthlessness, and social despair so widespread in black America." This nihilism has, in turn, led to the dissolution of black civil society. The main cause of this nihilism lies in the impact of the omnipresent consumer culture on black people who, in the main, lack the resources to be more than marginal players in that culture.

The images of the consumer society are linked to a wide array of other images that bombard consumers, black and white alike. Among these images are "comfort, convenience, machismo, femininity, violence and sexual stimulation" (West, 1994:27). West sees these images, and the consumer goods and consumer society that create and sponsor them, as the main causes of black nihilism:

> These seductive images contribute to the predominance of the market-inspired way of life over all others and thereby edge out nonmarket values—love, care, service to others— handed down by preceding generations. The predominance of this way of life among those living in poverty-ridden conditions, with a limited capacity to ward off self-contempt and self-hatred, results in the possible triumph of the nihilistic threat in black America.

> (West, 1994:27)

What does West propose as a solution to the problem of black nihilism? Viewing it as a disease of the "soul" (like alcoholism or drug addiction), West argues that what is needed is a process of "conversion," a "turning of one's soul . . . through one's own affirmation of one's worth—an affirmation fueled by the concern of others" (West, 1994:29). This process of conversion is *not* to take place under the auspices of some Great Society program run by the federal government but rather at the local level by those elements of black civil society still able to "promote self-worth and self-affirmation." (West, 1994:30). Furthermore, it is to be a decentered process taking place not in the limelight but "on the ground among the toiling everyday people" (West, 1994:31).

This analysis is clearly an example of multiculturalism and, just as clearly as it is informed, both consciously and unconsciously, by postmodern ideas. Yet, West is no postmodernist. For example, side-by-side with his local solutions is a call for a very modern sounding "large-scale public intervention to ensure access to basic social goods—housing, food, health care, education, child care, and jobs" (West, 1994:12).

We can get a clearer idea of West's theoretical orientation, and its relationship to his ideas, from an earlier essay on "The New Cultural Politics of Difference" (West, 1990). The new politics of difference rejects homogeneity and focuses instead on heterogeneity, prefers the concrete for the abstract, and historicizes, pluralizes, and contextualizes by focusing on the contingent, the provisional, and the changing. Those who adopt this perspective are not merely students of culture but seek to ally themselves with the disempowered to help empower them, perhaps through collective action, even collective insurgency. The new politics of difference involves politically engaged intellectuals.

Herein lies West's fundamental difference with most poststructural and postmodern theorists who he sees as creating ideas that do not further, and may even block, political action. Thus, while he finds Derrida's ideas on, for example, deconstruction an important resource, he also feels that they do not lead to, and may even prevent, collective action. He critiques the deconstructions of Derrida and his followers because they pay little attention to the larger social, economic, political, and military context in which they exist.

West argues that those who support the new politics of difference must draw on the best of intellectual currents like postmodernism, but they must not forget that they are allied with groups that are interested in resisting the status quo and altering its basic character. They may be scholars and intellectuals, but their cultural capital is to be used to improve the lot of those who are bearing the costs of the current system. Their goal is to work with those people to help ensure them a better future.

As is clear in the case of much of West's work, multiculturalists generally push the interests and concerns of a specific minority group. Thus, we could examine many different works in this section that adopt the viewpoint of gays, lesbians, Native Americans, women of color, and the like. However, to show the diversity of work in multiculturalism, let us close this section with a discussion of a piece of work which, while it operates from the vantage point of queer theory, seeks to articulate a broad theoretical objective.

Seidman (1994b; see also Hennessy, 1995; Morton, 1993) documents the silence of classical sociological theory on sexuality in general and homosexuality in particular. He finds it striking that while the classical theorists were dealing with a

wide range of issues relating to modernity, they had nothing to say about the making of modern bodies and modern sexuality. While the silence was soon to be broken, it was not until the work of Michel Foucault (1978/1980) on the relationship
among power, knowledge, and sexuality that the postmodern study of sexuality in
general, and homosexuality in particular, began (see Chapter 4) (Weeks, 1977;
Weeks, 1981/1989; D'Emilio, 1983). What emerged was the sense of homosexuality as both a subject and identity paralleling the heterosexual self and identity.

However, unlike many multicultural theorists who adopt the viewpoint of a specific group, Seidman argues that what distinguishes queer theory is a rejection of
any single identity, including homosexuality. Further, all identities are seen as multiple or composite, unstable and exclusionary. Thus, at any given time each of us is
a composite of a series of identity components (e.g., "sexual orientation, race,
class, nationality, gender, age, ableness" [Seidman, 1994b:173]) and they can be
combined and recombined in many different ways. As a result, Seidman does not
focus on the homosexual-heterosexual dichotomy but rather takes it as an object of
analysis and critique and seeks to move queer theory in the direction of a more
general social theory:

> Queer theorists shift their focus from an exclusive preoccupation with the oppression
> and liberation of the homosexual subject to an analysis of the institutional practices and
> discourses producing sexual knowledges and how they organize social life, with particu-
> lar attention to the way in which these knowledges and social practices repress differ-
> ences. In this regard, queer theory is suggesting . . . the study . . . of those knowledges
> and social practices which organize "society" as a whole by sexualizing—heterosexual-
> izing or homosexualizing—bodies, desires, acts, identities, social relations, knowledges,
> cultures, and social institutions. Queer theory aspires to transform homosexual theory
> into a general social theory or one standpoint from which to analyze whole societies.

> (Seidman, 1994b:174)

Thus, queer theory is put forth as but one of the "standpoint theories," that is, theories that view the social world from a specific vantage point (much as Marx viewed
capitalism from the standpoint of the proletariat) (Weeks, 1995). In fact, virtually
all of the multicultural perspectives mentioned above can be seen as standpoint
theories (Longino, 1993) or, in terms that fit better with the thrust of this book,
local narratives. However, while not surrendering the idea of a standpoint theory,
Seidman also aspires to have queer theory seen as a general social theory.

SUMMARY

In this chapter we deal with four largely American contributions to the literature on
postmodern social theory. We begin with the work of Daniel Bell, especially his
well-known concept of "postindustrial" society. While there are many similarities
between this concept and what we usually think of as postmodernity, Bell was a
modernist, not a postmodernist. Bell comes closer to the postmodernists in his
analysis of postmodern culture and its conflict with the postindustrial economy. In
contrast to most postmodernists, however, Bell is clearly critical of postmodern cul-

ture. While there are crucial differences in their perspectives, Bell, like most post-modern social theorists, accords great importance to consumer society and its ills.

Fredric Jameson adopts a Marxian orientation in viewing postmodernism as the cultural logic of late, multinational capitalism. As a result, he does not see a radical disjunction between modernity and postmodernity. Unlike most postmodernists, Jameson does not seek to distance himself from grand narratives in general, as well as the Marxian grand narrative in particular. Despite his Marxian roots, Jameson devotes far more attention to the cultural system than to its economic roots. In so doing, he accepts many of the basic ideas of postmodern social theory outlined throughout this book.

The core of Jameson's thinking is his comparatively clear image of a postmodern society composed of five major elements. First, postmodern society is distinguished by its superficiality and depthlessness. Second, there is a dwindling of emotion or affect in the postmodern world. Third, there is a loss of historicity with the result that the postmodern world is characterized by pastiche. Fourth, instead of productive technologies, the postmodern world is typified by reproductive technologies. Finally, at the base of all of this lies the multinational capitalist system.

Jameson's work is also characterized by interesting and important cultural analyses, including his thoughts on the hyperspace (and other postmodern characteristics) of the Hotel Bonaventure and the Gehry house. Unable to get our bearings in the hyperspace of the new postmodern world, Jameson argues that we are in need of new kinds of cognitive maps. Jameson also discusses the use of various homeopathic techniques to push postmodern society to the limit, and beyond.

Feminist theory has an extraordinary relationship with postmodern social theory. The positions range all the way from the idea that feminist theory is postmodern to the view that there are irreconcilable differences between the two theories. While they share a number of ideas such as the rejection of totalizations and grand narratives, there are many more differences as reflected in the wide array of feminist critiques of postmodern social theory. For example, feminists tend to reject the postmodern critique of the subject and of the idea of universal, cross-cultural categories. Especially worrisome to many feminists is postmodernism's seeming inability to develop a viable politics.

Despite the uneasy relationship between them, feminist theory has spawned a variety of postmodern perspectives. One is Judith Butler's effort to develop a postmodern sense of the feminist subject. While she makes the case for such a subject, it is one with multiple meanings allowing for the inclusion of a wide variety of types of women. Butler also warns feminist theorists to avoid the kind of foundationalism that has served to oppress them for centuries. The other is Donna Haraway's ideas on the cyborg in the postgender world. Included here is the erosion of boundaries between people and animals and, more important, between people and machines. The cyborg is subject to unprecedented control, but it is also ripe with new possibilities. Despite the problems associated with it, Haraway prefers the female cyborg to the female treated as a goddess.

Finally, we discussed the similarly ambivalent relationship between postmodern social theory and multicultural theory. While multiculturalists may reject some aspects of postmodern social theory, there is a strong affinity between many of the ideas derived from that theory and multiculturalism. The diversity of multiculturalism and its relationship to postmodernism is illustrated in a discussion of Cornel West's work on race and Steven Seidman's on queer theory. While not a postmodernist, West uses some postmodern ideas to address the problems of the contemporary world from a black standpoint. Seidman is interested not only in the gay standpoint but also in using it as a base to develop a more general social theory.

10

POSTMODERN SOCIAL THEORY AND CONTEMPORARY SOCIOLOGICAL THEORY

SOCIOLOGICAL THEORY IN THE POSTMODERN ERA
   Negative Lessons
   Positive Lessons

ALTHOUGH all of the thinkers discussed in this book developed social theories, or ideas that are related to such theories, very few of them were sociologists, or, more specifically, sociological theorists. Indeed, some of them were overtly critical of sociological (and even social) theory, and most, given their postmodern orientation, would reject the idea of something called a "theory," let alone one that somehow is the province of a field such as sociology. However, the primary audience for this book is students of sociology (and related disciplines) who are seeking an introduction to what, for many of them, is the very foreign set of ideas associated with postmodern theory. Thus, whatever the postmodernists might think of such an undertaking, this chapter and the next are devoted to the issue of the implications of the ideas covered throughout this book for social theory in general, especially sociological theory.

There clearly *are* a very wide range of such implications. Some of them are, in fact, beyond the purview of this book. For example, if we accept Baudrillard's ideas on the death of the social, then clearly sociology and sociological theory, at least as we know them, would be defunct since their subject matter is the (now dead) social.[1] For another, some of the ideas are so far out, so metaphysical, that it is nearly impossible to relate them in any meaningful way to sociological theory. However, the vast majority of the ideas associated with postmodernism do have a variety of implications for sociological theory; in fact, many of them *are* ideas that would traditionally be considered part of sociological theory. When one cuts through all of the underbrush, what one finds is a series of theoretical ideas, many of them very important theoretical ideas, that must be considered seriously by sociological theorists.

At one level, the issues raised by postmodern social theory are epistemological in nature. That is, in light of postmodern social theory, in what ways, if any, should

---

[1]To accept such a view would obviate the need for a book like this one. Obviously, in writing this book I am rejecting the idea that the social is "dead."

the practice of sociological theory change? Clearly, many of the epistemological ideas associated with postmodern social theory have powerful implications for sociological theory. It is not to be expected that sociological theory will close up shop, or even experience a complete renovation, as a result of postmodern social theory, but one can expect and think that it will change in significant ways.

I believe that Bauman is correct in his critique of the idea of a nonrational postmodern sociology (and sociological theory). In other words, I do not think that sociological theory ought to abandon its rational procedures and, for example, follow Baudrillard into pataphysics. A pataphysical sociological theory would have little, or nothing, in common with what we usually think of as sociological theory. However, that does not mean that sociological theorists ought not to read works like Baudrillardian science fiction. Clearly, there are useful ideas in such work, ideas that need to be translated so that they are applicable to the concerns of sociological theorists.

More generally, sociological theory needs to take into account the epistemological critiques and insights of postmodernists. For example, the attacks on the grand narrative and on the focus on the subject, among many others, are highly relevant to the practice of sociological theory.

At a second level, the issue is ontological. The world has changed in many of the ways suggested by postmodernists, and sociological theory must take cognizance of, and theorize, this changed social world. That is, in Bauman's terms, while we may not want to adopt a postmodern sociological theory, we do need a sociological theory of the postmodern social world. We will concern ourselves in Chapter 11 with such ontological issues; our focus in this chapter will be on the epistemological implications of postmodern social theory for sociological theory.

SOCIOLOGICAL THEORY IN THE POSTMODERN ERA

The issue of the state of sociological theory in the postmodern age can be addressed in two ways. First, there are a series of negative lessons about sociological theory to be derived from the postmodern critique. Second, there are a set of more positive implications for sociological theory embedded in that critique.

Negative Lessons

Sociological theory, like most modern undertakings, has tended to emphasize subjectivity. Such an emphasis has a number of implications including the tendency to focus on, if not deify, the (almost universally male) author of theoretical works. This is especially true in studies of classical sociological theory, which almost always involve analyses of the great man's[2] ideas (be it Marx, Weber, Durkheim, or others) as if they were a self-contained entity free of contact and linkage with the innumerable strands of theoretical ideas. Even in contemporary sociological the-

---

[2]For a discussion of the ignored role of women in classical sociological theory, see Lengermann and Niebrugge (1996).

ory, where the focus is more on schools (critical theory, symbolic interactionism, and so on) than people, there is still a tendency to hold one thinker, often regarded as a genius, up as the paradigm for a particular way of thinking theoretically—Talcott Parsons and structural functionalism, George Herbert Mead and symbolic interactionism, Harold Garfinkel and ethnomethodology, James Coleman and rational choice theory, and so on.

Postmodern thought is critical of such an emphasis on the author. The implication is that instead of concerning ourselves with people and the impact of their biographies and personalities on their thinking, we should concern ourselves more with ideas, their development, and their relationship with other ideas. Furthermore, contemporary sociological theorists could profit more than a little from less interest in individual fame; less interest in gaining credit, reknown, and a place in sociological theory texts of the future; less interest in generating eponymous fields such as Marxian and Parsonian theory. Conversely, the discipline could benefit from greater anonymity and a greater concern on the part of individual thinkers for the generation of creative new ideas that enhance our ability to understand the social world. Foucault is paradigmatic here in his often pronounced desire to be anonymous as an author.

One result of less focus on, and interest in, the author would be a sociological theory that would grow significantly more egalitarian. As it is, those who already have won fame and glory are more likely to have their ideas heard and thereby to gain even greater status (the "Matthew Effect") (Merton, 1973). On the other hand, those without status have a very hard time getting a hearing for their ideas. In a postmodern world where authorship, genius, charisma, and the like are deemphasized, ideas will become more important than the people who express them. Sociological theory will grow more democratic, and a plethora of voices and perspectives will be heard. The result will be more and different ideas. Many will prove dead-ends, but some will turn out to be gems that set theorizing off in some new and unanticipated directions.

To put this another way, in sociological theory in the postmodern era, the "text" replaces the "work" (or *oeuvre*). The idea of a work implies an author, a genius who alone was capable of producing such a work. Since, in a postmodern world, there are no more authors, there are no more works. Rather, there are texts, and, of course, texts bring with them the idea that what really matters is not the one who created the text but rather those who "read" the text. The power shifts from author to reader. This, too, implies great democratization. Every sociological theorist, indeed everyone, is an empowered reader of all theoretical works, even those emanating from the "geniuses" in the field. As a result, there will be (and, in fact, there are) almost as many interpretations as readers, and each of these interpretations is inherently no better or worse than the others or than the interpretations of the "authors" of their own work. The result: a massive proliferation of theoretical ideas, the raison d'être of sociological theory in the postmodern age where the goal is to "keep the conversation going."

Instead of the nature of the author, what matters is the relationship between a text and all other texts; in other words, the focus shifts to intertextuality. What readers need to come to understand is the relationship among the ideas expressed in a given text and the connection between those ideas and the ideas expressed in all other relevant texts. This, too, is empowering because the focus shifts from authors and their ideas to the relationship among ideas, and it is the readers who are the ones who are making those connections.

Accompanying the death of the author is the demise of the great work: *Capital, The Protestant Ethic and the Spirit of Capitalism, The Structure of Social Action,* and so on. Actually, it is not so much that these works have died as it is that they, and more important the ideas contained in them, have become part of the intertextual field that is sociological, or more generally social, theory. Again, the focus shifts from a given great work to the interrelationship of the myriad works and ideas that go into making up the intertextual field. Just as our focus has shifted away from the great author, it also needs to move away from a deification of canonical works.

Another very different implication of the postmodern critique of the subject relates to the tendency of many sociological theories to focus substantively on the subject and subjectivity. This ranges everywhere from the focus in various Marxian theories on the revolutionary subject to a focal concern with individual subjectivity among phenomenologists, symbolic interactionists, and the like. At the minimum, the postmodern critique alerts sociological theory to the fact that it has such a focus and to what some of the problems are in having such a primary interest. More strongly, postmodern social theory points sociological theory toward a more balanced interest in subject-object and subjectivity-objectivity. A more extreme implication would involve a wholesale shift in much of sociological theory away from its traditional focus on subject/subjectivity and toward a concern with object/objectivity. (While we are emphasizing the postmodern critiques of subjectivity, it should be made clear that a number of postmodernists, especially feminists and multiculturalists, do have a sense of agency, albeit one with multiple identities or positions. Other postmodernists do not so much reject the subject as they seek to decenter the concept, critique essentialist views of agency, and seek to provide sociohistorical accounts of the making of subjects.[3]) We get a glimpse of what such a sociological theory might look like in Baudrillard's work in which the focus does shift to the object (the masses, for example). It is obvious that such a sociological theory would be light years away from today's approach. What such a theory might look like, at least substantively, is touched upon in the following chapter.

Perhaps postmodern social theory's most serious epistemological attack on traditional sociological theory is the latter's historic reliance, indeed deification, of grand narratives. The vast majority of the giants in the history of sociological theory have earned their place, in large part, *because* they offered what appeared to many to be among the grandest of grand narratives. There is Auguste Comte and his law of the three stages, Herbert Spencer's evolutionary theories (militant to industrial, for example) driven by the universal dynamic of survival of the fittest, Karl Marx's theory of revolution and the emergence of communism, Max Weber's "iron cage" of rationality, Georg Simmel's "tragedy of culture," Emile Durkheim's

---

[3]I thank Steven Seidman for reminding me of this point.

theory of the evolution from mechanical to organic solidarity, Talcott Parsons's evolutionary theory driven by adaptive upgrading, Jürgen Habermas's theory of the colonization of the lifeworld, and many, many more. While all of these theorists and their grand theories have been accorded pride of place throughout the history of sociology, it is difficult, if not impossible, to hold a similar view of their work today. While they still have a role to play in sociology, it is clear that the era of the preeminence of grand sociological theories is over.

Why? For one thing, it is more difficult to believe in any one theory, answer, or point of view. Postmodern social theory has helped attune us to the fact that no single perspective can possibly grasp the complexity and diversity of the social world. For all of their complexities, sociological theory's grand narratives were all gross oversimplifications of the social world and its development. One comes closer to a fuller sense of the social world by immersing oneself in the enormous range of local narratives than by buying into, or trying to concoct, a single grand narrative.

For another, we have been alerted by many postmodern thinkers to the terroristic implications of such grand narratives. Thus, in light of Stalinism, the Gulag Archipelago, and other atrocities, it is impossible to ever look at Marxian theory (whatever the differences between Marxian theory and the realities of Soviet communism) in quite the same way ever again. While they may illuminate reality for some social groups, grand narratives inevitably cast others in the shadows, or perhaps even in total darkness. Such perspectives privilege some, but in the process they serve to doom others to a lesser, if not a horrible, fate.

The recent history of feminist sociological theory is instructive in this regard (see Chapter 9). It arose, at least in part, from a realization that the grand narratives in sociological theory relegated women to the margins, or beyond. In reaction, a variety of feminist theories arose that privileged females, that looked at the social world from the standpoint of women. However, women of color looked at these as a new set of grand narratives that marginalized them and they sought to compensate for this by creating narratives of their own (Collins, 1990). Out of this has emerged a wide range of narratives and an even greater realization of the dangers associated with grand narratives (Rogers, 1996b). As a result, it is difficult to imagine feminist theory falling victim to a new grand narrative, and, more generally, it is developments like these that also serve to make such a development unlikely in the field as a whole.

Many of the grand narratives in sociological theory have been oriented, even if they ultimately proved to be more enslaving, toward emancipating people from some sort of problem or difficulty. However, the death of the grand narrative brings with it the death of the notion of such emancipation. If we no longer accept a "story" about the origins and sources of a problem, it becomes equally impossible to accept "stories" about how to free ourselves from such a difficulty. Furthermore, there is the postmodern argument that emancipatory social theories more often than not bring with them the possibility of even greater problems. As we have seen on several occasions in this book, the model here is modernity as a grand narrative, which instead of emancipating people, as the Enlightenment thinkers imagined, enslaved many of them in places like Nazi Germany's concentration camps and the

Soviet Union's Gulag Archipelago. In light of such critiques, it is difficult today to create a theory that offers hope of emancipation when it appears at least as likely that such a theory would set in motion events that would lead to greater enslavement, at least for some.

While many social theorists may have emancipation as an overt objective, there is often a more covert goal of imposing their way of thinking on people and thereby gaining status and power for themselves. Among the most obvious in this regard is Comte's positivistic theory in which he sought to create, and attract people to, a new positivistic religion in which he was to have been installed as the Pontiff. Most sociological theorists since Comte's day have been far more subtle and somewhat more modest, and while they may not have had such lofty goals for themselves, they have often shared the objective of seeking (or at least hoping) to have their way of thinking imposed on large numbers of people. Marx, Durkheim, and Mannheim, among many others, come immediately to mind as falling into this category. Postmodern social theory leads to the view that sociological theorists need to be wary of falling into the trap of shortcircuiting peoples' ability to think for themselves.

The many critiques of grand narratives do not mean that there is no place in sociological theory for thinking that is broad in scope. In fact, in an era characterized by the proliferation of local narratives and the demise of traditional grand narratives, there may be more need than ever for such thinking. While they should have a wide sweep, these new perspectives must *not* pretend to be the ultimate answer. As long as they are presented, and read, as narratives not inherently better or worse than other narratives, then they are free to explore as wide a sweep of the social world as they wish. Those who support such narratives must not seek to impose them on readers as *the* answer. Rather, such narratives must be allowed to succeed or fail on the basis of how much of the social world they illuminate for how many different social groups. In other words, how "grand" a narrative is should be defined not only by its intellectual sweep but also by the degree to which it is embraced by diverse sets of readers.

Related to the critique of the grand narrative is the inability of postmodern critics to accept the totalizing character of most traditional sociological theories. Included here would be theories that see social systems as characterized by whether they are in conflict or in harmony (or enslaving or enabling); that see people as defined by their symbolic interaction; that see such a definition in peoples' exchange relationships, or, in interaction dominated by recipes and typifications. The postmodern critique has made it abundantly clear, if it was not already, that these, indeed all sociological theories, are at best partial, *not* total, perspectives. Sociological theorists should be forever alerted to the partial character of their perspectives and to the ludicrousness of, and dangers associated with, searching for and advocating a totalizing perspective.

Indeed, from its beginnings sociological theory has been badly hurt by its propensity to search for totalizations. For example, Durkheim did much damage to sociology by defining it as the study of social facts. In doing so, he excluded many relevant aspects (social psychological, for example) of the social world from consideration. The discipline has yet to overcome the difficulties created by

Durkheim's attempt to define the scope of sociological theory in such a limited manner. More generally, Durkheim's "sociologism" would also fall under the heading of a totalization that has done great harm to the discipline. Durkheim, of course, argued that only social facts could explain other social facts. This led to the view that only sociological phenomena could explain other sociological phenomena. Excluded, in the process, was the use of psychological or social-psychological factors to explain sociological factors. It is clear that in adopting such totalistic positions on what sociology was (and was not) about, Durkheim was severely limited and hampered the field.

Similarly, the supporters of specific theories, as well as of the paradigms of which they are part, have long sought to present their position as *the* all-encompassing, totalistic perspective (Ritzer, 1975). In so doing, they have sought to elevate partial perspectives to the status of world views. Not only were such efforts doomed to failure from the beginning, but they have created devastating problems for the field. For example, the exaggerated claims of the supporters of each paradigm have led to extraordinary political conflict within sociology as they fought over attaining hegemony within the field. It often has seemed as if more time is devoted to wrangling over which group has the most powerful world view than in pushing the field forward. Indeed, it could be argued that the discipline has been hampered in its development by all of this internal bickering and politicking.

Similarly difficult, if not impossible, to accept is the essentialism of most sociological theories. Many sociological theories have been grounded in the idea that there are certain necessary characteristics (needs, abilities, and so on) of people that must be built into sociological theories. The assumption is that to be human, one must have these essential characteristics. One version of this, best exemplified by Marx's theory, is that people have certain positive characteristics, and if those traits are negatively affected, or perhaps even denied, then there will be great trouble in the social world. Thus, Marx assumes that people need to think, act, associate with other people, work, and create. These essential human characteristics are denied in capitalism with the result that there is alienation, unrest, and ultimately a revolution aimed at overturning the forces that are serving to deny these traits. Another version, best exemplified by Durkheim (and Comte), is that people are most defined by essential characteristics that are largely negative in character and that unless they are controlled by society, there will be chaos in the social world. Thus, to Durkheim people are dominated by insatiable passions that, left unchecked, doom them to a life of perpetual frustration and dissatisfaction (hence the need for various societal controls that free people from the dominance of their passions).

Clearly, people cannot, at their essence, be both what Marx and Durkheim perceived that essence to be. More generally, people cannot be all of the essences defined or implied in innumerable other sociological theories. Or, to put it another way, all of those essences, and many more, may exist in people, but *none* of them is, or can be, *the* essential human characteristic. The search for such a characteristic is as untenable as the search for *the* totalization or *the* grand narrative.

While seemingly benign and purely of theoretical concern, the search for essences can have powerful political consequences that advantage some groups and disadvantage others. For example, Durkheim's ideas on the need to control passions leads to the view that there have to be some individuals (e.g., teachers) and groups (e.g., occupational associations) that ought to be in the position to regulate those passions. This, of course, leads to some people occupying positions of power and authority, positions that they can use to not only control but terrorize those whose passions are deemed to be not suitably controlled. This is even clearer in Comte's work, with similar assumptions about human passions, where a clear hierarchy is created headed by the Pontiff of Positivism. There is clearly great potential for terrorism in such a rigidly hierarchical system.

Lest we think that essentialism is restricted to classical sociological theory, consider James Coleman's (1990) argument for *homo economicus* and against *homo sociologicus*. The essentialism of Coleman's (1990:13–14) *homo economicus* involves actors purposively seeking to attain goals, with those goals and actions shaped by values or preferences. Furthermore, actors are seen as choosing those actions that will maximize utility or the satisfaction of their needs and wants. While accepting one version of essentialism, Coleman rejects others such as those that view action as purely expressive or that see action as completely determined by outside forces. Another contemporary example of essentialism is Habermas's (1984) ideas on free and open communication.

Just as essentialistic ideas now seem problematic, it is at least as difficult to accept the claims of sociological theorists that they, and only they, either individually or collectively, are the possessors of the truth. The more extreme postmodern position here is that since there is no such thing as truth, it is impossible to accept the truth-claims of any, indeed every, sociological theorist. The more moderate position is that what is considered to be truth depends upon one's theoretical standpoint. This leads to the view that either truth is dependent on one's standpoint and thus there is no ultimate truth or that the best we can hope for are partial truths. While there are both strong (no such thing as truth) and weak (the best we can hope for are partial truths) positions, the fact is that in either case it is impossible in light of postmodern theory to ever look at the truth claims of traditional sociological theorists in the same light. Marx (the exploitative character of capitalism), Weber (the iron cage of rationality), Habermas (the colonization of the life world), structural functionalism (consensus), and conflict theory (coercion), among many other theorists and theories, all purported to have discovered the "truth." All seem naive, if not archaic, in light of postmodern theory.

Then there is the issue of reality. Most sociological theories have operated on the basis of the premise that there is a reality "out there" and that they are representing and analyzing it using the theoretical (and methodological) tools at their disposal. The postmodern view is that reality can only be known interpretively or narratively; no one authority can claim to know reality. In one variant on the postmodern position on this, there is the view that all that exists are simulations of reality built upon other simulations. Such a view leads to the position that reality is nothing more than an array of simulations. Sociological theory clearly becomes a different endeavor when what it is studying are simulations, not reality. Furthermore, this postmodern perspective leads to the view that sociological theory itself may be nothing more than a set of simulations. Thus, sociological theorists may be seen as involved in the production of simulated perspectives on a simulated world.

All traditional sense of what sociological theory is, and is to concern itself with, collapses in an ecstasy of simulation heaped upon simulation.

Perhaps a more modest version of this is that, yes, the social world is made up of simulations, but it is the task of sociological theory to unmask the simulated character of the social world. This leads to a sociological theory not all that different from traditional theory oriented to the debunking of social myths. However, it is a theory that must be devoid of the traditional notion of unmasking simulations to get at some ultimate reality, some ultimate truth. In the postmodern epoch all that we can hope for is the peeling away of one simulated layer to get at yet another layer of simulations. Of course, this leads to the question: Why unmask simulations if all one will find are more simulations? And we continue to be faced with another question: How can a simulated sociological theory uncover simulations in the social world?

At least one answer to both questions is that we need to be ever-conscious of the simulations that pervade both the social world and sociology. In terms of the social world, while we may never uncover some ultimate truth, there are gains to be made from a continuing critique of the simulated nature of our lives. At the minimum, such a critique keeps simulations, and their dangers, at the forefront of our consciousness. At the maximum, this kind of critique can help prevent us from a total free fall into a simulated world in which nothing makes any sense at all.

In terms of sociology, what is suggested by this is a reflexivity which underscores the fact that sociology is not immune from the same processes that affect the social world. It also suggests a continuing self-criticism that can help prevent sociology from the same type of free fall that is possible in the social world. The extreme postmodernist position would suggest that free fall in both settings is inevitable, but a more moderate position would be that it could be slowed or stopped by a critically oriented sociological theory.

The rejection of the ideas of truth and reality brings with it the rejection of science as a privileged type of discourse. After all, science purports to study reality with the goal of uncovering its truth. Not all of sociological theory has wrapped itself in a scientific mantle, but a wide array of theories has, including Schutzian phenomenology, some varieties of Marxian theory, the Durkheimian study of social facts, exchange theory, rational choice theory, and many others. It is difficult to take the scientific pretensions of these theories seriously in light of their own highly limited contributions, let alone in terms of the wholesale rejection of science as a privileged discourse by postmodernists. At best, we can think of these theories as scientific narratives as long as we recognize that they are just that, narratives, with no inherently greater status or power than any other type of narrative.

From its inception, a large portion of sociological theory has sought to obscure and compensate for its weaknesses by adopting a scientific label. Notable, here, are Comte's (and many others) positivism and Durkheim's commitment to the scientific study of social facts. Since its inception, sociological theory has offered a series of narratives, some of them quite good and others not so good. But, they have been just that, narratives, no matter how much theorists may have tried to privilege them by wrapping them in a scientific cloak. Instead of trying to gain an unfair advantage by attaching a scientific label to their perspectives, sociological theorists ought to let their narratives compete freely with all other narratives. Those that have merit will succeed without need for a mystifying label.

Perhaps one way of summarizing much of what has been said up to this point in this chapter is to say that sociological theory needs to be decentered. That is, it needs to move away from many of the things—authorship, grand narrative, totalization, essentialism, truth, science, and so on—that have traditionally stood at its core. More generally, it needs to adopt the view that there is nothing inherently at its center. To seek a center, especially one that is enshrined there forever, is to doom many other things to the periphery. Those things shunted to the periphery do not get the attention they deserve and are also destined to be controlled by those things at the center.

It is far easier to say what sociological theory in the postmodern age ought not to be than it is to say what it should be. While there are positive lessons to be derived from this section, there are also more overtly positive lessons to be derived from postmodern social theory.

Positive Lessons

We can begin with the idea that we left off with at the close of the preceding section—decentering. While the negative lesson is to cease privileging certain ideas as the center, the positive implication is that sociological theory ought to devote more attention to, if not focus on, the periphery or the margins. When phrased this way, this is not very far from the approach of many sociologists who have, for example, focused on the "underdog." It is also very much in line with "third-wave" feminism where the focus has shifted to disempowered groups of women.

A central task of social theory from the point of view of postmodernism is deconstruction. While this is essentially a negative process, it has at least two positive implications for sociological theory. On the one hand, it involves the critical analysis, the tearing apart, the decomposition of all extant sociological theories. On the other, such deconstruction can be viewed positively as an effort to strengthen social theories by subjecting them to intense critical scrutiny.

In itself, deconstructionism is not a very foreign idea to those who do metatheoretical work, that is, carefully study extant sociological theories (Ritzer, 1991). In fact, Baudrillard's critique of Marx's theory for continuing to be in the thrall of the theorists of capitalism is an excellent example of a metatheoretical analysis done by the preeminent postmodern social theorist. The major difference between deconstructionism and traditional metatheoretical work is that the latter generally has positive objectives (a greater understanding of theory, new theories, new metatheories), whereas the goal of deconstructionism is the continual decomposition of extant theories. Such an objective is defined by the postmodernists' fear of allowing any theoretical perspective to gain hegemony. Among other things, terrorism looms on the horizon when any theory achieves hegemony. Some sociological metatheorists may share this concern while others may not, but in either case there is a need for the continual deconstruction of extant theories.

While much metatheoretical work might be quite respectful, there is also a great deal of it that is quite critical. Perhaps what deconstructionism points up is the fact that those who study theory (metatheorists) have sometimes been too respectful of extant theories; all theories ought to be systematically and continually deconstructed.

In addition to this general viewpoint, there are obviously practical lessons to be learned from deconstructionists in other fields about techniques to be used in going about this process. For example, Derrida emphasizes the importance of focusing the deconstructive effort on the key moment or central contradiction within a text. Most metatheoretical work in sociology has not had such a specific focus but has instead been involved in a more general deconstruction. An effort to find, and deconstruct, central elements in sociological texts might well prove worthwhile.

The other positive lesson to be derived from deconstructionism is the idea that since all of social life can be viewed as a series of texts, they all can and need to be deconstructed. Here deconstructionism comes very close to the idea of debunking (Berger, 1963) so central to much of sociological thinking. Even if there are important differences, it is not much of a stretch to go from debunking social myths to decomposing social texts. In this case, it is the sociological theorists, rather than the metatheorists, who have much to learn from deconstructionism.

Of course, the idea of texts itself opens up a number of possibilities for sociological theorists. If we view social life as a series of texts, then the array of techniques and approaches (e.g., deconstructionism) developed by postmodernists and poststructuralists becomes available to social theorists. Sociological theorists can see these as alternatives to current approaches or, more conservatively, as complements to them. Of course, most sociologists will see them as alternatives since the whole idea of texts is foreign to their realist orientation to the social world. A more acceptable view may be to say that whether or not the social world is a text, it can be treated as a text for the purposes of sociological analysis.

While it is not ordinarily used in this way, the idea of deconstruction can be extended to the postmodern idea that thinkers need to be continually reflexive about their own ideas. From this point of view, it is not advisable for theorists to dig in their heels and defend their perspective to the death. Rather, theorists are expected to continually deconstruct their own ideas. Sociological theorists need to be as wary of imposing a set of ideas on themselves as they do of imposing them on others.

One of Fredric Jameson's ideas is that while sociological theory may not be able to discover the truth, it can seek to root out that which is false. Again, this comes very close to the traditional sense of sociology as a field devoted to debunking social myths. While an attractive argument, sociologists would have the same problem that Jameson (and Baudrillard, among others) has: Without a sense of the truth, how do we know what is false? That is, while postmodernists are quick to make all sorts of judgments, including what is or is not false, they lack an Archimedian point upon which to base such judgments. This has been an important issue to some theorists, especially those associated with the various branches of Marxian theory, but most sociological theorists have traditionally not been deterred from making similar judgments even though they, too, lacked an Archimedian point. While this represents a crucial problem for postmodernists, it is the same problem that most sociological theorists have always had and failed to confront or resolve. The best we can say about postmodernists on this issue is that they are no worse off than most more traditional sociological theorists.

The lack of an Archimedian point also poses the problem of the difficulty of creating a meaningful political program when one has no clear idea of where one is headed. In fact, this is one reason why postmodernism is generally so lacking in political direction (another is the fear that such political direction could end up being a grand narrative with terroristic implications). This represents yet another problem for postmodern thinking, especially for those who believe that theories *should* be linked to political agendas. Again, however, postmodern theorists are no different from most sociological theorists who, lacking an Archimedian point, also lack such a political program, or, if they have one, it is not coherently tied to their theoretical perspective.

Another, more easily defensible idea, derived from Lyotard (as well as Rorty), is that instead of seeking definitive answers, what sociological theory ought to do is continually seek out new questions. The point of sociological theory is *not* to find *the* theory, or *the* answer, for there is *no* ultimate theory; there is no final answer. The point may be simply to keep the dialogue among sociological theorists alive through the constant generation of new theoretical ideas and perspectives. Idea generation is reduced or destroyed when theorists come to believe that they are in possession of the theory, the answer. It is the search for the unknown, not self-congratulation over what is (believed to be) known, that should be the center-piece of sociological theory. It is not in the interest of such theorizing to find the answer (even if we assumed there was such an answer, and there isn't), because such an answer, or even the belief that theorists' are in possession of such an answer, would end the process. Stasis occurs when theorists believe, undoubtedly erroneously, that they are in possession of the ultimate perspective. Instead of searching for the answer to *the* question, sociological theorists should be generating lots of questions and many answers to each question.

All theoretical ideas should be subject to intense intellectual scrutiny. In addition to surviving such scrutiny, theoretical ideas need to illuminate at least some aspect of the social world for at least some social groups. They don't need to be the answer, or even an answer, but they do need to help some people see and understand aspects of the social world that were previously obscured or hidden from view.

To my mind, this is the ultimate reason why postmodern social theory is so relevant to sociological theory. That is, postmodern social theory has generated an enormous number of new and interesting theoretical ideas (ideas that will be the focus of the following chapter). Not all of these ideas will prove edifying to everyone, but at least some of them will prove useful to some people. Furthermore, these new ideas, as well as the related critiques of traditional social and sociological theory, have certainly served to keep the debate going in sociological theory. The postmodern challenge has served to invigorate and enliven sociological theory.

Thus, instead of the search for hegemony, sociological theory involves the search for dissensus. Instead of searching for the answer, sociological theorists should be rooting out and exploring their fundamental differences. The tendency among sociological theorists has been to limit their search for differences to their analyses of other theoretical perspectives. The postmodern perspective suggests that in addition to this they should also be looking for differences with those who share their theoretical perspective. It is normative, for example, for structural functionalists to look for differences with symbolic interactionists or exchange theorists. Far less likely, but perhaps far more important, is the search for differences *within* each theoretical perspective. The search for such differences will raise new questions and keep every theoretical perspective alive and fresh. Conversely, it is deadening for theorists to celebrate their similarities with those who accept their theoretical orientation and to restrict their exploration of differences to other theories.

While postmodernists argue against grand narratives, that does not mean that sociologists ought not, and should not, produce narratives, as long as they restrict themselves to local or micronarratives. Sociological theory, by its very nature, will produce narratives. As discussed above, this is as it should be as long as the producers of each narrative do not aspire to have their story become the grand narrative; as long as it is seen as only one of many sociological narratives. In addition, sociological theorists need to recognize that narratives stem from many quarters (other areas of sociology, other disciplines) and that their narratives are not inherently better than any others. Sociological theorists bring a variety of distinctive perspectives and strengths to bear on the creation of their narratives; their narratives will have advantages over those emanating from other quarters, but they will also have disadvantages.

Sociological theorists ought to be more like Bauman's "interpreters" and less like "legislators." Since there are many narratives not only in sociology but in the many other fields that produce social narratives, it is necessary that sociological theorists become experts at interpreting narratives. They should be able to explain a given narrative to supporters of other narratives in terms the latter can understand. In addition, as interpreters, sociological theorists can serve to facilitate communication between narratives and seek to ensure that communication between narratives is not distorted. In a sense, the sociologist as interpreter becomes a "go-between" for extant narratives. This becomes especially important in a postmodern, multicultural world in which no single narrative, or even small number of narratives, can or should achieve hegemony.

Sociological theory, like all modern undertakings, is obsessed with the idea of progress. Firmly embedded in the minds of most sociological theorists is the idea that they need to operate from a firm base and that they need to be steadily and progressively building upon, expanding, that base. Theorists are urged not to veer off the straight and narrow path that is leading to progressive refinement and development of sociological theory. Clearly, this is a limiting perspective. The alternative is to emphasize not steady progress but continual new beginnings.[4] What is needed are more sociological theorists who not only veer off paths but repeatedly jump off them completely and start over on new paths. Over their careers, sociological theorists ought to set off on a number of new and different directions. This stands in stark contrast to the traditional notion that sociological theorists should

---

[4]Another way of saying this is that sociologists are interested in Brownian movement, not progress.

commit to a set path (the solidification of a given theory) early and stay with it throughout their careers.

Surrendering ideas like continual progress and grand narratives means that sociological theory will need to content itself with the idea that, at the minimum, some aspects of the social world will always remain unknown and inexplicable. Implicit in much sociological theory since Comte's day is that it is only a matter of time until we will be able to understand and explain all of social life. Whatever its present inadequacies and failings, there has been a faith among sociological theorists that something approaching complete knowledge awaited them down the road. Postmodern thinking leads to the realization that this will not be the case and, in a sense, it serves to liberate sociological theorists. They are freed to illuminate what they can without the burden of thinking that what they accomplish is never quite enough.

While I would not argue that sociological theory ought to abandon its rational procedures, there is an argument, derived from postmodern social theory, to be made that sociological theory could stand an infusion of irrationality. While rationality is to be prized and valued for many reasons, it can also serve to stultify creativity. A variety of more irrational procedures can serve to revive creative theorizing. For example, sociological theory is usually based on remembering, if not revering, the work of its forebears; indeed, theorists are urged to build upon the shoulders of their intellectual ancestors (Merton, 1965). While I, more than most given my interest in metatheorizing, would not reject the idea that we need to base our work on that which has come before, it is also important to realize that such an approach can produce blinders and limits just as easily as searchlights. Thus, there is an argument, following Lyotard, for learning and then perhaps forgetting, at least for a time, the ideas of the predecessors of contemporary sociological theory. On their own, without the burden of the weight of a century or more of social theory, perhaps sociological theorists can come up with some genuinely new theoretical ideas. To follow up on another of Lyotard's ideas, perhaps sociological theorists need to adopt a position less like responsible adults and more like "children" toward theoretical ideas.

The notion of more irrationality, more childishness brings us to the need to "play" more with theoretical ideas as well as with the pieces that remain of the social in the postmodern world. From a postmodern perspective, sociological theorists are a little too rigid, a little too stodgy, a little too mature. In addition to the disciplined study of theoretical ideas, theory could do with a lot more play with different theoretical ideas. In playing with various ideas, theorists are apt to waste a lot of time but also occasionally to come up with lots of new and interesting combinations. Most of them will prove useless, but a few of them may just end up being brilliant new insights. In any case, the point of sociological theory is not to come up with *the* answer, but instead it is to play with interesting theoretical differences in an effort to cast new light on the social world.

Relatedly, sociological theory ought to involve not just a focus on "reading" but a lot more "writing." This, of course, builds off the importance accorded to writing, to the creative process, by postmodernists. To studiously review the well-known work of forebears is not writing since it involves little or no creativity. Writing does not involve focusing on what we already know but on what we do not know. (However, we must not forget that good writing requires sufficient reading.) This means that theoretical writing should set off in uncharted directions rather than re-tracing well-worn paths. Clearly, the greatness of thinkers like Foucault and Bau-drillard stems, at least in part, from their willingness and ability to do just that. Un-fortunately, most contemporary sociological theorists are inclined by virtue of their training to follow well-known paths. Instead of, or at least in addition to, being ex-ercises in erudition, sociological theory also should involve exercises in imagina-tive thinking. While an emphasis on imagination is traceable to the postmodernists, it also has its roots in sociological theory, especially C. Wright Mills's (1959) *The Sociological Imagination.*

Similarly, Lyotard suggests the importance of mystical interpretations and the making of distorted images. This also brings us back to Baudrillard and his orien-tation to metaphysics, to say nothing of pataphysics, or his science of imaginary solutions; his science-fiction of the system. At one level, theorizing oriented to mysticism, metaphysics, science fictional accounts, and the production of distorted (rather than accurate) images is obviously a profound threat to the rational, even scientific, view of theory that has stood at the base of sociological theory since its inception in Comte's day. But is it really so different? After all, Comte's work cer-tainly had its mystical, metaphysical, fictional (even science fictional), and dis-torted qualities, and at least some of those characteristics continue to find their way into much of sociological theory to this day. But at another level, if the ultimate test of sociological theory is the generation of original ideas that cast new light on the social world, should we really care much about their basic character or funda-mental sources? Baudrillard's work, for example, has many of these qualities, but the bottom line is that it does succeed in offering us new insights into the social world. I don't want to push this too far and argue that sociological theory ought to have these qualities, but I do think that we ought not to exclude ideas simply be-cause they stem from perspectives that do not adhere to our traditional rational, scientific model.

Summarizing much of what has come before in this section, it could be argued, following Bauman, that since postmodernity is characterized by ambivalence, soci-ology must learn to adapt to it. Modern sociology, like modernity in general, was oriented to the eradication of ambivalence. It sought to understand the nature of the social world, but to postmodernists things like the "black box of the code" prevent us from ever achieving anything approaching a true understanding of the social world. In addition, it adopted a "gardening" mentality and sought total control over that which proved to be beyond control. Learning from the failures of modern soci-ology, sociological theory in the postmodern age will need to learn to be comfort-able with the ambivalence that is inherent in the study of the social world. It is going to be tougher to be a sociological theorist in the postmodern world than it was in the modern era with its grand hopes that the eradication of ambivalence was just around the corner.

One rather specific task for sociological theory, derived from Jameson's work, is the creation of cognitive maps. It could be argued that social theorists have al-ways created cognitive maps (Marx was mapping the then-new world of capitalism; Weber mapped the outlines of the then-new rational, bureaucratic world; more recently [see the next chapter], I have tried to map the terrain of the new Mc-Donaldized society). What is different now is, in part, the nature of the terrain being mapped (e.g., Jameson's new spatiality), but so is the status of the maps. No social thinker's map is any more privileged than any other's, and furthermore the social thinkers' maps have no greater or lesser status than those produced by novelists, poets, and so on. Nonetheless, it is important that sociological theorists keep on mapping the social terrain from their distinctive vantage point.

Sociological theory has traditionally focused on subjects, but one of the implications of postmodernism, especially the thinking of Baudrillard, is that instead of, or in addition to, such a focus, we ought to be concerning ourselves with objects. At its extreme, this suggests a drastic reorientation of sociological theory. In focusing on various subjects, sociological theorists have relegated large numbers of other people to the category of objects. That is, they have been relegated to the status of an undifferentiated group that is acted upon rather than acting. Directing our attention to this group can have various implications. For example, following Baudrillard, we might find that while they may not be powerful, agents, objects, or more specifically the masses have an interest, a charm, a power of their own (the "strength of the weak"). More modestly, sociological theorists may find much of interest in a shift in focus, at least to some degree, from subject to object.

Sociological theory in the postmodern age is, like postmodernity in general, both exhilarating and dangerous. For example, there is the thrill of being liberated from having to have all the answers, from needing to eliminate all ambiguity. On the other hand, there is the danger of feeling overwhelmed by a series of questions for which there are no answers. There is the additional danger of having sociology degenerate into a large number of warring tribes, or even to a situation where each individual sociologist has her own narrative that differs from the narratives of every other sociologist. Sociology could degenerate into the senseless babble of tens of thousands of different and conflicting voices. In such a case, who are newcomers to the discipline to listen to? Who are other theorists to listen to? Who is the larger public to listen to?

Sociology has a long history of concern with morality (Durkheim and Parsons are two notable examples). What is the place of morality in a sociology in the postmodern era when it is impossible to believe in the great overarching moral systems? One answer lies in Bauman's work where morality comes down to the individual, individual conscience, and the need for individuals to be *for* other individuals. Bauman's position won't satisfy all sociological theorists, but it is clear that moral concerns are not going to disappear in sociology, and therefore we need new ways of dealing with them.

Perhaps the ultimate epistemological challenge of postmodern social theory is the challenge to sociological and social theory to throw off its blinders and to look at the social world in a totally different way. The paradigm of this is Baudrillard's charge that Marx's focus on productive work blinded him to things like waste, play, and purely symbolic exchange. Whether or not one agrees with the specific foci of postmodern thinkers, the fact is that social theorists need to have their foci, and more generally the nature of what they do, challenged. While most traditional challenges are intra-paradigmatic and therefore ultimately mild in nature, there is also a need for the far more dramatic challenge from those who operate from a totally different paradigm. That is what is happening in the case of postmodern social theory. In the main, it represents a challenge to the most basic and sacred principles of traditional sociological and social theorists. It is healthy for such theorists to have to defend, rethink, and perhaps alter some of their most fundamental ideas in light of such an extreme challenge.

In fact, sociology itself is part of the postmodern world and therefore is subject to the same kinds of analyses and pathologies as every other aspect of that world. For example, we could view contemporary sociology as metastatic and hypertelic generating a neverending stream of signs in its huge and growing array of articles, books, research reports, and now items floating through the internet. This endless creation of ideas and data is far beyond the control of any given sociologist. It is also, in the main, largely without meaning to anyone, with much of it going largely unnoticed and unread. (Interestingly, this is most likely in the case of sociology on the highly postmodern internet.) Yet, the creation of sociological works spins on, largely out of anyone's control. Sociology, like the rest of the postmodern world, grows increasingly obese and cancerous; it involves increase without limits. As Baudrillard would put it, sociology is increasingly bloated with information. Just as the general public is bombarded by signifiers from the media, sociologists are overwhelmed not only by those signifiers, but also by signs emanating from the discipline itself. Again following Baudrillard, it could be argued that sociology in general, and sociological theory in particular, has become pornographic. Because there are so many signs, it is impossible to understand them. With so much information available, it is virtually impossible to distinguish the important ideas from those that are banal.

In the same spirit, perhaps the problem with sociology and sociological theory is that they have become hypervisible. A typical research study lays out everything, from inception of the project to conclusion, for the reader to see. A theoretical work is supposed to detail all of the intellectual twists and turns taken by the theorist. While such detail is prized in a rational, scientific discipline, might it not be that sociological theory has become hypervisible, obscene, and therefore unable to seduce its audience? Ultimately, is it not the case that theoretical works succeed or fail on the basis of their ability to seduce their relationship? Perhaps sociological theory has foundered in recent years because it has lost sight of the need to seduce its audience? Perhaps sociological theory has lost sight of the fact that in this need to seduce it is no different than poetry, novels, or art? Sociological theorists need to play more games with signs; they need to create more illusions for their readers. Baudrillard is certainly a model here since his works, especially the later ones, are elusive and nonlinear, but they certainly are seductive.

To begin this process, at least some thinkers should be oriented, following Baudrillard again, to injecting some "evil," some "death," some unreason, into sociological discourse. Sociological theory can be viewed as a domain too much in the thrall of reason; it could use an infusion of unreason to shake it up, to point it in some new directions. Indeed, the work of many postmodern thinkers can be seen as just that: efforts to inject some unreason into a mode of social thinking that has become lost in the endless proliferation of rational accounts.

SUMMARY

This chapter has been devoted to some of the epistemological implications of postmodern social theory for sociological theory. The first part of the chapter focused on some of the negative lessons of postmodern social theory, some of the things that sociological theory ought to stop doing, such as stop giving so much emphasis to the subject, the author, and the great work. Sociological theory is also critiqued for its tendencies toward privileging grand narratives, totalizations, essentialism, the search for truth, the belief in reality, and scientific discourse. Overall, it could be argued that all of the latter have been at the center of sociological theory, and in all of these it is in need of being decentered.

The second part of the chapter focuses on some of the more positive lessons of postmodernism. The decentering of sociological theory leads to a focus on more peripheral entities and orientations. Deconstructionism leads to critique that can ultimately strengthen sociological theory as well as to the view that all of social life is made up of texts in need of deconstruction. Deconstructionism can also be used to help the theorist be more self-conscious and self-critical. While it may not be able to unearth the truth, sociological theory in the postmodern age may be used to discover that which is false. Another, more modest, objective is merely to keep the process of theorizing going. Sociologists can and should continue to produce narratives as long as they recognize the dangers inherent in seeking grand narratives. Another, similarly modest, objective is for theorists to function like interpreters rather than legislators. Sociological theory could profit from an infusion of playfulness or childishness; it could do more creative writing and less reading. While there are innumerable other positive implications for sociological theory, in the end it is challenged to begin looking at itself and the social world in a different way.

11

POSTMODERN SOCIAL THEORY: AN APPLICATION

CONSUMER SOCIETY

A POSTMODERN ANALYSIS

DEALING WITH THE NEW MEANS OF CONSUMPTION

WE have now spent ten chapters amidst the abstractions of postmodern social theory. While surveying the theories and getting the ideas right are of great importance, it is difficult, to put it mildly, to fully understand those ideas when they are discussed purely in the realm of theory. It is also important to be able to think about the social world from a postmodern perspective; to apply postmodern theory to everyday experiences.

The objective in this chapter is to take many of the ideas associated with postmodern social theory and to apply them to a set of concrete examples. It should be made clear that this is essentially a modern application of postmodern ideas. In a way it constitutes a step toward the seemingly paradoxical modernization of postmodern social theory. Yet, if we accept Lyotard's perspective on the continuing relationship between the modern and the postmodern, this is not such an odd endeavor. A more modern postmodern perspective would serve to make postmodern social theory more generally accessible and usable. In addition, the modernization of postmodernism would likely lead to a counterreaction whereby some postmodernists seek to distance themselves from this hybrid. The result would likely be a flowering of new postmodern orientations.

The specific substantive concerns of this chapter can be combined under the heading of what I (Ritzer, forthcoming) and, more important, Baudrillard (1970/1988:54), call the "means of consumption." Specifically, I have in mind a number of relatively new means of consumption that are largely products of American society. These new means are already of great importance in the United States, and they are in varying stages of being exported to the rest of the world. Two of these new means of consumption are the fast-food restaurant (Ritzer, 1996a) and the credit card (Ritzer, 1995). Related innovations in the means of consumption include shopping (including mega-) malls, superstores, cybermalls, theme parks, home shopping via television, infomercials, telemarketing, and even the somewhat older supermarkets.

Before proceeding with this postmodern analysis, it should be pointed out that I have previously analyzed two of these new means of consumption from a *modern* point of view. For example, I have used the fast-food restaurant as the model for a grand narrative I have called the McDonaldization of society (Ritzer, 1996a). This approach is based on Max Weber's theory of rationality, especially his thinking on the increasing formal rationality (see below for a definition of this concept) of the Occident. To Weber, the model of a formally rational system was a bureaucracy, while today the fast-food restaurant represents an even better paradigm of this type of rationality. The bureaucracy is still with us, but the fast-food restaurant better exemplifies this type of rationality. This implies that not only is formal rationality still an important phenomenon but so is the modern world of which this type of rationality is a key component.

There are four dimensions of formal rationality: efficiency, predictability, an emphasis on quantity rather than quality, and control through the substitution of nonhuman for human technologies; then there is the likelihood that this form of rationality brings with it the irrationality of rationality. Efficiency means the search for the best means to whatever end is sought. In the fast-food restaurant the drive-through window is a good example of a highly efficient means for obtaining a meal. Predictability means a world of no surprises; the Big Mac one eats in Los Angeles is indistinguishable from the one being eaten in New York; similarly, the Egg McMuffin we consume tomorrow or next year will be just like the one we eat today. Rational systems tend to emphasize quantity, usually large quantities, rather than quality. The Big Mac is a good example of this emphasis on quantity rather than quality. Instead of the human skills and abilities of a chef, fast-food restaurants rely on nonhuman technologies like unskilled cooks following detailed directions and assembly-line methods applied to the cooking and serving of food. Finally, such a formally rational system brings with it various irrationalities, most notably the demystification and dehumanization of the dining experience.

Thus, the fast-food restaurant brings with it new heights in formal rationality in general, as well as in each of its specific dimensions. Furthermore, innumerable other businesses and many other sectors of the social world are emulating some or all of the innovations put in place by the fast-food restaurant. If we equate formal rationality with modernity, then the success and spread of the fast-food restaurant, as well as the degree to which it is serving as a model for much of the rest of society, indicate that we continue to live in a modern world. Buttressing this argument is the fact that the fast-food restaurant is Fordist in various ways (Kumar, 1995), most notably in the degree to which it utilizes assembly-line principles and technologies. Fordism is usually associated with modernity, while post-Fordism is better linked to a postmodern world (Clarke, 1990). Similarly, the fast-food restaurant is built on modern industrial principles, thereby standing in contradiction to the view that we have moved into a postindustrial society (Bell, 1973; Hage and Powers, 1992) often linked with postmodernism. While there may be other changes in the economy that support the idea of a postindustrial society, the fast-food restaurant and the many other elements of the economy that are modeled after it, in the main, do not.[1]

Ritzer (1995) has also examined credit cards from the point of view of the rationalization thesis. It could be argued that what credit cards have served to do is to McDonaldize the receipt and expenditure of credit. Instead of fast food, what the modern bank is doing is dispensing fast money. Each of the dimensions of McDonaldization applies to the credit card. The whole process of obtaining a loan has been made more efficient. Instead of a long and cumbersome application process, there are just a few simple questions to answer. And if that is not efficient enough, many people are frequently offered preapproved cards. Predictability is best exemplified by the fact that the credit card serves to make consumption more predictable; people can even consume without any cash at all on hand. The emphasis for most people is on quantitative matters such as the number of credit cards they can acquire and the collective credit limits of those cards, with little regard to the adverse effect a large amount of debt has on the quality of their lives. Decisions about whether or not to issue a new card or to raise a credit limit are increasingly left to ever-more sophisticated nonhuman computer programs with little or no input from humans on a case-by-case basis. Ultimately, the highly rationalized credit card business has a series of irrationalities, including the dehumanization associated with dealing with nonhuman technologies and robot-like bank employees who engage in tightly scripted interaction with customers (Leidner, 1993).

Thus, the credit card, like the fast-food restaurant, can be seen as part of our McDonaldized, formally rationalized, and therefore ultimately modern society. The two examples discussed here–the fast-food restaurant and the credit card—both indicate advancement in rationality, and therefore in modernization, over their predecessors: the local diner and the personal loan.

This raises an immediate issue: How can these phenomena be discussed under the heading of postmodernism in this chapter when two of them have already been discussed as modern phenomena? The answer is that in this context I am not adopting the chronological view that postmodernity supplants modernity (in fact, Lyotard [1988/1993:76] argues that the "idea of linear chronology is itself perfectly 'modern' ") but rather that one can analyze any social phenomenon from the point of view of *both* modern *and* postmodern theory. Having previously analyzed these phenomena from a modern perspective, my intention in this chapter is to now look at them, and more generally the new means of consumption, from a postmodern perspective.

In fact, it may be far more useful to regard modernism and postmodernism not as epochs that follow one another but as different "modes" of analysis (Lyotard, 1988/1993:24). In analyzing social phenomena alternately from a modern and then

---

[1]One way that they do is in producing large numbers of service jobs, although they are in low-paying, low-status occupations that are different from the professional and technical service occupations emphasized by analysts of the postindustrial society.

a postmodern perspective, one would be following the logic employed by Weinstein and Weinstein in their recent postmodern analysis of Simmel:

> To our minds "modernism" and "postmodernism" are not exclusive alternatives but dis-
> cursive domains bordering each other. . . . We could be working the modernist side of
> the border (as we have in the past) if we didn't think that the postmodernist side con-
> tained more resources for mapping present culture.

> (Weinstein and Weinstein, 1993:21)

Having worked the modern side of the border in my earlier work, in this chapter
I will be working the other side of the border to discuss fast-food restaurants and
credit cards and, more generally, the new means of consumption. One is quite safe
in doing so since the postmodernists, themselves, have tended to look at phenomena like the fast-food restaurant as representative of postmodernism. Take, for example, the following description of postmodernism by Lyotard:

> Eclecticism . . . of contemporary general culture: one listens to reggae, watches a west-
> ern, eats *McDonald's* food for lunch and local cuisine for dinner, wears Paris perfume in
> Tokyo and "retro" clothes in Hong Kong; knowledge is a matter for TV games.

> (Lyotard, 1979/1984:76,; italics added)

It should be pointed out that I (and many others) tend to look at the new means
of consumption in a very material (Marxian) sense, but most postmodernists (and
poststructuralists) tend to focus far more on the signs associated with such phenomena and their place in the code. However, these two approaches are not mutually exclusive, and we will have many things to say about signs and the code in the
context of a discussion of these means of consumption.

CONSUMER SOCIETY

The place to begin a postmodern analysis of these means of consumption is with
the view that postmodern society is a consumer society (Featherstone, 1991); indeed one often sees the terms used synonymously. Baudrillard's early work was
focused on consumer society, and, more recently, Bauman has viewed postmodernity in these terms. As we have seen, capitalist society *has* undergone a shift in
focus from production to consumption. In the early days of their economic system,
capitalists focused almost exclusively on controlling production in general and
production workers in particular. As factories have moved out of advanced capitalist nations, the focus in those nations has moved toward controlling consumption
in general, especially the thoughts and actions of consumers. While producing
more and cheaper goods remains important, attention is increasingly being devoted
to getting people to consume more, and a greater variety of, things.

In the realm of consumption, the focus is usually on marketing and advertising.
While these are certainly important, what I want to focus on, as pointed out above,
are the new means of consumption as both social structures that constrain people
and as signs (and as producers, sponsors, and so on of signs). In doing so, I am fol-

lowing Baudrillard (1970/1988) who discussed such means of consumption in some of his early work. Baudrillard focused on the distinctively French drugstore as such a (then-) new means, but closer to my foci he also discussed the shopping mall in these terms.

The new means of consumption are just that, means to allow people to consume. The concept is obviously derived from Marx's focus on the means of production—tools, raw materials, machines, factories, and so on. Just as such means are necessary to, and facilitate, production, means of consumption perform the same roles in the sphere of consumption. Furthermore, this helps us to see, once again, that there are important analogies between workers and consumers. In fact, as we will see, consumers now "work" in conjunction with these new means of consumption, and to the constant joy of capitalists (and their profit margins) they perform that work without compensation.

On the surface, means of consumption and their functions seem benign enough, even quite positive. But, looked at more deeply, they are means to gently, and not so gently, lead consumers to consume in ways that are most advantageous to manufacturers and sellers. This means that at least some of the time they act to the detriment of consumers. For example,

- Fast-food restaurants offer people foods that tend to be high in cholesterol, sugar, salt, and so on that are harmful to their health.
- Credit cards induce people to spend more than they should and beyond their available means, buying things they do not need and may not even want.
- Shopping malls entice people into buying things they may not need.
- TV shopping networks and cybermalls permit people to shop 24 hours a day, seven days a week, thereby increasing the likelihood that they will spend more than they should.
- Catalogues allow people to purchase products from anywhere in the world, and they may be induced into buying unnecessary products.

The point is that these and other new means of consumption *enable* people to do things they could not do before, but they also *constrain* them financially, psychologically, and materially to buy more than they need; to spend more than they should.

The fact is that capitalists need customers to do so to keep the economy operating at a high and growing level. Thus, capitalism is a major force in the invention of these new means of consumption. Furthermore, capitalism needs[2] to keep on having them invented so that it can continue to be the kind of economic system we have known it to be. In fact, more attention seems to be devoted these days to inventing new means of consumption than to the more traditional course of creating new means of production. If postmodern society is consumer society, at least in part, then these new means of consumption are key elements of the postmodern world.

---

[2]Of course, capitalism does not "need" things; it is the capitalists who do if their enterprises are to remain profitable.

There is an enormous amount of money spent on advertising the glories of the various new means of consumption, and this is reflective of the growing importance of consumption in modern capitalism. While we usually associate labor with production, Baudrillard has made it clear that consumption has become a kind of labor. Thus, in a sense, we all perform labor in trekking to a half-dozen or more fast-food restaurants each week. Not only must we (usually) drive to them and back, but we must often also wait on lines in or out of our cars. If we eat in the restaurant, we must literally perform a series of jobs (serve as waiters by carrying our own food; serve as buspersons by cleaning up after ourselves) that restaurants of old had to pay people to perform. If we go through the drive-through and take the food with us, we do the work of sanitation workers by disposing of the debris left over after our meal is completed. Similarly, we work during our treks to shopping malls, supermarkets, and even Las Vegas casinos. All of this, and much more associated with the new means of consumption, is work, and capitalism must keep us at it to keep expanding and to prevent the consuming masses from thinking about anything remotely resembling a social revolution. In addition, capitalism wants to keep us at it because instead of paying workers, people are willing, even eager, to pay for the "privilege" of working as consumers. Most important, capitalism needs us to keep on spending at ever-increasing levels to be and to remain capitalism. Without ever-increasing consumerism, capitalism as we have come to know it would collapse. As a result, the focus of capitalism has shifted from exploiting workers to exploiting consumers.

The new means of consumption also lead to the proliferation of goods and services. Bauman (1992) recognizes this and relates it to Simmel's tragedy of culture. The tragedy is that our capacities do not develop fast or far enough to allow us to deal with the enormous profusion of commodities. In addition to the expected goods and services, in the postmodern world virtually every aspect of culture (art, music, and so on) is for sale; such cultural products add enormously to the commodities to be sold in the consumer society. In other words, we come to be overwhelmed by objects of consumption, to say nothing of the increasingly wide array of means in existence to dispense these goods and services.

Given this contextualization of this discussion of the new means of consumption from a postmodern perspective, let us turn to a more general postmodern analysis of these phenomena. Since, as the reader has seen, postmodernism is not a coherent theory, indeed it generally denies the possibility of such a theory, in the following section we will present a "pastiche" of postmodern ideas and their applicability to an analysis of the new means of consumption. In the concluding section we will address a rather surprising topic (although we have encountered it in the discussion of Baudrillard's work), given the usual association of postmodern social theory with nihilism—ways of dealing with the new means of consumption.

A POSTMODERN ANALYSIS

One of the things that we will certainly be doing in this chapter is deconstructing the new means of consumption. In one sense, we will seek to critique, to undermine, to subvert this phenomenon and the larger system and code that it represents and is manifest in it. Relatedly, but in another sense, we will be decomposing this phenomenon, taking it apart (at least intellectually). However, unlike modern efforts, our purpose in this deconstruction will not ultimately be the creation of a new construction out of the shards of what we have taken apart. Rather, it will be left with you, the reader, to play with the pieces that remain after the new means of consumption have been deconstructed in these pages. It is such play, rather than the provision of yet another ultimate answer, that is of greatest importance to a postmodernist. It is not my task as the "author" to offer such an answer, to make such a construction; rather, it is your task as "readers" to do so. Were I to offer yet another construction of how we really ought (or ought not) to be consuming, I would be committing the modern error of engaging in a kind of terrorism designed to constrain or control your thoughts and actions. If postmodernism stands for nothing else, it stands for the empowerment of the reader and the dethronement of the author.

As a result, this chapter will be composed of a series of different interpretations of the meaning of this deconstruction and of what is left after the means of consumption have been deconstructed. Again, leaving it at this is just fine from a postmodern perspective, in part because the modern alternative has been characterized by too many perspectives that purport to be *the* answer and not enough satisfied to be one of many possible answers.

Such an orientation is, of course, related to the idea of decentering, as well. In one sense, we are engaging in decentering the analytical process by moving away from an answer provided by the author to a range of different perspectives emanating from the readers. Furthermore, the set of perspectives to be offered in this chapter is lacking in a center; it is a pastiche of postmodern positions on the new means of consumption without some overarching theme such as is to be found in my modernist interpretation (see above) of fast-food restaurants as paradigmatic of the McDonaldization of society. This analysis is decentered in yet another sense; instead of examining high culture, as is usually the case in modernist academic works, the focus here is on low or popular culture. Postmodernism is characterized by its refusal to privilege high culture or even to differentiate between high and low culture. Jameson (1991), for example, moves back and forth between examples of high (the paintings of van Gogh) and low (the popular movie, *Body Heat*) culture. Clearly, fast-food restaurants and the like are part of low culture, but their popular character makes them, if anything, more important than aspects of high culture as objects of critical analysis.

Jameson's (1984b, 1991) work, especially his five basic characteristics of postmodernism, while it relies heavily on the work of others (especially Baudrillard), provides us with a useful organizing framework and starting point for a more substantive postmodern take on the new means of consumption.

First, to Jameson, postmodern society is characterized by superficiality and depthlessness. The creators of its cultural products are satisfied with surface images and do not delve deeply into underlying meanings. Clearly, fast-food restaurants fit well into this aspect of postmodern society. Social relations within the fast-food restaurant are certainly superficial and depthless. As Robin Leidner (1993) has shown, the employees are generally mindlessly following scripts, and the customers are undoubtedly responding with what Alfred Schutz (1932/1967) would call "recipied" action. That is, customers are mindlessly following what they consider tried-and-true social recipes, either learned or created by them previously, on how to deal with restaurant employees and, more generally, how to work their way through the system associated with the fast-food restaurant. Social relations are similarly superficial in the credit-card world, especially those involving customer and merchant and customer and employee of the credit-card firm. For example, there are the numerous phone calls in which an employee of the credit card company "reads" a script offering us a new card, and we respond (assuming we don't hang up immediately) with a recipe that has been developed to handle the situation ("sorry, I don't take phone solicitations").

Similarly depthless are our relationships with those who make sales pitches or answer the phones on home-shopping networks, the telemarketers who call to purvey their wares, and the clerks who work behind endless counters at the shopping mall, the superstore, and the supermarket. With the coming growth of cybermalls, our relationships with those who sell us things will grow even more depthless and superficial as we communicate with them exclusively through keystrokes or mouse clicks on the computer.

The foods sold in a fast-food restaurant (and more generally the products marketed in the wide variety of McDonaldized chains) can be said to be lacking in depth. Clearly, the foods are of the most basic types, using common ingredients, and prepared in the simplest of ways. Complex foods using unusual ingredients and involving sophisticated preparation simply do not fit into the fast-food model; for example, they make it difficult to satisfy one of the most fundamental precepts of McDonaldization—efficiency. As a general rule, the more complex the product, the more unusual the ingredients, and the more sophisticated the preparation, the more inefficient it is to produce a meal (or virtually anything else). While there are exceptions, most of the new means of consumption work best when the simplest and most generic of products are being marketed. For example, the few seconds or minutes at the disposal of the telemarketer make telemarketing most useful in selling simple, known, and easily explained products.

Relatedly, the new means of consumption are characterized, and to a very high degree, by simulacra which, by definition, are superficial; lacking in depth. For example, instead of "real" human interaction with servers in fast-food restaurants, with clerks in shopping malls, with telemarketers, and so on, we can think of these as simulated interactions. Employees follow scripts, and customers counter with recipied responses, with the result that no genuine, authentic interaction ever takes place. In fact, so many of our interactions in these settings are simulated, and we become so accustomed to them, that we lose a sense of genuine interaction. In the end, all we have are simulated interactions; there are no more "real" interactions. In fact, the entire distinction between the simulation and the real is lost; simulated interaction *is* our reality.

The same point applies to objects associated with other new means of consumption. Any given credit card is a simulation of all other cards of the same brand; there was no "original" card from which all others are copied; there is no "real" credit card. Furthermore, credit cards can be seen as simulations of simulations. That is, credit cards simulate currency, but each bill is a simulation, a copy, of every other bill and, again, there was no original bill from which all others have been copied. But currencies, in turn, can be seen as simulations of material wealth, or of the faith one has in the Treasury, or whatever one imagines to be the "real" basis of wealth. Thus, the credit card shows how we live in a world characterized by a never-ending spiral of simulation built upon simulation.

Of perhaps greatest importance, in this regard, is the fact that credit cards are simulated means that allow people to purchase all of the other simulated goods and services[3] being churned out in contemporary society and being sold through other new means of consumption—for example, shopping malls, theme parks, and catalogues. (Thus, the credit card can be seen as a means to all the other means of consumption; a "meta-means.") For example, to build on one of Jameson's (1984a, 1991) examples, we could charge a copy (a simulation) of Andy Warhol's (simulated) painting of Campbell soup cans. Or, we could even charge a copy (a simulation) of a second artist's reproduction (another simulation) of Andy Warhol's "original" (yet another simulation). We could even go so far as to charge a "real" can of Campbell's soup (which is, of course, a copy of perhaps billions of other such cans in label, design, physical structure, and contents) in our local supermarket (which is undoubtedly a simulation of many other such markets). Most generally, we can say that the credit card is a simulation that helps to enable all other simulations. Thus, as credit cards (and other forms of electronic funds transfer) increase in importance in the coming years, we will see a society dominated even more by simulations.

Simulations also characterize the fast-food industry. For example, there are the simulated playgrounds that grace the entrances to many fast-food restaurants. Then, there are the foods—the hamburgers, the pizza, the tacos—which, while they may be very good simulations of others of their genre, are poor copies of their ancestors bearing only the faintest resemblance to the homemade hamburgers, pizzeria pizzas, and roadside-stand tacos that some can still remember. In fact, such "real" food, if it ever existed, has disappeared under an avalanche of simulacra. Today, to most Americans under the age of thirty or forty, the McDonald's burger is the "real" burger, or to put it more accurately, there is nothing but simulated hamburgers. One who wants to unmask these simulacra for what they are runs the risk of discovering that there are no "real" hamburgers, there is no "true" hamburger (or anything else, for that matter). Then, there are the completely invented foods, for example, the millions, perhaps billions, of virtually identical (and simulated) Chicken McNuggets. The latter fits perfectly Baudrillard's idea of a simulacrum as an identical copy for which no original ever existed. The original, the chicken, had the temerity to be created with bones, skin, gristle, and so on. But then chickens themselves, given modern factory farming, are nothing more than simulations that bear little resemblance to the dwindling number of their "free-ranging" brethren.

---

[3]Theoretically, credit cards could be used to purchase "originals," but in postmodern society about all we have are simulations.

Then, of course, there is the structure and decor of the fast-food restaurant. The Roy Rogers' chain is modeled, I suppose, after the movie cowboy's ranch house, a ranch house that never existed, except perhaps in the movies where, of course, it was already a simulation. The whole western atmosphere created by the chain, and its commercials, has much more to do with the movies (simulations) than it does with the "real" old west (whatever that was).[4] Another example that comes to mind is the "Arthur Treacher" chain of restaurants, which is modeled after an old English fish and chips shop (whatever that may be). For those of you too young to remember, Arthur Treacher was a British actor who was most associated with butler roles in the movies.[5] This simulated British butler was the symbol of this chain of simulated fish and chips shops. A similar point could be made about the fictional Long John Silver (known best to the public, of course, from the movie [i.e., simulated] version of *Treasure Island* rather than the original book) chain of seafood restaurants, as well as many other simulated purveyors of simulacra. By the way, these examples reflect the importance that the media (movies, TV) play in the postmodern world. In the above instances they are affecting us indirectly, but they of course also have a more direct impact on us that has been the concern of many postmodernists.

As simulated worlds selling simulated products, the new means of consumption in general, and the shopping mall in particular, have a hyperreal quality to them; they seem more real than real. A typical mall has a cold sterile quality; it is not quite of this world; it is not quite real, or rather it is a little bit more real than "real" shopping plazas in large cities as well as in small towns. The malls are outdone by the theme parks (although malls are coming to look more and more like theme parks) like Disney World in which Disney products are sold in a world that seems more real than reality. The same sort of thing can be said about Las Vegas casinos and cruise ships, which create a hyperreal world to separate us from our money without the need to give us any goods at all in return. The products purveyed in glossy catalogues (e.g., the lingerie marketed in the Victoria's Secret catalogue, to say nothing of the women who model the nighties) and on the home-shopping networks are made to appear far more real than they will be when they find their way into our homes and onto our backs. Obviously, even more hyperreal are the new cybermalls. Can we be far from "virtual shopping"?

Second, to Jameson, postmodernism is characterized by a waning of emotion or affect. The world, and the people in it, have become fragmented; affect, such as it is, is free-floating and impersonal. There is certainly little if any genuine emotion or affect in our relations with those who serve us in fast-food restaurants, shopping malls, modern hotels, and supermarkets. Relations between customers and employees are mechanical and devoid of emotion. Even the major acts in such a society—say, purchasing a hamburger, charging a CD (which can now be done via an 800 phone number, yet another new means of consumption), reserving a room, paying for groceries—are generally mechanical and unemotional.

---

[4]Of course, the real old west has been filtered for so long through the simulations of movies and TV shows that it is difficult to even have a glimmer of what it "really" was.

[5]I remember him best, however, as the announcer on a talk show starring Merv Griffin.

Relatedly, Baudrillard describes America as a desert, and it is not surprising that fast-food restaurants, perhaps the quintessential American product, are similarly desert-like. Lacking in depth and emotion, every fast-food restaurant seems like every other. Ultimately, the entire terrain of fast-food restaurants seems like some vast desert in which it is difficult to differentiate one superficial landmark from another. Each fast-food restaurant seems like one more meaningless outpost in the desert. People are dashing from one outpost to another, but there is nothing meaningful about any of the outposts or in the monotonous process of moving from one to another. People seem to be coming from nowhere and headed to nowhere. (Much of what has been said about the fast-food restaurant in this paragraph describes the shopping mall equally well.) And, America is rapidly exporting this mode of consumption to much of the rest of the world, which eagerly awaits it, or at least the seemingly desirable signs that go with it. From Baudrillard's perspective, the rest of the world is rushing headlong in the direction of creating a similar consumer, and ultimately social, desert.

While they are characterized by a certain flatness, there is, as Jameson points out, a peculiar kind of euphoria ("intensities") associated with these postmodern settings. There is, for example, the sense as one arrives at the fast-food restaurant that one is in for excitement, or at least some fun. Indeed, what fast-food restaurants really sell is not food but a (simulated) kind of fun. The clowns, the cartoon characters, the setting (a carnival, a ranch, a pirate ship) all promise excitement, even if the food is of the most prosaic type one can imagine. What could be less exciting to most Americans than eating yet another fast-food hamburger, chicken wing, or pizza slice? Yet, we seem to be fooled (or to fool ourselves) continually by the peripherals into believing that we are in for some excitement when we pass through the portals of the fast-food restaurant.

Of course, this excitement pales in comparison to the intensity of feeling on the part of the consumers who enter yet another shopping mall with credit card at the ready. Malls, like fast-food restaurants, promise, and seem to deliver on, excitement, especially those like the Mall of America in Minneapolis with its amusement park, including even a roller coaster. Just as fast-food restaurants are not really peddling food, malls are not really selling goods, or at least they are not selling themselves on the basis of the goods they have to offer, since those same goods can be purchased almost anywhere else. What they are peddling is their version of an enchanted environment in which to buy those goods. And lo and behold, in come the customers, and what do they have at the ready? The magical credit card; the keys to the kingdom! What could be more exciting. Here we are in a magical world and we've got the golden key that will unlock every door. Better yet, and even more magical, it appears as if it's all free! Merchants gladly take our plastic, we sign our names, and off we go with as many goods as we can carry (and as our credit limits will allow). Of course, we know that a downer (the credit-card bill) awaits us down the road, but who cares? We're too excited to worry about such future consequences. Even if we "max" out on one card, some other bank will admire our profligacy and give us another card. We might even be able to take a cash advance on the new card to make a minimal payment on an overdue bill from the old card.

Related to the idea of intensities is the sense that Bauman and others (Debord, 1977) convey that postmodern systems are intent on offering "spectacles." Examples include the garishness of fast-food restaurants and their amusement-park qualities such as playgrounds for children, the modern malls that are more shows with some, as we've seen, even including amusement parks within their confines, as well as the amusement parks themselves, which often seem little different from shopping malls oriented to the sale of products associated with the park's theme. Thus, Disney World seems to be only marginally different from Mall of America (Fjellman, 1992). Disney World has a few more attractions, a few less shops, than Mall of America, but both have a healthy mix of both, and both are oriented to using the spectacle to attract as many buyers as possible. Cruise ships, casinos, hotels, even supermarkets seek to present themselves as spectacles so that they can elicit that intensity that is otherwise made so difficult to experience by the unemotional and affect-less character of most postmodern systems.

Third, there is a loss of historicity, and this is certainly true of fast-food restaurants. They either tend to seem timeless (McDonald's golden arches) or to be a pastiche of things from different time periods (what are those 1990s style technologies doing in a Roy Rogers' cowboy ranch house, circa 1880?). Similarly, adrift in yet another day of charging things at the mall, one finds it difficult to differentiate one hour or day from the next. Indeed, malls (and Vegas casinos) are infamous for not having any visible clocks to give the shopper the illusion of the absence of time passing.

More important is the fragmented and discontinuous character of life associated with the new means of consumption. Tacos today, burgers yesterday, and pizza tomorrow add up to fragmentation and discontinuity. Credit cards are perhaps the ultimate means to a fragmented and discontinuous life. Limited only by the number of cards in our possession and their collective limit, we can be anywhere we want, buy anything we wish. We can spend a little time here, and a bit more time there, and we can put it all on the card. We can buy a new leaf blower today, skis tomorrow, and swimsuits the next day. The only continuity in this fragmented and discontinuous life is the constant spending and the fact that that inevitable reckoning will be appearing in our mailboxes. The package tour is another wonderful example of this as vacationers whirl through a series of fragmented sites often so quickly that they hardly know where they are, let alone the significance of what they are seeing.

Baudrillard describes much of this experience with the term "ecstasy." Each and every fast-food restaurant can be seen as but one of a series of empty forms that endlessly differentiate themselves from one another (even though they are all essentially alike). In the process, they are constantly reinventing the same products (other empty forms) over and over again, with only slight variation from one to another. Fast-food restaurants and their products are hypertelic, increasing at astronomical rates without any reason (save new or greater sources of profit) for their increase; there is an ecstasy associated with this pure movement. Involved in this is a kind of empty inflation. As a result, we find ourselves asea in an ecstatic system in which fast-food restaurants (or shopping malls, supermarkets, superstores) and their endlessly different, yet surprisingly similar, products whirl about us. This brings with it a massive proliferation and differentiation of signs that ultimately end up being an incoherent blur. We are lost in a world of relentless, yet meaning-less, expansion. Thus, customers, fast-food restaurants, their products, the resulting signs are all madly and meaninglessly spinning about in this hyperreal world. Fast-food restaurants (and the other new means of consumption) are contributing to a world in which there is too much meaning (we actually know the meaning of "Chicken McNuggets" and "Egg McMuffin"), much of it superfluous (do we re-ally need to know the difference between a Whopper and a Big Mac?). We are left with a feeling of vertiginousness. Things in the world of fast food go round and round at a dizzying pace, but there is no essential meaning to the process.

It is worth noticing here that as significant and highly visible sponsors, the fast-food restaurants play a key role in the proliferation of signs by the media, perhaps the main source of sign overload in contemporary society. Through the media, the fast-food restaurants not only bombard us with all of their own signs but through their sponsorship they help support a media system that produces a daily avalanche of signs. In so doing, the fast-food restaurants help contribute to the perception that everything is available for communication, signification, banalization, commer-cialization, and consumption.

Of course, all of this is much more true of credit cards and the world of shop-ping it has helped spawn; communication, signification, banalization, commercial-ization, and consumption are all very apt terms to describe that world. As means to means, credit cards have not only increased enormously but they have con-tributed to the hypertelic expansion of all of the other means of consumption.[6] Shopping malls, casinos, cruise ships, package tours and the like have exploded because, at least in part, credit cards have permitted people to use them more quickly and easily and, more important (at least sociologically), they have permit-ted people to spend far beyond their cash on hand. An interesting case in point is the coming growth in cybermalls. At the moment, the use of cybermalls is limited by the fact that there is no reliable means to protect peoples' credit card numbers when they are used to charge things over the internet. However, the major credit card companies have promised that they will soon have the capacity to offer such protection. Once such protection is in place, once people feel sure about using their credit card numbers on the internet, we can expect to see a hypertelic proliferation of such malls, the businesses that participate in them, and the consumers who buy through them.

Fourth, there is a new technology associated with postmodern society. All of the new means of consumption, especially the fast-food restaurant and the credit card, can be seen as implosive technologies. They are not technologies that produce anything new (at least directly). Rather, they are technologies that better permit us to get what we want and that entrepreneurs want us to purchase. In the vast array of fast-food restaurants, the range of different foods available to us implodes into an undifferentiated black hole of hard-to-differentiate salty-sweet foods. Subtlety of taste is not the strong suit of fast-food restaurants. Similarly, in the mad race to acquire as many goods as we can with our credit cards, they implode into a mass

---

[6]Fast-food restaurants were slow to incorporate the use of credit cards because, at least in part, of the small amount of money associated with any given purchase, but that is now changing.

of largely undifferentiable stuff, stuff that we don't really want, don't need, and will likely replace as soon as our credit card limits will allow. Again, there is no explosive production of goods with credit cards but rather an implosive consumption of wares.

While they may be implosive technologies, they are undergoing explosive growth; that is, there is enormous expansion of fast-food restaurants, credit cards, and the other new means of consumption in postmodern society. One could say, following Baudrillard, that, like cancer, they are metastasizing throughout American society and around the rest of the world. Much the same can be said about virtually all, if not all, of the new means of consumption.

Finally, at least in Jameson's schema, there is the postmodern multinational capitalistic system that, from his perspective, lies at the base of the development and expansion of these new means of consumption. While the same could be said for all of the new means of consumption, the fast-food restaurant and the credit card fit well into this aspect of Jameson's approach; they are central aspects of contemporary capitalist society. Instead of exporting automobiles or steel, we are exporting burgers and pizza. More generally, and important, we are exporting the means to consume them—the various franchises—with a large portion of the profits from each franchise returning to American corporations. The credit card is an American innovation that has led people to buy more than they otherwise would. In fact, as we have pointed out previously, the credit card allows people to spend money they do not have. Much like the Treasury, credit cards create money. Of course, Visa doesn't actually print currency, but it does imprint credit cards with varying limits. With these cards, people can spend all the currency in their possession printed by the Treasury, and then they can spend the additional "money" available in the collective credit limits of their cards. This additional money has been created by the credit card companies (not the Treasury), and it allows capitalism to operate at a far higher level than it could if it was limited to extracting all of the consumer's available cash.[7]

Most of the other new means of consumption assist the capitalist system by devoting themselves to getting people to buy things they otherwise would not or to spend more than they intend. Take the example of megastores like Price Club. The whole idea behind these stores is to get people to buy things they do not need and, more important, to buy things in far larger quantities than they ordinarily would, sometimes in larger quantities than they could ever use. Thus, multiples of a given item are packaged together so that instead of one, several must be purchased. Similarly, enormous containers, jars, bottles, bags, and so on are used so that people buy far larger quantities of things. People go to outlets like Price Club to save money. While the unit prices are ordinarily lower, people in fact often end up spending more money than they otherwise would. Going to Price Club is a sign that one is a wise shopper, but that sign conceals the fact that one is buying and spending more than one would in other settings.

---

[7]In fact, the majority of economic transactions, not just credit card charges, are now done electronically. Enormous transactions among large businesses and even among nations are accomplished with a few computer keystrokes. Modern capitalism would be impossible without these new technologies.

This is a case where the postmodern sign (careful shopper) is at odds with what the means of consumption lead people to do (buy more than they need; be careless). This raises the interesting issue of the precise nature of the relationship between postmodern signs and postmodern means of consumption. As is clear in this case, they are not necessarily always consonant with one another.

Today, credit card firms (and fast-food restaurants) are concentrating on international expansion. This will mean greater profits for them. More important, it will allow more and more people around the world to do what Americans are doing— spend far beyond their available cash resources. Consuming more like Americans, they will inevitably consume more American goods as well as the goods of other capitalist nations. The result will be a more active capitalist system and greater profits to the capitalist firms.

International expansion is certainly not restricted to fast-food restaurants and credit cards. Disney's theme parks are now found in both Asia and Europe (even the troubled EuroDisney is now earning a profit); shopping malls and supermarkets are finding greater international acceptance; television shopping networks are now found outside the confines of the United States; and of course the cybermalls, like the internet of which they are part, are inherently international in scope. Indeed that is a great source of the attraction to sellers of a wide array of goods and services.

Of course, Jameson is an atypical postmodernist in viewing postmodernism as continuous with capitalism and therefore modernity. In contrast, for example, Baudrillard sees us as having moved from the industrial era in which there is serial production of simulacra by the industrial system to an era in which the code predominates and in which simulacra are reproduced by the code. The era of the code brings with it a possibility of control that far exceeds that of the industrial-capitalist system. Furthermore, while the industrial-capitalist era is marked by production, the era of the code is one of reproduction (see above).

The new means of consumption, of course, produce virtually nothing. Rather, they reproduce the same products over and over, and, more generally, they serve to reproduce the code and the system. For example, while the fast-food restaurant exerts control through more modern industrial-capitalist mechanisms and contributes to capitalistic expansion, it is also a significant contributor to, and part of, the code, and it is through that code that it also manifests control. We can, following Baudrillard, think of the code as a "code of signification"; that is, the code is a set of signs that exerts control over people. In the postmodern world, objects and commodities are signs; in using or consuming them we are using or consuming signs. Thus, in using or consuming fast-food restaurants and their products we are making statements about ourselves. Of course, those statements are controlled and kept in a narrow range by the code. It is much like the referenda to which Baudrillard devotes so much attention. In a referendum, our ostensibly free choices are defined for us in advance; our free choices are tightly constrained. Similarly, our ostensibly free choice of food is constrained by the fact that fast-food restaurants are driving the alternatives out of business. More important, the differences that they appear to offer turn out to be, at best, superficial. Thus, following Baudrillard's notion of the referendum, when we "vote" on which fast food to eat in a given day, that choice can hardly be deemed to be a free one.

Let me use an example of a new means of consumption, one not used previously, to further illustrate this point—Wal-Mart. A discount department store focusing at least initially on small towns eschewed by other large retailers, Wal-Mart clearly qualifies as an example of one of the new means of consumption. Typically, when a Wal-Mart arrives in a small town it drives out many of the competing "downtown" businesses. In a sense, it becomes virtually the only game in town. Thus, when people choose to shop at Wal-Mart it is because, in many instances, it has helped create a situation in which there are no alternatives to it.

Jameson argues that these postmodern settings exemplify hyperspace where modern conceptions of space are useless in helping us to orient ourselves. While the interiors of fast-food restaurants do not have this characteristic, the typical "strip" on which a vast array of fast-food restaurants, and other McDonaldized systems are found, does. It is difficult to get one's bearings when one is adrift in a seemingly endless sea of such McDonaldized businesses. The strips are characterized by things Jameson associates with postmodernism—an "existential messiness," and the feeling of a "bad trip" (Jameson, 1991:117). Even better examples of hyperspace are to be found in modern hotels (see Jameson's discussion of the Hotel Bonaventure in Chapter 9), and shopping malls, especially the megamalls. Las Vegas, as well as many of the enormous new casinos (MGM Grand, for example), are also characterized by hyperspace.

In addition to material constraints and characteristics, and of far greater importance to most postmodernists, is the fact that the new means of consumption are busy fabricating and manipulating signs, and it is those signs that are controlling our behavior. For example, fast-food restaurants clearly signify "fast." To the degree that the sign "fast" has become part of the code, we are led in the direction of doing many things, not just eating, quickly and efficiently, and conversely we are led away from slow, cumbersome processes in most, if not all, settings. Concretely, this means that we will be drawn to fast-food restaurants and away from traditional restaurants where it might take an hour or two to dine.

Another sign associated with fast-food restaurants is "fun" (the bright colors, the clowns, the toys, and so on). Again, with fun food part of the contemporary code we are going to gravitate toward the fast-food restaurants and away from the "old-fashioned" restaurants that offer only good food in staid surroundings. More generally, we are led to look for fun in most, if not all, other settings. In Neil Postman's (1985) terms we are intent on "amusing ourselves to death." Thus, one of the cruise lines is the *Carnival* line; we are not just getting a cruise but a carnival, and what could be more fun than that?

The code, and the fact that we all implicitly understand it, enables us to understand what people are saying about themselves when they utilize one of the new means of consumption. In eating in one fast-food chain rather than another, or in eating one type of food rather than another, we are saying, at least implicitly, that we are like some people and different from others. In other words, our eating habits constitute a text that it is possible to read. "Reading McDonald's" might involve such things as understanding what some people are saying when they consume "value meals" and what others are saying by eschewing such meals. Those who are regulars at Taco Bell are telling us something about themselves and how they differ from those who are habitués of Burger King, Kentucky Fried Chicken, or Popeye's. To take one other example, those who eschew McDonald's for higher status McDonaldized chains like Red Lobster are communicating a message, and that message is even stronger from those who avoid all fast-food restaurants of any type and frequent only traditional, up-scale restaurants where meals are cooked from scratch with fine ingredients by culinary experts. Because it is all coded, there is no end to our ability to read the signs associated with peoples' eating habits.

To take another example, there are the signs associated with different credit cards. Use of American Express, Diner's Club, and Carte Blanche communicates that one is of higher status than one who uses the more prosaic and widely used Visa and MasterCard. Using a gold or platinum card, rather than one of the basic cards (and colors), communicates the same message. (There are even reports of a mysterious black American Express card for really big spenders [Lewis, 1995].) Then there is the need to read the significance of using cash rather than a credit card. A wealthy person using cash may be saying one thing, while a poor person who pays in cash is saying something quite different. Thus, one can read credit card use (or its absence) just as one can read fast-food preferences; indeed, utilization of all of the new means of consumption is coded and therefore can be, and is, read.

From the perspective of signs and the code, eating, shopping, vacationing, and so on have little or nothing to do with "needs" as they are conceptualized conventionally. For example, we do not eat in fast-food restaurants because we need to eat there (as opposed, for example, to at home). More to the point, we do not eat Chicken McNuggets (as opposed to any other food) because we need them, and only them. The desire to eat Chicken McNuggets has been manufactured, like all other needs, by the code (and the economic system). Indeed, the human race survived quite nicely for the eon before the Chicken McNugget was "invented." We do not eat what we need, but what the code tells us we should eat; the code produces our needs (if they can still be called needs when they are manufactured externally). In general, we eat to express our similarities and differences with other humans and not to satisfy our need for food and, more generally, to survive. When we eat a Big Mac we may think that we are consuming a glorified hamburger, but in fact we are eating an object-sign. In eating that object-sign and not others, we are expressing much about our position within the system.

One tangential point worth mentioning briefly relates to the focus of postmodernists (and poststructuralists) on expressing differences in the signs we consume. While there is certainly much truth in this, it is *also* the case that we use signs to express our commonalities with others. The consumption of signs associated with fast-food restaurants is clearly much more an expression of commonality than difference. Indeed, with the massification of signs, it seems clear that people are being led in the direction of "needing" to express far more commonality and far less difference in sign consumption. There will always be signs of difference, but they are increasingly dwarfed by signs of commonality—McDonald's golden arches and, to take an example from another realm, Nike's "swoosh" logo.

Returning to the thrust of the argument on signs, many of the same kinds of things said about fast-food restaurants can be said about the other means of consumption. When we whip out our credit card at the mall we are saying, among other things, that we are "players" in the postmodern economy. A similar sign is communicated when we take a cruise or gamble in a Vegas casino (many cruise ships offer casinos). In these cases we are demonstrating that we are not merely players but "high rollers" (when, of course, most of us are not and will need to spend months or years paying off the trip and/or the gambling debt), but there are also times when we demonstrate that we are knowledgeable and cautious consumers. A trip to Price Club might be designed (although not consciously) to demonstrate that fact, even though, as we have already seen, we often spend more money and buy more goods than we intended or should have. Then, there is making a purchase via a cybermall, which is a sign that we are among the most progressive of consumers utilizing the latest technological advances.

In the preceding pages we have been dealing, in the main, with Baudrillard's third stage, but as we saw in Chapter 6 Baudrillard has recently added a fourth, fractal stage. Here, we are talking about endless proliferation, the end of difference, the interpenetration of everything. All negativity has been eliminated, and all we are left with is a vacuous positivity, the "Hell of the same." Fast-food restaurants, shopping malls, Las Vegas casinos, TV shopping networks are all well described by their efforts to remove all negativity; to create at least the illusion of total positivity. While many other things could be discussed under the heading of the fractal order, perhaps the most important relates to the end of differences. For example, while there are many different kinds of fast-food, they all end up being pretty much the same: a vast "black hole" of fast food.

An even better and broader example is the erosion of the distinction between shopping and nonshopping areas. It could be argued that more and more places are taking on the characteristics of a shopping mall. We have already discussed how amusement parks are growing more and more like malls. Then there are college student unions, airport and train terminals, and the like, which are looking increasingly like shopping malls. With the arrival of TV home-shopping networks, our living rooms and dens have become outposts of the malls. Soon our studies and offices will be extensions of the cybermalls. There used to be many areas where one could escape from, be free of, shopping. Those areas are being drastically reduced as more and more of them become malls, or at least extensions of them. Following Baudrillard, we could say we are in the era of "transconsumerism."

DEALING WITH THE NEW MEANS OF CONSUMPTION

Postmodern theorists identify, although many times only implicitly, a number of ways of responding to the problems associated with postmodernism, and many of them can be applied to the new means of consumption. As we saw in Chapter 6, Jean Baudrillard's work is particularly rich in such responses. This is somewhat ironic since Baudrillard (and postmodernism more generally) is often seen as nihilistic. But, given the great diversity of work that exists under the heading of postmodern social theory, it is virtually impossible to make such generalizations about it in general and Baudrillard's perspective in particular.

While Baudrillard's work is rich with explicit and implicit responses, it should be pointed out that in his view, it was far easier to respond to the modern capitalist system where the proletariat had a clear adversary (the capitalist) than it is to cope with the postmodern code (to say nothing of the fractal order) since there is no obvious antagonist associated with it. Furthermore, capitalist hegemony was largely restricted to the economy, while the code is and seems everywhere; it is omnipresent. Therefore, it is difficult to figure out ways of combatting the code, and even if one is successful in one domain, problems are likely to persist in many other areas. Given these caveats, let us look at several of the responses in postmodern theory and their application to the new means of consumption.

Like many other postmodernists (and not a few modernists), Baudrillard sees the contemporary world as plagued with disenchantment. In various ways he seeks to reenchant the world, and reenchantment constitutes a way of dealing with the excesses of contemporary society. Thus, for example, one of the problems with exchanges between customers and employees in superstores (among other new means of consumption) is that they have lost their symbolic qualities. This is not only true for the economic exchange of money for commodities but also the social exchanges between customers and employees in these settings which have taken on a mechanical, nonhuman quality. To put this another way, a world of simulation (including simulated human relationships) has replaced symbolic exchanges between humans. This implies that one way of responding to this, and more generally to the disenchantment in settings like the superstore, is by reestablishing symbolic exchange among and between workers and customers. Involved in such symbolic relationships is a continual cycle of giving and receiving rather than the self-limiting exchanges that characterize settings like superstores. Furthermore, a wide range of things would need to be exchanged rather than the highly specific and very limited types of exchange found in superstores. That is, not just money and goods would be exchanged but also things like emotions, feelings, experiences, knowledge, insight, and so on. Work in such settings would involve unlimited giving and receiving rather than the limited exchange of money for services. To customers, employees in superstores are like the dead discussed by Baudrillard; they are physically separated from customers and prevented (by such things as scripts, rules, counters and the like) from engaging in symbolic exchange with them. In engaging in symbolic exchange with employees, customers would be striking a blow against the powerful, but fragile, code that serves to keep both in their places.

Similarly, Baudrillard suggests that we respond to the system, in this case the new means of consumption, by offering it "gifts" to which it is constitutionally unable to reciprocate. Thus, I suppose, in the case of the fast-food restaurant, we might take to overpaying for our food, performing unpaid and unexpected services for those restaurants, or literally bringing them gifts on anniversaries and openings. This would make their inability to engage in symbolic exchange even more glaring and hasten their downfall. How this downfall might occur is left unclear by Baudrillard, but even Marx was more than a little vague on the details of the communist revolution and the overthrow of capitalism. Unless one buys into Baudrillard's argument fully, it does seem to strain credulity to believe that such acts as overpaying for a Big Mac would jeopardize the current system.

The ability of such minor actions to make a difference, let alone bring down the system, is based on Baudrillard's belief that while it appears to be omnipotent, it has in fact grown progressively unstable. Thus, such mundane actions do, in fact, have the capacity, at least in Baudrillard's view, to topple the hegemony of fast-food restaurants, the system, and the code. Of course, these actions cannot occur only in fast-food restaurants, or even just in the new means of consumption, but must take place at every site in which the code is represented and re-created (which, of course, is close to all, if not all, social sites).

Paying extra for food at McDonald's is related to another of Baudrillard's suggestions—reckless expenditure. Squandering money on a series of useless expenditures (a cynic might say that this is already what most consumers do in the postmodern society and culture) is, in a sense, making gifts to the code and the system that they do not know what to make of and to which they are unable to respond. Baudrillard believes that this, like more specific gifts to entities like the fast-food restaurant, will help set the system on a course to self-destruction.

Alternatively, Jameson's ideas on homeopathic remedies can be applied to the issue of dealing with the new means of consumption. Instead of responding with things postmodern systems cannot produce or respond to (like symbolic exchange), homeopathic remedies involve responding to postmodern systems in the same way that they deal with us: using the elements of that world to push it to its limits and beyond. In the case of fast-food restaurants, this might involve formally rational responses to the formally rational system. For example, customers might adhere strictly to all of the rules, formal and informal, that govern the fast-food restaurant. Such adherence would be time consuming and demanding of the system and its staff; it might well cause the system to slow to a crawl, thereby giving the lie to the label "fast food."

The world of fast-food restaurants and many other new means of consumption (Price Club would be another excellent example) may be viewed, in Baudrillard's terms, as an obscene world in which seemingly everything is visible, indeed hypervisible. Note, for example, the visibility of the food-preparation area in contrast to the traditional restaurant where the kitchen is almost always hidden from view, the obvious and abundant trash receptacles rather than the way trash and its disposal is hidden from view in a traditional restaurant. To Baudrillard, the traditional restaurant is a "scene" where some things are hidden; where some mystery (e.g., just how the foods are prepared; how trash is disposed of) continues. Fast-food restaurants are obscene because almost nothing is hidden; everything is visible. A solution to Baudrillard to this problem is the return of some invisibility, some mystery; in other words the return, to use another of his terms, of seduction. Instead of hypervisible fast-food restaurants, we need restaurants that retain some, even a great deal of, mystery. Instead of fast-food restaurants that bludgeon customers into submission, we need restaurants that retain the ability to seduce, rather than overwhelm, customers.

Take the issue of the taste of the food. Fast-food tends to overwhelm our taste buds with strong and obvious (obscene) tastes, especially very sweet and highly salty. Our taste buds are not seduced by a wide variety of subtle flavors but over-whelmed by a few strong tastes. In contrast, of course, a gourmet restaurant (or a home-cooked meal) is oriented to seducing our taste buds. Even the decor of such restaurants is seductive, in contrast to the bright, loud, and powerful colors and decorations of the typical fast-food restaurant. The logic of Baudrillard's argument leads us to see the creation and patronage of seductive restaurants as a way of cop-ing with the contemporary world.

This, of course, easily lends itself to the accusation that the postmodern perspec-tive is elitist. After all, such restaurants are costly to build, and such meals are apt to cost the diner a great deal of money. However, one wonders whether one could combine low cost and seductiveness in a restaurant? More generally, are there af-fordable but more seductive alternatives to the various new means of consumption? Is there a necessary contradiction between cost and seductiveness? In fact, the an-swer is no. One could prepare a seductive meal at home for less than it would cost to dine at a fast-food restaurant. One could also imagine quite a seductive restau-rant being built for far less than the cost of the average fast-food restaurant.

Could one go a step further and envision a chain of franchised, but still gen-uinely seductive, restaurants? The answer is undoubtedly no. Once one moves be-yond a single restaurant, to a chain, one is immediately in the realm of simulacra. Simulation is not a characteristic that Baudrillard would ascribe to the process of seduction. Thus, as one tries to institutionalize and replicate seduction from one site to another, it would lose its seductive qualities. Yet, it is possible to simulate seduction, and the time will undoubtedly come when we will see a chain of restau-rants that offers simulated seduction. The creators of such chains will recognize that some segment of the population that frequents fast-food restaurants is tiring of being bludgeoned into culinary submission, and there is money to be made in of-fering them simulated seduction, both in the food and in the setting.

Seduction is related in Baudrillard's work on the fatality of the objects, in this case those—the customers—who frequent fast-food restaurants (or utilize the other means of consumption). Instead of being constrained by these restaurants, Baudrillard suggests that it is possible that it is the restaurants that are being se-duced by the customers (objects). For example, the seemingly ever-increasing pa-rade of customers is seducing the fast-food chains into endless rounds of expan-sion and proliferation, a game that will ultimately prove fatal as fast-food restaurants eventually proliferate beyond their ability to survive. The same process, of course, affects all of the other new means of consumption. To take another ex-ample, millions and millions of people can be seen as seducing the credit-card companies by accepting offer after offer for new credit cards and overture after overture to increase their spending limit once the old limit has been exceeded. The result is that the banks and credit-card firms are extending untold billions of dol-lars in unsecured credit. This could eventually cause this vast "house of cards" (lit-erally) to collapse when it becomes clear that there is no way that the masses will be able to repay much of this debt, or even the interest on it.

The above are two examples of the mass's "fatal strategies." Baudrillard be-lieves that such strategies will lead the world into an ever-spiraling downward tra-jectory that will end only in catastrophe for the system and the code. The fatal strategies of the "evil genies," the masses, will not lead to revolution in the traditional, grand-narrative sense of the term but rather to a gradual devolution as the code, and the system on which it is built and which sustains it, gradually unravels.

As to looking for agents[8] (the masses, as objects, cannot be seen as agents) to respond to the new means of consumption, one can, for example, point to those people who have avoided their pervasive presence and influence. The problem is that in the United States, and increasingly in many other parts of the world, it is difficult to identify very many who have been able to avoid their effects. The young, those most likely in most conditions to form the base of a subversive movement, are the most profoundly affected by the influence of the new means of consumption. The working class, the traditional revolutionary subject, would be similarly affected and, in any case, would have no obvious material reason to be the vanguard of such a revolution. One can only hope that isolated pockets of people relatively immune to the influence of the new means of consumption (say, the Amish) can provide the base for a social movement whose objective is to at least limit their impact.

More promising is the postmodern idea that the revolution is not the grand product of a group of revolutionary agents, but such a transgression is possible, even necessary, here and now in the everyday practices of individuals. In postmodern terms, especially in the work of Derrida, everyone, all of the time, has the capacity to "write," that is, to create innovative responses to the code and more specific oppressive structures. By, for example, demanding things of fast-food restaurants that they do not want to deliver (a rare hamburger; extra-brown french fries) people are engaging in a form of writing that can alter the nature of the fast-food restaurant and perhaps ultimately the code. Clearly, we are talking here of millions of very specific behaviors repeated over and over again; we are talking about innumerable micro lines of resistance.

A related set of actions would involve scrambling the signs associated with the code. Baudrillard sees graffiti artists as playing this role within the city, but what form might it take in a setting like the fast-food restaurant? Graffiti on the walls of the local McDonald's would certainly represent an assault on its fetish for cleanliness and, more generally, on it as a system. A more specific example might involve a deliberate misreading of the signs that dominate the fast-food restaurant. People might come in and sit down and wait for service rather than following the code and waiting on line to order their own food. Or, people might do the latter but then leave their food on the counter, indicating an expectation that the food be delivered to them. Or they might respond to the high speed demanded of them by the system by being as tortoise-like as possible in the way they do things in the fast-food restaurant. Taking one's time while deciding what to order, or slowly wending one's way through and out of the drive-through, would be highly effective devices. These efforts to scramble the code (Deleuze and Guattari also seek this goal through schizoanalysis and the schizophrenic process) at the fast-food restaurant might serve to destabilize what, as we've seen, Baudrillard regards as an already fragile system.

---

[8]Most postmodern social theorists would reject the idea of an agent, let alone a search for one.

Ultimately, Baudrillard favors any sort of indeterminacy as a way of responding to the determinacy of the code with its reproduction and endless repetition. Death, not as a final event, but as a model of indeterminacy, is Baudrillard's paradigm for responding to the system. This, of course, does not mean that people should take to dying in droves at the counters of fast-food restaurants, but it does mean that any sort of indeterminacy would serve to disrupt the smooth operation of the system and the code. More specifically, Baudrillard recommends that we inject some risk, some small measure of death, into otherwise meticulously regulated systems like fast-food restaurants. This suggests a range of actions anywhere from taking the chance and ordering a Big Mac without special sauce to actually eschewing fast-food restaurants and taking the plunge and preparing a meal from scratch at home. We are in the realm of the "infinitesimal lines of escape" discussed by Deleuze and Guattari, but they are all that is available in an epoch when the great revolutions are deemed no longer possible or desirable.

Similarly, Deleuze and Guattari's ideas on freeing desire and the desiring machine would fit here. That is, the fast-food restaurant, and the revolution in the means of consumption of which it is part, would be seen as constraining such freedom in a Weberian iron cage. Weakening, destabilizing, and ultimately destroying this process and such settings would help free desire. Liberated desire would clearly wreak havoc on the code.

Most of the responses discussed thus far may be combined under the heading of the "strength of the weak" (Genosko, 1994). There is no better example of this than the hundreds of billions of dollars of uncollateralized credit extended to the masses by the credit-card companies. The masses accept every new card, and every increase in the credit limit, offered to them. In the process, the economic system grows more and more unstable. Before it falls, the masses will have taken and used much of the credit offered them.

While most of the responses discussed in this section are nonrational or irrational, there are more rational responses to be found in postmodern social theory. One example is Jameson's suggestion that what we need are new cognitive maps. Adrift in the hyperspace of postmodernity, we need new kinds of guides to help us find our way. On the one hand, this means that we need, and need to do, new kinds of social analyses and critiques of the world of the new means of consumption. On the other, we need maps that will help us find the increasingly scarce alternatives to those things.

A more rational task, mainly for scholars and intellectuals, would be to engage in Jameson's transcoding. That is, a scholar can examine what one can say, think, and do in the fast-food restaurant and compare and contrast that to the possibilities in other systems (say, the kitchen of a traditional French restaurant). Such a contrast might serve to point up the problems in the fast-food restaurant as well as some alternatives to it.

SUMMARY

Clearly, the ideas dealt with in this chapter are only suggestive of what a postmodern analysis of the new means of consumption would look like. In fact, the objective has been more to offer concrete applications of various postmodern ideas than it has been to do a postmodern analysis of these new means. Since postmodern social theory necessarily involves micro narratives, any given postmodernist would do a very different analysis of these phenomena. It is out of a set of such analyses that we would get a fuller sense of what postmodern social theory has to offer in this realm. This chapter only serves to give us the flavor of what such analyses would look like.

12

CRITICISMS OF, AND THE MOVE BEYOND, POSTMODERNISM

BASIC CRITICISMS

BEYOND POSTMODERN SOCIAL THEORY

*T*HIS book has been devoted to a reasonably dispassionate portrayal of postmodern social theory. However, the general reaction in sociology, as well as in many other fields, has been far from dispassionate. In fact, debates about postmodern social theory ordinarily generate an enormous amount of heat. Supporters are often gushing in their praise, while detractors are frequently driven into what can only be described as a blind rage. To give the reader a flavor for the tenor of the critiques of postmodern social theory, we begin with a few acid quotations from John O'Neill's (1995) aptly named, at least from his point of view, *The Poverty of Postmodernism*:

- There exists what can only be called "the insanity of postmodernism" (p. 16).
- Postmodernism offers "a great black sky of nonsense" (p. 191).
- "The postmodern celebrants of the irreal, of the screen and its simulacra ought to be understood as religious maniacs, or as iconoclasts breaking the gods, and not at all as sophisticates of modern science and art" (p. 197).
- We are confronted with "the new illiterati who espouse the postmodern condition" (p. 198).
- Postmodern social theory is "an already dead moment of the mind" (p. 199).

While such rhetoric is eye-catching, if not eye-popping, by the standards of academic discourse, it does little to advance the debate over postmodern social theory. The purpose of the first part of this chapter is to survey some of the more dispassionate critiques of postmodern social theory.

However, while we will review some of the major criticisms, it should be borne in mind that given the diversity and idiosyncratic nature of postmodern social theories, general criticisms of those theories are of questionable validity and utility. The critics often seem to focus on stereotypes of postmodern theory rather than on its details as articulated by specific postmodern theorists. In fact, the criticisms seem to apply more to the derivatives of the great sets of ideas covered in this book than to those ideas themselves (Kroker and Cook, 1991). To keep these problems to a minimum, we will try to connect general criticisms of postmodern social theory to the concrete ideas of specific postmodern social theorists. On occasion, we will see that while a given criticism might apply to one (or more) postmodern social theorist, it does not apply to others.

BASIC CRITICISMS

1. Most criticisms of postmodern social theory stem from its failure to live up to modern scientific standards, standards that postmodernists eschew.

It should come as no surprise that postmodern social theory has come under attack from modernists who critique it on a variety of grounds, most often its failure to measure up to (modern) scientific standards. To be fair, most postmodernists would find these criticisms irrelevant since they stem from the kind of modern perspective from which they are seeking to disassociate themselves. Despite the postmodernists' lack of sympathy for these critiques, it is important that we enumerate at least a few of them.

To the scientifically oriented modernist, it is impossible to know whether or not the contentions of postmodernists are true. To put it in more formal terms, virtually everything that the postmodernists have to say is viewed by modernists as not being falsifiable; that is, their ideas cannot be disproved, especially by empirical research (Frow, 1991; Kumar, 1995). Of course, this criticism assumes the existence of a scientific model, of reality, and of a search for and existence of truth. All of these assumptions would, naturally, be rejected by postmodernists.

Since the knowledge produced by postmodernists cannot be seen as constituting a body of scientific ideas, it might be better to look at postmodern social theory as ideology (Kumar, 1995). Once we do that, it is no longer a matter of whether or not the ideas are true but simply whether or not we believe in them. Those who believe in one set of ideas have no grounds to argue that their ideas are any better or worse than any other set of ideas.

It is argued that the ideological character of postmodernism leads most of its practitioners to be dogmatic and closed to competing perspectives. Postmodern thinkers clearly tend to dismiss scientific perspectives and scientific findings. Furthermore, there is a tendency to adhere to one postmodern viewpoint and to dismiss others. Baudrillard, for example, clearly believes in his perspective and, at the same time, has little sympathy for Foucault's perspective, which is, in his view, better forgotten.

Because they are unconstrained by the norms of science, postmodernists are free to do as they please, to "play" with a wide range of ideas, sometimes in a highly ludic manner. Broad generalizations are offered, often without qualification. Furthermore, in expressing their positions, postmodern social theorists are not restricted to the dispassionate rhetoric of the modern scientist. The excessive nature of much of postmodern discourse makes it difficult for most of those outside the perspective to accept its basic tenets.

Unlike modern science, postmodern social theory does not aspire to, and is not, a coherent body of ideas. In fact, it often constitutes little more than a pastiche of ideas drawn from many different domains. Because it is so eclectic, it fails to offer a coherent view of the social world.

In addition to rejecting the basic tenets of science, postmodern social theorists also tend to reject many of the approaches—macrotheory, systemic analysis, grand historical narratives—that have brought sociological and social theory what modernists consider to be its greatest intellectual advances.

It could be argued that postmodernists have not only given up on science but on knowledge, at least systematic knowledge, as well. This can be traced, at least in part, to the tendency, especially in Foucault's work, to conflate power and knowledge. Opposed to those who have used knowledge to advance their own power, it can be argued that at least some postmodernists have eschewed what we conventionally think of as knowledge altogether.

2. The antimodernism of the postmodern social theorists creates many other problems for them, including a tendency toward a lack of clear conceptualization.

Postmodern ideas are often so vague and abstract that it is difficult, if not impossible, to connect them to the social world (Calhoun, 1993). Relatedly, meanings of concepts tend to change over the course of a postmodernist's work, but the reader, unaware of the original meanings, is unclear about any changes.

For example, there are a number of conceptual problems in Foucault's work. While power is central to Foucault, he fails to define it carefully in his early work, and even when he does come to define it later, the definition has a nebulous and elusive quality. For another thing, he fails to carefully differentiate among the different types of power (Fraser, 1981). Similar kinds of things can be said about his definition and conceptualization of knowledge (Best, 1994). Such conceptual failings cast doubt on his entire effort to link power and knowledge. More generally, Foucault's antimodernist propensity to not define his terms carefully makes it difficult to understand, evaluate, and build upon his work.

Many critics express great frustration over Baudrillard's terminology. Many of his major terms (code, for example) are not defined and, as a result, his work is difficult, if not impossible, to comprehend fully. Similarly, the meanings of some of his terms (evil, for example) change over time, but the reader is unaware that Baudrillard is using the same term, but with a different meaning.

To take one other example, Derrida's tendency to use different terms, albeit with subtle differences among them, to describe much the same phenomenon makes it extremely difficult to get a clear sense of what he is saying. A good example is found in the overlapping meanings of terms like writing, arche-writing, trace, and *differance* in Derrida's work.

3. Despite their propensity to criticize the grand narratives and totalizations of modern theorists, postmodern social theorists often offer their own varieties of such narratives and totalizations.

As we saw in Chapters 3 and 4, Foucault is one of the postmodern social theorists who is critical of the tendency of modern theorists to offer totalizations and grand narratives. Despite such criticisms, the reader often has the feeling that Foucault is offering both (Dean, 1986). For example, the contentions that we have moved from a society that tortures to one that disciplines or that we have witnessed an explosion of discourse about sexuality sound strikingly like grand narratives. One certainly recognizes Foucault's argument that changes like these do not take place in a linear fashion, but even with that, the reader still emerges with the sense that Foucault is offering a series of grand narratives about such things as madness, medicine, prison, sexuality, and the rise of the human sciences. How can we take Foucault's critiques of modern grand narratives seriously when he often appears to be offering grand narratives of his own?

Another example is Jameson's acceptance of the kind of totalizing theory of the world offered by a Marxian perspective. Like other Marxists, Jameson accepts a totalizing view that accords overwhelming importance to the mode of production (albeit with counterforces). Jameson (1991:400), himself, accepts this viewpoint, "It has not escaped anyone's attention that my approach to postmodernism is a 'totalizing' one."

Jameson is also criticized for utilizing the kind of grand narrative, emancipatory subject, and telos of modern Marxist thinking. Take, for example, the following assertion by Jameson:

> The postmodern may well in that sense be little more than a transitional period between two stages of capitalism, in which the earlier forms of the economic are in the process of being restructured on a global scale. . . . *That a new international proletariat (taking forms we cannot yet imagine) will reemerge from this convulsive upheaval it needs no prophet to predict*: we ourselves are still in the trough, however, and no one can say how long we will stay there.
>
> (Jameson, 1991:417; italics added)

However, it should be pointed out that while Jameson may be guilty of employing totalizations (and grand narratives), he is overtly critical of most totalizations because to him they do not simply mean unification, but unification in search of power. He sees totalizations as reflecting the power relations hidden behind humanist and positivist systems. But, this argument can be turned against Jameson, and his totalizations can be seen as empowering some and disempowering others.

Jameson defends his use of (Marxian) totalities in the context of the postmodern discussion of difference. He dismisses most of the postmodern defense of difference as little more than liberal tolerance. In any case, he feels that difference and totalities are not inimical; differences can be dealt with within the context of totalities; "difference relates" (Jameson in Stephanson, 1989:46). In his terms, "a system that constitutively produces differences remains a system," and it is possible to deal with "the non-centered subject that is part of an organic group or collective" (Jameson, 1991:343, 345). Or, more generally, "the apparent celebration of Difference, whether here at home or on the global scale, in reality conceals and presupposes a new and more fundamental identity" (Jameson, 1991:357). We are unable to see this fundamental identity, this new totality, precisely because we exist in a world of multinational capital; since everything is systematic, we begin to lose our sense of the system.

In defense of Jameson and his totalizations, Best (1989) distinguishes between two types of totalities. The first is "a reductive analysis which forces all particulars within a single theoretical perspective at the expense of 'textual' difference and complexity," while the second is "a contextualizing act which situates seemingly isolated phenomena within their larger relational context and draws connections (or mediations) between the different aspects of a whole . . . which grasps systemic relationships while respecting difference, discontinuity, relative autonomy, and un-even development" (Best, 1989:344). Best rejects the first and accepts the latter, which is the totalizing perspective he associates with Jameson (although he recognizes that Jameson sometimes falls into the trap of excessive totalization).

While most often criticized for their totalizations, going to the other extreme, postmodernists are sometimes critiqued for being excessively narrow, offering only local narratives (Munz, 1992). O'Neill (1995:194) sees the postmodernists as offering "aggressive 'mini-logues' that, in my view, distract us from the corporate monologue which is, in fact, well served by the postmodern babel of tongues." While he may be implicitly offering grand narratives, Foucault can be seen as advancing a series of such "mini-logues" on madness, medicine, crime, sexuality, and so on. There are many who continue to believe in the importance of broad generalizations.

4. In their analyses, postmodern social theorists often offer critiques of modern society, but those critiques are of questionable validity since they generally lack a normative basis with which to make such judgments.

In his historical studies, Foucault excels at describing problems, especially the oppression of the mad, the sick, the criminal, indeed people in general. One comes away from Foucault's work with a strong sense of his anger over the oppressive-ness that he finds throughout the "carceral archipelago." However, the reader has no theoretical idea *why* Foucault is so upset at what he finds in the realms of mad-ness, crime, medicine, and sexuality. That is, in formal terms he fails to offer us a vision of the normative framework (Fraser, 1981) that he uses to make his judg-ments. One can guess at that normative framework (or Archimedian point), or even piece it together from his work, but neither is a substitute for an explicit articula-tion of that framework. Of course, Foucault is seeking to get away from the mod-ern practice of operating with such a framework (as, for example, Marx does with his concept of species being), but that effort cannot be deemed successful if all one succeeds in doing is making one's normative framework implicit rather than ex-plicit. If that is all Foucault accomplishes in this domain, then the modernist propensity to make the normative framework explicit is far more preferable.

Lacking a normative basis, postmodern social theory tends to encourage a "babel of tongues." Such a babble of co-equal voices serves the interests of those in power. All voices are encouraged and of similar validity, even the voices of those in positions of power. With so many conflicting viewpoints and no clear ad-versary, those in power are better able to stay right where they are.

5. Obsessed as they are with contemporary (postmodern) developments, one is often led to question the assertions of postmodern social theorists about the past.

One of the defining characteristics of Foucault's approach is his interest in writ-ing the history of the present. That is, in writing about the past, he is guided in his choice of topics and mode of analysis by present-day concerns. There is no ques-tion that this serves to make his historical analyses far more relevant and interest-ing to contemporary readers than were he interested in history for history's sake.

However, one often gets the feeling that his presentism (there is also a presentism in Derrida's thinking about writing) adversely affects his ability to analyze the past (Habermas, 1986). For example, one is led to wonder whether his obvious anger over the degree of surveillance that exists in contemporary society biases his analysis of the Panopticon and causes him to give it, and related phenomena, undue attention? A presentist bias can help to illuminate past realities, but it can also serve to distort the past and obscure as much as it illuminates.

Baudrillard spends most of his time analyzing and critiquing the contemporary world, but his ventures into the past include a tendency to romanticize primitive societies as havens of symbolic exchange. As criticized as they are, Baudrillard's observations about the present are far more fully developed and credible than are his ideas about the past.

6. Given their rejection of an interest in the subject and subjectivity, postmodernists often lack a theory of agency.

Not only does Foucault not offer us a normative framework, he also lacks a theory of agency (Best, 1994). The careful reader can piece together a sense of agency from Foucault's work, but that is not the same as explicitly offering a theory of agency as do such modernists as Marx and Giddens. Perhaps because he lacks a theory of agency, Foucault also fails to offer any ideas on how people can deal with the problems he describes and emancipate themselves from the oppressive society he spends so much time describing and analyzing. In contrast, of course, a modernist like Marx not only describes the evils of capitalism but also offers his thoughts on how it can be overthrown. Lacking such ideas, Foucault is often thought of as offering an "iron cage" perspective on the modern world, much like the one offered by Weber (who also found himself in that predicament because, at least in part, he too lacked a theory of agency).

This lack of a theory of agency is even more serious in the case of the work of Fredric Jameson. After all, Jameson adheres to a Marxian orientation, and such an orientation would seem to require such a theory. In fact, not only does he not have a theory of agency, Jameson never identifies a subject of revolutionary practice.[1]

7. Postmodern social theorists are best at critiquing society, but they lack any vision of what society ought to be.

Postmodernists generally lack any vision of the future. The mild version of this critique is that postmodern social theory is lacking in such a vision, but the more extreme argument is that because it lacks such a vision the theory is subversive of viable political programs and objectives (Gitlin, 1988).[2]

For example, as a result, at least in part, of his lack of a normative framework and a theory of agency, Foucault is often accused of being nihilistic and failing to offer either an affirmative ethic or a positive vision of a future society (Coles,

---

[1]Although Jameson (in Stephanson, 1989:63) hints at one, "a *collective subject.*"
[2]For a case for a more critical postmodern social theory, see Yeatman (1991).

1991). Of course, if Foucault did offer all of those things—normative framework, theory of agency, affirmative ethic, positive vision of the future—he would be considered a modern theorist; he would not be considered one of the key figures in the break with modernist theoretical practices. In a sense, Foucault is being critiqued for not being a modernist, a critique he would likely accept as praise.

As we saw, Baudrillard does, at least implicitly, have a vision of his alternative society (one characterized by symbolic exchange), and even though he generally offers quite dismal views, he does offer some glimmers of hope. However, many criticisms can be leveled at these hopeful possibilities in Baudrillard's work. For example, Baudrillard sometimes has the tendency to romanticize certain groups— examples include the youth or the graffiti artists. His thinking on these groups and their revolutionary potential is among the least convincing in his work. To take just one example, it simply strains credulity to believe that graffiti artists and their scrambling of signs really pose a threat to the control exercised by the code (a similar criticism can be made of Deleuze and Guattari and their faith in schizophrenia).

The real hope in Baudrillard's work, and some of his most creative theorizing, involves the strength of the weak and the fatal strategies of the masses. While in this case Baudrillard presents a very interesting and creative line of thinking about the future, it is not without its problems. To take just one of many examples, it is hard to believe that the system is going to crumble just because people begin to engage in symbolic exchange with it. More specifically, offering gifts to a system incapable of receiving such gifts seems, if anything, even more preposterous. These ideas follow from the logic of Baudrillard's thinking about symbolic exchange and its disappearance in the (post)modern world, but that does not mean that they make any kind of practical sense.

Unlike most postmodernists, Jameson has a clear Marxian vision of a way out of our present predicament. However, at least in part because of this, Jameson is dismissed by some postmodernists as really being a modernist with an emancipatory grand narrative.

8. Postmodern social theory leads to profound pessimism.

Despite hopeful signs here and there, in general postmodern social theory tends to be pessimistic about the future. The pessimism, along with the willingness to accept the babble of competing positions, leaves many postmodernists without any firm convictions. O'Neill (1995:18) argues that postmodernists have a "will to willessness."

Beyond that, there is the sense that all one can hope to do is to destroy. Recall, for example, Deleuze and Guattari's (1972/1983:311) injunction, "Destroy, destroy. The task of schizoanalysis goes by way of destruction." Such a view is unlikely to fill one with optimism.

9. Some postmodern social theorists have a disturbing tendency to reify at least some social phenomena.

Baudrillard tends to reify some social phenomena, most notably the code. The code tends to take on a life of its own in Baudrillard's work, causing people to do certain things and not others. For example, the code leads people to make a series of choices in the realm of consumption that serves to differentiate them from others. Clearly, there is no reified code, but Baudrillard fails to offer us a view of the way in which the code is intertwined with our everyday thoughts and actions.

A similar criticism can be made of Foucault who fails to clearly define power or, when he does, tends to reify it.

10. There are major discontinuities in the work of postmodern social theorists, and this leads to many unresolved issues and ambiguities.

There are discontinuities in Foucault's work, especially between his earlier, more institutional work and the later studies of the self (Best, 1994). The result is that these two sets of work tend to stand side-by-side with little to integrate them. A central, but unresolved, issue is the relationship between the more macro-level institutions that concerned Foucault in his early work and the later, more microscopic, work on the self. For example, a reader would want to know about the relationship between the Panopticon and the self-image of the prisoner and, more generally, about the relationship between the carceral archipelago and the self-images of people in general. Such critically important linkage questions remain unanswered in Foucault's work, perhaps because he came to the issue of the self late in his life and did not live long enough to integrate it with his more institutional concerns.

Similarly, there is discontinuity between Baudrillard's early, more modern work and his later work in which he is far more postmodern. Substantively, for example, it is difficult to relate his early material interest in the means of consumption with his later nonmaterial interest in things like signs and the code.

11. While postmodern social theorists grapple with what they consider to be major social issues, they often end up ignoring what many consider the key problems of our time.

Postmodern social theory is often accused of being silent on many crucial social, political, and economic issues (Best and Kellner, 1991). Despite his presentist concerns with oppression, Foucault fails to deal with such centrally important contemporary forms of subjugation as class and gender oppression (Porter and Poster, 1991). Thus, Foucault is all but silent on the pressing problems of our time. Furthermore, he is even far from explicit about the oppression confronted by gays and lesbians. While his later work indicates a concern for the growing separation and oppression of the "love of boys," Foucault clearly does not go nearly far enough in his analysis of this contemporary form of oppression.

Perhaps the ultimate critique of Baudrillard stems from the fact that he tends to reduce life to images, simulations, and the like. In so doing, he fails to deal with the more material aspects of life. Bauman is one who makes this argument:

To many people, much of their life is anything but simulation. To many, reality remains what it always used to be: tough, solid, resistant and harsh. They need to sink their teeth into some quite real bread before they abandon themselves to munching images [in front of the TV].

(Bauman, 1992:155)

In fact, this critique goes beyond Baudrillard to a more general indictment of postmodern social theory for its failure to focus on the material issues that really make a difference in people's lives (Wenger, 1993–1994).

Jameson is one postmodern social theorist who is not vulnerable to this latter kind of critique given his Marxian orientation to economic phenomena. In fact, however, although it is central to his analysis, Jameson has little to say about the economy. He plays down the role of social classes and social movements. Nor does he offer much on the linkages between economy and culture. However, Jameson does devote a great deal of attention to cultural analysis and in that sense is open to the criticism that even he is not dealing with the material issues of greatest importance to most people.

Of course, feminists and multiculturalists who operate from a postmodern perspective have served to rectify this problem, at least to some degree. Clearly, they are far more focused on the problems of the day, albeit ordinarily only from a particular "standpoint."

12. When postmodern social theorists seek to integrate the postmodern perspective with those of other, more traditional perspectives, they often fail to satisfy supporters of any theoretical persuasion.

The great strength of Jameson's work is his effort to synthesize Marxian theory and postmodernism. In fact, Zuidervaart (1989:203) contends: "Were it not for the dance of Fredric Jameson, Marxism and postmodernism might well seem incompatible." While he is to be praised for this integrative effort, the fact is that his work often displeases *both* Marxists and postmodernists:

Generally, poststructuralists and others claim that Jameson is guilty of excessively totalizing, subjectivizing, historicizing, and of utilizing humanist and reductive modes of thought . . . while Marxist and other critics claim that Jameson goes too far in the direction of dissolving and fragmenting subjectivity and in accepting postmodernism . . . or they criticize him for pessimistically reifying society into a massive systemic totality, invulnerable to political struggle.

(Kellner, 1989b:39).

Most generally, to postmodern critics he seeks to retain a centered perspective in a decentered postmodern world. Operating from a Marxist point of view, Best and Kellner (1991:192; see also Jay and Flax, 1993) contend, "His work is an example of the potential hazards of an eclectic, multiperspectival theory which attempts to incorporate a myriad of positions, some of them in tension or contradiction with each other, as when he produces the uneasy alliance between classical

Marxism and extreme postmodernism." More specifically, for example, some Marxists object to the degree to which he has accepted postmodernism as a cultural dominant.

Jameson is not taken with the postmodernists' critiques of his position and replies that the cultural criticism of texts must be supplemented with economic and market analyses. In fact, ever the Marxist, Jameson (1991:208) argues that economics is "the ultimate consequences, the ultimate stake, in this kind of literary or cultural analysis."

However, Jameson is not arguing for a return to "modern" dialectical thinking. Rather, we live in a postdialectical age in which the goal is not new syntheses but the simultaneous presentation of incompatibilities. Postdialectical thinking is spatial, like jumping around spaces on a game board. In that, it is like TV channel switching, which many postmodernists see as the paradigm of attention in a postmodern world. It is in the spatial imagery of moves around a game board that Jameson embeds postmodern thinking. Indeed, he argues that "such interfection is then the very prototype of what we call the postmodern mode of totalizing" (Jameson, 1991:373). It is in such a mode of thinking (which is at least somewhat like schizophrenia) that Jameson seeks to rescue the Marxian dialectical approach to totalities without falling victim to its historic inadequacies.

13. While in some cases the form of their work is undifferentiable from that of modernists, in other cases the form of their work creates problems for postmodern social theorists.

The form of Baudrillard's work, especially much of his later work, is a source of great frustration to the critics. While many of his early books are conventional academic works that follow a more or less standard format, many of his later works take on a more "postmodern" form. For example, instead of reasoned argumentation and a systematically developed thesis, the reader is often offered a seemingly random set of aphorisms with little or nothing to connect one to the others. Of course, this criticism, like most others of Baudrillard and other postmodernists, belies a modernist bias and orientation. Modern readers want an "author" like Baudrillard to do the work for them. However, the postmodernists put the burden on the reader, not the author. Reading Baudrillard's collections of aphorisms certainly succeeds in the latter, and in that sense they are paradigmatic postmodern texts.

A related problem, especially in the later texts, is that Baudrillard is fond of hyperbole (other examples include Deleuze and Guattari's valorization of the schizophrenic process) with the result that his work often lacks sustained systematic analysis. A good example is *America*, which is loaded, as we saw in Chapter 6, with highly quotable and highly exaggerated statements about America and its place and role in the postmodern world. However, the reader in search of a sustained, systematic critique of American society is not going to find it in the pages of *America*.

America also serves to exemplify a related set of criticisms of the form of Baudrillard's work. For one thing, he offers a series of generalizations and totalizations about America (and much else), usually without qualifications (Virilio does a similar thing in his analyses of speed). For another, he focuses on particular issues and places (for example, the desert, Los Angeles) and, in the process, ignores many other important topics. Then, he tends to ignore contradictory evidence. For example, he critiques the media without discussing its many benefits. Finally, he is not afraid to offer dismal views of America and its future based on very limited data. Furthermore, he uses his limited exposure to generalize about the fate of the world since he sees America and its destiny as the paradigm for the rest of the world.

14. While one can find adherents among them, the feminists have been particularly strong critics of postmodern social theory.

We have reviewed some of the feminist criticisms in Chapter 9. Just to remind the reader, feminists have tended to be critical of the postmodern rejection of the subject, of its opposition to universal, cross-cultural categories (like gender and gender oppression), of its excessive concern with difference, of its rejection of truth, and of its inability to develop a critical political agenda.

We could obviously enumerate many other criticisms of postmodernism in general, to say nothing of many more specific criticisms of each postmodern theorist. However, the above gives the reader a good sense of the range of those criticisms. While there is much validity to each of them, the reader is urged to think more in terms of specific theorists and their ideas than in gross generalities. Further, whatever the merits of these critiques, the central issue is whether or not postmodernism has produced a set of interesting, insightful, and important theoretical ideas that are apt to affect social theory long into the future. It should be clear from the body of this book that, at least in my opinion, such ideas exist in profusion within postmodern social theory.

BEYOND POSTMODERN SOCIAL THEORY

While postmodern social theory is only beginning to have a powerful impact on American sociology, in many areas it is long past its prime and in decline. Interestingly, it is in French social theory, the source of the best in poststructuralism and postmodernism, that we find the most determined efforts to move beyond postmodern theory. Let us look at some of the most important examples of what might be termed, albeit more than a little awkwardly, "post-postmodernism."

That French thinkers have moved beyond the body of work discussed in this book must come as a shock to readers for whom most of the substance of this work is largely, if not entirely, new. Furthermore, many of the thinkers who received great attention in these pages are still alive and producing important new scholarly works (Bauman, Baudrillard, Derrida, and Virilio, for example). And, the works of many of these scholars are increasingly the subject of scholarly attention. This is even, and perhaps particularly, true in the case of the major thinker covered in this book who is no longer alive, Michel Foucault. Finally, it is clear, as pointed out above, that the works of these thinkers, individually and collectively, are going to affect social theory profoundly for the foreseeable future.

Yet, it is also the case that most of the thinkers and many of the works discussed in this book can be traced back to the 1960s. This is certainly true, for example, for many of Foucault's important works, and even Baudrillard, still active today, began publishing in the 1960s. Thus, we can see how, to contemporary French intellectuals, work that is new to many of us appears to be somewhat antiquated.

A good example of the latter point is Luc Ferry and Alain Renaut's (1985/1990) *French Philosophy of the Sixties*. As the title suggests, the authors are looking back on the literature of the 1960s, especially its antihumanist, death-of-the-author, and death-of-the-subject orientations. They focus on four paradigmatic poststructural thinkers of the period, three of whom were of great importance in this book (Foucault, Derrida, and Lacan), and a fourth (Pierre Bourdieu) who was omitted because he is better thought of as a modernist (although we will have a bit more to say about him below). They summarize this body of literature by offering a Weberian ideal type composed of four elements, elements that are central to the poststructural/postmodern orientation presented in this book:

1—The end of traditional philosophy. Philosophy was defined by the sixties' thinkers as problematic and well suited to deconstruction.

2—The paradigm of genealogy. History, too, was seen as problematic and subject to multiple interpretations. Instead of grand abstractions, history involved the study of discourses in "their concrete historical conditions" (Ferry and Renaut, 1985/1990:11).

3—The disintegration of the idea of truth. Instead of truth, there was simply deconstruction leading to yet further deconstructions.

4—All categories were to be historicized, and there was to be an end to all references to anything universal.

In addition, stylistically the sixties' theorists tended to demand complexity, if not to reject clarity altogether, and to position themselves on the margins from which they saw mainly conspiracy wherever they looked.

All of this led sixties' theorists in the direction of what some contemporary French theorists now see as "the very costly (perhaps ruinous) antihumanist route" (Ferry and Renaut, 1985/1990:30; Todorov, 1994). Thus, what Ferry and Renaut (and Todorov, among others) are seeking to do is to rescue humanism (and subjectivity) from the postmodern critique that had presumably left such an idea for dead. They are not clear on precisely the form such a humanism might take, but they are certain that it can and must be rescued. Lilla (1994b:20) is more specific arguing that what is being sought is "a new defense of universal, rational norms in morals and politics, and especially a defense of human rights."

Another strand of "post-postmodernism" involves an effort to reinstate the importance of liberalism in the face of the postmodern assault on the liberal grand narrative (Lilla, 1994b). The works of the poststructuralists / postmodernists (e.g., Foucault's *Discipline and Punish*), even when they were couched in highly abstract theoretical terms, were read by the French as attacks on structures in general, especially the structure of liberal bourgeois society. Not only did postmodernism question such a society, it also led to the view that there was no way of escaping the reach of that society's power structure. However, all of this changed in the

1980s following, among other things, the election of the socialist, François Mitterand, as president of France:

> During the eighties, discussions of political philosophy centered on the books that would have been unwritten, unpublished, or unread ten years earlier: studies of important political thinkers of the past [e.g., Tocqueville, Locke, Montesquieu; see Manent, 1987/1994], theoretical treatises on human rights, essays on liberal government and society, even translations of Anglo-American political and moral philosophy of the "analytic" variety.

(Lilla, 1994b:15)

Issues thought dead during the heyday of postmodernism—"human rights, constitutional government, representation, class, individualism" (Lilla, 1994b:16)—have attracted renewed attention. The nihilism of postmodernism has been replaced by a variety of sympathetic orientations to liberal society. One could say that this revival of interest in liberalism (as well as humanism) indicates a restoration of interest in, and sympathy for, modern society.

We can close this section with a discussion of a major example of post-postmodernism, Gilles Lipovetsky's (1987/1994) *The Empire of Fashion: Dressing Modern Democracy*. Lipovetsky takes on, quite explicitly, the poststructuralists and postmodernists. Most direct is his attack on the poststructuralist, Pierre Bourdieu, and his effort to explain fashions in consumption on the basis of class conflict and competition. More generally, Lipovetsky challenges the poststructural/postmodern tendency to be hypercritical of contemporary society. Those perspectives would be especially critical of something so seemingly trifling, superficial, and fleeting as Lipovetsky's focal concern—fashion.

In contrast to Bourdieu's emphasis on the role played by class, class distinctions, and class pretensions in consumption and, less directly, in fashion, Lipovetsky (1987/1994:5) argues that "in the history of fashion, modern cultural meanings and values, in particular those that elevate newness and the expression of human individuality to positions of dignity, have played a preponderant role." The source of the contemporary interest in fashion (and consumption), and more generally individuality, is traced to cultural factors rather than to economic, class-related factors. Thus, Lipovetsky (1987/1994:48) unabashedly accords primary importance to what are, in Marxian terms, "superstructures."

However, while he challenges the Marxian orientation, the bigger intellectual adversaries as far as Lipovetsky is concerned are the poststructuralists/postmodernists. Here is the way he articulates the position taken by them and to which he is opposed, at least to some degree:

> In our societies, fashion is in the driver's seat. In less than half a century, attractiveness and evanescence have become the organizing principles of modern collective life. We live in societies where the trivial predominates. . . . Should we be dismayed by this? Does it announce the slow but inexorable decline of the West? Must we take it as a sign of the decadence of the democratic ideal? Nothing is more commonplace or widespread than the tendency to stigmatize—not without cause, moreover—the consumerist bent of democracies; they are represented as devoid of any great mobilizing collective projects,

lulled into a stupor by the private orgies of consumerism, infantilized by "instant" culture, by advertising, by politics-as-theater.

(Lipovetsky, 1987/1994:6)

In contrast, while he recognizes the problems associated with it, Lipovetsky (1987/1994:6) argues that fashion is "the primary agent of the spiraling movement toward individualism and the consolidation of liberal societies." Thus, Lipovetsky does not share the gloomy view of the postmodernists; he sees not only the negative but also the positive side of fashion and has a generally optimistic view of the future of society.

To take a more specific example, Lipovetsky looks at haute couture as a modern bureaucratic system, but he fails to see in it one of Michel Foucault's disciplinary systems:

instead of the production of useful bodies, with haute couture there is a glorification of luxury and frivolous refinement; instead of stylistic uniformity there is a plurality of models; instead of prescriptive programming and the minutiae of rules, there is an appeal to personal initiative; instead of regular, constant, impersonal coercion, there is the seduction of the metamorphoses of appearance; instead of a micro-power exercised over every little detail, there is a power that relinquishes control over accessory elements to individuals and concentrates on the essentials. Quite clearly, even though it was bureaucratic, haute couture as an organization put into play not the technologies of disciplinary constraint but previously unknown processes of *seduction* that inaugurated a new logic of power.

(Lipovetsky, 1987/1994:77–78)

Lipovetsky sees seduction[3] as a new supple, open, and flexible form of power that stands in stark contrast to the terrorism of Foucault's disciplinary power.

While Marxist and postmodernist critics attacked the superficiality of things like fashion, Lipovetsky argues that there is a "ruse" to fashion's irrationality:

we need to understand that seduction now serves to limit irrationality; that the artificial facilitates access to the real; that superficiality permits increased use of reason; that playful displays are springboards to subjective judgment. Fashion does not bring about the definitive alienation of the masses; it is an ambiguous but effective vector of human autonomy . . . fashion has allowed public questioning to expand; it has allowed subjective thoughts and existences to take on greater autonomy. *Fashion is the supreme agent of the individualist dynamic in its various manifestations.*

(Lipovetsky, 1987/1994:9–10; italics added)

In fact, Lipovetsky (1987/1994:10) sees "fashion as the ultimate phase of democracy."

While Lipovetsky has much that is positive to say about fashion, consumerism, individualism, democracy and modern society, he also recognizes the problems associated with each. He concludes that we live in "neither the best of worlds nor the worst. . . . Fashion is neither angel nor devil. . . . Such is the greatness of fashion,

---

[3]This is a very different sense of seduction than that of Baudrillard.

which always refers us, as individuals, back to ourselves; such is the misery of fashion, which renders us increasingly problematic to ourselves and others" (Lipovetsky, 1987/1994:240–241). Intellectuals are warned not to dismiss fashion (and the rest) just because it offends their intellectual sympathies. It is for being dismissive of such important phenomena as fashion (and liberalism, democracy, and so on) that Lipovetsky attacks the poststructuralists/postmodernists and others (e.g., critical theorists). In any case, the assault on fashion (and other aspects of modern society) has led us to lose sight of the fact that "the age of fashion remains the major factor in the process that has drawn men and women collectively away from obscurantism and fanaticism, has instituted an open public space and shaped a more lawful, more mature, more skeptical humanity" (Lipovetsky, 1987/1994:12).

While his paradigm is clothing, Lipovetsky argues that fashion is a form of social change that is a distinctive product of the Occident. In contrast to the postmodernists who were resistant to the idea of origins, Lipovetsky traces the origins of fashion to the upper classes in the West in the late Middle Ages. Fashion is a form of change characterized by a brief time span, largely fanciful shifts, and the ability to affect a wide variety of sectors of the social world. A number of factors came together in the West to give birth to the fashion form, especially its consecration of both individuality and novelty.

Fashion has been a force in the rise of individuality by allowing people to express themselves and their individuality in their clothing even while they might also be attending to collective changes in fashion. Similarly, it has been a factor in greater equality by allowing those lower in the stratification system to at least dress like those who ranked above them. Fashion also permitted frivolous self-expression. Most generally, it is linked to increasing individualism and the democratization of society as a whole.

While Lipovetsky offers us a genealogy of the recent history of fashion, he is particularly interested in its most recent phase, which he labels "consummate fashion" and is characterized by the extension of the fashion form to more and more sectors of society:

> Fashion is not so much a particular peripheral sector, now, as a general form at work in society as a whole. Everyone is more or less immersed in fashion, more or less everywhere, and the triple operation that specifically defines fashion is increasingly implemented: the operation of *ephemerality, seduction,* and *marginal differentiation.*

> (Lipovetsky, 1987/1994:131)

Lipovetsky proceeds to examine the role of fashion in the production and consumption of goods of various types, advertising, culture in general (movies, television), and even intellectual ideas (like poststructuralism and postmodernism).

While he has criticisms of the role of fashion in all of these realms, what stands out in Lipovetsky's analysis is his counter-intuitive case *for* something as seemingly trivial and destructive as consummate fashion:

> The era of consummate fashion is one that allows very large numbers of people to think for themselves; this is because the timeless order of tradition has exploded and terrorist

systems of meaning have lost their hold on humanity. People are subject to a great variety of influences, but no single one of them is strictly determining any longer; no single one does away with the capacity to reconsider. The critical spirit is expanding in and through the mimicry of fashion, in and through the fluctuations of 'opinion': such is the greatest paradox of the dynamics of enlightenment. Autonomy is inseparable from the mechanisms of heteronomy.

(Lipovetsky, 1987/1994:224)

While Lipovetsky makes such an argument over and over, he also warns us of the dangers of fashion and of becoming too self-satisfied with the current world dominated as it is by fashion.

The discussion in this section should not be taken to mean that post- or anti-postmodernism exhausts contemporary French theory, but it is clearly one of the dominant themes in that theory. Postmodernism is not dead in contemporary France. Jean Baudrillard and Paul Virilio, among others, continue to write, and there are others whose work we have not had time to discuss.

More important for our purposes, postmodern social theory is not only alive and well but on the ascendancy in the United States. However, we need to look beyond intellectual fashion in the United States (or France) and realize that whether or not postmodern/poststructural ideas are in or out of fashion in any given place at any given moment, they will be of continuing significance to social theory in general for some time to come. We will eventually move beyond postmodern theory, but social theory in general will never be quite the same again.

SUMMARY

This concluding chapter has been devoted to two final tasks. First, we reviewed many of the major criticisms of postmodern social theory. Where possible, we sought to link those criticisms to the ideas of specific postmodern social theorists. Second, we outlined the effort in France to move beyond postmodernism, to post-postmodernism. While both the criticisms and the latter movement are strong, postmodern social theory remains a powerful force whose impact is yet to be felt fully within the discipline of sociology.

REFERENCES

Alexander, Jeffrey C.
1995   *Fin de Siècle Social Theory: Relativism, Reduction, and the Problem of Reason.* London: Verso.

Antonio, Robert J.
1991   "Postmodern Storytelling versus Pragmatic Truth-Seeking: The Discursive Bases of Social Theory." *Sociological Theory* 9:154–163.

1995   "Nietzsche's Antisociology: Subjectified Culture and the End of History." *American Journal of Sociology* 101:1–43.

Artaud, Antonin
1976   *Antonin Artaud: Selected Writings.* S. Sontag (ed.). New York: Farrar, Straus and Giroux.

Asante, Molefi Kete
1987   *The Afrocentric Idea.* Philadelphia: Temple University Press.
1996   "The Afrocentric Metatheory and Disciplinary Implications." In M. Rogers (ed.), *Multicultural Experiences, Multicultural Theories.* New York: McGraw-Hill: 61–73.

Banks, Alan, Billings, Dwight, and Tice, Karen
1996   "Appalachian Studies and Postmodernism." In M. Rogers (ed.), *Multicultural Experiences, Multicultural Theories.* New York: McGraw-Hill: 81–90.

Barthes, Roland
1964/1967   *Elements of Semiology.* New York: Hill and Wang.
1970/1982   *Empire of Signs.* New York: Hill and Wang.

Baudrillard, Jean
1968/1988   "The System of Objects." In M. Poster (ed.), *Jean Baudrillard: Selected Writings.* Stanford: Stanford University Press: 10–28.

1970/1988   "Consumer Society." In M. Poster (ed.), *Jean Baudrillard: Selected Writings.* Stanford: Stanford University Press: 29–56.

1972/1981   *For a Critique of the Political Economy of the Sign.* United States: Telos Press.

1973/1975   *The Mirror of Production.* St. Louis: Telos Press.
1976/1993   *Symbolic Exchange and Death.* London: Sage.
1977   *Oublier Foucault.* Paris: Galilee.

1979/1990	*Seduction.* New York: St. Martin's Press.
1980–1985/1990	*Cool Memories.* London: Verso.
1983	*Simulations.* New York: Semiotext(e).
1983/1990	*Fatal Strategies.* New York: Semiotext(e).
1986/1989	*America.* London: Verso.
1990/1993	*The Transparency of Evil: Essays on Extreme Phenomena.* London: Verso.
1992/1994	*The Illusion of the End.* Palo Alto: Stanford University Press.

Bauman, Zygmunt

1987   *Legislators and Interpreters: On Modernity, Post-Modernity and Intellectuals.* Cambridge: Polity Press.

1989   *Modernity and the Holocaust.* Ithaca: Cornell University Press.

1991   *Modernity and Ambivalence.* Ithaca: Cornell University Press.

1992   *Intimations of Postmodernity.* London: Routledge.

1993   *Postmodern Ethics.* Oxford: Basil Blackwell.

1995   *Life in Fragments: Essays in Postmodern Morality.* Oxford: Blackwell.

Beck, Ulrich

1992   *Risk Society: Towards a New Modernity.* London: Sage.

Bell, Daniel

1973   *The Coming of Post-Industrial Society.* New York: Basic Books.

1976   *The Cultural Contradictions of Capitalism.* New York: Basic Books.

Benhabib, Seyla

1995   "Feminism and Postmodernism: An Uneasy Alliance." In S. Benhabib, J. Butler, D. Cornell, and N. Fraser (eds.), *Feminist Contentions: A Philosophical Exchange.* New York: Routledge: 17–34.

Berger, Peter

1963   *Invitation to Sociology.* New York: Doubleday.

Bertens, Hans

1995   *The Idea of the Postmodern: A History.* London: Routledge.

Best, Steven

1989   "Jameson, Totality, and the Poststructuralist Critique." in D. Kellner (ed.), *Postmodernism, Jameson, Critique.* Washington, D.C.: Maisonneuve Press: 333–368.

1994   "Foucault, Postmodernism, and Social Theory." In D. R. Dickens and A. Fontana (eds.), *Postmodernism and Social Inquiry.* New York: Guilford Press: 25–52.

Best, Steven, and Kellner, Douglas

1991   *Postmodern Theory: Critical Interrogations.* New York: The Guilford Press.

Bevis, Phil, Cohen, Michele, and Kendall, Gavin
1993   "Archaeologizing Genealogy." In M. Gane and T. Johnson (eds.), *Foucault's New Domains*. London: Routledge: 193–215.

Bogard, William
1991   "Discipline and Deterrence: Rethinking Foucault on the Question of Power in Contemporary Society." *Social Science Journal* 28:325–346.

Bordo, Susan
1990   "Feminism, Postmodernism, and Gender-Scepticism." In L. Nicholson (ed.), *Feminism/Postmodernism*. London: Routledge: 133–156.

Bourdieu, Pierre
1977   *Outline of a Theory of Practice*. London: Cambridge University Press.
1984   *Distinction: A Social Critique of the Judgment of Taste*. Cambridge, MA: Harvard University Press.

Bowie, Malcolm
1991   *Lacan*. Cambridge: Harvard University Press.

Brown, B., and Cousins, M.
1980   "The Linguistic Fault: The Case of Foucault's Archaeology." *Economy and Society* 9:251–278.

Brown, Richard
1987   *Society as Text: Essays on Rhetoric, Reason, and Reality*. Chicago: University of Chicago Press.
1990   "Rhetoric, Textuality, and the Postmodern Turn in Sociological Theory." *Sociological Theory* 8:188–197.

Buffalohead, W. Roger
1996   "Reflections on Native American Cultural Rights and Resources." In M. Rogers (ed.), *Multicultural Experiences, Multicultural Theories*. New York: McGraw-Hill: 154–156.

Burris, Val
1979   "Introduction." In "The Structuralist Influence in Marxist Theory and Research." *Insurgent Sociologist* 9:4–17.

Butler, Judith
1990   *Gender Trouble: Feminism and the Subversion of Identity*. New York: Routledge.
1995   "Contingent Foundations." In S. Benhabib, J. Butler, D. Cornell, and N. Fraser (eds.), *Feminist Contentions: A Philosophical Exchange*. New York: Routledge: 35–57.

Calhoun, Craig
1993   "Postmodernism as Pseudohistory." *Theory, Culture and Society* 10:75–96.

Callari, Antonio, Cullenberg, Stephen, and Biewener, Carole (eds.)
1995   *Marxism in the Postmodern Age: Confronting the New World Order.* New York: Guilford Press.

Christie, John
1993   "The Human Sciences: Origins and Histories." *History of the Human Sciences* 6:1–12.

Chua, Beng-Huat
1981   "Genealogy as Sociology: An Introduction to Michel Foucault." *Catalyst* 14:1–22.

Cixous, Helen
1981   "The Laugh of the Medusa." In E. Marks and I. de Courtivron (eds.), *New French Feminisms.* New York: Schocken Books: 245–264.

Clarke, Simon
1990   "The Crisis of Fordism or the Crisis of Social Democracy." *Telos* 83:71–98.

Clough, Patricia Ticineto
1992   *The End(s) of Ethnography: From Realism to Social Criticism.* Newbury Park, CA: Sage.
1994   *Feminist Thought: Desire, Power and Academic Discourse.* Oxford: Blackwell.

Coleman, James
1990   *Foundations of Social Theory.* Cambridge: Belknap Press of Harvard University Press.

Coles, Romand
1991   "Foucault's Dialogical Artistic Ethos." *Theory, Culture and Society* 8:99–120.

Collins, Patricia Hill
1990   *Black Feminist Thought: Knowledge, Consciousness and Empowerment.* Boston: Unwin Hyman.

Connell, R. W.
1996   "Men and the Women's Movement." In M. Rogers (ed.), *Multicultural Experiences, Multicultural Theories.* New York: McGraw-Hill: 409–415.

Cooper, Davina
1994   "Productive, Relational and Everywhere? Conceptualising Power and Resistance within Foucauldian Feminism." *Sociology* 28:435–454.

Craib, Ian
1992   *Anthony Giddens.* London: Routledge.

Crook, Stephen, Pakulski, Jan, and Waters, Malcolm
1992   *Postmodernization: Change in Advanced Society.* London: Sage.

Crossley, Nick
1993   "The Politics of the Gaze: Between Foucault and Merleau-Ponty." *Human Studies* 16:399–419.

Culler, Jonathan
1976   *Ferdinand de Saussure.* Harmondsworth, England: Penguin.
Dahrendorf, Ralf
1979   "Towards the Hegemony of Post-Modern Values." *New Society* Nov. 15:360–362.

Dean, Mitchell
1986   "Foucault's Obsession with Western Modernity." *Thesis Eleven* 14:44–61.

Debord, Guy
1977   *Society of the Spectacle.* Detroit: Black and Red.
Deleuze, Gilles, and Guattari, Felix
1972/1983   *Anti-Oedipus: Capitalism and Schizophrenia.* Minneapolis: University of Minnesota Press.

D'Emilio, John
1983   *Sexual Politics, Sexual Communities: The Making of a Homosexual Minority in the United States, 1940–1970.* Chicago: University of Chicago Press.

Denzin, Norman
1989   "Re-Reading The Sociological Imagination." *American Sociologist* Fall: 278–282.
1993   "The Voyeur's Desire." *Current Perspectives in Social Theory* 13:139–158.
1994   "Postmodernism and Deconstructionism." In D. R. Dickens and A. Fontana (eds.), *Postmodernism and Social Inquiry.* New York: Guilford Press: 182–202.

Derrida, Jacques
1967/1974   *Of Grammatology.* Baltimore: The Johns Hopkins University Press.
1978   *Writing and Difference.* Chicago: University of Chicago Press.
Derrida, Jacques, Brault, Pascale Anne, and Naas, Michael
1994   "'To Do Justice to Freud': The History of Madness in the Age of Psychoanalysis." *Critical Inquiry* 20:227–266.
Diamond, Irene, and Quimby, Lee (eds.)
1988   *Foucault and Feminism: Reflections on Resistance.* Boston: Northeastern University Press.
Di Stefano, Christine
1990   "Dilemmas of Difference: Feminism, Modernity, and Postmodernity." In L. Nicholson (ed.), *Feminism/Postmodernism.* London: Routledge: 63–82.

Docker, John
1994   *Postmodernism and Popular Culture: A Cultural History.* Cambridge: Cambridge University Press.
Donnelly, Michael
1982   "Foucault's Genealogy of the Human Sciences." *Economy and Society* 11:363–380.

Donougho, Martin
1989   "Postmodern Jameson." In D. Kellner (ed.), *Postmodernism, Jameson, Critique.* Washington, D.C.: Maisonneuve Press: 75–95.

Doran, Chris
1994   "Codifying Women's Bodies? Towards a Genealogy of British Victimology." *Women and Criminal Justice* 5:45–70.

Dunn, Robert
1991   "Postmodernism: Populism, Mass Culture, and Avant-Garde." *Theory, Culture and Society* 8:111–135.

Dutton, Michael
1992   "Disciplinary Projects and Carceral Spread: Foucauldian Theory and Chinese Practice." *Economy and Society* 21:276–294.

Eco, Umberto
1976   *A Theory of Semiotics.* Bloomington, IN: Indiana University Press.

Elazar, Daniel J.
1980   "Meaning of the Seventies." *Society* 17:7–11.

Ellis, John M.
1994   "Fredric Jameson's Marxist Criticism." *Academic Questions* 7:30–43.

Farganis, Sondra
1994   "Postmodernism and Feminism." In D. R. Dickens and A. Fontana (eds.), *Postmodernism and Social Inquiry.* New York: Guilford Press: 101–126.

Featherstone, Mike
1989   "Postmodernism, Cultural Change, and Social Practice." In D. Kellner (ed.), *Postmodernism, Jameson, Critique.* Washington, D.C.: Maisonneuve Press: 117–138.

1990   "Global Culture: An Introduction." In Featherstone (ed.), *Global Culture: Nationalism, Globalization and Modernity.* London: Sage: 1–14.

1991   *Consumer Culture and Postmodernism.* London: Sage.

Ferguson, Marjorie
1991   "Marshall McLuhan Revisited: 1960s Zeitgeist Victim or Pioneer Postmodernist?" *Media Culture and Society* 13:71–90.

Ferry, Luc, and Alain Renaut
1985/1990   *French Philosophy of the Sixties: An Essay on Antihumanism.* Amherst: University of Massachusetts Press.

Fiedler, Leslie
1969/1975   "Cross the Border–Close that Gap: Postmodernism." In Marcus Cunliffe (ed.), *American Literature Since 1900.* London: Sphere Books: 344–366.

Fjellman, Stephen M.
1992   *Vinyl Leaves: Walt Disney World and America.* Boulder: Westview Press.

Flax, Jane
1990   "Postmodernism and Gender Relations in Feminist Theory." In L. Nicholson (ed.), *Feminism/Postmodernism.* London: Routledge: 39–62.

Flynn, Bernard
1978   "Michel Foucault and Comparative Civilizational Study." *Philosophy and Social Criticism* 5:145–158.

1981   "Sexuality, Knowledge and Power in the Thought of Michel Foucault." *Philosophy and Social Criticism* 8:331–348.

Foucault, Michel
1961/1967   *Madness and Civilization.* London: Tavistock.
1963/1975   *The Birth of the Clinic.* New York: Vintage.
1966/1973   *The Order of Things: An Archaeology of the Human Sciences.* New York: Vintage.

1969, 1971/1976   *The Archaeology of Knowledge and The Discourse of Language.* New York: Harper Colophon.

1975/1979   *Discipline and Punish: The Birth of the Prison.* New York: Vintage.

1978   "Politics and the Study of Discourse." *Ideology and Consciousness* 3:7–26.

1978/1980   *The History of Sexuality, Vol. 1, An Introduction.* New York: Vintage.

1983   "Preface." In Gilles Deleuze and Felix Guattari, *Anti-Oedipus: Capitalism and Schizophrenia.* Minneapolis: University of Minnesota Press: xi–xiv.

1984/1985   *The Use of Pleasure: Volume 2 of The History of Sexuality.* New York: Pantheon Books.

1984/1986   *The Care of the Self: Volume 3 of The History of Sexuality.* New York: Pantheon Books.

Foucault, Michel, and Simon, John K.
1991   "Michel Foucault on Attica: An Interview." *Social-Justice* 18:26–34.

Fox-Genovese, Elizabeth
1993   "From Separate Spheres to Dangerous Streets: Postmodernist Feminism and the Problem of Order." *Social-Research* 60:235–254.

Fraser, Nancy
1981   "Foucault on Modern Power: Empirical Insights and Normative Confusions." *Praxis International* 1:272–287

Fraser, Nancy, and Nicholson, Linda J.
1990   "Social Criticism without Philosophy: An Encounter between Feminism and Postmodernism." In L. Nicholson (ed.), *Feminism/Postmodernism.* London: Routledge: 19–38.

Freundlieb, Dieter
1988   "Rationalism vs. Irrationalism? Habermas's Response to Foucault." *Inquiry* 31:171–192.

Frisby, David
1991   "The Aesthetics of Modern Life: Simmel's Interpretation." *Theory, Culture and Society* 8:73–93.

Fritzman, J. M.
1990   "Lyotard's Paralogy and Rorty's Pluralism: Their Differences and Pedagogical Implications." *Educational Theory* 40:371–380.

Frow, John
1991   *What Was Postmodernism?* Sydney, Australia: Local Consumption Publications.

Fuchs, Stephan, and Ward, Steven
1994   "What is Deconstruction, and Where and When Does it Take Place? Making Facts in Science, Building Cases in Law." *American Sociological Review* 59:481–500.

Gane, Mike
1991a   *Baudrillard's Bestiary: Baudrillard and Culture.* London: Routledge.
1991b   *Baudrillard and Critical and Fatal Theory.* London: Routledge.

Gane, Mike (ed.)
1993   *Baudrillard Live: Selected Interviews.* London: Routledge.

Garland, David
1990   *Punishment and Modern Society.* Chicago: University of Chicago Press.

Genosko, Gary
1992   "The Struggle for an Affirmative Weakness: de Certeau, Lyotard, and Baudrillard." *Current Perspectives in Social Theory* 12:179–194.
1994   *Baudrillard and Signs: Signification Ablaze.* London: Routledge.

Gergen, Kenneth
1991   *The Saturated Self: Dilemmas of Identity in Contemporary Life.* New York: Basic Books.

Giddens, Anthony
1984   *The Constitution of Society: Outline of the Theory of Structuration.* Berkeley: University of California Press.
1990   *The Consequences of Modernity.* Stanford, CA: Stanford University Press.

1991 *Modernity and Self-Identity: Self and Society in the Late Modern Age.* Stanford: Stanford University Press.

1992 *The Transformation of Intimacy: Sexuality, Love and Eroticism in Modern Societies.* Stanford: Stanford University Press.

Gitlin, Todd
1988 "Hip-Deep in Post Modernism." *New York Times Book Review* Nov. 1:35–36.

Godelier, Maurice
1972a *Rationality and Irrationality in Economics.* London: NLB.
1972b "Structure and Contradiction in *Capital.*" In R. Blackburn (ed.), *Readings in Critical Social Theory.* London: Fontana: 334–368.

Gottdiener, Mark
1993 "Ideology, Foundationalism, and Sociological Theory." *Sociological Quarterly* 34:653–671.

1995 *Postmodern Semiotics: Material Culture and the Forms of Modern Life.* Oxford: Blackwell.

Habermas, Jürgen
1981 "Modernity versus Postmodernity." *New German Critique* 22:3–14.

1984 *The Theory of Communicative Action. Vol. 1, Reason and the Rationalization of Society.* Boston: Beacon Press.

1986 "The Genealogical Writing of History: On Some Aporias in Foucault's Theory of Power." *Canadian Journal of Political and Social Theory* 10:1–9.

1987 *The Philosophical Discourse of Modernity: Twelve Lectures.* Cambridge, MA: MIT Press.

1991 "A Reply." In A. Honneth and H. Joas (eds.), *Communicative Action: Essays on Jürgen Habermas's The Theory of Communicative Action.* Cambridge, MA: Cambridge University Press: 215–264.

Hage, Jerald, and Powers, Charles H.
1992 *Post-Industrial Lives: Roles and Relationships in the 21st Century.* Newbury Park, CA: Sage.

Haraway, Donna
1990 "A Manifesto for Cyborgs: Science, Technology, and Socialist Feminism in the 1980s." In L. Nicholson (ed.), *Feminism/Postmodernism.* London: Routledge: 190–233.

1991 *Simians, Cyborgs and Women: The Reinvention of Nature.* New York: Routledge.

Harding, Sandra
1986 *The Science Question in Feminism.* Ithaca: Cornell University Press.

1990   "Feminism, Science, and the Anti-Enlightenment Critiques."
                              In L. Nicholson (ed.), *Feminism/Postmodernism*. London:
                              Routledge: 83–106.
1991   *Whose Science? Whose Knowledge? Thinking from Women's
                              Lives*. Ithaca: Cornell University Press.

Harrison, Paul Raymond
1987   "From Bodies to Ethics: The Second and Third Volumes of
                              Foucault's History of Sexuality." *Thesis Eleven* 16:128–140.
1993   "Bourdieu and the Possibility of a Postmodern Sociology."
                              Thesis Eleven 35:36–50.

Hartsock, Nancy
1987   "Rethinking Modernism: Minority vs. Majority Theories."
                              Cultural Critique 7:187–206.

Harvey, David
1989   *The Condition of Postmodernity: An Inquiry into the Origins
                              of Cultural Change*. Oxford: Blackwell.

Hassan, Ihab
1971   "POSTmodernISM: A Paracritical Bibliography." *New Liter-
                              ary History* 3:5–30.

Hawkes, Terence
1977   *Structuralism and Semiotics*. London: Methuen.

Hayim, Gila
1980   *The Existential Sociology of Jean-Paul Sartre*. Amherst: Uni-
                              versity of Massachusetts Press.

Hengehold, Laura
1994   "An Immodest Proposal: Foucault, Hysterization, and the
                              'Second Rape'." *Hypatia* 9:88–107.

Hennessy, Rosemary
1995   "Incorporating Queer Theory on the Left." In A. Callari, S.
                              Cullenberg, and C. Biewener (eds.), *Marxism in the Post-
                              modern Age: Confronting the New World Order*. New York:
                              Guilford Press: 266–275.

Hewitt, Martin
1983   "Bio-Politics and Social Policy: Foucault's Account of Wel-
                              fare." *Theory, Culture and Society* 2:67–84.

Hollinger, Robert
1994   *Postmodernism and the Social Sciences: A Thematic Ap-
                              proach*. Thousand Oaks, CA: Sage.

Holub, Robert C.
1991   *Jürgen Habermas: Critic in the Public Sphere*. London:
                              Routledge.

Huyssen, Andreas
1990   "Mapping the Postmodern." In L. Nicholson (ed.), *Femi-
                              nism/Postmodernism*. London: Routledge: 234–277.

Irigaray, Luce
1981   "The Sex Which is Not One." In E. Marks and I. de
                Courtivron (eds.), *New French Feminisms*. New York:
                Schocken Books: 99–106.

Jameson, Fredric
1972   *The Prison House of Language: A Critical Account of Struc-
                turalism and Russian Formalism*. Princeton: Princeton Uni-
                versity Press.
1981   *The Political Unconscious: Narrative as a Socially Symbolic
                Act*. Ithaca: Cornell University Press.
1984a   "Foreword." In Jean François Lyotard, *The Postmodern Con-
                dition: A Report on Knowledge*. Minneapolis: University of
                Minnesota Press: vii–xxi.
1984b   "Postmodernism, or, The Cultural Logic of Late Capitalism."
                New Left Review 146:59–92.
1989   "Afterword—Marxism and Postmodernism." In D. Kellner
                (ed.), *Postmodernism, Jameson, Critique*. Washington, D.C.:
                Maisonneuve Press: 369–387.
1991   *Postmodernism, or, The Cultural Logic of Late Capitalism*.
                Durham: Duke University Press.

Jay, Martin, and Flax, Jane
1993   "Forum: On Fredric Jameson, Postmodernism, or the Cul-
                tural Logic of Late Capitalism." *History and Theory*
                32:296–310.

Jencks, Charles
1975   "The Rise of Post-Modern Architecture." *Architecture Asso-
                ciation Quarterly* 7:3–14.
1977   *The Language of Post-Modern Architecture*. New York: Riz-
                zoli.

Jones, W. T.
1992   "Deconstructing Derrida: Below the Surface of *Différance*."
                Metaphilosophy 23:230–250.

Kamolnick, Paul
1994   "Marxism, Postmodernism, and Beyond: A Critical Analysis
                of David Harvey's Theory of Contemporary Culture." *Cur-
                rent Perspectives in Social Theory* 14:71–88.

Kellner, Douglas
1989b   "Introduction: Jameson, Marxism, and Postmodernism." In
                D. Kellner (ed.), *Postmodernism, Jameson, Critique*. Wash-
                ington, D.C.: Maisonneuve Press: 1–42.

Kellner, Douglas (ed.)
1989a   *Postmodernism, Jameson, Critique*. Washington, D.C.:
                Maisonneuve Press.

1989d	*Jean Baudrillard: From Marxism to Postmodernism and Beyond.* Cambridge: Polity Press.
1994	*Baudrillard: A Critical Reader.* Oxford: Blackwell.

Keohane, Kieran
1993   "Central Problems in the Philosophy of the Social Sciences after Postmodernism: Reconciling Consensus and Hegemonic Theories of Epistemology and Political Ethics." *Philosophy and Social Criticism* 19:145–169.

Knorr-Cetina, Karin
1981   *The Manufacture of Knowledge: An Essay on the Constructivist and Contextual Nature of Science.* Oxford: Pergamon.

Kristeva, Julia
1981   "Oscillation Between Power and Denial." In E. Marks and I. de Courtivron (eds.), *New French Feminisms.* New York: Schocken Books: 165–167.

Kroker, Arthur
1985   "Television and the Triumph of Culture: Three Theses." *Canadian Journal of Political and Social Theory* 9:37–47.
1992   *The Possessed Individual.* New York: St. Martin's Press.

Kroker, Arthur, and Cook, David
1991   *The Postmodern Scene: Excremental Culture and Hyper-Aesthetics.* Montreal: New World Perspectives.

Kroker, Arthur, and Levin, Charles
1991   "Cynical Power: The Fetishism of the Sign." *Canadian Journal of Political and Social Theory* 15:1–3, 123–134.

Kumar, Krishan
1995   *From Post-Industrial to Post-Modern Society.* Oxford: Blackwell.

Kurzweil, Edith
1980   *The Age of Structuralism: Lévi-Strauss to Foucault.* New York: Columbia University Press.
1986   "The Fate of Structuralism." *Theory, Culture and Society* 3:113–124.
1995   *Freudians and Feminists.* Boulder, CO: Westview.

Lacan, Jacques
1966/1977   *Ecrits: A Selection.* New York: W. W. Norton & Co.
1966–1982/1985   *Feminine Sexuality.* New York: W. W. Norton & Co.
1973/1978   *The Four Fundamental Concepts of Psycho-analysis.* New York: W. W. Norton & Co.
1986/1992   *The Ethics of Psychoanalysis, 1959–1960.* New York: W. W. Norton & Co.

Laclau, Ernesto, and Mouffe, Chantal
1985   *Hegemony and Socialist Strategy: Towards a Radical Democratic Politics.* London: Verso.

Lamont, Michele
1987   "How to Become a Dominant French Philosopher: The Case
                        of Jacques Derrida." *American Journal of Sociology*
                        93:584–622.

Lash, Scott
1991   "Introduction." In S. Lash (ed.), *Post-Structuralist and Post-
                        Modernist Sociology.* Aldershot, England: Edward Elgar
                        Publishing Limited: ix–xv.

Latour, Bruno
1987   *Science in Action.* Cambridge: Harvard University Press.

Latour, Bruno, and Woolgar, Steve
1979   *Laboratory Life: The Social Construction of Scientific Facts.*
                        Beverly Hills, CA: Sage.

Leidner, Robin
1993   *Fast Food, Fast Talk: Service Work and the Routinization of
                        Everyday Life.* Berkeley: University of California Press.

Lemert, Charles
1990   "The Uses of French Structuralisms in Sociology." In G.
                        Ritzer (ed.), *Frontiers of Social Theory: The New Syntheses.*
                        New York: Columbia University Press: 230–254.

Lemert, Charles (ed.)
1994   "Social Theory at the Early End of a Short Century." *Socio-
                        logical Theory* 12:140–152.

Lengermann, Patricia Madoo, and Niebrugge, Jill
1996   "Early Women Sociologists and Classical Sociological The-
                        ory: 1830–1930." In G. Ritzer, *Classical Sociological The-
                        ory,* 2nd ed. New York: McGraw-Hill: 294–328.

Levin, Charles
1981   "Translator's Introduction." In J. Baudrillard, *For a Critique
                        of the Political Economy of the Sign.* United States: Telos
                        Press: 5–28.

Lévi-Strauss, Claude
1967   *Structural Anthropology.* Garden City, NY: Anchor Books.

Lewis, Michael
1995   "The Rich: How They're Different . . . Than They Used to
                        Be." *New York Times Magazine* November 19:67ff.

Lilla, Mark (ed.)
1994a   *New French Thought: Political Philosophy.* Princeton:
                        Princeton University Press.

Lilla, Mark
1994b   "The Legitimacy of the Liberal Age." In M. Lilla (ed.), *New
                        French Thought: Political Philosophy.* Princeton: Princeton
                        University Press: 3–34.

Lipovetsky, Gilles
1987/1994   *The Empire of Fashion: Dressing Modern Democracy.* Princeton: Princeton University Press.

Lloyd, Moya
1993   "The (F)utility of a Feminist Turn to Foucault." *Economy and Society* 22:437–460.

Long, John
1992   "Foucault's Clinic." *Journal of Medical Humanities* 13:119–138.

Longino, Helen E.
1993   "Feminist Standpoint Theory and the Problems of Knowledge." *Signs* 19:201–212.

Lovejoy, Arthur
1936/1940   *The Great Chain of Being: A Study of the History of an Idea.* New York: Harper Torchbooks.
1948   *Essays in the History of Ideas.* Baltimore: Johns Hopkins University Press.

Lovibond, Sabina
1990   "Feminism and Postmodernism." In R. Boyne and A. Rattansi (eds.), *Postmodernism and Society.* New York: St. Martin's Press: 154–186.

Lyon, David
1991   "Bentham's Panopticon: From Moral Architecture to Electronic Surveillance." *Queen's Quarterly* 98:596–617.

Lyotard, Jean-François
1979/1984   *The Postmodern Condition: A Report on Knowledge.* Minneapolis: University of Minnesota Press.
1988/1993   *The Postmodern Explained.* Minneapolis: University of Minnesota Press.

Maffesoli, Michel
1995   *The Time of Tribes.* London: Sage.

Mahon, Michael
1993   "Michel Foucault's Archaeology, Enlightenment, and Critique." *Human Studies* 16:129–141.

Mandel, Ernest
1975   *Late Capitalism.* London: New Left Books.

Manet, Pierre
1987/1994   *An Intellectual History of Liberalism.* Princeton: Princeton University Press.

Marks, Elaine, and de Courtivron, Isabelle (eds.)
1981   *New French Feminisms: An Anthology.* New York: Schocken.

McBride, William L.
1991   "Sartre and His Successors: Existential Marxism and Post-modernism at Our *fin de siècle.*" *Praxis International* 11:78–92.

McCaughey, Martha
1993   "Redirecting Feminist Critiques of Science." *Hypatia* 8:72–84.

McDermott, Patrice
1987   "Post-Lacanian French Feminist Theory: Luce Irigaray." *Women and Politics* 7:47–64.

Meadmore, Daphne
1993   "The Production of Individuality through Examination." *British Journal of Sociology of Education* 14:59–73.

Merton, Robert
1965   *On the Shoulders of Giants: A Shandean Postscript.* New York: Free Press.
1973   *The Sociology of Science.* Chicago: University of Chicago Press.

Mestrovic, Stjepan G.
1993   *The Barbarian Temperament: Toward a Postmodern Critical Theory.* London: Routledge.

Miller, James
1993   *The Passion of Michel Foucault.* New York: Anchor Books.

Mills, C. Wright
1959   *The Sociological Imagination.* New York: Oxford University Press.

Minh-ha, Trinh T.
1989   *Woman, Native, Other: Writing Postcoloniality and Feminism.* Bloomington: Indiana University Press.

Morgan, Kathryn Pauly
1991   "Women and the Knife: Cosmetic Surgery and the Colonization of Women's Bodies." *Hypatia* 6:25–53.

Morton, Donald
1993   "The Politics of Queer Theory in the (Post) Modern Moment." *Genders* 17:121–150.

Munz, Peter
1992   "What's Postmodern, Anyway?" *Philosophy and Literature* 16:333–353.

Nicholson, Linda
1992   "On the Postmodern Barricades: Feminism, Politics, and Theory." In S. Seidman and D. G. Wagner (eds.), *Postmodernism and Social Theory.* Cambridge, MA: Blackwell: 82–100.

Nicholson, Linda (ed.)
1990   *Feminism/Postmodernism.* London: Routledge.
Nietzsche, Friedrich
1887/1974   *The Gay Science.* New York: Vintage Books.
1992   *Basic Writings of Nietzsche.* New York: The Modern Library.
Norris, Christopher
1985   *The Contest of Faculties: Philosophy and Theory after Deconstruction.* New York & London: Methuen.
Norton, Bruce
1995   "Late Capitalism and Postmodernism: Jameson/Mandel." In A. Callari, S. Cullenberg, and C. Biewener (eds.), *Marxism in the Postmodern Age: Confronting the New World Order.* New York: Guilford Press: 59–70.
Nuyen, A. T.
1992   "The Role of Rhetorical Devices in Postmodernist Discourse." *Philosophy and Rhetoric* 25:183–197.
O'Neill, John
1986   "The Disciplinary Society: From Weber to Foucault." *British Journal of Sociology* 37:42–60.
1995   *The Poverty of Postmodernism.* London: Routledge.
Paden, Roger
1987   "Foucault's Anti-Humanism." *Human Studies* 10:123–141.
Pecora, Vincent P.
1992   "What Was Deconstruction?" *Contention: Debates in Society, Culture, and Science* 1:59–79.
Pettegrew, John
1992   "A Post-Modernist Moment: 1980s Commercial Culture and the Founding of MTV." *Journal of American Culture* 15:57–65.
Phelan, Shane
1990   "Foucault and Feminism." *American Journal of Political Science* 34:421–440.
Plant, Sadie
1993   "Baudrillard's Woman: The Eve of Seduction." In C. Rojek and B. S. Turner (eds.), *Forget Baudrillard?* London: Routledge: 88–107.
Poggi, Gianfranco
1993   *Money and the Modern Mind: Georg Simmel's Philosophy of Money.* Berkeley, CA: University of California Press.
Porter, Roy, and Poster, Mark
1991   "Is Foucault Useful for Understanding Eighteenth and Nineteenth Century Sexuality?" *Contention: Debates in Society, Culture, and Science* 1:61–81.

Poster, Mark (ed.)
1988   *Jean Baudrillard: Selected Writings.* Stanford: Stanford University Press.

Postman, Neil
1985   *Amusing Ourselves to Death: Public Discourse in the Age of Show Business.* New York: Viking, 1985.

Richardson, Michael
1994   *Georges Bataille.* London: Routledge.

Ritzer, George
1975   *Sociology: A Multiple Paradigm Science.* Boston: Allyn and Bacon.

1981   *Toward an Integrated Sociological Paradigm: The Search for an Exemplar and an Image of the Subject Matter.* Boston: Allyn and Bacon.

1991   *Metatheorizing in Sociology.* Lexington, MA: Lexington Books

1993   *The McDonaldization of Society.* Thousand Oaks, CA: Pine Forge Press.

1995   *Expressing America: A Critique of the Increasingly Global Credit Card Society.* Thousand Oaks, CA: Pine Forge Press.

1996a   *The McDonaldization of Society,* revised ed. Thousand Oaks, CA: Pine Forge Press.

1996b   *Sociological Theory.* 4th ed. New York: McGraw-Hill.
1996c   *Modern Sociological Theory.* 4th ed. New York: McGraw-Hill.

forthcoming   *Consuming Society.* Thousand Oaks, CA: Pine Forge Press.
Robertson, Roland
1992   *Globalization: Social Theory and Global Culture.* London: Sage.

Rogers, Mary (ed.)
1996a   *Multicultural Experiences, Multicultural Theories.* New York: McGraw-Hill.

Rogers, Mary
1996b   "Introduction." In M. Rogers (ed.), *Multicultural Experiences, Multicultural Theories.* New York: McGraw-Hill: 1–10.

Rojek, Chris
1993   "Baudrillard and Politics." In C. Rojek and B. S. Turner (eds.), *Forget Baudrillard?* London: Routledge: 107–123.

Rojek, Chris, and Turner, Bryan S.
1993   Introduction: Regret Baudrillard?" In C. Rojek and B. S. Turner (eds.), *Forget Baudrillard?* London: Routledge: ix–xviii.

Rorty, Richard
1979   *Philosophy and the Mirror of Nature.* Princeton: Princeton University Press.
1984   "Habermas and Lyotard on Post-Modernity." *Praxis International* 4:32–44.
Rosenau, Pauline Marie
1992   *Post-Modernism and the Social Sciences: Insights, Inroads, and Intrusions.* Princeton: Princeton University Press.
Ross, Howard
1983   "Derrida: A Discussion." *Quarterly Journal of Ideology* 7:58–65.
Sartre, Jean-Paul
1943   *Being and Nothingness.* New York: Pocket Books.
1963   *Critique of Dialectical Reason.* London: NLB.
Sass, Louis A.
1994   "The Epic of Disbelief: The Postmodernist Turn in Psycho-analysis." *Partisan Review* 61:96–110.
Saussure, Ferdinand de
1966   *Course in General Linguistics.* New York: McGraw-Hill.
Schutz, Alfred
1932/1967   *The Phenomenology of the Social World.* Evanston, IL: Northwestern University Press.
1973   *Collected Papers I: The Problem of Social Reality.* The Hague: Martinus Nijhoff.
Schwartz, Martin D., and Friedrichs, David O.
1994   "Postmodern Thought and Criminological Discontent: New Metaphors for Understanding Violence." *Criminology* 32:221–246.
Seem, Mark
1983   "Preface." In Gilles Deleuze and Felix Guattari, *Anti-Oedipus: Capitalism and Schizophrenia.* Minneapolis: University of Minnesota Press: xv–xxiv.
Segura, Denise A., and Pesquera, Beatriz M.
1996   "Beyond Indifference and Antipathy: The Chicana Movement and Chicana Feminist Discourse." In M. Rogers (ed.), *Multicultural Experiences, Multicultural Theories.* New York: McGraw-Hill: 395–409.
Seidman, Steven
1989   "Introduction." In S. Seidman (ed.), *Jürgen Habermas on Society and Politics: A Reader.* Boston: Beacon Press: 1–25.
1991   "The End of Sociological Theory: The Postmodern Hope." *Sociological Theory* 9:131–146.
1994a   *Contested Knowledge: Social Theory in the Postmodern Age.* Oxford: Blackwell.

1994b	"Symposium: Queer Theory/Sociology: A Dialogue." *Sociological Theory* 12:166–177.

Sewell, Graham, and Wilkinson, Barry
1992   "'Someone to Watch over Me': Surveillance, Discipline and the Just-in-Time Labour Process." *Sociology* 26:271–289.

Sheridan, Alan
1980   *Michel Foucault: The Will to Truth.* London: Tavistock.

Shumway, David
1989   "Jameson/Hermeneutics/Postmodernism." In D. Kellner (ed.), *Postmodernism, Jameson, Critique.* Washington, D.C.: Maisonneuve Press: 172–202.

Shusterman, Richard
1991   "The Fine Art of Rap." *New Literary History* 22:613–632.

Singer, Linda
1992   "Feminism and Postmodernism." In J. Butler and J. Scott (eds.), *Feminists Theorize the Political.* New York: Routledge: 464–475.

Smart, Barry
1983   *Foucault, Marxism and Critique.* London: Routledge and Kegan Paul.
1985   *Michel Foucault.* Chichester, England: Ellis Horwood.
1993a   *Postmodernity.* London: Routledge.
1993b   "Europe/America: Baudrillard's Fatal Comparison." In C. Rojek and B. S. Turner (eds.), *Forget Baudrillard?* London: Routledge: 47–69.

Smith, Adam T.
1994   "Fictions of Emergence: Foucault/Genealogy/Nietzsche." *Philosophy of the Social Sciences* 24:41–54.

Sontag, Susan
1964/1967   "Against Interpretation." In S. Sontag (ed.), *Against Interpretation and Other Essays.* New York: Dell: 3–14.

Spivak, Gayatri
1974   "Translator's Preface." In J. Derrida, *Of Grammatology.* Baltimore: The Johns Hopkins University Press: ix–lxxxvii.
1992   "French Feminism Revisited: Ethics and Politics." In J. Butler and J. Scott (eds.), *Feminists Theorize the Political.* New York: Routledge: 54–85.

Spivak, Gayatri Chakravorty, and Gross, Elizabeth
1984–1985   "Criticism, Feminism and the Institution: An Interview with Gayatri Chakravorty Spivak." *Thesis Eleven* 10–11:175–187.

Stabile, Carole A.
1995   "Feminism Without Guarantees: The Misalliances and Missed Alliances of Postmodernist Social Theory." In A. Callari, S. Cullenberg, and C. Biewener (eds.), *Marxism in*

the Postmodern Age: Confronting the New World Order. New York: Guilford Press: 283–291.

Stavro-Pearce, Elaine
1994   "Towards a Posthumanist Feminism." Economy and Society 23:217–245.

Stephanson, Anders
1989   "Regarding Postmodernism: A Conversation with Fredric Jameson." In D. Kellner (ed.), Postmodernism, Jameson, Critique. Washington, D.C.: Maisonneuve Press: 43–74.

Still, Judith
1994   "'What Foucault Fails to Acknowledge . . .': Feminists and The History of Sexuality." History of the Human Sciences 7:150–157.

Strinati, Dominic
1995   An Introduction to Theories of Popular Culture. London: Routledge.

Todorov, Tzvetan
1994   "Lévi-Strauss." In M. Lilla (ed.), New French Thought: Political Philosophy. Princeton: Princeton University Press: 38–53.

Valverde, Mariana
1996   "Bisexuality and Deviant Identities." In M. Rogers (ed.), Multicultural Experiences, Multicultural Theories. New York: McGraw-Hill: 246–248.

Venturi, Robert
1966   Complexity and Contradiction in Architecture. New York: Museum of Modern Art.

Venturi, Robert, Scott Brown, Denise, and Izenour, Steven
1972   Learning From Las Vegas. Cambridge, MA: MIT Press.

Vidich, Arthur J.
1991   "Baudrillard's America: Lost in the Ultimate Simulacrum." Theory, Culture and Society 8:135–144.

Virilio, Paul
1983   Pure War. New York: Semiotext(e).
1986   Speed and Politics. New York: Semiotext(e).
1991a   Lost Dimension. New York: Semiotext(e).
1991b   The Aesthetics of Disappearance. New York: Semiotext(e).
1995   The Art of the Motor. Minneapolis: University of Minnesota Press.

Walkerdine, Valerie
1993   "Beyond Developmentalism?" Theory and Psychology Nov. 3:451–469.

Warnke, Georgia
1993   "Feminism and Hermeneutics." Hypatia 8:81–98.

Waters, Malcolm
1995   *Globalization.* London: Routledge, 1995.
Weeks, Jeffrey
1977   *Coming Out: Homosexual Politics in Britain, from the Nine-teenth Century to the Present.* London: Quartet.
1981/1989   *Sex, Politics and Society: The Regulation of Sexuality Since 1800,* 2nd ed. London: Longman.
Weeks, Kathi
1995   "Feminist Standpoint Theories and the Return of Labor." In A. Callari, S. Cullenberg, and C. Biewener (eds.), *Marxism in the Postmodern Age: Confronting the New World Order.* New York: Guilford Press: 292–300.
Wei, William
1996   "Reclaiming the Past and Constructing a Collective Culture." In M. Rogers (ed.), *Multicultural Experiences, Multicultural Theories.* New York: McGraw-Hill: 346–360.
Weinstein, Deena, and Weinstein, Michael A.
1993   *Postmodern(ized) Simmel.* London: Routledge.
Wenger, Morton G.
1993–1994   "Idealism Redux: The Class-Historical Truth of Postmodernism." *Critical Sociology* 20:53–78.
Wernick, Andrew
1991   "Sign and Commodity: Aspects of the Cultural Dynamic of Advanced Capitalism." *Canadian Journal of Political and Social Theory* 15:152–169.
West, Cornel
1990   "The New Cultural Politics of Difference." In R. Ferguson, et al. (eds.), *Out There: Marginalization and Contemporary Cultures.* Cambridge, MA: MIT Press: 19–36.
1994   *Race Matters.* New York: Vintage Books.
Wickham, Gary
1983   "Power and Power Analysis: Beyond Foucault?" *Economy and Society* 12:468–498.
Wolff, Janet
1990   "Postmodern Theory and Feminist Art Practice." In R. Boyne and A. Rattansi (eds.), *Postmodernism and Society.* New York: St. Martin's Press: 187–208.
Yeatman, Anna
1991   "Postmodern Critical Theorising: Introduction." *Social Analysis* 30:3–9.
Zeitlin, Irving M.
1994   *Nietzsche: A Re-Examination.* Cambridge: Polity.
Zuboff, Shoshana
1988   *In the Age of the Smart Machine.* New York: Basic Books.

Zuidervaart, Lambert
1989   "Realism, Modernism, and the Empty Chair." In D. Kellner
              (ed.), *Postmodernism, Jameson, Critique.* Washington, D.C.:
              Maisonneuve Press: 203–227.
Zurbrugg, Nicholas
1993   "Baudrillard, Modernism, and Postmodernism." *Economy
              and Society* 22:482–500.

NAME INDEX

SUBJECT INDEX